DATE DUE			

The Development of Self-Regulation Through Private Speech

The Origins of Behavior

Michael Lewis and
Leonard A. Rosenblum, Editors

Volume 1
The Effect of the Infant on Its Caregiver

Michael Lewis and
Leonard A. Rosenblum, Editors

Volume 2
The Origins of Fear

Michael Lewis and
Leonard A. Rosenblum, Editors

Volume 3
Structure and Transformation:
Developmental Aspects

Klaus F. Riegel and
George C. Rosenwald, Editors

Volume 4
Friendship and Peer Relations

Michael Lewis and
Leonard A. Rosenblum, Editors

Volume 5
Interaction, Conversation,
and the Development of
Language

Michael Lewis and
Leonard A. Rosenblum, Editors

Volume 6
The Development of Self-Regulation
Through Private Speech

Gail Zivin, Editor

The Development of Self-Regulation Through Private Speech

Edited by

Gail Zivin

A Wiley-Interscience Publication

JOHN WILEY & SONS

New York • Chichester • Brisbane • Toronto

Library of Congress Cataloging in Publication Data:

Main entry under title:
The Development of self-regulation through private speech.

(The Origins of behavior; v. 6)
"A Wiley-Interscience publication."
Includes index.
1. Self-control in children. 2. Children—Language. I. Zivin, Gail, 1943-
II. Series. [DNLM: 1. Child behavior.
2. Child development. 3. Speech—In infancy and childhood. W1 OR687 v.6 / WS105 D48914]
BF723.S25D48 155.4′18 78-27615
ISBN 0-471-98380-2

Printed in the United States of America

10 9 8 7 6 5 4 3 2 1

Contributors

Jean-Paul Bronckart
Faculté de Psychologie et des Sciences de l'Éducation
Université de Genève
1211 Genève 4, Switzerland

Karen C. Fuson
School of Education
Northwestern University
Evanston, Illinois 60201

Sherryl Goodman
Department of Psychology
Emory University
Atlanta, Georgia 30322

Adrienne Harris
Department of Psychology
Rutgers University-Newark
Newark, New Jersey 07102

Ann E. McCabe
Department of Psychology
University of Windsor
Windsor, Ontario N9B 3P4
Canada

John A. Meacham
Department of Psychology
State University of New York at Buffalo
Buffalo, New York 14226

Donald Meichenbaum
Department of Psychology
University of Waterloo
Waterloo, Ontario N2L 3G1
Canada

Richard N. Roberts
Department of Psychology
University of North Carolina
Greensboro, North Carolina 27412

Kenneth H. Rubin
Department of Psychology
University of Waterloo
Waterloo, Ontario N2L 3G1
Canada

Madeleine Ventouras-Spycher
Faculté de Psychologie et des Sciences de l'Éducation
Université de Genève
1211 Genève 4, Switzerland

James V. Wertsch
Department of Linguistics
Northwestern University
Evanston, Illinois 60201

Gail Zivin
Department of Psychology
Beaver College
Glenside, Pennsylvania 19038
and
Annenberg School of Communication
University of Pennsylvania
Philadelphia, Pennsylvania 191

To Jerome S. Bruner

Series Preface

"The childhood shows the man,
as morning shows the day."
Milton, Paradise Regained

None can doubt that the study of man begins in the study of childhood. Few would contend that the newborn lacks the challenge of his evolutionary heritage. This series addresses itself to the task of bringing together, on a continuing basis, that confluence of theory and data on ontogeny and phylogeny which will serve to illustrate *The Origins of Behavior*.

Whether our social, human, and professional concerns lie in the psychological disorders of childhood or adulthood or merely in the presumptively normal range of expression in development in different cultures, varied environments, or diverse family constellations, we can never hope to discern order and regularity from the mass of uncertain observation and groundless speculation if we fail to nurture the scientific study of development. Fortunately, the last two decades have seen an enormous burgeoning of effort toward this end, both at the human and nonhuman level. However, despite this growth of effort and interest, no single means of pooling our growing knowledge on development in children and animals and communicating that fusion of material to the broad scientific community now exists. This series seeks to fill the gap. It is our intention to have each volume deal with a specific theme that is either of social or of theoretical relevance to developmental issues. In keeping with the integrated perspective that we consider to be vital, and to provide a meaningful context within which these issues may be considered, each volume in the series will contain a broad range of material and will seek to encompass theoretical and sound empirical studies of the behavior of human infants as well as pertinent aspects of animal behavior with a particular emphasis on the primates. It is our view, furthermore, that not only is it necessary to focus our interest on both human infants and animals, but that the levels of analysis which will explicate the processes of development that are our concern must ultimately involve the study of behavior at all levels of discourse. Thus studies of developmental significance may be found in genetic, physiological, morphological, dyadic, and societal levels and an increased interdigitation of these separate disciplines is among the major goals of this series.

In light of the diversity of topics to be considered, the breadth of material to be covered, and the variety of orientations that will be included in these discourses on the origins of human behavior, we expect this series to serve the needs of the broad social science community, not merely of those interested in behavioral development alone. Just as the series itself will draw upon the knowledge and research of psychologists, ethologists, sociologists, psychiatrists, pediatricians, obstetricians, and devoted scientists and clinicians in a number of related disciplines, it is our hope that the material in this series will provide both stimulation and guidance to all among us who are concerned with man, his past, his present, and his future.

Michael Lewis
Leonard A. Rosenblum
Editors

Preface

This is the first book-length Western work devoted to research on the child's development of self-regulation through speech. It grew out of a need noted by a subset of the present contributors when they collaborated in 1973 to present two symposia. They frequently regretted the lack of a central, authoritative text on the topic—a book that might dispel some of the contradictions among different seminal theorists and also provide one commonly shared collection and clarification of the classic Russian, French, and English work on self-regulation and private (or egocentric) speech. Besides aiming to serve those two functions, the present volume collects a representative sampling of current Western thinking on Soviet-inspired approaches to verbal self-regulation—including the historical-philosophical roots of Soviet theories, their paths of reinterpretation in the West, their points of conflict and mesh with current Piagetian thought, and Vygotsky's fit as a contemporary speech-act theorist. It also presents new empirical work from naturalistic perspectives, includes a comprehensive review of research on children's verbal self-regulation—including studies often thought to be primarily about cognitive strategies—and provides a full international bibliography. It is shaped to give perspective on and contemporary interpretation of research and theory concerning the child's development of self-regulation through speech, and should serve well as a sourcebook on the topic.

Gail Zivin

Philadelphia
Autumn 1979

Acknowledgments

The momentum for this book began in the two cumulative symposia that I chaired in 1973, one at the Society for Research in Child Development meetings in Philadelphia and one in Ann Arbor at the Meeting of the International Society for the Study of Behavioral Development—the latter published in 1976 in Reigel and Meacham's first volume of *The Developing Individual in a Changing World*. The participants in those symposia, Jean-Paul Bronckart, Adrienne Harris, John Meacham, Donald Meichenbaum, Larry Wilder, Robert Wozniak, Sheldon White, and myself, are the originators of the idea that a book focused on classic and new Soviet-related work on the development of verbal self-regulation should be attempted.

Particular people were pivotal in the transformation of that idea into this volume. Rochel Gelman, on the SRCD Program Committee gave the initial impetus to the idea of the value of a book with such a focus. Klaus Reigel, whom the contributors miss and particularly appreciate for his teaching and influence, further propelled the project by his encouragement of the ISSBD symposium. Added support came from Sheldon White's enthusiastic participation in the first symposium and his evaluation of the idea of a book in the area. I especially thank him for the cumulative effect on my development of his teaching and colleagueship. Ultimately, however, it was Michael Lewis who provided the link to publication through Wiley. We hope that this book adds, at the same high level, to the contributions recently made by the several volumes on cognitive-social development under his and Leonard Rosenblum's editorship of this series.

During the task of editing this book, I have had reason to be thankful for the generous support of some fine colleagues. The ever-present comradeship of Adrienne Harris has been more sustaining than she is likely to imagine. The promptness and patience of Ann McCabe, John Meacham, and Donald Meichenbaum who were contributors from the start—and Don's useful forging of new links to others in the field—greatly furthered the likelihood of the project's completion. An important addition must be noted in Karen Fuson's energy and dedication in undertaking and in shaping and reshaping her comprehensive review. And special appreciation is felt for Richard Solomon who throughout has been such a wise and helpful colleague and friend.

A very particular thanks is due Jerome Bruner. As my dissertation advisor (along with Eric Wanner whose elegant logic, gentle teaching, and friendship I greatly prize), he sponsored and did his utmost to bring wisdom to my early way of studying verbal self-regulation—a way that rather justifiably did not meet with his enthusiasm. His unflagging support, from student days through the present, and the cast of mind he taught have been of indescribable importance to me. The latter has been a valued touchstone, even as my research focus and skills change. I thank him and hope he is not displeased with its influence on this student.

Special thanks are due to Adele Stotland and Tybie Levit for their invaluable, patient help with the manuscript and index.

Ultimately I thank the remarkable person who is my friend and husband, Craig SanPietro. His joyful way of being there nurtures all the rest.

G. Z.

Contents

The Development of Self-Regulation Through Private Speech

Introduction

This book appears two years after the death of A. R. Luria. Largely through his energetic efforts in the 1950s to have writings of Soviet psychology translated into English, Western psychology came to know, and indeed accept, the Soviet theory of the role of speech in the development of self-regulation. Doubtless the interest generated by Luria's efforts (e.g., 1961) was partially responsible for the translation into English of Vygotsky's 1934 book. While Vygotsky may be the anterior source of rich theorizing on verbal self-regulation and while others, such as Leont'ev, Gal'perin, Anokhin, and Elkonin, may have had major roles in building theories of action and mind that assume and explain verbal self-regulation, Luria is primarily responsible for the promulgation in the West of a basic theory of verbal self-regulation and for belief in the importance of this phenomenon in human development.

This book examines in depth the pioneering work of both Luria and Vygotsky on children's development of self-regulation through speech. Among the particular questions explored in this book are: the historical flow of ideas that altered and was altered by each, the intellectual value of their models of organized human functioning, the points of mesh and conflict of each with other psychological world views, more precise or more current interpretations of their explanations, points where they inspire practical application, the adequacy of the approaches to the problems, as well as empirical validation of the claims of each.

Understanding the development of verbal self-regulation is the common goal of this volume's contributors. The Soviet framework is their starting place. They take seriously the Soviet viewpoint and Soviet empirical reports. They focus on them in order to elucidate, evaluate, and further develop them in ways consonant with several positions in Western psychology. In their aim to disseminate the newest relevant Soviet work on children's development of verbal self-regulation, in their presentation of drastic reinterpretations of new non-Soviet explanations, and in their isolation of points of empirical support and lack of support, the editor and contributors have attempted to foster Luria's goals of international communication on the development of verbal self-regulation.

ORGANIZATION AND CONTENTS

The chapters group themselves in two sets. The first set untangles confusions about, and provides contemporary perspectives on, the theoretical bases of the classic research on verbal self-regulation and egocentricity. The second set presents new empirically grounded extensions of the classical works. A comprehensive international review of research on verbal self-regulation heads this section. Most of the chapters in this section speak to the need for naturalistic studies on the spontaneous occurrence of self-regulating speech in order to assess its importance in the actual occurrence of daily behaviors. Two of the chapters aim to fill this need.

In the first chapter of Part I, Zivin demarcates distinctions between the overlapping and the confused use of terms that have been associated with verbal self-regulation (egocentric speech, private speech, speech-for-self, inner speech). She then traces a brief history of United States interpretations and recastings of Soviet and Piagetian egocentric speech and derives 12 dimensions of theoretical importance on which she contrasts and compares the six major researchers whose writings on such speech are most often cited and confused (Vygotsky, Piaget, Luria, Reese, Flavell, and Kohlberg).

Harris then traces and analyzes the historical development of the psychological and political assumptions that, since before Pavlov, have been the frame for Russian ideas on self-regulation, action, and society. She helps the Western reader discern splits within Soviet psychology, which is usually perceived monolithically in the West. Her analysis of the "psychophysiological and philosophical traditions, with their shared commitment to materialism," makes clear in a new way for the Western reader the mysterious "first and second signal systems," on which all Soviet explanations of the development of self-regulation depend, but which are not adequately construed as Western verbal mediation.

Wertsch provides a linguistically inspired analysis of Vygotsky's translated and untranslated work to show that he was essentially a speech-act theorist in harmony with our most contemporary psycho- and sociolinguistic theorizing. He explicates Vygotsky's definitions of psychological subject and predicate, shows how they correspond respectively to the "given" and the "new" of what the child's attention presents to itself during the use of speech, dispels the paradox around how a child can tell himself something that is "new" (that he does not already know), and suggests an empirical approach to validating whether this given-new structure is (partially) responsible for the effectiveness of speech's form during self-regulation.

Bronckart and Ventouras-Spycher bring Part I back to its initial focus on the dispute between Vygotsky and Piaget. Although they may not accept the term, both are neo-Piagetians (the senior author worked with Piaget and H. Sinclair). They focus on what was identified in the first chapter as the ultimate point of contrast between Piaget and Vygotsky: the importance attributed to the role of the social origin of thought and language. They detail why Piaget could have no conception of self-regulation as construed in the Soviet-inspired literature. Finally they present a Saussurian analysis of representation and suggest a Vygotsky-based application of some of Piaget's ideas to the study of the opposite of egocentric speech: schemes of increasingly competent interpersonal communication.

Fuson frames Part II with her extensive review of Western, Soviet-related research on verbal self-regulation. Her detailed consideration of this vast set of studies organizes them by research paradigm for easy reference to whether a reader's question of interest was posed in previous research. With this organization (using the dual axes of who, child or experimenter, chose the speech the child uttered *versus* the degree of naturalness of the action during which the child was studied), she points out the lack of studies that collect spontaneous speech during wholly natural actions of the child's choice. In addition to its rich bibliographic service, this chapter points out methodological problems, areas of empirical agreement across studies, and suggests cognitive mechanisms that seem to underlie different sets of studies.

McCabe presents a unique argument and empirical demonstration of the interaction of speech and motor systems that emphasize the opposite direction of influence from the one usually studied: the effect of motor activity upon concurrent speech. She finds that its effect is to degrade the logical quality of the uttered content. This work raises questions of shared impulse segmentation across systems and hints that semantic concreteness is the level most apt to mesh with concurrent motor activity.

Meacham examines, in a quasi-naturalistic situation, the curious phenomenon (reported in Lurian bulb-pressing situations) of self-regulating speech following, rather than preceding, the action to which it applies. He develops a memory-in-ongoing-behavior-integration explanation of the phenomenon that invites comparison with Vygotsky's earliest and most abstruse form of self-regulating speech. In explanation he develops a comparator model of the phenomenon that focuses on memory of intended goals as a crucial element in the integration of ongoing behavior.

Rubin presents one of the first naturalistic studies that codes children's speech in its entirety, while the child is playing alone with real-world toys of his own choosing. He examines whether the incidence of self-regulating private speech appears with sufficient frequency to be important. He demonstrates how a positive finding depends on a particularly fine-grained set of speech categories and categorizing criteria that take account of the temporal relation between speech and action. His findings also show the contextual selection of likely private speech type by the kind of concurrent activity.

Roberts offers a unique naturalistic study of the spontaneous speech of first-grade children. Its uniqueness rests on: (1) the academic and reading-laden nature of the activity in which the children were observed and (2) the application of a conditional probability analysis as well as a more traditional frequency-of-speech category analysis to the data. He provides the singular addition of a strict operant interpretation of self-regulation, which is only slightly modified by the Soviet perspective. Both his convincing analysis of reading aloud (a highly task-specific form of frequent and effective self-regulating speech during the studied activity) and his finding that more general forms of traditionally considered self-regulatory speech (questions, strategy statements, and feedback) are infrequent and unhelpful point up—in accord with Rubin—the crucial importance of the grain of the category system in locating self-regulating speech. His findings further highlight the key roles played by the contextual variables of familiarity of task and task competence in affecting frequency and type of self-regulating speech.

Meichenbaum and Goodman's contribution offers a highly practical review of methodological considerations for capturing spontaneous private speech. Citing the need for more naturalistic research, they note concerns that range from procedures for guaranteeing codability of audio transcripts to theoretical criteria for activities that are most likely to answer questions on self-regulation. They then discuss some of their laboratory's successes in the application of analyses of self-regulatory speech to clinical problems.

NEW THEMES

There are several new themes arising from many contributors' independent considerations. Two are new directions in the theoretical perspectives that frame the central questions of whether and how speech comes to aid self-regulation. Two are new findings about when self-regulatory speech occurs. Two are developments based on older concerns.

Inseparability of Self-Directed and Social Aspects of Self-Regulatory Speech

Given the current upsurge of interest in the child's social cognition, it is not surprising to see contemporary workers show new sensitivity to the possible social origin and social relevance of self-regulatory speech. This appropriately revises Vygotsky's primary importance as the original theorist to emphasize how the regulation of one's action by others is rooted in interpersonal life. Thus we see Wertsch focus on Vygotsky as a speech-act theorist and apply the originally social given-new distinction to Vygotsky's explanation of regulation. Bronckart and Ventouras-Spycher also adopt a Vygotsky-consistent view in their critique of Luria and their proposal for a systematic study of social communication. Harris explicates the history of the Marxist political view that coincides with Vygotsky's focus on social origins of capacities. Rubin, taking his lead more from Kohlberg than Vygotsky, comes back to the Mead-derived hypotheses that a major function of the most frequent private (if not self-regulating) speech is to aid social development. Fuson points out how social origin is assumed by several proposed self-regulatory mechanisms, particularly the child's adoption of parental teachings.

Naturalistic Observation and Ecological Validity

Both the chapters by Fuson and the one by Meichenbaum and Goodman call for naturalistic studies that, in accord with the tenor of the 1970s, test whether what has heretofore been induced in laboratories can be shown to be valid in the natural ecology of the child. Indeed the editor had attempted to entice several researchers to undertake the difficult analysis of the corpora of natural utterances in the home, which have accumulated through the recent interest in the natural course of language acquisition. Such a review would tap the ecology of the home and provide more random sampling of activities, but would be greatly hindered by the absence of adequate contextual glossing. The studies that are quasi-naturalistic (Meacham's) and naturalistic (Rubin's, Roberts', Goodman's, and Fuson's) research provide the child with activities very much like those he encounters in his natural preschool or school life. These studies occur in similar spaces (for Roberts it is school itself), but are not, except for Fuson's, wholly embedded in the free selection and daily routine of the child. These studies do nevertheless capture the child's spontaneous speech and they use important timing equipment (not easily installed in the home) to examine the precise natural relations between speech and action.

Although it had been an original concern for Vygotsky and Luria, timing of speech and motor acts gets a new emphasis in these chapters. Rubin, Roberts, and Meichenbaum and Goodman use the criterion of whether speech precedes, is during, or follows action to infer whether the speech could be regulating the action. In so doing speech that occurs before and/or during action was considered to be self-regulating in the manner of primitive plans. Roberts, however, also speaks to the more complex interactional nature of ongoing action organization when he combines differing elements of his conditional probability analysis to derive an overall organization of speech and action alternately "cueing" each other in the process of achieving each answer in the task. Meacham, on the other hand, takes the obviously relevant content and the seeming overall effectiveness of speech that occurs after (a portion of the) action and argues for an even more complexly structured model of overall goal-directed action in which speech after action aids in the memory of a more ultimate goal.

The Aid of Speech in Making Transitions

A striking finding in three of these studies deserves to be highlighted. In both Meacham's and Rubin's work the place most likely to show speech that appears self-regulatory by content is in transitions: (1) for Meacham it is between following incorrectly and following correctly one adult-given instruction; (2) for Rubin it is between different types of freely chosen types of play activity. A less obvious but consonant finding by Roberts is that self-regulating speech occurs with differing parts of the task that alternate with each other. Vocalizations are thus in the position of accompanying acts that are transiting to reality and which, as Roberts phrases it, "cue" the next segment of action. Whether speech is seen to occur in transition positions or to occur before, during, or after an act of course is partly determined by the observer's choice of criteria for relating a piece of speech to a particular segment of ongoing action and by whether he views the action as composed of little acts or as segments of one goal-controlled action. Nevertheless these chapters' new focus on the transitional role of self-regulatory speech and on the complex structural quality of action is a new sophistication in the Western conception of verbal self-regulation.

Contextual Selection of Speech Types

While rarely considered in earlier Western work on self-regulation, the influence of the activity type, the actual materials, and the familiarity of the action on the likelihood of concurrent self-regulating speech implicitly contributed to the experimenter's selection of circumstances in which to study verbal self-regulation. In this volume we see Rubin pointedly analyzing activity type for its most frequent concurrent type of speech (and finding non-random distributions) and Roberts noting familiarity of, and competence in, a task to explain why task-specific self-regulating speech is more frequent than general self-regulating speech and why it is particularly so for the most task-competent children. This newly heightened attention to contextual selection in this area of research is also reflected by Meichenbaum and Goodman's suggesting specific activity features that would most contribute to particular explorations of self-regulatory speech, and by Fuson's pointing out how differences in particular task and environment variables appear to account for differences in findings of amounts, types, and effects of self-regulatory speech.

Cybernetic Models of the Role of Self-Regulatory Speech

As pointed out in Harris' historical review, earlier Soviet theorizing, particularly by Anokhin, used cybernetic principles to model the neurophysiological processes underlying the control of action. This approach to verbal self-regulation, as noted by several contributors, was first promulgated in the West by Wozniak (1972,1976). Several contributors offer their own refinements of such a model. They are made explicit in the chapter by Meacham who emphasizes the comparator function of feedback that is effected by labeling the action. Rubin, Roberts, Fuson, and Meichenbaum and Goodman also include feedback as a speech-type category and thus incorporate one element of cybernetic functioning into their views, rather than assimilating the entire self-regulatory process to a cybernetic model. The comparator aspect of a cybernetic model thus appears increasingly useful to contemporary theorists.

Impulse and Rhythmic Aspects of Self-Regulatory Speech

Concern with the impulse aspect of speech and particularly its structure into rhythm, appears to the editor—who has a particular interest in this problem—to be underrepresented in this volume. Regulative segmentation of a concurrent motor action by the structure of the motor impulses of accompanying speech was identified in the 1950s by Luria who cited Tikhomirov's (1958/1975) findings of rhythmic coordination across speech and manual systems. In this book the rhythmic segmentation hypothesis is cited by McCabe in partial resolution of the paradox she has discovered, and Bronckart and Ventouras-Spycher assert the universal role of rhythm in control of communication, while vitiating it of any explanatory power in Luria's bulb-press paradigm. However no new work on regulation through speech impulse appears in this volume.

Western work to explore the positive contribution of rhythm to verbal self-regulation began with Meacham, Harris, and Blaschko (1973) who attempted to demonstrate empirically the entrainment of manual rhythms by speech rhythms; Harris (1976) who recruited far-ranging neurophysiological evidence for the existence of a central timing mechanism of all motor efference; and Zivin (1976) who argued for speech rhythm in Luria's bulb-press research as a ubiquitous artifact that made rhythm a more important factor in his explanations. A chapter reviewing writings on rhythmic regulation and focusing on new empirical study was planned for this volume by Harris and Zivin. That research showed only suggestive trends, thus it was judged insufficient for a chapter. It is briefly summarized here:

> The aim of the study was to demonstrate that when paired with differing separate rhythms, manual rhythm was more likely to become distorted toward verbal rhythm than vice versa. The study looked to find which (if either) system was more distorted in its internal rhythm when a child concurrently activated the other system in a separate rhythm. Age differences in effect, between twelve 6- to 7-year-olds and twelve 10- to 11-year-olds, were also sought.
>
> The manual system could be activated in tapping a weak (. . . .) or a strong (. . _, . . _) rhythm. The speech system could be activated in a weak ("1,2,3,4 . . . 10") or a strong ("1 potato, 2 potato, 3 potato . . .") rhythm. Eight conditions were created by combining each type of manual action (after 30 sec. of it alone) with each type of speech activity (for three rounds) and by combining each type of speech activity (after three rounds alone) with each type of manual activity (for 30 sec.). Thus there were eight sequences, one starting with each strength of one system's activity and becoming paired with one strength of the other system's activity. Separate channels of an Esterline-Angus event recorder per unit time recorded beats.
>
> Three mean rates of beats per unit time were calculated for each child in each sequence: the system alone at the start, that system after it had been joined by the other, and the second system after it had joined the first. Then for each child and for each sequence, the rate differences were calculated. These rate differences reflected whether the rate of one system, after it had been joined by the other, was more similar to its own rate *before it had been joined* or to the rate of the system *that joined it*. The results are best seen in the percentage of children at each age for whom: (one strength of) one system "pulls" the rate of (one strength of) the other system versus those for whom the starting system's rate stayed the same. The one effect that seems to appear is that for young children only the strong manual rhythm is pulled by the introduction of either strength of the speech system (for 9 out of 12 children by the weak; for 10 out of 12 by the strong). The weak manual rhythm is not affected, nor is either strength of the speech system by either manual rhythm strength.

This global measure of deformation of rate of the starting system falls short of a picture of the changing emphasis of beats as a rhythm changes. Such a measure would be necessary to be sure that the actual rhythm is being entrained and not just that the global rate has changed. This precise rhythm measure was not available from the event recorder which, even though it had been electronically modified to approximate an analog recorder, was activated too quickly to allow accurate recording of the degree of beat emphasis. The question of general capacity of speech rhythm to structure other accompanying motor rhythms thus remains a plausible hypothesis, but an imprecisely researched question.

THE PROBLEM OF COMMON NOMENCLATURE

An original goal of this volume was to introduce one clear new term for all speech phenomena that are considered to be acommunicative (i.e., not intended for, or not effectively adapted for, communication with others) as well as one term for that subset of acommunicative speech that is hypothesized to have self-regulating functions. The term, "private speech," was to be avoided in this volume because it seemed too exclusive to function as the more inclusive term and too inclusive to be used for the self-regulation subset. Two realizations that prevented the creation and use of two such new terms across chapters might be informative for the reader.

(1) Upon analysis of the definitions of the speech phenomena proposed as potentially self-regulating, it became clear that there is sufficient lack of coextention to prevent a term which encompasses all suggested self-regulating speech from providing any important clarification. The term for this all-inclusive subset would be precise for no particular position (it would include too many phenomena not proposed as self-regulatory by any specific theorist), and it would almost indistinguishably approximate the extension of the more inclusive term. This distribution of the overlapping, but multimodal attributes, of self-regulatory speech is most visibly divided between those who take self-regulation to be explained by: (a) intraindividual processes (neurophysiology and/or cognitive processing of translations between activation and sign significance, as in Lurian positions) or by (b) interindividual processes (the internalization of others' social effect, as in original Vygotskian and recent Kohlbergian positions). The greatest problem in common terminology for this less extensive term is that some theorists combine positions, while others take them to be mutually exclusive. When this is realized it becomes clear that little aid to reference could be accomplished by carving out one term (or a mutually exclusive subset of terms) that would distinguish all suggested self-regulating speech from the residue of acommunicative utterances, such as make-believe, (some) emotional expressions, and poorly adapted utterances directed at others.

(2) The other realization concerns a more extensive term, such as "acommunicative speech," and the current communicative power of the

term, "private speech." Several contributors found "private speech" the most comfortable way of referring to all speech that is not aimed at, or efficient in, communicating with others. Long discussions followed to determine whether the high recognition value and previously published indexing of "private speech" outweighed the theoretical precision to be gained by a new term. As the reader can tell, and is likely to agree, "private speech," with disclaimers for idiosyncratic modifications of its referent set, was judged the least egocentric way to refer to the set of speech phenomena that is not socially communicative. It is therefore used throughout this sourcebook to refer to the speech phenomena that compose the focus of its field.

REFERENCES

Harris, A. E. The function of speech rhythms in the regulation of non-speech activity, in K. Reigel and J. A. Meacham, eds., *The developing individual in a changing world*, vol. 1. The Hague: Mouton, 1976. (Originally presented at the Biennial Meeting of the International Society for the Study of Behavioral Development, Ann Arbor, 1973.)

Luria, A. R. *The role of speech in the regulation of normal and abnormal behavior*, J. Tizard, trans. New York: Liveright, 1961.

Meacham, J. A., Harris, A. E., and **Blaschko, T.** Integration of verbal and motor activities. (Paper presented at the Biennial Meeting of the Society for Research in Child Development, Philadelphia, March, 1973.)

Tikhomirov, O. K. "The formation of voluntary movements in children of preschool age." *Soviet Psychology*, 1975, *14* (1-2), 48-135. [Originally published, 1958.]

Vygotsky, L. S. *Thought and language,* E. Hanfmann and G. Vakar, eds. and trans. Cambridge, Mass.: M.I.T. Press, 1962. [Originally published, 1934.]

Wozniak, R. H. Verbal regulation of motor behavior—Soviet research and non-Soviet replications. *Human Development*, 1972, *15*, 13-57.

______. Speech-for-self as a multiply reafferent human action system, in K. Reigel and J. A. Meacham, eds., *The developing individual in a changing world,* vol. 1. The Hague: Mouton, 1976. (Originally presented at the Biennial Meeting of the International Society for the Study of Behavioral Development, Ann Arbor, 1973.)

Zivin, G. Developmental aspects of rhythm in self-regulation, in K. Reigel and J. A. Meacham, eds., *The developing individual in a changing world,* vol. 1. The Hague: Mouton, 1976. (Originally presented at the Biennial Meeting of the International Society for the Study of Behavioral Development, Ann Arbor, 1973.)

PART I

THEORETICAL BASES OF CLASSIC WORK

CHAPTER 1

Removing Common Confusions About Egocentric Speech, Private Speech, and Self-Regulation

GAIL ZIVIN
Beaver College and The University of Pennsylvania

Soon after developing an interest in verbal self-regulation, the researcher finds that the associated literature is indexed under "egocentric speech," a term referring to phenomena as diverse as empathy and aphasia. The confusion only increases when dealing with the phrase's supposed synonyms, "private speech" and "inner speech." The researcher's hypotheses and experimental design hang on slippery definitional questions, and the definitions resist clarification even (or especially) on several rereadings of the major authors in the area—Piaget, Vygotsky, and Luria. The answers to these definitional questions have important implications for how the phenomenon is conceived and studied, for example, whether a subject must be in isolation to demonstrate self-regulation through egocentric speech, whether verbal self-regulation should be expected to be absent in adult populations, whether the absence of overt speech is evidence for one particular explanatory theory or merely the absence of information, or what verbal content (or forms) should be counted as instances of attempted verbal self-regulation. The originators of the term, "egocentric speech," Piaget and Vygotsky, would disagree on each of these points. The difficulty for the researcher is not that they would disagree; the difficulty is the obscurity of the disagreements (Zivin, 1972). Each new researcher spends months clarifying the phenomena, labels, and theoretical assumptions in the area, but without passing this on to give either the next researcher the benefit of that labor or to provide a set of common understandings on which a new set of conceptually compatible studies could build. The goal of this chapter is to provide such clarities.

In preview of the arguments presented, two main sources of confusion can be summarized. One is that although Vygotsky (1934/1962) and Piaget (1923/1955) each wrote arguments criticizing the other's and defending his own theory of egocentric speech, they really were not referring to the same phenomenon. Their use of the same phrase, "egocentric speech," for some—but far from all—of the same behaviors hides the phrase's incompatibility for the two writers. Worse, Piaget's vague suggestions of functions of egocentric speech (1923/1955) include several functions that are irrelevant to his major conception of egocentricity, but which are central to the Soviet view. Moreover, Piaget's (1962) style of indirect disagreement with Vygotsky gives the erroneous impression of sufficient common ground to cloud the sources of their dispute. Their true disagreement is on the relation between thought and language. Both writers' definitions of egocentric speech are grounded in their views of this relation. They thus cannot agree on what the phenomenon of egocentric speech is, even though they may agree that some behaviors appear to be examples of it. No third party can come to a definition of egocentric speech that accords with both of these authorities unless, like Kohlberg, Yaeger, and Hjertholm (1968), one posits a transition in the nature of egocentric speech between different developmental stages and assigns Vygotsky's conception to one period and Piaget's to another.

A second source of confusion is that Luria is usually interpreted as a spokesman for Vygotsky's position. Although attempting to demonstrate the truth of Vygotsky's hypothesis that stage-like changes in egocentric speech eventuate in silent verbal planning, Luria emphasized a rather different phenomenon. Vygotsky was concerned with the constant effect of the semantic side of egocentric speech while its physicalization in utterances changed and diminished. Luria noted and emphasized a stage before the supremacy of the semantic effect of egocentric speech in which the effect of the child's speech is due solely to the motor system of speech. A merger of these two views into one "Soviet position," as Luria is thought to present, seriously changes Vygotsky's hypothesis. Furthermore, most of Luria's tests (e.g. 1959, 1960, 1961*a*, 1961*b*, 1969) induce the child's speech, while Vygotsky's main claim was that the overt use of egocentric speech is natural and spontaneous. To fail to support Luria's findings, especially in regard to the motor (or impulse) aspect of speech, is not relevant to Vygotsky's hypothesis.

Are there not reliable secondary sources available to point out such difficulties? Unfortunately the secondary sources seem to be concerned with interpreting any of the three positions (Piaget's, Vygotsky's, or Luria's) into a framework more compatible with the psychology of American learning theory. These interpretations did not explicitly convey the preinterpretation viewpoints that they operated on. They did contribute to a proliferation of somewhat, but not entirely, overlapping definitions of "egocentric," "private," and "inner" speech. It will therefore be useful to review not only the viewpoints of the three major writers, but also the positions of their primary American interpreters—Reese, Flavell, and Kohlberg.

It must be noted that Bruner and Birch did much to further the study of verbal self-regulation and Soviet theory by their support of several students who were drawn to the area. Although Bruner and Birch were themselves involved in studying issues peripheral to verbal self-regulation, reports of those works (e.g. Bruner, 1965; Bruner, et al., 1966; Birch, 1966, 1971) stimulated interest in self-regulatory phenomena and Soviet theory. Bruner in fact wrote the introduction to the English translation of Vygotsky (Bruner, 1962). Because their interpretations of Vygotsky's and Piaget's work on egocentric speech are not published, their contributions cannot easily be reviewed. But the force of their influence can be mentioned.

Cole's contribution to the field should also be pointed out. The uninterpreted dissemination of a large body of Soviet psychological knowledge was greatly aided by his interest and energy, which resulted in the fine handbook he edited with Maltzman (1969), the collection of Vygotsky's work on higher psychological prophecies that Cole edited with several colleagues (Vygotsky, 1978), and the recent anthology of developmental research reprinted from the journal *Soviet Psychology* (Cole, 1978). These, the bulk of the uninterpreted English translations of developmental Soviet psychology, became available through Cole's efforts.

This chapter will first detail Piaget's view of egocentric speech which is embedded in his overall idea of egocentrism. From Piaget's position on egocentric speech, which was in print before that of Vygotsky, 12 dimensions will be drawn. The positions of others working in this area can be contrasted along these 12 dimensions. Then detailed explications of Vygotsky and Luria will be contrasted with each other and with that of Piaget. Finally contrast among the three American psychologists who actively interpreted the Soviet and Piagetian theories of speech and self-regulation will be presented.

As the present chapter moves from figure to figure, it becomes clear that the properties of the speech phenomena they analyze change, although the labels for the phenomena may not. Alternatively the labels for the speech phenomena may differ but maintain reference to many of the same properties. There are even aspects of some phenomena which may not properly be called speech. In these cases, some level of internal speech or speech-like associative effect is inferred from performance. There are however two properties which together are common to the various phenomena reviewed here: (1) a lack of communicative effectiveness to others or (2) an apparent lack of intent to communicate with others.

How can one refer with ease to the speech phenomena with which these properties associate? Flavell (1964/1966) suggested the term, "private speech," to cover the multiplicity of speech phenomena loosely aggregated around the idea of egocentric speech and inferred speech-like cognitive activity. Although "private speech" has become commonly used to refer to all speech that is not obviously aimed at others, its strong connotations of voluntary use of the meaning of words implicitly excludes speech which is used involuntarily and/or whose effect on concurrent action is through the motoric impulse of speech. It is therefore useful to create yet a new term to denote explicitly the full set of phenomena that have been associated with self-regulatory speech. This term should point to the above noted features of absence of communication (shared by both the lack of intention and lack of effectiveness to communicate), but it should also be neutral with regard to intention, effect, presumed underlying mechanism, and the apparent recipient of speech. Such neutrality admits all the speech phenomena (overt and covert) that have been suggested as self-regulatory plus those non-regulatory ones that have been associated with the labels of "egocentric" and "private" speech. The simplest new term with this range appears to be "acommunicative speech."

"Acommunicative speech" will be used in this chapter to provide a neutral umbrella for all related speech phenomena that will be contrasted. While one can hope for widespread adoption of such a broad unbiased term to refer to this entire area of research, it is unlikely. "Private speech," which does label a central (even if vaguely bounded) subset of acommunicative speech phenomena, has become widely used. By contrast, "speech-for-self" which was jointly coined by several researchers (Zivin, 1973) to capture that subset of acommunicative speech which was presumably self-regulating has tended to be used less precisely and now is frequently interchangeable with "private speech."

PIAGET

Piaget is the father of the idea and the label, "egocentric speech." While his first book-length work on childhood cognition (published in French in 1923, in English in 1926, and usually cited in the Meridian edition of 1955), focused on the child's communicative egocentricity, it established the central role of general egocentricity of mind. Egocentric speech was taken as an index of overall intellectual immaturity which Piaget termed "egocentricity." Then, as now (see Chapter 4; Sinclair-de Zwart, 1969; Sinclair, 1976), speech was for Piaget a window to the mind.

In this book Piaget (1923/1955) attempted to categorize exhaustively all speech forms of 6-year-olds, and accordingly generated eight categories, three of which he characterized as "egocentric," that is, as reflecting in different ways the egocentric quality of the child's mind. Approximately 45% of the peer-situated utterances during constructive school activities fell in one of these categories, resulting in the conclusion that approximately half of these 6- to 7-year-olds' utterances were egocentric speech. The criteria for coding utterances into these three categories and the passing references that Piaget (1923/1955) makes to the reasons (or motivations or functions) for these three types are:

1. *Repetition (echolalia):* Imitation of others' words, often "completely unconscious" (p. 35). The motivation for (or function of) echolalia is "the pleasure of using words...for the sake of playing with them," or "for the pleasure they give" (p. 35).
2. *Monologue:* Speech that accompanies action, often describing the action, the object of the action, or a desire for something. There are two types of motivation for (or function of) simple monologue: being "impelled...to speak as he acts" (p. 36) and to "use words to bring about what the action itself is powerless to do" (pp. 36-37).
3. *Collective monologue:* Essentially the same in content as monologue itself but is marked with some indication (for example "I say,...") that the child intends to interest or thinks he is interesting others in his thoughts or activities (p. 40). Thus it is communicative in intent, but it is not effective as communication. To be so classified by Piaget, this speech must take place in the presence of others. The motivation for (or function of) collective monologue is simply the feeling that one is being interesting to others.

In order to understand the lack of common properties among the phenomena and functions which he noted throughout the book under "egocentric speech," it is necessary to note that this first work was an attempt to characterize general intellectual immaturity (or egocentricity) which presumably could have many manifestations. Even in this first book one sees the emphasis on "being unable to see from another person's point of view" as the most important feature of all manifestations of central egocentricity. And in later work, this emphasis continues (see especially Piaget and Inhelder, 1956, 1966/1969; Inhelder and Piaget, 1958). These manifestations are best distinguished from the communicative egocentricity this is revealed in egocentric speech by noting and labeling them as separate phenomena:

1. The infant's inability to experience himself as an objectifiable object among other such objects (bodily egocentricity).

2. The preschooler's inability to know that a viewed object appears differently to someone who does not share his spatial relation to the object (perceptual egocentricity).
3. The young elementary schooler's inability to select his words and tone to fit the informational needs and social appropriateness of his audience (communicative egocentricity).
4. The preadolescent's difficulty in grasping the assumptions of his conversational partner (role-taking egocentricity).
5. The adolescent's difficulty in accepting the viability of social views other than his own (world-view egocentricity).[1]

The emphasis in this first book on speaking without regard for the usual consensual (or as Piaget terms it, "social" or "adapted") constraints on communicative speech allows the term, "egocentric speech," to cover all acommunicative speech that may arise for any reason. Piaget mentions various reasons (or motivations or functions) for the appearance of such speech, and this is where his misleading overlap with the egocentric speech of Vygotsky arises. Piaget is not particularly interested in why instances of egocentric speech occur, just that they do and thereby bear witness to an egocentric (or not yet socially adapted) quality of mind. He cites reasons for (or motivations or functions for) such egocentric speech, seemingly to make its reality more comprehensible to the reader. In this listing of motivations (as well as in his characterizing the egocentric mind as an only partially socially adapted transformation of the "natural" autistic state of the newborn's mind), Piaget (1923/1955) was strongly influenced by "Janet and the psycho-analysts" (p. 36) "and Psycho-analysts...as Bleuler" (p. 63). Piaget is rarely characterized as having been influenced by psychoanalysis (see Wolff, 1968), perhaps because the nonreductionistic structuralism that he later developed as an explanation of (certain aspects of) psychological development appears incompatible with or irrelevant to more motivational or functional reasons for specific actions. Indeed several explanatory gambits in his first book (1923/1955), such as the equation of some instances of monologue with the "magical language" of psychoanalysis (p. 37), do not fit with what we know by hindsight will become Piaget's theory.

[1]The ages mentioned for each type of egocentricity reflect the upper age at which Piaget (or Flavell et al., 1968, for role-taking egocentricity) sets the measurable diminution of the phenomenon. These upper ages are now in dispute, particularly for aspects of communicative egocentricity, for example Gelman and Shatz (1977). Piaget has no consistent labels for these various manifestations. I devised the labels to aid the distinctions.

The reader of that early book, especially if he aims to compare Piaget's views on acommunicative speech with the Soviets', is bound to be confused by not knowing how seriously to take the rather motivational and functional characterizations of egocentric speech that appear in the 1923 work. These appear while Piaget simultaneously develops the structural approach to which these characterizations will be irrelevant. For the clarification purposes of this chapter, these secondary and perhaps superfluous motivational and functional characterizations are important. If one takes them seriously, then Piaget and Vygotsky definitely *are* referring in some instances to the same phenomenon by the term, "egocentric speech." In his few references to "simple monologue," which magically creates a social presence by words or is an energizing stimulus to one's own actions, Piaget comes very close to describing what might be imagined as examples of the Soviet view of egocentric speech. Apparently Vygotsky (1934/1962) saw such similarities and based his criticism of Piaget on them.

Vygotsky (1934/1962) focused on Piaget's references to the motivations for egocentric speech and labeled them, "accompaniment to activity," (communicative-emotional) "expression," and (emotional) "release" functions (p. 45). He seized on the potentially effect-creating aspect of expressive and magical language functions as a link to the function that was central in his conception of egocentric speech: the planning function. Thus Piaget's secondary enumeration of motivations behind acommunicative speech gave Vygotsky a seeming point of overlap which he then systematically argued to be the central defining function of egocentric speech.

However, as can be told from the bulk of emphases in Piaget's book (1923/1955), and from the tenor of his later consolidated theorizing, Piaget is much more seriously interested in collective monologue and his own more structural (not functional) view of echolalia and simple monologue. Thus viewed there is no important Piagetian interpretation of acommunicative speech forms that are "for" or "to" the child himself: echolalia, simple monologue, and collective monologue all appear because the child does not yet realize that he is a social object among others and who is inappropriately (unadaptedly) uttering words. Piaget is not concerned with the immediate motivations for the utterances, only that their form is "unadapted." If one sees Piaget's serious emphasis to be on communicative misfiring and socially inappropriate use of words, then it becomes clear that, as defined by function, Piaget is referring to one kind of speech and Vygotsky to another. Piaget means using or not using words in accord with consensually agreed upon social convention. Vygotsky is talking about using words for one's own idiosyncratic cognitive-motoric self-regulation.

The confusion as to what Piaget and Vygotsky mean by egocentric speech can thus be seen as due to their both seeming to accept defining aspects that are peripheral to their own theories (for both writers these include the accompaniment to activity, expressive, and release functions), while each ultimately ignores those functions and asserts as centrally defining a feature that is wholly irrelevant to the theory of the other. Piaget emphasizes lack of understanding of others' viewpoints; Vygotsky emphasizes the potential for self-regulation. Piaget seems to recognize (1962), with a tact that obscures the point, that his concern with egocentric speech and Vygotsky's concern are unrelated to each other and therefore not worthy of contrast. In the same piece he also notes the direct clash of his earlier use of the term, "social," as in "social speech," with Vygotsky's use of the term. His 1962 *Comments on Vygotsky's Critical Remarks* illustrates that Piaget recognized that: (1) he and Vygotsky were referring to entirely different features as centrally defining properties of egocentric speech and (2) that the true difference between them rested in their views of the course of intellectual development and the role of language in it. Those details are given in this chapter under "Central Contrasts between Piaget and Vygotsky."

A final note should be made of one seeming point of contrast between Piaget and Vygotsky that tends to seduce comparison-makers into an empirical test of which view of egocentric speech, Piaget's or Vygotsky's, is confirmed in fact. Piaget hypothesizes that egocentric speech is the trailing tip of an atrophying phenomenon, such that its time course of appearance should differ from Vygotsky's. According to Piaget at around 6 or 7 years the child is learning to adapt his speech to others' communicative needs. What one observes at that age is the remaining non-adapted residue of still unsocialized utterances. Egocentric speech is becoming nonexistent at age 7 and presumably has disappeared by adulthood or the end of the development of formal operations. Vygotsky on the other hand sees egocentric speech becoming internalized at 5 to 6 years. Thus egocentric speech stops its spontaneous prevalence at around age 7, but it should be able to be re-evoked in older people of all ages by placing difficulties in their way when problem-solving or concentrating. It has not disappeared. It has simply gone underground. The two theorists thus appear to make differing time-course predictions about the same phenomenon.[2]

[2]This apparent avenue for a critical experiment between Piaget's and Vygotsky's positions was influentially suggested by Kohlberg, Yaeger, and Hjertholm (1968).

Dimensional Characterization of Piaget's Acommunicative Speech

The following 12 dimensions can be derived from Piaget's (1923/1955) book-length definition of egocentric speech and his 1962 *Comments*. These are dimensions that allow comparison across the other views of acommunicative speech reviewed in this chapter. The list includes features which were peripheral for Piaget, but important for other writers. For example, such issues as the three motivations behind specific speech occurrences and the relevance of being isolated while speaking are listed for comparison with other writers, but they are hardly relevant to Piaget.

For Piaget the 12 characterizations of acommunicative speech are:

1. *Self-Directedness:* Acommunicative speech is not in any sense directed toward oneself.
2. *Self-Regulation:* Acommunicative speech has no direct or indirect effect on one's own action or behavior.
3. *Isolation:* Acommunicative speech can occur in others' presence or in isolation; neither condition is relevant to its definition.
4. *Motivation by noninhibition:* Acommunicative speech may occur as a difficult-to-inhibit accompaniment to action (in echolalia or simple monologue); this is not a defining property, but an epiphenomenal expression of a certain egocentric level of mind.
5. *Motivation for effect:* Acommunicative speech may occur to further the pleasure of sound-play or the magical evocation of fantasized reality (in echolalia or simple monologue); these are not defining properties, but epiphenomenal expressions of a certain egocentric level of mind.
6. *Motivation for social communication-contact:* Acommunicative speech may occur in order verbally to contact or interest others (in collective monologue); this is not a defining property, but one of several transitory eliciting conditions.
7. *Modification for effective communication:* Acommunicative speech is not modified to meet the communication needs or expectations of an audience (should there be one); this is a defining property of all instances of Piaget's acommunicative speech.
8. *Diagnostic indication of developmental level:* Acommunicative speech's presence is a symptom of an as yet unadapted level of intellect; this is a defining property.
9. *Transitoriness:* Acommunicative speech is a transitory, stage-linked

phenomenon that disappears due to transformations of the underlying state of intellect by the time the child is 7 or 8 years old.

10. *Overtness:* A communicative speech is always overt. There is no sense in which this unconventionalized form of talking could be understood as having a covert form.

11. *Semantic versus motoric mechanism:* It is the meaning, not the physical stimulation of sound or speech-motor production, that is the aspect of the spoken word that is of theoretical interest concerning acommunicative speech.

12. *Spontaneity:* The acommunicative speech of interest is produced spontaneously by the child; he is not instructed to speak by someone else.

VYGOTSKY

In 1934 Vygotsky's work on *Thought and Language* was published posthumously in Russian. It was published in English in 1962. One chapter of the seven in the Vygotsky book is devoted to a vigorous attack on Piaget's views of the developmental course of language and thought. The chapter focuses on the nature of egocentric speech.

Vygotsky's (1934/1962) primary concern was to present a general theory of the development of the human mind. For Vygotsky, language and the social origin of each child's experience are crucial components of man's intellectual development. Drawing parallels and differences between human thought (and Yerkes' and Koehler's) findings on the problem-solving of apes, Vygotsky argued that preverbal children had a practical intelligence like that of apes. It appeared to be independent of any capacity to use symbol-based language. (Symbol-based here means language whose component signs have arbitrary relations to their referents. These signs can evoke awareness of the referents regardless of whether the referents are perceptually available; the referents are not limited to the emotions or desires of the sign-maker.[3]) This practical intelligence forms one root of intellectual develop-

[3]It is noteworthy that in 1934 Vygotsky suggested the now familiar essential test of whether apes have human-like language capacities: Could they learn to treat signs in one medium (which need not be vocal-oral; he suggested manual sign language) in such a way that they appeared to have internal representations of physically unavailable referents and such that the signs were not treated as properties of the referents? Vygotsky would have been among the first to accept Premack's (1976) evidence of apes' capacity to learn and use symbolic representations, some of which (e.g., distinguishing between referent and medium) was more stringently derived than the test Vygotsky had proposed. However because of Vygotsky's emphasis on the social context and spontaneousness of language-learning in man, which has not been found in apes, it is not clear that Vygotsky would change his claim that the practical thought that apes and children share is language-independent.

ment. The other root is social speech, which Vygotsky considered to originate in the child's earliest cries and babbling. Thus there is a preverbal root of intelligence and a separate preintellectual root of speech. Gradually in the preschool years, after the rudimentary speech behaviors of spoken language are mastered, these two processes merge. This interaction changes the nature of each process and makes a qualitative difference in the structure of intellectual development: a large proportion of the intellectual process becomes verbalizable, creating the process of thinking in words; almost all social speech becomes fully comprehended and laden with meaning for the child social-speaker; and intellectual development is now influenced by the new meanings, by verbalizable thought, as well as by information acquired through conversation with others. The essence of the new major influence on the course of intellectual development is the structuring of intellectual processes by the category structure that underlies (or is) word meaning.[4] As the two original roots of verbalizable thought unite, the child starts thinking in words for problem-solving and for organizing his activity. However at first he neither realizes that this thinking should be kept to himself nor has he sufficient fluent-economical facility in verbal thinking to allow all of this thinking to be silent. Gradually, starting around age five, the child begins to master the conventional rules for and facility in silent thinking. This silent verbal thought is called "inner speech" (see Sokolov, 1968/1972). It is predominantly internalized by 7 or 8, but can be re-externalized by obstacles at any age. It should be noted that Vygotsky proposes that some practical-spatial-intuitive thought remains ununited with words and that some purely expressive vocalizations remain nonintellectual. Egocentric speech is for Vygotsky the form of the transition from overt verbalized thought to inner speech. In the course of the transition, the form becomes more condensed for efficiency.[5]

Egocentric (overt) speech and inner (covert) speech are assumed by Vygotsky to have all the functions of orderly thought; however it is their use in the planning function (self-regulation) upon which Vygotsky focuses. Egocentric speech may, for Vygotsky, also epiphenomenally accom-

[4]It is no wonder, then, that Vygotsky devoted much energy and creativity to the study of the development of different category structures at different ages. Indeed he is now best known in America for his hypothesis—promulgated and detailed by Bruner (1965) and Bruner et al., (1966)—that there are three main stages of category structure: whimsical "heaps," intersecting but noncoextensive "complexes," and, superordinated and label-carrying "true concepts." Progress through these structures for scientific categories (as opposed to more casually used concepts in mundane or emotion-laden activities) is traced in Chapters 5 and 6 of Vygotsky's *Thought and Language*. It is also immortalized in the diagnostic Vygotsky Block Test (Hanfmann and Kasanin, 1942, pp. 30-31).

[5]Wertsch (Chapter 3) details Vygotsky's explanation of the orderliness of the form taken in this condensation.

pany activity, provide emotional release, or be socially-emotionally expressive. In the first case (accompanying activity), it may *accidentally* regulate the child's own action. This is demonstrated in Vygotsky's famous anecdotal illustration of the child who says of the pencil with which his is drawing, "It's broken!" and then suddenly includes the property of brokenness in the car he is drawing: the meaning of a word in the *accidentally*[6] spoken thought exerted pressure on the form of the concurrent action. This is Vygotsky's most primitive form of verbal self-regulation. The second, more mature form (emotional release) appears to remain accidental and occurs as description *during* activity. The third, most mature form (social-emotional expression) appears as a brief (element of a) plan *before* action (Vygotsky, 1934/1962, p. 17). For later contrast with Luria, note that Vygotsky focuses on word meaning (not on the motoric-neural medium of speech) as the only source of the regulating effect of words.

For Vygotsky there is a sense in which *all* verbalizable thinking is self-regulation. It is necessary to understand this in order to see that Vygotsky was not being sloppy or opportunistic in adopting, as examples of a function that was essentially self-regulating, all of Piaget's suggested functions of egocentric speech. Vygotsky could see all instances of speaking one's thoughts aloud as instances of potential (and not necessarily intentional) self-regulation because of his interpretation of the functioning of the second signal system[7] suggested by Pavlov. The interpretation of the second signal system by Vygotsky and other Soviet psychologists continues today in the Soviet Union as a dominant set of assumptions about the nature of man. It makes comprehensible man's creativity through symbols and his capacity to control his own behavior in spite of the human infant's complete dependence on, and presumed behavioral determination by, the forces of conditioning and social materialism.

The functioning of the second signal system may be briefly described. The first way in which the infant relates to his environment is as an organism that is wholly conditionable by physical contingencies. This relation is based on the conditioning principles of the *first signal* system: the

[6]See Meacham (Chapter 7) for an interpretation of how post-activity description may (purposely) aid self-regulation. This interpretation is consonant with Vygotsky's more vague suggestion implied in this anecdote.

[7]For more exacting detail on how Soviet theory explains the start and developmental relationship between the two signal systems, particularly in their relation to the orienting reaction (a general attentional exploratory and preparatory response, as in Lynn, 1966) the reader is referred to Harris (Chapter 2), A. N. Sokolov (1969), and E. N. Sokolov (1964/1969), in conjunction with Luria (1961*a*). The general Soviet theory of action under which this falls has been developed by Leont'ev and is explicated by Wertsch (Chapter 3). Further useful explication of the Soviet view of thought and action is available in Anokhin (1966/1969) and Gal'perin (1969).

sheer stimulus properties of his environment are the only ones the young child understands and uses in his social interactions, much like a dog who can solve problems in prediction and social interaction based on repetition of perceptible contingencies in his environment. As language and thought merge in the late preschool years, however, intangible meaning acquires a physical carrier through the spoken word. The young, first-signal-system-level child masters word comprehension and functional utterance by first reacting to and controlling his behavior by the physical-perceptible sound of a word, just as he previously reacted to other perceptible conditioned stimuli such as touches, glances, and sights of food. At this point the perceptible properties of the child's own speech are self-influencing. Gradually the special kind of conditioned stimulus that is a spoken word becomes differently attended to, so that the *second signal system* comes into effect: the significance (or meaning or underlying extension of a label) of words becomes understood and reacted to more strongly than the perceptible properties of the spoken word. As the child comes to react more and more to the meaning of the words that are presented to him, he becomes able, by presenting himself with spoken words, to elicit his own behavior. He thus becomes the executive of his own behavior through verbal self-regulation.

Soviet theorizing does not provide an explanation of this shift that is satisfying to most Western psychology. For the Soviets, however, the transition is based in the differential reorganization of neural excitations as a function of the special properties of language whose elements were originally material (at the level of the first signal system) and which is mapped in the nervous system by an intrinsically more "concentrated and mobile" (Luria, 1961*a*, p. 75) system of irradiations. Vygotsky focused on the properties of the second signal system, while Luria, as is illustrated below, focused on the transition from the first to the second signal system and thus emphasized physical stimulation in contrast to Vygotsky's emphasis on word meaning. By understanding the idea of the second signal system, it should be evident how, for Vygotsky, an unintentional utterance of words can "catch" one's own behavior and "regulate" it, particularly at the point of transition between the first and second signal systems' predominance.

Central Contrasts between Vygotsky and Piaget

Vygotsky found in Piaget's descriptions of egocentric speech an observable characteristic of the speech that should characterize his own hypothesized transition toward inner speech: socially inappropriate utterances that reflect what the child is thinking. Both writers characterize the preschool child as speaking socially inappropriately, and both writers refer to the child's lack of awareness about refraining from utterances that are not well adapted to others' understanding. Thus the fact of the child inappropriately uttering what is on his mind, the general age at which this becomes prevalent (about 5), and the age at which it becomes infrequent (about 8) combine to invite Vygotsky to identify his hypothesized transitional form of speech with what Piaget had already labeled, "egocentric speech." It should now be clear however that the two writers were referring to two very different processes as underlying and defining these surface features.

Confusion about the comparability of egocentric speech for Piaget and Vygotsky is increased by the nature of Piaget's *Comments on Vygotsky's Critical Remarks.* This is a small pamphlet that was distributed by MIT Press along with the first hardcover edition of Vygotsky's *Thought and Language.* Piaget had been provided with the Vygotsky manuscript in order to write such accompanying comments. This was particularly apt in light of the directly critical nature of Vygotsky's chapter devoted to reinterpretation of Piaget's work in the late 1920s and early 1930s. But it must be noted that Piaget read Vygotsky (one presumes for the first time) and wrote his comments in 1961 or 1962.

Piaget is highly respectful and correspondingly indirect in the *Comments.* He acknowledges the novelty and plausibility of Vygotsky's hypothesis that unintelligible speech may be a step toward something construed as interiorized speech. But it is crucial to note that Piaget could not consider this process of interiorization as central to an understanding of intellectual development: by 1961 Piaget already believed that the effective substrata of prelogical and logical thinking are nonverbal actions. Actions, not verbalizations, are for Piaget (e.g., Piaget and Inhelder, 1966/1969) the element of early life that develops into the operations of mind that act on abstract (not verbal) representations of propositions. While not much interested in the interiorization of speech, he bases his entire theory of intellectual development on the interiorization of nonverbal action. His one example of inner speech is highly socialized and adapted: it is a rehearsal of a scholarly defense of his theorizing that he might address to his colleagues.

Vygotsky's deepest disagreement with Piaget is with the latter's view that the speech and thought of the child start life as unsocialized. By "unsocialized," Vygotsky seems to mean (1) uninfluenced by the adaptive social effects that others' behavior must have on the child's behavior and (2) unable to affect the necessary adaptations for survival through gross communication of needs to others. For Vygotsky, whatever communication skills are present from birth, whether in sound or gesture, are adaptive for survival. From birth the use of these skills is adapted to, and shaped by, others' communication and these skills is adapted to, and shaped by, others' communication and responsiveness, through the action of the first signal system. The progress of development is from this socially adapted little being to a full human intellect whose thoughts may be quite individualized and unique. He objects to Piaget's course of development which is just the opposite: from an "autistic," fantasy-bound, and isolated little mind to a "socialized" one (that is for Piaget a scientifically objective and rationally valid thinker). In his attack he challenges Piaget's explanation of the phenomenon called "egocentric speech."

Piaget does write in the *Comments* as though he and Vygotsky were disagreeing about the ramifications of the same concept, but he succinctly states the difference between the functions each assigns to the acommunicative speech which both call, "egocentric." He concedes (indeed, complains) that he, Piaget, is speaking of the condition of mind that influences consensual communicability, while Vygotsky is not at all interested in communicability as an index of mental structure. If one reads the *Comments* carefully however, one notes that Piaget recognized that he and Vygotsky were really theorizing about two different processes between which there need be no choice. He says,

> But I call such behavior, [which does] not manage to understand the difference between two points of view, unadapted from the point of view of intellectual cooperation. This point of view is the only aspect of the problem which has concerned me but which does not seem to have interested Vygotsky. [1934/1962, p. 8]

In other words, Piaget was really interested in working on a structural level—with structural, not with functional (nor motivational), interpretations of instances of egocentric speech. He could well nod in his *Comments* to the value of Vygotsky's work on egocentric speech because it was, by the time that Piaget read it, irrelevant to his own view. The point for us is that Piaget recognized the irrelevance of the two views of egocentric speech, but did not explicitly say so, perhaps out of politeness or out of his continuing acceptance of responsibility for the theoretically peripheral functional explanations that appear in his 1923 work.

This chapter's main argument toward clarification is, in sum: (1) that Piaget's 1923 work presented interpretations of egocentric speech simultaneously in two realms (the functional and the structural); (2) that Vygotsky's 1934 comparison and those of others focused on the functional plane where comparison seemed possible; but (3) that Piaget more seriously meant (and later focused exclusively on) the structural plane, while Vygotsky made one of Piaget's irrelevant functions the whole of his own interpretation of egocentric speech. According to this argument there is no overlap between the egocentric speech of Piaget and Vygotsky, hence there is no place for comparison on this phenomenon.

The place for comparison between these thinkers, indeed the place of irreconcilable difference, is on two sets of views: (1) whether the developing mind goes from an autism-like lack of awareness of the world outside the infant's own idiosyncratic experiences to an adapted or socialized structure of mind that comprehends the world in an objective (consensual) way, or whether the infant starts with socially originating and socially conditioned similar experience of the world and develops toward greater individuality that arises from using language to explore experience, meaning, and implications; (2) whether language use simply follows and mirrors intellectual structure or actively contributes to its change. The first positions in each set obviously are Piaget's (as well as Freud's, 1935; Werner's, 1948; and James', 1890), while the second positions in each set are Vygotsky's. These two polarities are easy enough to trace in Piaget's and Vygotsky's writings, and thus require no elaboration here. Further details contrasting these two sets of views on mind, language, and social functioning between Vygotsky and Piaget are found in Chapter 4 by Bronckart and Ventouras-Spycher.

Dimensional Characterization of Vygotsky's Acommunicative Speech

The details of other features of Vygotsky's position can be itemized along the 12 dimensions derived from Piaget:

1. *Self-Directedness:* Vygotsky's acommunicative speech begins developmentally as undirected utterances. Unlike Piaget's, it soon acquires unaware and, later, aware direction to one's self as description and plan.
2. *Self-Regulation:* Contradictory to Piaget's phenomenon, Vygotsky's is always (at least potentially) self-regulatory. Even in the early years when speech follows behavior, it is considered at least potentially self-regulatory through the diffuse effects of description.
3. *Isolation:* Similar to Piaget's phenomenon, Vygotsky's can occur in others' presence or in isolation.
4. *Motivation by noninhibition:* Similar to one type of motivation cited by Piaget, Vygotsky's acommunicative speech may be emitted, during the early years, as involuntary accompaniment to action, both following it and being coterminous with it.
5. *Motivation for effect:* There is no parallel in Vygotsky to Piaget's notion that acommunicative speech can be motivated by primitive play. However the peripheral magical function of creating reality for Piaget is similar to the earliest form of the main effect for Vygotsky: the influence on outcomes through description.
6. *Motivation for social communication-contact:* Such motivation is not present in Vygotsky's acommunicative speech even though one of the

developmental roots of this speech is in vocal contact and instrumental (nonverbal) vocalizations.

7. *Modification for effective communication:* Similar to Piaget's, Vygotsky's acommunicative speech is not modified to fit an audience's communication needs. For Vygotsky there is no way in which it makes sense to think of a relevant audience for his egocentric speech besides the speaker himself.

8. *Diagnostic indication of developmental level:* Contrary to Piaget's, Vygotsky's acommunicative speech is not merely a symptom of level of development. For Vygotsky this speech does not appear until preschool years and later diminishes in overt appearance, but it can be re-evoked by stress at all ages.

9. *Transitoriness:* Again in contradiction to Piaget's view, for Vygotsky the seeming disappearance of egocentric speech is not due to its going out of existence, but rather to the inhibition of it (which then warrants the label, "inner speech," for its inhibited, covert form).

10. *Overtness:* For Vygotsky as well as Piaget, their forms of acommunicative speech are always overt. If covert, it would be called "inner speech."

11. *Semantic versus motoric mechanism:* As with Piaget, it is the meaning of the uttered words that is important to the theoretical interest of the phenomenon.

12. *Spontaneity:* Also in agreement with Piaget, reported instances of acommunicative speech were spontaneously produced by observed children.

LURIA

Luria's theoretical framings of his empirical work (e.g., 1957, 1959, 1960, 1961*a*, 1961*b*, 1969; Luria and Vinogradova, 1959; Luria and Yudovich, 1959) usually draw a direct line of development from Vygotsky through himself, concerning research on one form of acommunicative speech. For example, at the outset of his major book in English (1961a) he says:

> It [egocentric speech] was first a kind of *verbal orientation to surroundings,* as it were, reflecting the surrounding objects and checking the possibilities of using them to find a way out; and then it began to spread beyond the confines of the immediate situation, various systematized and generalized signs of the child's *previous experience* appearing in his "egocentric" speech.
>
> The use of verbal links to overcome a given difficulty seems here to have played a decisive part: this showed that the child's *own speech was involved in his practical activities*... he had begun to form *new func-*

> *tional systems* in whose innermost structure speech was involved. [pp. 33-34]

And he proceeds to introduce his experiments demonstrating how the speech of adults and, later, the child's own speech regulate the child's behavior.

It is little wonder then that almost all researchers of acommunicative speech equate the basic phenomena on which both Vygotsky and Luria worked. It is instructive however that Luria rarely uses the term, "egocentric speech," but rather uses the term, "self-regulatory speech," to refer to the child's speech that occurs in his laboratory.

There is more than a mere difference in methodology that separates the speech phenomena of Vygotsky and Luria. The latter conducts quantifiable motor and speech measurements in the laboratory; the former relies mainly on unsystematic observation of natural tasks. Although they both point to the self-affecting function of the child's own speech, Luria has an importantly limited phenomenon under consideration and also has a different theoretical goal. The goal will be considered first.

Luria's main purpose is to create an empirical demonstration, interwoven with common Soviet theory (including Vygotsky's), to demonstrate that a model of the ontological development of voluntary behavior can be created within the Marxist-Pavlovian materialist framework. This framework makes the conditioning of neurological irradiations to external stimuli the initial assumption in the explanation of any behavior. Luria is solving a Soviet version of the question of free will, given Marxist-Pavlovian materialism. He is creating a demonstration of what could be produced within the age dependent limits on conditionability. He is not discovering (or uncovering) the spontaneous course of developmental events that do occur naturally.

Hence most Western psychologists understand Luria to be presenting a developmentally timed description of how Vygotsky's egocentric speech becomes incorporated into the preschool child's natural self-regulation, when at most, Luria was presenting the limits for conditioning. Within these limits the child's self-directed overt speech might be effective in natural life *if* it happens that the child does use it spontaneously. Luria does not demonstrate such spontaneous use.

Other sources of disjunction between Vygotsky's and Luria's acommunicative speech become clear in examining Luria's empirical work. The experiments were varied and ingenious. Only the most famous set will be summarized here. Luria suggests that his experiments give psychological detail to the developmental course suggested by Vygotsky. The present summary includes the age points at which Luria (or his colleagues) found different limits on the conditionability of various aspects of self-regulatory speech.

For Luria's experiments to be intelligible to the Western reader one must understand that the Soviet materialist position separates the effects of the *impulse* aspect of speech from the *semantic* aspect of speech. Both aspects are potentially effective on behavior, and hence each is regulatory. The former refers to both the stimulation by sheer sound in hearing and by the efferent and reafferent motor excitation when one is the producer of the speech. The impulse side of speech can be either initiating or inhibiting, depending on the net of prior neural stimulation; both effects are aspects of the neurophysiological irradiation patterns that, in Soviet psychology, play important roles in the explanation of all awareness and behavior.

The semantic aspect is the one on which Vygotsky focused. Soviet work after Vygotsky details the semantic aspect as including: (1) the power to isolate properties denoted by categorical labeling through a word and (2) the power of word meaning to make idiosyncratic nets of association with other word meanings through experience and conversation (Luria, 1969). This latter was given less attention by Vygotsky but its behavioral aspect has become widely studied in the West as semantic conditioning or verbal conditioning.

To be subject to conditioning, or even to the elicitation of behavior by the impulse side of speech, is to be at the level of the first signal system. Moving to the distinctively human semantic aspect of speech, as discussed earlier, is moving to the level of the second signal system.

Luria's best known experiments to demonstrate the steps by which the child might establish voluntary regulation of his movements are the bulb-press studies. The experimental situation of these studies has the child pressing a rubber bulb as he is instructed by the experimenter to start, stop, or coordinate his presses with a flashing light and/or with his own words. At 1½ to 2½ years there is: (1) the initating function of speech by another person, but there is not yet the (2) inhibiting function of speech by another; and there are neither (3) initiating nor (4) inhibiting functions of the child's speech. (Inititating and inhibiting here refer to stimulus effect on the child's behavior, not to the Soviets' often invoked underlying excitation or inhibition within neural patterns that sum to inititation or inhibition of motor action.) The presence of (1) and the absence of (2) are evidenced by the child intensifying his pressing when the experimenter tells him to stop. The absence of (3) and (4) is shown by the child's mediocre coordination when he is to say "Go!" at each light flash: instead random pressing accompanies each light flash, although the child is supposed to coordinate his verbalizations and his presses with each flash. At 3 to 4 years there are both initiating and inhibiting functions of another's speech and the initiating function of the child's own speech, but the inhibiting function of his own speech has not yet developed: he can do the two tasks the younger children failed. However if he is asked to say "Press" to one light and "Don't press" to another light and to act in accord with his two different statements, he presses to both lights (although he can easily make the correct coordinated verbalizations). Another experiment similarly illustrates the lack of the full regulating function of the child's own speech before 4½ years. If the 3- or 4-year-old is asked to say, "I shall press twice," he will verbalize correctly, but make one protracted press that lasts for the duration of his utterance; on the other hand if he says "Go! Go!" he will press correctly (Luria, 1961*a*; Tikhomirov, 1958/1975). Luria takes this last contrast as strong evidence that the control still rests in the patterns of generalized excitement in the motor effector system and has not yet been fully transferred to the semantic aspect of what the child says. By 4½ to 5½ years this task is easily passed, and control has supposedly been transferred to the full language system.

Luria is not directly interested in the interiorization of this control once it has been established. In fact his more frequent clinical interests were in reexternalizing or relearning external means of verbal control when control has been lost through various pathologies (e.g., 1959). In line with this, all the evidence for verbal control that he reports is overt speech. The oldest age cited in the above series of studies is 5½ years, while Vygotsky would indicate that 8-year-olds must be studied to see the interiorizing of spontaneous self-regulatory speech.

Central Contrasts between Luria and Vygotsky

Having seen Luria's stages of self-regulation, one can examine whether Luria and Vygotsky mean the same thing by self-regulation. First, do they both have the same answer for the question "Why tell yourself something you must already know?" (Wozniak, 1973). Vygotsky would answer by the developmental claim that during preschool years the child simply does much thinking aloud; he does not yet know how to inhibit the thought which has newly united with speech. Luria would give a neurophysiological answer attuned to efficient mutual influence of interacting systems. He emphasizes how much more "mobile" (that is, conditionable, discriminating, and generalizable) the verbal system is in comparison with all other motor systems. The verbal system is also seen to mature more quickly. Thus Luria implies that it is organismically functional to put control of nonverbal motor behavior under the control of verbal behavior. In Luria's view his children are not failing to inhibit the overt expression of thought; they are employing an external control circuit to augment the faulty internal one. For Luria the children are talking *to* control themselves; for Vygotsky they are happening to talk while they are thinking, and talk happens to affect behavior. In this sense Luria sees children acting (albeit unawaredly) as agents on their own behavior by speaking "to" themselves. Vygotsky does not see such a gulf between agent and object.

A second point on which these two writers differ in their interpretation of self-regulation is what aspect of speech (impulse, semantic, or both) affects the speaker's behavior. Vygotsky focuses exclusively on the semantic aspect of speech. It is meaning, not content-free physical stimulation, which interests Vygotsky. Luria, on the other hand, emphasizes the sheer activational role of speech during the early years, but sees both impulse and semantic aspects contributing to full self-regulation.

The third and most far-reaching difference between the two theorists' work on self-regulation is in the phenomena they actually studied. Vygotsky saw and elicited (by creating stresses and frustrations) the natural spontaneous speech of children engaged in usual daily activities. Luria instructed his children on what to say and when to say it. All his bulb-press findings came from situations in which the subjects might not have used speech had they been left to their own proclivities. Thus all one can tell from these experiments are the ages at which particular utterances, by adults or by children, could and could not regulate the child's behavior—if the speaker had naturally chosen to make these (or similar) utterances.

It is clear, then, that while Luria and Vygotsky share a theoretical thread, the speech instances that each actually examined are similar only in that they require, by age 4½, parallelism between self-regulating speech content and goal (or form) of behavior. The areas of nonoverlap (impulse aspect, ages examined, and difference in spontaneity) indicate quite dissimilar types of acommunicative speech under study by each. For later comparison with some American interpreters, it is useful to note one similarity in the self-regulation by speech function which both invoke: the regulation concerns the goal (or form) of active, generally concurrent behavior; it has nothing to do with using speech for priming or mnemonic strategies in verbal memory tasks. In sum if the self-regulatory speech which Luria actually studied is taken to exemplify his accommunicative speech, the similarity of this speech with Vygotsky's is only moderate in theoretical emphases and not demonstrably similar as empirical phenomena.

Dimensional Characterization of Luria's Acommunicative Speech

The phenomenon studied in Luria's laboratory can be summarized through the 12 familiar dimensions:

1. *Self-Directedness:* Unlike Piaget but coincident with Vygotsky, Luria's acommunicative speech is (always) self-directed.

2. *Self-Regulation:* In contrast to Piaget but like Vygotsky, Luria's acommunicative speech is (always) self-regulatory.

3. *Isolation:* Similar to both Piaget and Vygotsky, Luria's acommunicative speech can occur alone or in others' presence.

4. *Motivation by noninhibition:* Like one form of motivation for Piaget and for Vygotsky, Luria's speech may involuntarily accompany action in the early years before that speech becomes voluntary. This is asserted, but not demonstrated, by Luria.
5. *Motivation for effect:* Unlike Piaget and like Vygotsky, Luria's speech is always aimed at self-regulation.
6. *Motivation for social communication-contact:* As with Vygotsky, social contact is not a motivation for Luria's communicative speech, despite its roots in social interaction.
7. *Modification for effective communication:* For Vygotsky's reasons, not Piaget's, Luria would not characterize this speech as being modified to fit the communicative needs of an external audience. In practice, the utterance given to the child by the experimenters is shaped by their idea of the form that would be the most efficient for the demonstration of effect. The child does not determine content or form.
8. *Diagnostic indication of developmental level:* Contrary to Piaget and somewhat like Vygotsky, for Luria the first appearance of this speech is linked to developmental level; its lack of regulatory effect, not its presence, would be a symptom of intellectual level.
9. *Transitoriness:* Contrary to Piaget's, but identical to Vygotsky's position, the purported disappearance of this speech would be considered by Luria not as going out of existence, but as becoming internalized. (Recall that Luria suggests, but never demonstrates, such a decline).
10. *Overtness:* As with Piaget and Vygotsky, the speech referred to as "egocentric speech" is always overt; if it were covert, it would be called "inner speech." Both forms have a self-regulatory function for Luria and Vygotsky.
11. *Semantic versus motoric mechanism:* Luria's point of clear departure from Vygotsky as well as from Piaget is that the neuromotor aspects of hearing and speaking are, at an early developmental level, as important as are the effects of word meaning at a later level.
12. *Spontaneity:* While spontaneity of acommunicative speech is hypothesized in natural settings by Piaget, Vygotsky, and Luria, spontaneity does not characterize Luria's studied phenomenon.

REESE

The Soviet work of both Vygotsky and Luria became linked to the American study of verbal mediation by Hayne Reese in an influential article in 1962. Summarizing earlier United States work showing maturing children's decreasing difficulties with various aspects of discrimination tasks, he cited the work of Kuenne (1946) and of Kendler, Kendler, and Wells (1960) to illustrate developmental states in which spontaneous labels were apparently used by older children to mediate responses but were not (presumably) within the capacity of preschoolers. The 1960 Kendler paper was the first to frame the "mediational deficiency" hypothesis: at early stages children do not use self-produced labels to aid their discriminations either overtly or covertly. The Reese paper was the one to publicize Luria's bulb-press experiments and link them to the mediation deficiency hypothesis.

Reese provided several clear characterizations of the self-regulatory aspects of verbal mediation. This clarity seems to have been ignored by subsequent workers. One characterization was that verbal mediation acted on concurrent action and/or perception rather than on memory tasks. Reese did not introduce memory as a relevant domain; he simply equated United States discrimination tasks with Luria's bulb-press problems and noted the potential for verbal mediation in both. A second point was that the ages at which words became useful in aiding discrimination could vary with differing discrimination tasks. A third important distinction was made between the voluntary versus involuntary uses of verbal mediation. He noted that we did not (as we still do not) know to what degree the effects of verbal mediation are under voluntary control. Rehearsal itself surely is voluntary, but there is no reason to believe, as later workers seemed to assume, that mediation is rehearsal.

The main force of the Reese paper was to propose the mediation deficiency hypothesis as the result of developmental stages and to link the Lurian work with a solution to the problems of the nature of the stages and of verbal mediation itself. It should be noted that Reese never used the phrases, "self-regulatory speech," "egocentric speech," or "inner speech." He wrote only of "verbal mediation." In this he did not distinguish between overt and covert forms of verbal mediation; the covert form is simply assumed to be a more mature package for the same fundamental function.

Dimensional Characterization of Reese's Acommunicative Speech

While presenting these clear parallels between Soviet and Western concerns, Reese did little to modify Luria's characterization of semantically, self-regulatory speech. On the 12 dimensions, Reese's verbal mediation has the following attributes:

1. *Self-Directedness:* Reese's acommunicative speech is always self-directed by definition, but this does not imply that its use is always at the level of voluntary awareness.

2. *Self-Regulation:* Reese's acommunicative speech is always self-regulatory, if the verbal response does occur.

3. *Isolation:* Reese's acommunicative speech can occur alone or in others' presence.
4. *Motivation by noninhibition:* Whether occurrence of Reese's acommunicative speech is involuntary or voluntary is opened as a question.
5. *Motivation for effect:* The only effect of acommunicative speech that Reese considers is self-directed aid in problem-solving, that is, self-regulation.
6. *Motivation for social communication-contact:* This is never characteristic of Reese's acommunicative speech.
7. *Modification for effective communication:* Fit to audience needs is irrelevant for Reese's phenomenon.
8. *Diagnostic indication of developmental level:* Whether speech is used to mediate task performance would be a symptom of developmental level; non-use would indicate preschool level, and silent use would indicate greatest maturity.
9. *Transitoriness:* Little is said about the transition from overt to covert speech; hence the questions of the disappearance of the speech and the timing of its disappearance are not raised.
10. *Overtness:* Contrary to the three writers already reviewed, Reese makes the complete equivalence of the function of overt and covert forms; in almost all the work he cites, the existence of the covert form is inferred from improved performance.
11. *Semantic versus motoric mechanism:* Only the semantic aspect, not the impulse aspect, is relevant to Reese's acommunicative speech.
12. *Spontaneity:* Spontaneous and instructed wordings, are treated as having equally mediating powers, and hence as equivalent in Reese's review.

FLAVELL

Flavell and his colleagues were inspired by Luria and Vygotsky toward two lines of investigation and by Piaget toward a third. Flavell's (1964/1966) paper, outlining the boundaries of "private speech," indicates that he initially saw as related all phenomona that had been associated in print with "egocentric speech." By 1970 he had clearly divided self-regulatory studies from ones concerned with perspective-taking. This followed his making new distinctions in the study of self-regulation.

Production Deficiency versus Mediation Deficiency

The first branch of Flavell's work made a finer distinction than had Reese in examining preschoolers' apparent lack of verbal self-regulation. The most often cited paper in this series is by Flavell, Beach, and Chinsky (1966). It expands the lead of Maccoby (1964) in making a distinction between speech not being produced (and thus not being available for mediation) versus speech being produced, but being unable to provide mediating links with behavior. Flavell, Beach, and Chinsky (1966) dubbed the former position as the "production deficiency hypothesis," and called the latter position the "mediation deficiency hypothesis." This distinction cast Reese (1962) in support of the mediation deficiency hypothesis, while Flavell (Flavell, Beach, and Chinsky, 1966; Keeny, Cannizo and Flavell, 1967; Corsini, Pick, and Flavell, 1968) eventually found evidence more supportive of the production deficiency hypothesis.

Flavell, Beach, and Chinsky, (1966) were wise enough to realize that the conditions for testing the production deficiency hypothesis differed from those for testing the mediation deficiency hypothesis by requiring that there be an opportunity to see whether spontaneous production of potentially mediating words would occur. This could be observed by electromyographic readings of throat and tongue muscles at the subvocal level as studied by Sokolov (1968/1972), but they chose to examine only the overt level that would be voiced or shown in lip movements. They emphasized that to *test* the production deficiency hypothesis one had to use, as the dependent variable, the presence versus the absence of spontaneous vocalizations, not the effect versus the noneffect of induced speech. They recognized that Luria did not test the production deficiency hypothesis, but rather tested only the mediation deficiency hypothesis by his procedure of supplying the words that the child was to utter.

In fulfilling what they detailedly analyzed to be the ideal conditions for testing the production deficiency hypothesis, Flavell, Beach, and Chinsky (1966) suggested a new function that the speech in question had to perform: it had to aid recall. They looked for verbal production in a delayed serial recall task because it appeared to them to have the highest probability of eliciting verbalization and of inviting the child to use its aid overtly. Thus an entirely new function of self-regulating speech was introduced. Whereas before it had been thought to foster general activation and goal-orienting self-guidance, it now was also to cover strategies for memory encoding during tasks that find little parallel in daily intellectual life.[8]

If the speech in question is defined by its attributed function, Flavell, Beach, and Chinsky (1966) broadened the meaning of the acommunicative speech

[8]Meacham (Chapter 7) develops a memory-aiding conception of self-regulating speech. By focusing on behavioral integration during ongoing activity, Meacham is quite in agreement with the Soviet servomechanistic "receptor of action" (Luria, 1969) and the "acceptor of effect" (Anokhin, 1966/1969) view of mechanisms underlying self-regulation. Flavell's recall (as task) suggests another function that has its own goal.

whose basic functions on the semantic side had stayed in agreement from Vygotsky through Reese. There does not appear in the literature any notice of this change; and ignoring Reese's implication that the stages for differing tasks might differ, there does not appear any suggestion until 1966 that findings of preschoolers' production deficiency on recall tasks might be inconsistent with other work on verbal self-regulation.

It is worth noting that Flavell introduced two further modifications of Reese's notion of self-regulation through speech. For the first time since Piaget implied that acommunicative speech is mere accompaniment to action or word play, the suggestion is made, via the mediation deficiency hypothesis, that acommunicative speech might miss its mark and have no self-regulative function at all. The second modification is the implication that verbal mediation is a phenomenon of an isolated person. Although Flavell and his coworkers take the position of requiring isolation primarily to safeguard experimental logic in testing for production of speech (which may or may not be correlated with improved performance), the requirement of isolation tends to suggest that overt verbal self-regulation would not occur in the presence of others.

Interpretation and Replication of Soviet Studies of Verbal Self-Regulation

The second branch of Flavell's work on acommunicative speech focuses on his synthesis of Vygotsky's and Luria's work and his conclusion that neither reported solid, replicable phenomena. By paraphrasing the Lurian stages and adding the Vygotskian final stage, Miller, Shelton, and Flavell (1970) promote the impression that all the Soviet stages are of the same level of empirical support, are all theoretically integrated with each other, and all have been found to be naturally occurring steps in self-regulation. Thus, failure to replicate either Luria or Vygotsky would cast doubt on the whole.[9]

Much energy in this branch of work went into replicating Luria's bulb-press studies. Jarvis (1964, 1968) and Miller, Shelton, and Flavell (1970) were reports of attempts to replicate Luria. They saw Luria as testing the mediation deficiency hypothesis. Such replications thus fit Flavell's program of testing both production and mediation deficiency hypotheses.

These attempted replications did not repeat Luria's results (nor did several other attempted replications, i.e., Beiswenger, 1968; Rondal, 1974, 1975; Wilder, 1968; and others reviewed by Wozniak, 1972. It is interesting that Flavell eventually dismissed the Soviet work on verbal self-regulation and did not exempt from dismissal Soviet studies wherein spontaneous speech production deficiency. He did not, however, see the need (for reasons of

[9]The actual synthesizing theory is to be found in the work of Leont'ev, as described by Wertsch (Chapter 3).

clarity in introducing the necessity for allowing spontaneity in tests of production deficiency. He did not, however, see the need (for reasons of ecological validity) of allowing spontaneous speech in tests of mediation deficiency. Neither did he consider that induced speech may be a different phenomenon from spontaneous speech. It is particularly ironic that Flavell did not see the need for spontaneity in all tests concerning the mechanisms of verbal self-influence since he was the first sponsor of an American attempt to replicate Vygotsky's naturalistic observations. On the questions of whether the child overtly verbalizes, whether the content is related to the task, and whether performance improves with more task-relevant speech, Klein's (1964) doctoral dissertation found ambiguous but seemingly positive answers. However, the power of the naturalistic stance in determining that the phenomenon actually exists in the child's development went unnoted by Flavell and was not continued in his later work.

Flavell took the failures to replicate Luria as casting doubt on the whole Soviet position, including Vygotsky's initial hypothesis of spontaneous self-regulating speech. This is not so easily assumed if one is clear that Vygotsky and Luria were not studying the very same phenomenon. As noted, Vygotsky studied and theorized about spontaneously produced speech, while Luria studied induced speech which he claimed only as a model of possible function, not as a claim of naturally found stages.

Role-Taking

This third branch of Flavell's work is the rather large collection of studies on the child's capacity to take the role of the other. The research questions and strategies in this body of work are rooted in Piaget's concept of egocentricity and egocentric speech. These studies are summarized in a book by Flavell and many co-workers (1968). Happily they do not confuse the two primary meanings of egocentric speech (oblivious to other viewpoints and self-regulation). They take their heritage from Piaget's focus on his original interpretation of egocentric speech as a symptom of a structure of mind that prevents one from knowing that there are other viewpoints and hence from taking the role of the other to whom one is speaking. Such role-taking is commonly associated with empathy. In this research Flavell is interested in replicating and expanding Piaget's (1923/1955) exploration of the child's capacity to take another's role by meeting the other's communication needs.

In no sense does this work deal with self-regulation through speech. It should be obvious that its relation to the non-Piagetian work is simply through the historical association of Piaget's inquiry into consensual perspective-taking in conversation with Vygotsky's inquiry into language and self-regulation. There would thus be little profit in comparing this third branch of Flavell's work with other work reviewed in this chapter.

Dimensional Characterization of Flavell's Acommunicative Speech

A summary of the self-regulatory acommunicative speech studied by Flavell through 1970 is of direct relevance in this review. He ignores acommunicative speech in his role-taking research. The resulting characterization is quite similar to that of Reese's acommunicative speech.

1. *Self-Directedness:* The speech may or may not be directed to oneself, depending upon whether it is effective in mediation; if preschoolers' produced acommunicative speech is mediation-deficient, then it is not self-directed. When produced, this acommunicative speech is mediating and thus self-directed.
2. *Self-Regulation:* The speech may or may not be self-regulating, depending upon whether it is effective in mediation; if preschoolers' produced acommunicative speech is mediation-deficient, then it is not self-regulating. When produced, this acommunicative speech is mediating and thus self-regulating.
3. *Isolation:* Although in principle Flavell's acommunicative speech could occur in isolation or in the company of others, he emphasizes that there would be more convincing demonstration of its existence if the child were isolated; this makes isolation an operationally, if not substantively, defining property for Flavell. It has not been a discriminating property for any of the researchers reviewed here until Flavell.
4. *Motivation by noninhibition:* Flavell does not consider whether mediating speech may be involuntarily elicited and resistant to inhibition; rather, he is concerned with inability to produce it. Flavell's analysis suggests that production is voluntary, but that mediation is an effect of maturity beyond the reach of volition.
5. *Motivation for effect:* The only effects of acommunicative speech that Flavell considers are self-regulatory, such as verbal mediation. He expands on Reese's similar position by adding memory aid as a mediating process.
6. *Motivation for social communication-contact:* This is not relevant to Flavell's acommunicative speech.
7. *Modification for effective communication:* This is not relevant to Flavell's self-regulatory acommunicative speech. His acommunicative role-taking speech, begins to be mastered around age 9.
8. *Diagnostic indication of developmental level:* The absence of acommunicative speech, and hypothetically, its lack of effect despite its presence, is a symptom of a preschool level of development for Flavell.
9. *Transitoriness:* Little attention is given by Flavell to how transitory the overt form may be. It is not clear that Flavell sees the overt form as substantially less mature than the covert form.

10. *Overtness:* Overt and covert forms are considered equivalent by Flavell.
11. *Semantic versus motoric mechanism:* Only the semantic aspect of speech is relevant for Flavell.
12. *Spontaneity:* Both spontaneous and nonspontaneous speech were studied for their mediating effects. Nonspontaneous speech is considered capable of mediating; spontaneity is considered necessary only to test for whether the speech is produced.

KOHLBERG

Historically, Kohlberg is the last figure to promote widespread interest in the acommunicative speech associated with Piaget and Vygotsky. The primary article that did this (Kohlberg, Yaeger, and Hjertholm, 1968) draws on the student research of Yaeger (1968) and Hjertholm (1968). These efforts invite one back to the original apparent dispute between Piaget and Vygotsky, provide the promise of crisp empirical tests to distinguish between their explanatory adequacies, outline a category system for recording different forms of acommunicative speech, and suggest a stage-wise hierarchical ordering for the appearance of these forms. The unique position that Kohlberg put forth includes the points: (1) that all of his coded forms of acommunicative speech could be organized into a hierarchy of stages and (2) that the whole of the hierarchy was best understood through George Herbert Mead's (1934) view that the child builds a differentiated self through conversations of gestures (or poorly articulated speech) with aspects of the self that represent the "generalized other." This may be a valuable new view of acommunicative speech, but the 1968 article left a legacy of confusion about the original positions of Piaget and Vygotsky.

As detailed below, the central source of confusion is the manner in which Kohlberg reinterprets Piaget, Vygotsky, and even Luria. The reader has great difficulty squaring the reinterpretations with the original work or in being able to retrace the original points that lead Kohlberg to his new interpretations. Less important in creating long-term confusion, but nevertheless presenting obstacles to understanding the Piagetian and Soviet roots of Kohlberg's argument, are difficult aspects of the article's style. the argument frequently shifts its apparent aim, and terminology slips between various labels for acommunicative speech in a way that hinders the student from tracing the theoretical lineage of a speech form.

Kohlberg's empirical approach proceeds from his valuable suggestion about the basis for dispute between Piaget and Vygotsky. He highlights the one feature of the surface phenomena that seems common to both theorists' descriptions as the relatively poor audibility of acommunicative speech. He aptly generalizes the meaning of this common feature: "speech which is not addressed or adapted to a listener" (Kohlberg, Yaeger, and Hjertholm,

1968, p. 692). This is in fact very much like this chapter's assertion of the common acommunicative property that encompasses the phenomena cited by the writers reviewed here. Rather than pointing to a lack of basic similarity between Vygotsky and Piaget, suggested by the singularity and level of abstraction of this property, Kohlberg focuses on this property as evidence of basic comparability and testability between these two views. As argued earlier the assumption of such comparability between Vygotsky's and Piaget's explanations of egocentric speech suggests a misunderstanding of their overall theories of thought and language.

Kohlberg's six forms of acommunicative speech draw upon a close reading of motives for speech occurrences that Piaget suggested in his 1923 work, as well as upon an integration of Vygotsky and Luria, and upon Kohlberg's own observations of child speech. The reader will recognize the first and third forms as originating with Piaget and the fifth as having Vygotsky's self-regulating function. The six forms are:

1. Word play and repetition
2. Remarks to nonhuman objects
3. Description of one's own activity
4. Questions answered by one's self
5. Self-guiding comments
6. Inaudible muttering

Because it is covert, Kohlberg adds silent inner speech, the most mature type of acommunicative speech, as a final but not wholly comparable category.

Kohlberg marshalls the patterns that were found in these categories (of nonisolated children's spontaneous utterances) to make these three suggestions: all acommunicative speech is due to poor differentiation of self from other; there will be greater diversity of speech forms in isolation than in others' presence; the developmental course of the speech forms that are uttered in isolation should differ from the course of speech forms in the company of others. These suggestions bear on the sense of others' presence and the interiorization of a generalized other, which Kohlberg argues are central factors in the appearance of acommunicative speech.

It does not further the purpose of clarifying Kohlberg's position to detail problems in his suggestions for a hierarchy. Such problems include the lack of justification of the developmental order suggested and the absence of criteria for determining why these particular acommunicative phenomena and not (all) others compose the hierarchy. However it is important to note the central unity that Kohlberg claims for the forms in the hierarchy. They are all self-communicative, in the sense of being directed to aspects of the self for the purpose of developing ways of communicating with imaginable others. It is apparent that self-communication would have an important function from a position like Kohlberg's (or Mead's), wherein aspects of the self stand in social relation to each other as the components of the more complex, socialized self (which includes a well-differentiated central self and a generalized other). Self-communication is what Mead cites as the major manner of differentiating the self, by differentiating and integrating the generalized other. Kohlberg's hierarchy is proposed as the set of forms speech takes as this one function develops.

The confusing reinterpretations of Piaget and particularly of Vygotsky, seem to arise out of Kohlberg's rhetorical strategy of pitting predictions from these two theorists against each other and of noting phenomena for which neither could account. To cast Piaget and Vygotsky in these roles, Kohlberg presented their positions as more neatly opposing and mutually relevant than they are. Kohlberg suggests, for example, that Vygotsky could not account for the appearance after age 7 of overt acommunicative speech. Reader confusion arises in two ways from such an erroneous assertion. One arises simply because an incorrect interpretation of Vygotsky's position is promoted; Vygotsky indeed accounts for such appearances as due to processing augmentation during difficulty. The second is an indirect distortion of Vygotsky's entire theory of the development of thought and language. If the student attempted to make his understanding of Vygotsky agree with the impossibility of stress evoking overt acommunicative speech at any age, he would then have to distort his accurate understanding of Vygotsky's overall view of verbal self-regulation, which is that self-regulating speech can go underground precisely because the regulated activity no longer presents any great difficulty.

A final source of difficulty in gaining an accurate understanding of Vygotsky's position through Kohlberg's presentation is that Kohlberg takes Luria's emphases and attributes them to Vygotsky. Even granting that no Western theorist had drawn a clear set of distinctions between Luria and Vygotsky, and that Flavell's interpretation of Luria's nonreplications had weakened the total Soviet position, to build an analysis of Vygotsky on points he never made, had to foster misinterpretation of his position.

Dimensional Characterization of Kohlberg's Acommunicative Speech

Kohlberg's six acommunicative speech forms can be characterized along the 12 familiar dimensions as follows:

1. *Self-Directedness:* Kohlberg considers all six speech categories as directed to an aspect of the differentiating self. Of all the writers reviewed, Kohlberg has the clearest implication of the speaker conceptualizing the self as an audience of his speech. This is a defining feature of his self-communative acommunicative speech.
2. *Self-Regulation:* Only one of Kohlberg's six categories is self-regulating.
3. *Isolation:* Kohlberg is the one writer reviewed who makes isolation a centrally defining feature of the type of speech elicited. The presence of a

real other to whom one could speak appears, in Kohlberg's view, to prevent overt speech that is truly directed to the self.

4. *Motivation by noninhibition:* Kohlberg's emphasis on direction to oneself suggests that this speech does not occur simply because it cannot be inhibited.
5. *Motivation for effect:* All six forms have the same overall effect of furthering the differentiation of self; each form appears for a more specific (and for Kohlberg, wholly secondary) reason which suggests the label for each form.
6. *Motivation for social communication-contact:* Kohlberg is the one theorist reviewed who sees this speech as having a major communicative function; the object of this communication is the self or society as internalized as an aspect of the self.
7. *Modification for effective communication:* This, for Kohlberg, is the shaping of one's dialogue to fit the role of the imagined other being explored.
8. *Diagnostic indication of developmental level:* The six forms are proposed as developmental steps reflecting each type's prevalence; silent inner speech is the most mature step.
9. *Transitoriness:* Kohlberg considers each form to be transitional to the next form in the hierarchy; and a high frequency of overt speech is considered transitional on the way to inner speech. However, all overt forms can be re-evoked at all ages.
10. *Overtness:* Kohlberg sees basic equivalence between overt and covert forms.
11. *Semantic versus motoric mechanism:* Only the semantic aspect of speech is relevant for Kohlberg.
12. *Spontaneity:* Only spontaneously produced speech would be instances of Kohlberg's self-differentiating self-communication.

SUMMARY

It has been the purpose of this chapter to clarify the use of the terms "egocentric speech," "private speech," and "inner speech," as they relate to self-regulation when used by six major theorists in the area. Lack of clarity and comparability probably accounts for much of the noncumulative development of knowledge on these topics, leaving each student of the field to define for himself, afresh, the basic terms and assumptions of his predecessors.

This chapter has argued that much of the conceptual confusion in the area has arisen because Piaget and Vygotsky really are referring to two very different phenomena by the term "egocentric speech:" Piaget's is structurally, and Vygotsky's is functionally defined. Despite the impression given by Vygotsky's (1934/1962) critique of Piaget's explanation of egocentric speech, despite Vygotsky's own suggestion (1934/1962) of an alternate interpretation of a phenomenon called "egocentric speech," and despite Piaget's polite *Comments* (1962) that gave the impression that his egocentric speech and Vygotsky's were comparable, this chapter pointed out how the feature which each writer considers central is irrelevant to the concern of the other. Piaget is interested in the child's progress toward consensual (objective) or "adapted" thought and speech. Vygotsky's concern is with how the child uses speech to regulate his activities.

This chapter also indicated two fundamental differences between the phenomenon studied by Luria and that studied by Vygotsky: (1) Luria adds a theoretical place in self-regulation for nonsemantic, impulsive speech effects, and (2) he studies only induced, nonspontaneous speech. Instances of each writer's phenomenon do share similarities: besides being self-regulating, both seem not to be fashioned for, or successful in, effective communication with another person.

These two similarities (self-regulation and ineffective communication) can also characterize the speech phenomena referred to by the other researchers reviewed, who draw upon, but modify, the meanings of Vygotsky and Piaget. The term "acommunicative speech" was used to encompass, with the least amount of inherited theoretical bias, these two general features of the diverse speech phenomena associated with the terms "egocentric speech," "private," and "inner speech."

The unique theoretical emphases of each new researcher, the features attributed to acommunicative speech, and the explanations suggested for acommunicative speech—all oscillate around several properties or dimensions that can be found in Piaget's original 1923 delineation of egocentric speech. There is no particular pattern to, or progress in, the field's understanding shown by these oscillations. In order to render them coherent and easily comparable for the reader, 12 dimensions were noted which seem to capture the central concerns of and contrasts between the six major researchers reviewed here. Brief characterizations of each theorist's position, based on these 12 dimensions, are supplied at the end of each section detailing their work. These summaries are aimed to facilitate clear delineation of the embedded issues and of the reader's own position in relation to the thinking that has gone before. Perhaps cumulative knowledge will be more likely than oscillation with the availability of these comparisons.

References

Anokhin, P. K. Cybernetics and the integrative activity of the brain, in M. Cole and I. Maltzman, eds., *A handbook of contemporary Soviet psychology*. New York: Basic Books. 1969. [Originally published, 1966.]

Beiswenger, H. Luria's model of the verbal control of behavior. *Merrill-Palmer Quarterly,* 1968, *14*, 267-284.

Birch, D. Verbal control of nonverbal behavior. *Journal of Experimental Child Psychology,* 1966, *4*, 266-275.

______. Evidence for competition and coordination between vocal and manual responses in preschool children. *Journal of Experimental Child Psychology,* 1971, *12*, 10-26.

Bronckart, J.-P., and **Ventouras-Spycher, M.** The Piagetian concept of representation and the Soviet-inspired view of self-regulation, in G. Zivin, ed., *The development of self-regulation through private speech.* New York: Wiley, 1979.

Bruner, J. S. Introduction, in L. S. Vygotsky, *Thought and language.* Cambridge, Mass.: MIT Press, 1962.

______. The growth of mind. *American Psychologist,* 1965, *20,* 1007-1017.

Bruner, J. S., Olver, R., Greenfield, P. M., Hornsby, J. R., Kenney, H. J., Maccoby, M., Modiano, N., Mosher, F. A., Olson, D. R., Potter, M. C., Reich, L. C., and **Sonstroem, A. McK.** *Studies in cognitive growth.* New York: Wiley, 1966.

Cole, M. ed., *Soviet developmental psychology: an anthology.* White Plains, N.Y.: Sharpe, 1978.

Cole, M., and **Maltzman, I.,** eds., *A handbook of contemporary Soviet psychology.* New York: Basic Books, 1969.

Corsini, D. A., Pick, A. D., and **Flavell, J. H.** Production deficiency of non-verbal mediators in young children. *Child Development,* 1968, *39,* 53-58.

Flavell, J. H. Private speech. Paper presented at the Annual Meeting of the American Speech and Hearing Association, San Francisco, November 1964. (Le language prive. *Bulletin de Psychologie,* 1966, *19,* 698-701.)

Flavell, J. H., Beach, D. R., and **Chinsky, J. M.** Spontaneous verbal rehearsal in a memory task as a function of age. *Child Development,* 1966, *37,* 283-299.

Flavell, J. H., Botkin, P. T., Fry, C. L., Wright, J. W., and **Jarvis, P. E.** *The development of role-taking and communication skills in children.* New York: Wiley, 1968.

Freud, S. *A general introduction to psychoanalysis.* New York: Washington Square Press, 1935.

Gal'perin, P. Y. Stages in the development of mental acts, in M. Cole and I. Maltzman, eds., *A handbook of contemporary Soviet Psychology.* New York: Basic Books, 1969.

Gelman, R., and **Shatz, M.** Appropriate speech adjustments: The operation of conversational constraints on talk to two-year-olds, in M. Lewis and L. Rosenblum, eds., *Interaction, communication and the development of language.* New York: Wiley, 1977.

Hanfmann, E., and **Kasanin, J.** Conceptual thinking in schizophrenia. *Nervous and Mental Disorders Monographs,* 1942, *67* (Whole number).

Hjertholm, E. Comparison of Norwegian and American children on independence behavior and training. Unpublished masters thesis, University of Chicago, 1968.

Inhelder, B., and **Piaget, J.** *The growth of logical thinking from childhood to adolescence.* New York: Basic Books, 1958.

James, W. *The principles of psychology*, vol 2. New York: Holt, 1890.

Jarvis, P. E. The effect of self-administered verbal instruction on simple sensory-motor performance in children. Unpublished doctoral dissertation, University of Rochester, New York, 1964.

———. Verbal control of sensory-motor performance: A test of Luria's hypothesis. *Human Development,* 1968, *11,* 172-183.

Keeny, T. J., Cannizo, S. R., and **Flavell, J. H.** Spontaneous and induced verbal rehearsal in a recall task. *Child Development,* 1967, *38,* 953-966.

Kendler, T. S., Kendler, H. H., and **Wells, D.** Reversal and nonreversal shifts in nursery school children. *Journal of Comparative Physiological Psychology,* 1960, *53,* 56-60.

Klein, W. L. An investigation of the spontaneous speech of children during problem-solving. Unpublished doctoral dissertation, University of Rochester, New York, 1964.

Kohlberg, L., Yaeger, J., and **Hjertholm, E.** Private speech: Four studies and a review of theories. *Child Development,* 1968, *39,* 691-736.

Kuenne, M. Experimental investigation of the relation of language to transposition behavior in young children. *Journal of Experimental Psychology,* 1946, *36,* 471-490.

Luria, A. R. The role of language in the formation of temporary connections, in B. Simon, ed., *Psychology in the Soviet Union.* Stanford, Stanford University Press, 1957.

———. The directive function of speech in development and dissolution. *Word,* 1959, *16,* 341-352.

———. Verbal regulation of behavior, in M. A. B. Brazier, ed., *The central nervous system and behavior.* New York: Josiah Macy, Jr., Foundation, 1960.

———. *The role of speech in the regulation of normal and abnormal behavior,* J. Tizard, trans. New York: Liveright, 1961*a*.

———. The genesis of voluntary behavior, in N. O'Connor, ed., *Recent Soviet psychology,* New York: Liveright, 1961*b*.

———. Speech development and the formation of mental processes, in M. Cole and I. Maltzman, eds., *A handbook of contemporary Soviet psychology.* New York: Basic Books, 1969.

Luria, A. R., and **Vinogradova, O. S.** An objective investigation of the dynamics of the semantic systems. *British Journal of Psychology,* 1959, *50,* 89-105.

Luria, A. R., and **Yudovich, F. I.** *Speech and the development of mental processes in the child.* London: Staples, 1959.

Lynn. R. *Attention, arousal and the orientation reaction.* New York: Pergamon, 1966.

Maccoby, E. E. Developmental psychology. *Annual Review of Psychology,* 1964, *15,* 202-250.

Meacham, J. A. The role of verbal activity in remembering the goals of actions, in G. Zivin, ed., *The development of self-regulation through private speech.* New York: Wiley, 1979.

Mead, G. H. *Mind, self, and society*. Chicago: University of Chicago Press, 1934.

Miller, S. A., Shelton, J., and Flavell, J. H., A test of Luria's hypothesis concerning the development of verbal self-regulation. *Child Development,* 1970, *41,* 651-665.

Piaget, J. *The language and thought of the child.* M. Gabain, trans. London: Routledge & Kegan Paul, 1926; New York: Meridian, 1955. [Originally published, 1923.]

______. *Judgment and reasoning in the child.* New York: Harcourt Brace, 1928.

______. Comments on Vygotsky's critical remarks. A. Parsons, trans.; E. Hanfmann and G. Vakar, eds., Cambridge, Mass.: MIT Press, 1962. [Pamphlet published in conjunction with Vygotsky's *Thought and Language.*]

Piaget, J., and **Inhelder, B.** *The child's conception of space.* London: Routledge & Kegan Paul, 1956.

______. *The psychology of the child.* H. Weaver, trans. New York: Basic Books, 1969. [Originally published, 1966.]

Premack, D. *Intelligence in ape and man.* New York: Halsted, 1976.

Reese, H. W. Verbal mediation as a function of age level. *Psychological Bulletin,* 1962, *59*, 502-509.

Rondal, J. A. The role of speech in the regulation of behavior. Paper presented at the Annual Meeting of the Canadian Psychological Association, Windsor, Ontario, June 1974.

______. Contrôle de la latence des réponses dans certaines tâches motrices avec et sans auto-accompagnement verbal. *Revue Belge de Psychologie Pedagogique,* 1975, *37*, 29-42.

Sinclair, H. Developmental psycholinguistics and the psycho-biological approach. Paper presented at Psychology and Biology of Language and Thought: A Symposium in Memory of Eric H. Lenneberg, Ithaca, N.Y., May 1976.

Sinclair-de-Zwart, H. Developmental psycholinguistics, in D. Elkind and J. H. Flavell, eds., *Studies in cognitive development.* New York: Oxford University Press, 1969.

Sokolov, A. N. *Inner speech and thought.* G. T. Onischenko, trans. New York: Plenum, 1972. [Originally published, 1968.]

______. Studies of the speech mechanisms of thinking, in M. Cole and I. Maltzman, eds., *A handbook of contemporary Soviet psychology.* New York: Basic Books, 1969.

Sokolov, E. N. The modeling properties of the nervous system, in M. Cole and I. Maltzman, eds., *A handbook of contemporary Soviet psychology.* New York: Basic Books, 1969. [Originally published, 1964.]

Tikhomirov, O. K. The formation of voluntary movements in children of preschool age. *Soviet Psychology,* 1975, *14*, (1-2), 48-135. [Originally published, 1958.]

Vygotsky, L. S. *Thought and language*, E. Hanfmann and G. Vakar, eds. and trans. Cambridge, Mass.: MIT Press, 1962. [Originally published, 1934.]

Vygotsky, L. S. Mind in society: the development of higher psychological processes. M. Cole, V. John-Steiner, S. Scribner; and E. Souberman, eds., Cambridge, Mass.: Harvard University Press, 1978.

Werner, H. *Comparative psychology of mental development.* New York: Science Editions, 1948.

Wertsch, J. V. The regulation of human action and the given-new structure of private speech, in G. Zivin, ed., *The development of self-regulation through private speech.* New York: Wiley 1979.

Wilder, L. The role of speech and other feedback signals in the regulation of the sensorimotor behavior of three- and five-year-old children. Unpublished doctoral dissertation, Pennsylvania State University, 1968.

Wolff, P. H. *The developmental psychologies of Jean Piaget and psychoanalysis.* New York: International Universities Press, 1968.

Wozniak, R. I. Verbal regulation of motor behavior—Soviet research and non-Soviet replications. *Human Development,* 1972, *15,* 13-57.

______. Speech-for-self as a multiply reafferent human action system, in K. Reigel and J. A. Meacham, eds., *The developing individual in a changing world,* vol. 1. The Hague: Mouton, 1976. (Originally presented at the Biennial Meeting of the International Society for Behavioral Development, Ann Arbor, 1973.)

Yaeger, J. A. Self-directing speech and puzzle-solving in children. Unpublished doctoral dissertation, University of Chicago, 1968.

Zivin, G. Functions of private speech during problem-solving in preschool children. Unpublished doctoral dissertation, Harvard University, 1972.

______. chm., Self-regulation through vocalization: Really? How? Symposium presented at the Biennial Meeting of the Society for Research in Child Development, Philadelphia, March, 1973.

CHAPTER 2

Historical Development of the Soviet Theory of Self-Regulation

ADRIENNE HARRIS
Rutgers University

Soviet work on verbal regulation has its most complete and sustained articulation in the developmental and clinical work of A. R. Luria (1959, 1960, 1961, 1966a, 1966b). Verbal regulation is the process through which some component of the language system moniters, controls, organizes, structures, or plans behavior arising in some nonverbal system in the individual. Self-control through language is assumed to operate on motor activity, on cognitive or on perceptual processing. For a number of Soviet theorists, language in this regulatory role *is* voluntary activity (Tikhomirov, 1958). By virtue of its specialized structure, its unique physiological properties, and its communicative function in human interaction, language is considered in Soviet theory to have regulatory power both in the maintenance of behavioral systems running in parallel (Kosilov, 1960; Meleshko, 1958; Merlin, 1961) and in the organization of hierarchically structured behaviors (Sokolov, 1967, 1972; Anohkin, 1969).

Luria is best known in North America for the genetic or developmental aspects of his theory. His stage model treats both the process of internalization of verbal control and the transformation of control from impulsive, motoric forms into increasingly abstract ones. In addition Luria has identified a rehabilitative function for the speech system. Dynamic and functional relationships, hypothesized at the level of neurophysiology, are assumed to tie the speech system to other behavioral systems in the organism. Under these assumptions language can have a prosthetic role in the maintenance or initiation of behavior in damaged, immature, or dysfunctional organisms.

The study of the specialized regulatory role for language, although currently dominated by Luria's work, has been a major preoccupation of Soviet psychologists and psychophysiologists. Certain features in this research have their inception in nineteenth century physiology (Yaroshevski, 1968) in the study of voluntary activity (Sechenev, 1963), and in the pre- and post-Soviet research of Pavlov (1928) and his followers (Anohkin, 1969, Ivanov-Smolenskii, 1955, 1956a). This chapter reviews experimental research and both the philosophical and psychological theory that bear directly on the

Soviet analysis of self-regulation. Since Luria's model is the cornerstone of Soviet work on this topic, key features of that model will be identified and their genesis and development in Soviet and pre-Soviet psychology described. Chapter 3 by Wertsch details Leont'ev's general theory of action. That theory, based on Vygotsky's work, shares common assumptions with those associated in this chapter with Luria's model.

In reviewing Soviet work on self-regulation two distinct but interdependent research traditions, with important influences on the study of self-regulation, can be identified. On the one hand the regulatory function of language has been investigated in psychophysiological studies which treat the problem in terms of the relationship of conditioned connections arising in the first (direct, motoric) and second (linguistic, symbolic) signal systems (Ivanov-Smolenskii, 1954). In a neurophysiology dominated by Pavlovian models, self-regulation is cast in the language of conditioned responses operating through processes of irradiation, excitation, generalization, inhibition, and disinhibition. The research which identifies processes of control at the neurophysiological level will be reviewed and influences on this work will be traced from Sechenev's reflexology and identified most clearly in the work of Pavlov and Behkterev.

On the other hand a second tradition is specific to the post-revolutionary period. Soviet psychology has been deeply and consistently involved in an explicit attempt to develop theoretical principles and empirical work in psychology which are consistent with Marxism (Payne, 1969; Volosinov, 1973; Rahmani, 1973). Soviet psychologists appear to have been particularly influenced by Lenin's critique of idealist psychology and the positivism and psychophysical parallelism characteristic of Mach (Lenin, 1970).

Several principles dominate Soviet theory and are explicitly indebted to the influences of Marxism (Brozek, 1963; Smirnov, 1964): (1) Soviet psychology stresses a Hegelian-influenced stage model in which development is characterized as a series of functional and qualitative reorganizations of existing structures both intra- and interindividual in nature; (2) the tradition is consistently a materialist one, devoted to an account of problems of being, of consciousness, of any mental activity as rooted and observable in physical and objective phenomena (Badmayev, 1966). Matter is matter in motion and processes of higher mental activity, in which verbalization and self-regulation can be included, are ultimately describable in terms of the organization of matter; (3) a central role is assigned to the social and historically determined interactions of individuals. Both the structure and function of social interaction is directly implicated in the formation of higher mental functions, such as thinking, speaking, and the regulation of nonverbal behavior through language.

In this chapter the psychophysiological and the philosophical traditions, with their shared commitment to materialism will be outlined and their effect on the study of verbal regulation identified. Compatibility, interdependence, and points of contradiction in these two research areas will be outlined, and the two influences on self-regulation will be treated dynamically. A genetic and historical account of the development of Soviet work on self-regulation must examine the work in its periods of reductionism and mechanism and in its more dialectical phase. A thesis explored in this chapter is that the analysis of self-regulation, arising in Soviet psychology in the past 50 years, and developed most thoroughly by Luria, depends in large measure on the particular tensions, contradictions, and shifts in ascendency in the psychophysiological and the social-historical Marxist analyses.

A comment is in order concerning the quality of experimental work. It is conventional to claim that research outside the North American tradition inevitably fails to meet the standards of rigor present in the empirical- and positivist-based tradition. Certainly assessment of the Soviet work described here is made difficult due to problems of the presentation of statistical evidence, the report of individual protocols and raw data rather than summary statistics, problems of translation, and lack of discussion of design features. In this chapter however I have been less interested in assessing the experimental validity of the work (for which there seems insufficient information) than in drawing the historical connections between interpretations of work on the dynamic interaction of the two signal systems and the work on self-regulation and verbal control.

PSYCHOPHYSIOLOGICAL BACKGROUND: INTERPRETATION OF HIGHER NERVOUS ACTIVITY

The analysis of voluntary activity and the special properties of the speech system in the service of complex activity is initiated most dramatically in the work of Pavlov (1928) and Behkterev (Schniermann, 1930). It is perhaps most mechanistically reproduced in Kornilov's reactology and in the work of some of Pavlov's followers who conceptualize self-regulation as a set of conditioned responses which although elaborated in the speech system are rooted in and analogous to simpler conditioned responses (Ivanov-Smolenskii, 1956b).

Sechenev

The study of voluntary activity can be traced to Sechenev's (1963) analysis of reflex activity. The Soviet treatment of cortical functioning as a dynamic and active process owes a great deal to the physiology and objective materialist psychology of Sechenev.

Review articles in psychology often begin like a medieval prayer with a catalogue of critical patron saints somehow seen to bless and legitimize the undertaking. Russian analyses are no exception and in accounts of work on verbal regulation or verbal control, Sechenev inevitably appears as the important initiator in the research tradition. His work cast nineteenth-century Russian physiology and, subsequently (via Pavlov) Russian psychology in an explicitly materialist and mechanistic form.

Regarding the study of verbal regulation and voluntary activity organized through language, we can identify three central features of Sechenev's model for voluntary action which retain their identity and importance even in quite contemporary accounts of psychological functioning. First, reflexive activity is viewed as the common building block for both involuntary and voluntary activity and for all complex or higher order psychic phenomena. Complex or higher nervous activity (under which Sechenev subsumes thinking, speaking, and feeling) arises with the coordination and association of chains of simple reflexes which, when coordinated, give rise to a new order of reflexive activity, the psychic reflex. In fact a close reading of Sechenev's account of the reflexive origins of voluntary or purposive activity reveal a remarkable similarity to that of Piaget (1952). Purposive or intelligent activity arises with the repetition of motor reflex acts, for example grasping and orienting (a sensory reflex act). Thus elementary concrete knowledge is primarily motoric or sensory and is the result of involuntary learning which arises with the repetition of particular sets of reflexive acts (that is schemes). The identification of the reflex (a tripartite structure with receptor coupled to central event and effector) as the single building block for complex activity remains as a cornerstone of Russian psychology: through Pavlov, Behkterev, and Kornilov, influencing the work begun in the 1920s and developed through the 1950s by Ivanov-Smolenskii and his coworkers on the interaction of the first and second signal systems.

Secondly, Sechenev also introduced into Russian physiology the notion of reafference. This principle, although also present in the European and British tradition in neurophysiology, seems to have been earlier and more consistently a feature of models of psychological functioning in the Soviet tradition. In an explanation of the mechanism for verbal control that utilizes reafference of the verbal signal, Luria draws on a tradition initiated by Sechenev and evolved substantively by Soviet psychologists like Bernstein (1967), Boyko (1973), and Anohkin (1969).

Finally, Sechenev identified the central role in voluntary activity played by inhibition. Inhibitory capacities, activated first externally and subsequently internally, have a developmental history—a history which reappears in Luria's stage model for verbal regulation. Inhibition, once established, permits a smoother orchestration or organization of voluntary activity and can be established in two ways. First inhibition (here it is reflexive in origin) can result from the sequencing of antagonistic muscle systems. This technique for inhibition surfaces later in Luria's model as the double starting paradigm (Wozniak, 1972), whereby children who cannot stop some ongoing motor act, either through the commands of others or their own verbal instruction, can effectively inhibit ongoing activity through the initiation of a contradictory or competing motor act.

Inhibition can also be central in origin, and here inhibition performs a crucial task in the development of thought. Sechenev thought that thinking is two-thirds of a psychic reflex, that is that thinking is an evolution of the reflexive act of speaking in which the final component of the reflex act, motor output, is withheld. Thought as inhibited or internalized speech, which appears first in Sechenev's work, has thus a long history in Soviet research on thinking (Sokolov, 1967; 1972). Internalization of speech activity achieved through inhibition prefigures Luria's use of the same mechanism for the control and regulation of activity.

In any historical treatment it is probably important not to make early figures appear clairvoyant and all-knowing. Much of Sechenev's writing on reflexive acts, reafference, and inhibition is speculative and schematic. It is simply that his preoccupations, his particular brand of mechanism, and the physiological cast to psychological speculation grounds and initiates Russian psychology in the pre-Soviet period.

Pavlov

The analysis of voluntary reflex acts develops most systematically in the hands of Pavlov, to whom we turn next in an examination of the roots of modern accounts of verbal regulation. Pavlov's articulation of the laws of conditioned responses and his speculations on conditioned connections specific to human activity and elaborated through the speech system have influenced much Soviet research on the role of speech in nonspeech activity. It is interesting to note that it is Behkterev's method of studying reflexive acts that is actually utilized by Pavlov in his work on the interaction of the first (motoric) and second (speech) signal system and by Luria in the study of verbal regulation. For Pavlov's salivary response in conditioning paradigms, Behkterev substituted the associated motor reflex (that is bulb press) as a response system more appropriate to the study of human reflexive activity.

Pavlov's contribution to, and influence over, Soviet analyses of verbal regulation is extremely interesting to examine. Pavlov's speculations on higher nervous activity in humans leads to the identification of two response systems in which conditioned connections and voluntary learned responses can be elaborated. This analysis of the first and second signal system influenced a generation of Soviet psychologists who investigated the interaction and interdependence of speech and nonspeech systems.

Pavlov identified two signal systems. The first direct system links analyzers (perceptual encoding systems) to motor output; the second signal system, a system of "signs of signs," is elaborated through the speech system. The second signal system has special powers for the discrimination of cues and for generalization to complex response systems. It is unique to human functioning and higher mental processes.

This analysis is an interesting psychophysiological mate to Lenin's theory of reflection. Lenin proposed a dialectical path to consciousness of the real world: (1) the individual is in active contemplation of the real world (first signal system); (2) there is a process of abstract contemplation (second signal system); and (3) there is a reintegration of thought and practical execution. If one examines the evolution of Pavlov's model for interacting signal systems and the role of speech in regulation, it is interesting to note that it is Luria who stresses the role of second signal system functioning in the control of action and who is truer to the dialectical analysis of Lenin than are Pavlov's direct inheritors, for example Ivanov-Smolenskii. His inheritors study regulation at the most mechanical level, looking for laws determining the formation and generalization of conditioned responses.

Pavlov's pronouncements on the nature of psychology and the importance of physiological investigation for the understanding of psychic functioning constitute a dominant influence on Soviet psychology. The persistent tendency to neurologize can be tied to Pavlov's insistence that the experimental analysis of the subjective psychological world was grounded, indeed reduced to, physiological forms. For example Pavlov suggests that the cerebral hemispheres, viewed globally, have two functions: analyzing and coupling. These are roughly parallel to the psychological classifications of discrimination and association. Higher nervous activity is an aggregate of reflexes. We shall see in the work on the signal systems a persistent tendency to make tight and immediate connections of function with psysiological structure, a tendency from which Luria is perhaps the freest.

Following Pavlov's direction some Soviet researchers persistently reduce motor functions, voluntary activity, and all the speech-related behaviors routed through the second signal system to a set of conditioned connections. Psychological analyses thus operate on a two-tiered model with the subjective and phenomenological level abandoned in favor of a behavioral level of explicit or overt responses reduced to physiological functions. These functions are derived and modeled through Pavlovian laws of conditioning, that is excitation or inhibitory reflexes, irradiation of excitation, and concentration of reciprocal induction. Such functions depend at base on the relative strengths of excitation and inhibition. What Pavlov establishes for psychology is a rigid form of mechanistic materialism in which complex psychic phenomena are seen as a direct reflection of simple mechanical and physiologically manifested laws. This is Pavlov's direct effect on psychology in the Soviet Union. However in the post-Soviet period this tendency is formally legitimized with the "pavlovization" of psychology occurring after

1950. This tendency not only simultaneously organizes research on verbal control, but also develops in critical opposition to Luria's stage model for verbal regulation, which is informed by a more dialectical treatment of materialism. Ivanov-Smolenskii (1955), in his introduction to empirical work on the implications for psychiatry of first and second signal system functioning, specifically targets Luria as an idealist and dualist. The substance of the criticism is that Luria's model assumes that language can have a relatively autonomous and dominant role in control of nonspeech activity and could exist relatively independently of the first signal system. This criticism in fact can be sustained only by ignoring what Pavlov himself said about the second signal system, namely that speech-specific connections had the particular properties of speech, lability and persistence, which were thus unique to human psychological functioning. Luria's analyses of verbal regulation persistently capitalizes on the unique character and structure of the speech system to explain its particular power to regulate nonspeech activity.

In comparing Luria's model with the psychophysiological analyses of the interaction of the first and second signal systems, we see in the second signal system the relative dominance of mechanistic over dialectical materialism and the insistence on a reflexive base to voluntary action. One obvious point of contrast is the relative equilibrium of speech and nonspeech systems, with Ivanov-Smolenskii and his coworkers stressing functional balanced interdependence and Luria investigating the particular regulatory role of the speech system upon other action.

INTERACTION OF FIRST AND SECOND SIGNAL SYSTEMS

Let us examine in some detail both the empirical method and the interpretation of researchers on the first and second signal systems, which characterizes substantial sectors of Soviet work on verbal regulation. Ivanov-Smolenskii (1956b) defines the first signal system as utilizing direct objective stimuli and motoric responses, while the second signal system utilizes symbols and the verbal system as, respectively, distinctive stimuli and response system. He notes that conditioned responses can be elaborated through either system, and that dynamic transmission can operate within a signal system and across the speech and motor systems.

Conditioned responses can be divided into two groups. One arises when the conditioned response reproduces or replicates the unconditioned response from which it was generated. These Ivanov-Smolenskii terms "unconditioned conditioned responses" (UCR). The second is a type of conditioned response in which the effectors do not replicate the UCR. These conditioned conditioned responses are acquired in ontogenesis, and whenever such temporal conditioned connections are formed via speech (operating either as a signal, as instruction, or as reinforcement), these responses are characterized as falling within the second signal system. Such second-signal-system connections customarily supplant first-signal-system connections. In contrasting the slower elaboration by direct methods (reinforcement of responses in the first signal system) with the immediate connections formed through the speech system, Ivanov-Smolenskii reflects on the particular character and strength of the second signal system, which he identifies as "the result of the special interrelationship of humans among themselves" (1956a). However, while he touches on the social and dialectical implications of the second signal system, the research tradition he initiates examines the interaction of the two systems in a quite mechanistic fashion and reduces individual functioning on voluntary speech or nonspeech tasks to conditions and interactions of systems of conditioned responses.

The methods for demonstrating its effect reveals important assumptions about the role and operation of the second signal system embedded in the technique for establishing conditioned responses. Voluntary activity is demonstrated through the establishment of temporary conditioned responses. When the speech system is involved in the elaboration of such responses, voluntary activity takes on a unique and specifically developed character. Activity is established faster, more smoothly, more consistently, and with more stability. Voluntary activity is, through the intervention or control of the second signal system, generalizable on abstract and higher order principles. The second signal system can intervene in the development of temporary conditioned connections in several different ways. The speech system may be involved in the conditioned response. Correspondingly verbal stimuli may replicate or be offered in conjunction with direct stimuli. Finally verbal instructions may provide the basis for forming conditioned connections. Methods for forming conditioned connections include direct and indirect reinforcement, imitation in conjunction with orienting responses to salient signals, and spontaneous exploration. What is important to note is that a parallel structure is proposed between conditioned responses which are elaborated in the classic fashion (through pairing of conditioned and unconditioned stimuli) and conditioned responses which are elaborated on a single trial through verbal instructions. That is the experimental instruction, "press the bulb to the red light," is the second signal system mechanism which creates immediate conditioned connections between objective stimuli and the individual's motor response. Correspondingly the special generalizations in conditioned responses elaborated to verbal stimuli are second signal system phenomena and speak to the rich structural system and interrelationships that characterize human language.

Kolitsova (1960) notes the evolution of the second signal system from situations where the word organizes a reflexive act first as a direct stimulus, then in generalizable form. Finally words integrate systems of generalized responses. In this analysis the conditioned responses organized for verbal estimation mirror semantic organizations, with single words operating as direct stimuli and superordinate terms activating a system of conditioned responses to verbal stimuli by semantic classifications.

These methods are the core of the experimental work on the character and impact of second signal system connections and of their interaction with first signal system connections. This impact is, in essence, the relationship of speech to voluntary nonspeech activity. Through the demonstration of verbal and motor responses conditioned via either signal system, a model for complex voluntary activity is developed. By virtue of such Pavlovian laws of conditioning as irradiation of excitation and inhibition, generalization (diffuse or selective), and reciprocal induction, the two systems are assumed to be interdependent on both a functional and physiological level. Since the speech system represents a higher level of organization and functioning (due to its speed, lability, systemic structure), the second signal system has a special capacity to organize other action systems to which it is linked. This essentially physiological, indeed almost hydraulic, model is the explanatory structure for: voluntary activity in normal functioning; pathological conditions, such as schizophrenia or depression; activity levels under specific environmental or organic conditions, such as fatigue, work or school schedules or disease and, curiously, analyses of personality types. We can consider representative examples of this work in more detail.

The impact of verbal stimuli on the development of associations has been studied in very young children (Degtyar, 1961). A group of children, 21 to 38 months old, were conditioned to make eyeblink responses to a set of complex conditioned stimuli: a bell accompanied either by the sound of another bell, a metronome, or flowing water. After conditioning was established, the presence of second order conditioning was examined by the presentation of the extra stimuli in the absence of the bell. In another experimental condition the original conditioning paired the bell with the extra stimuli and its verbal representation. Only about half of the subjects (primarily the older subjects) showed and generalized a conditioned response to the acoustic stimulus paired with the bell. There was however better transfer for the eyeblink response when the bell was accompanied by the word equivalent. This finding is interpreted as evidence of the positive and efficacious role of verbal stimuli in conditioning paradigms appearing quite early in development.

In a more typical study of the interaction of the first and second signal system, Kurbatov (1956), using 7- to 8-year-old subjects, established a motor response (bulb pressing) to the sound of a bell. The sound stimulus was then replaced with a verbal signal, "bell." Characteristically in such experiments subjects produce no response immediately, but then the conditioned response generalizes to the verbal analogue of the stimulus object. This is viewed as evidence of the transmission of responses across the signal systems.

In an extension of this work again using young school-age children, a motor response is conditioned to a red light (Kurbatov, 1958). The generalization of the response and accompanying orienting response are measured with a direct verbal analogue used as a stimulus: "red flame." Control words which were unrelated semantically were also introduced. The conditioned response generalized only to the semantically related verbal signal.

Interestingly generalization of response is more immediate and stable when the stimuli involve only one perceptual modality or analyzer. Kurbatov reports greater generalization across signal systems when the direct stimulus of a bell sounding was replaced by the word, "bell," than when a direct visual stimulus was replaced by its auditorially presented verbal referent.

The theoretical explanation for these phenomena relies heavily on Pavlov: ontologically prior to these experimental manipulations, conditioned responses (that is associations in language learning) are formed between direct stimuli and their verbal designates. Therefore generalization always has a double character. The direct stimuli cause irradiation of excitation (that is a potentiality for response is created) in analyzers of the first signal system. But the stimuli also cause irradiation to the earlier established conditioned responses, thus uniting the first signal system response to the associated verbal referent.

A number of studies examine the regulatory effect of the second signal system in motor responses. Ivaschenko (1960) replicates the phenomenon of generalization of conditioned responses to verbal signals tied in some association of meaning. In a discrimination task with colored lights and visual presentation of the words, "green" or "red", as the stimuli, Ivaschenko reports greater speed and greater frequency of conditioned verbal responses when the stimuli were verbal and therefore not direct. It was also possible to reverse the connection. That is when the conditioned response was presented as a stimulus, it elicited from the subject the verbal response, "green" (the prior stimulus word). These demonstrations are interpreted as evidence of the speed of elaboration of verbal conditioned connection, their reversibility, and the substitutive function of language.

Asratyan (1973), in a discussion of causally conditioned reflexes, assumes bilateral conductivity. That is a two-way relationship between neural structures so that conditioned responses to cue events can have cue properties. This assures that when two phenomena are associated, a signal connection is formed and the functional unit (which may be word-word, word-direct, direct-word, or direct-direct) has real epistemological significance. Conditioned connections are thus in this work reflections at the physiological level of objective cause and effect relations in the environment. This viewpoint is consistent with Lenin's theory of reflection and a materialism that stresses the relationship and interdependence of external and internal connections.

Extending the analysis of generalization of responses within the second signal system, Ratner (1960) examined generalization of a motor response to verbal signals which were varied along a phonological and semantic dimension. He found both dimensions salient and operable. Kostomarova (1961) looked at difference in response to verbal signals within a set of logical or semantic relations. Here reaction time was the measure, rather than the occurrence or nonoccurrence of a response. She reports that if the stimulus word was a superordinate category of which the response word was a member, responses were faster than in the inverse case. Where the set of relations and semantic associations were particularly dense and elaborate, differentiation with responses was hampered and reaction times were slower in a discrimination task.

Samsonova (1960) found that visual discrimination performance (in a task involving depth perception) improved when the response required during learning was verbal and not motor. When the discrimination was well learned, motor responses proved less disruptive and more effective. In the task, she investigated a judgment: equal depth of stimuli was signalled by a motor bulb-press or by the verbal response, "equal." If the two stimuli to be discriminated were not at equal distance from the subject, the response was a forearm abduction, used (designed) as a cross-modal matching. When the response was verbal and not motor, accuracy of the movement of the forearm was improved. Although it is possible that in the motor condition were two competing motor activities were the discriminative responses, the planning and execution of the task was more complex than in the condition where one response was verbal and one motor. The interpretation placed on this work by Samsonova was based on the greater speed and efficiency of second-signal-system connections.

Maraev (1961) studied the effect of warning (a second-signal-system stimulus) on galvanic skin response (GSR) as compared to the direct stimulus of electrical shock. Warning of the onset of weak or strong shock was accompanied by either weak or strong current, giving four combinations of warning plus direct stimulus. No description is offered of experimental design and only individual results are reported, but it is noted that some subjects show greater GSR to the warning than to the actual direct stimuli. Kosilov (1960) found that the effect of supplementary stimuli in motor action was more efficacious when the additional stimuli were verbal rather than direct. This study notes the differential effects of disinhibition originating from the first or second signal system. The motor response studied was a rhythmic one for which language (where a rhythmic structure is easily elaborated) may be particularly appropriate.

These studies examine the transmission of *excitation* between the two signal systems. In addition experimental work has been done on the selective and diffuse irradiation of *inhibition*. In general this latter work suggests the frailer character of inhibitory processes, particularly in children. Fuflygina (1956b) demonstrates the generalization of inhibition in a four-step procedure. Verbal associations are formed and stabilized to verbal stimuli. Subsequently motor responses are conditioned to light stimuli. Instructions are given to inhibit the effect of the original verbal stimuli, then the light stimuli are presented again. Providing no summary statistics, Fuflygina notes that some subjects show long latencies before making the motor response (selective inhibition), while others inhibit the motor response altogether (general irradiation of inhibition.)

Sokolova (1962) has pursued developmental aspects of the mechanism of inhibition. Using groups of 6-, 9-, and 13-year-olds, she looks at the differential impact of inhibitory instructions on a verbal response to verbal stimuli. Inhibition was hardest to achieve in the youngest subjects, while restoration of the prior response was fastest for this group. Her interpretation, consistent with Luria's analysis, is that excitatory systems dominate inhibitory. Similarly Fuflygina (1956a) reports that the capacity of an external signal to disinhibit extinguished responses is greatest with younger subjects (approximately 8 years old).

What this work typifies is the Soviet tendency, consistent with Pavlov's particular interpretation of materialism, to reduce behavior to a set of reflexive acts, to neurologize. In the clinical applications of work on the second signal systems, this tendency is even more apparent. Ivanov-Smolenskii (1955) describes disorders of personality, or psychological functioning, in terms of imbalance in the transmission of conditioned connections within and across the signal systems. Changes in the capacity of the second signal system to monitor and control voluntary activity are the explanatory mechanisms for hysteria and obsessional neurosis (Seredina, 1955; Raevna, 1955). Schizophrenia (Kostandov, 1955) and even alcoholism are identified with a stereotyping of response and stagnation of temporary conditioned connections. Catatonics and depressives are viewed as exhibiting overly strong inhibitory connections (Gartsshtein, 1955).

There has even been work on typologies in character or personality-functioning linked to signal system interaction. Briks (1956), following a suggestion by Pavlov, identifies four response types in which individuals can be characterized. Excitable subjects form fast conditioned responses, show broad generalization, and the strong impact of external inhibition. Subjects termed labile show more balanced excitory and inhibitory responses. Inhibited subjects show a predominance of inhibitory responses, slower responses, and a difficulty in responding to disinhibitory stimuli. One can highlight the special character of Soviet research by comparing this work to the analysis developed in North America of cognitive tempo. At the behavioral level the observations of excitable, labile, and inhibited subjects sound remarkably close to the dichotomy of reflexive-impulsive identified for example by Kagan and Kogan (1970).

Typically however the Soviets do not model a psychological process, but reduce behavior to the strength and status of conditioned responses, that is to the physiological level. More specifically, individual variation and functioning are translated into types of dysfunction in the interaction of signal systems. The capacity of the speech system to organize inhibitory or excitatory responses, the flexibility of the transmission of effects within these responses to the first signal system, is the determiner of the four styles of functioning. This interpretive strategy is developed by Luria in his clinical work. And the entire research area is thus compatible both with Kornilov's reactology of the 1920s and Behkterev's psychology as reflexology in the systematic avoidance of psychological or subjective levels of interpretation.

Physiological Modeling of Second-Signal-System Interaction

Recognizing that Pavlov's analysis often operated at a considerable distance from actual physiological evidence, there has been some attention in Soviet work to describe physiological systems operating in dynamic and temporary conditioned connections. Of particular interest to this discussion is the work on modeling conditioning where speech is implicated. Kreindler (1960) identifies what he terms a morphological unit observed at three points when conditioned responses are formed through speech: physiological effects are observed subcortically, in the primary analyzers (first signal system), and in the speech system. Particular identifiable physiological events arise under conditions of dynamic transmission. Latency measures reflect the stability and strength of irradiation. In addition, orienting responses customarily accompany generalization of conditioned responses from direct to verbal stimuli. Kreindler (1960) and Chuprikova (1972) note the overlapping, but functionally distinguishable, components of generalized responses, that is, orienting reflexes and conditioned responses. Chuprikova notes the increased excitation arising from nonspecific activating systems in both the reticular formation and in nonspecific thalamic structures. He notes also concomitant electrical changes in the cortex which rise and fade more immediately for the orienting response and are more gradual and sustained for conditioned motor or verbal responses.

Aleksanian (1958) investigated mechanisms for internal inhibition. In forming any conditioned connection, he claims two foci of excitation are developed, excitatory and inhibitory. Connections are thus "double in sign or nature but not in number." Conditioned inhibition is thus the remodeling of prior conditioned responses in which the signal significance of formerly positive stimuli is eradicated and a new negative connection strengthened. The development of internal inhibition is thus a "process of strengthening of the negative component of the conditioned response." A neurophysiological base for conditioned responses elaborated in the speech system has been described by Chuprikova (1972). In accounting for the role speech plays in the development of conditioned responses, one must be able to explain why and how a cue value is assigned to a stimulus via instruction and what changes in the central nervous system result from such an instruction. Sokolov (1963) explains the phenomenon as an instance of a stimulus endowed through language with orienting properties. Chuprikova claims that instruction changes the levels of excitation and the general conditions of arousal. That is, verbal cues create the preconditions for new conditioned corrections; there is an observable movement of excitation from speech areas to primary projection areas; and foci of heightened excitation permit the establishment of new functional links. Thus the effect of second-signal-system stimuli is to alter "the general functional state of the cortex." Since there is the additional assumption that verbal signals create the same foci of excitation as do direct stimuli, the claim is thus that the signal will have a specific as well as a general potential for arousal. In claiming a regulatory or modulating function for language, Chuprikova is claiming that the "functional state of direct projections" can be modified over long periods of time.

Boyko (1973) has modeled conditioned responses in a scheme which appears to combine Pavlovian laws and reflex-based action patterns with more contemporary schemes of cortical switching and circuitry for decision-making. Conditioned responses formed through the discriminative action of verbal stimuli, Boyko terms, "dynamic." There is a "physiological interaction of prior associations brought about by the mutual intensification of excitation in shared neuron aggregates" (Boyko, 1973, p. 36).

The role of second-signal-system functioning is modeled in a problem-solving task in which subjects must discover the match between one of four bulbs and one of four keys. Intervening clues are given in which separate pairs of lights are triggered by two sets of two keys. A three-part process is envisioned. First-signal-system analyzers reflect the set of events (keys and lights), and these events are also registered or represented in the second signal system. A generalized response via the speech system is thus developed. In subsequent trials nonrecurring events lead to the selective second-signal-system inhibition of some components of the response and intensifications of connections that are replicated. The model assumes a two-tiered level of cortical functioning with summation effects operating on representations of direct stimuli in the speech system. The speech system, because of its capacity to generalize, again provides a model of the problem, with which particular trial events can be matched. Here the second signal system appears to be a representational space available for internal operations on stimuli and therefore capable of participating in complex problem-solving and planned action.

What is outlined here is a neurological account of the efficacy of verbal stimuli in conditioning (that is the role of instruction) and the mechanisms for transmission of verbal effects to first signal (nonverbal motor) systems. This modeling of verbal regulation is consistent with the mechanistic tradition established by "pavlovization." Recently however there has been a shift in explanation of regulation away from laws of conditioning.

CYBERNETIC MODELS OF REGULATION

Information theory, systems analysis, and cybernetics provide a more contemporary and dynamic model for self-regulation. The mechanism of reafference (which in protean form was suggested by Sechenev) replaces systems of association, conditioned connections, and orienting responses. In the modeling of regulation or speech connections by Anohkin (1969), Bernstein (1967), and others, verbal signals or responses modulate via feedback, rather than through parallel and interconnected tracks of excitation and inhibition.

Anohkin's model for voluntary purposive acts allows reafference a key role in the maintenance of controlled action. Afferent synthesis is the general term for a set of dynamic processes whereby behavior is initiated and sustained and modulated. One critical component of this process is the comparison of reafferent signals (which could arise in the acoustic-articulatory speech system) with a central and general plan for the action in question. The outcome of this comparison, via the acceptor of effect, then permits the reactivation, continuence, or reconstruction of ongoing activity.

Bernstein has an analogous model, while not dealing directly with language as a source of reafference. The acceptor of effect has its counterpart in Bernstein's system as the motor act or "solution to a problem of action," which is a general model of a "required future" against which ongoing acts can be compared. Bernstein explicitly counters the notion of point-to-point projections as the underlying mechanism for first- and second-signal-system responses.

Luria has made use of the principle of reafference in his analysis of self-regulation. For Luria language appears to operate within this cybernetic model in two ways. Language in some unspecified form (that is internal and external speech may well have different features) is the format in which the general plan of action is specified. That is the motor problem or acceptor of effect is specified linguistically and is available for correction or for referencing ongoing action. The plan to speak, the act of speaking, and some form of articulatory (kinesthetic) or acoustic reafference from speech (emitted by self or other) can operate either as a corrective, as an inhibitor of action, or as a disinhibitor of previously extinguished action.

SOCIAL-INTERACTIONIST PERSPECTIVE: MARXISM-COMPATIBLE PSYCHOLOGY

The post-revolutionary imperative to develop a materialist psychology consistent with Marxism lead to certain tendencies and developments in the analysis of psychic events, consciousness, and mental functioning. After a pluralistic period in the early 1920s, there was a long struggle to rid psychology of idealist conceptions and to promote a materialist analysis of higher mental functioning through the application of the dialectical method. A dialectical analysis examines relationships between concrete and moving objective events. Applied to questions of epistemology, this constitutes the study of interdependent relations and the reciprocal and active reflection of internal matter in motion (brain functioning), mental activity, and objective external events.

Dialectical materialism treats mental functioning (and consciousness in particular) as a by-product or emergent property of matter in motion. The process, both of mental development and of moving relations in the world, is assumed to follow dialectical laws articulated by Hegel: negation of the negation, interpenetration of opposites, and qualitative transformations built on quantitative change. We shall give these laws specific reference when discussing Luria's model for self-regulation in more detail.

Lenin's attack on Mach, *Materialism and empirio-criticism* (Lenin, 1970) is the most sustained treatment of epistemological problems and thus had particular impact on Soviet psychology (Kupalov, Volokhov, and Voronin, 1960). This theory sets in opposition the psychic and the physical (that is matter and sensation), but binds them in a dialectical activity of mutual reflection. The dualism then is essentially at the epistemological level. A material unity of reality is maintained while the reduction of mental functioning to matter is avoided (contrary to the strategy of Pavlov). Higher nervous activity, of which self-regulation or voluntary control are clear examples, is a special property of matter which in the human brain has evolved a unique degree of organizational complexity. Although reflection is a property of all matter in Lenin's view, reflection inherent in brain functioning (and therefore in psychic functioning) takes a particular form. Subjective experience reflects the objective external dialectic. The knower acts on the world and in that action reflects the objective and moving material conditions. It is a reflection with consequences for the formation and organization of interiorized experience. Developmentalists should recognize a theoretical statement consistent with Piaget's model of assimilation and accomodation for the development of intellectual structures. This process of active reflection and internalization of external relations is however concretized and worked out explicitly by Luria in his developmental model for self-regulation.

Closely dependent on this treatment of mental functioning is the Marxist view of the effect of social relations on internal activity. Social relations, which are tied to (and determined by) the relations of individuals to the material and productive base, are themselves material and objective conditions, which can be reflected in subjective experience. This idea is developed speculatively by Vygotsky (1962), and Rubinstein (1955; Payne, 1969), and concretely by Luria (1961). It must be stressed that in making nonreductionist claims and in stressing the interaction of social and internal cognitive relations, this particular brand of materialism exists in some contradiction with the more mechanistic and reductionist materialism of Sechenev, Pavlov, and others. What is so interesting is that Luria's work, examined in all its facets—clinical, experimental, and theoretical—shows the influences of both traditions. The tension Payne (1969) notes between mechanistic monism (inherited from Sechenev) and dialectical materialism (instantiated in Marxism) persists in Luria's work and in his treatment of language functions in the control of voluntary behavior.

LURIA'S VERBAL REGULATION

In an introduction to an experimental study of the effects of speech therapy on twins (Luria and Yudovich, 1959), Luria seemed to be charting a careful course between mechanism and the potential charge of idealism. He was simultaneously against treating behavior either as a set of motor habits or as some inner force. His resolution was to treat language as the critical tool for complex mental activity and for voluntary behavior in particular, but to insist that language was rooted in material and social interactions. Internalized language was one of "complex functional formations which are built up as an outcome of concrete forms of interaction between the organism and its environment" (Luria and Yudovich, 1959, p. 9).

The theoretical position developed by Luria and his coworkers, fleshed out with extensive experimental and clinical work, is the most sustained contemporary analysis of verbal regulation in Soviet psychology. Luria's work draws eclectically on many of the earlier tendencies and analyses already outlined in this chapter. In discussing Luria's work attention will be paid both to the historical antecedents to, and influences on, his study of verbal regulation as well as to the tensions between Luria's model and less dialectical or mechanistic approaches to the analysis of behavior (that is observable in work on the interaction of the signal systems).

Luria's work is by now well known in the West. It is interesting to note that the Soviet work on verbal regulation transplanted to North America has been incorporated in the standard paradigms in Western psychology. In this case verbal mediation, the verbal deficiency hypothesis with its underlying s-r framework (for example Miller, Shelton, and Flavell, 1970), and operant conditioning (Meichenbaum and Goodman, 1969a, 1969b) have been the interpretive apparatus through which verbal control has been understood. It is however more appropriate and more elucidating to embed all Soviet analysis of the voluntary control of behavior in the theoretical and philosophical context in which it has arisen. Luria's treatment of verbal regulation is only comprehensible when viewed through the particular prism of dialectical materialism and the materialist-based psychophysiology which begins with Sechenev and Pavlov.

Wozniak (1972) has provided a detailed discussion of the experimental paradigm through which Luria describes a stage model for the evolution of verbal control over nonverbal behavior. We shall not replicate that exercise. Instead Luria's model will be introduced quite generally and specific focus will be on features of Luria's work that draw on the philosophical and experimental background already developed.

What is at issue is an analysis of how individuals come to be able to initiate, sustain, and modify voluntary acts. Luria says, voluntary behavior "is the ability to create stimuli and to subordinate them" (1932). The distinction between voluntary and involuntary behavior (a conception treated first by Sechenev) is tied to the distinct behavioral outcomes after particular signal properties accrue to stimuli. Voluntary acts arise with the creation of temporary associations formed between such stimuli and behavioral acts. Central to Luria's position is the view that language has some features and attributes that are unique allowing it to act both on external stimuli (endowing them with cue distinctiveness) and on internal foci of excitation (forging associations between stimuli and particular responsive acts). Language is thus the essential tool for the development and maintenance of voluntary activity.

A second crucial feature of Luria's theory is that the ability of language to affect voluntary activity is acquired gradually and trails the simpler processes of the acquisition, production, and comprehension of utterances. We might summarize the direction of development of verbal regulation as involving three critical processes: (1) One can chart the development and transformation of a mechanism for inhibition. How does the individual come to be able to withhold action permanently or temporarily to offset the irradiating or perseverating effects of excitation? It is of course an underlying assumption that inhibiting output and orchestrating inhibitory and excitatory effects are prerequisites for skilled or complex serial activity; (2) There is an internalization of the source of commands and control. That is the system of control is initially social and finally individual. In this preoccupation we see the most dialectical aspect of Luria's work. Mental functioning, higher nervous activity in the individual, is the reflection of material and social relations. It is a formulation resonant with Lenin's theory of reflection. It is also crucial that the format for the internalization be linguistic, since the speech system is the modality for social interaction and is initially the medium for social control. It is this linguistically mediated interaction that is internalized and comes to operate on individual activity. Luria's claim is essentially that the dyadic model of social control is acquired and run off by the individual as he monitors and controls his own activity; (3) Luria notes the increasing impact of the semantic component of the verbal signal. This theory thus acknowledges the multilevel and multifunctional nature of the speech system and records the change from motoric, impulsive influences to semantic influences in the regulatory power of language. Again Luria is utilizing the unique capacity of the speech system to act as a regulatory mechanism. Speech has a motor component through which impulsive effects can have a structural or perhaps prosthetic effect on simultaneously occurring behaviors. However verbal stimuli are also generalized signals or signifiers. Because they make direct reference they can endow cue distinctiveness to real-world events and by virtue of the structural richness (semantic and syntactic) of the language system, they permit (to restate Chuprikova's analysis) cortical closure between: verbal stimuli and the direct referent, response acts, and afferent and efferent pathways. Language can thus have a unifying and organizing effect on disparate stimuli and disparate responses. This view of language is compatible with Jakobson's account of system in language by metonymy (syntagmatic association) and metaphor (paradigmatic association). Luria asserts that this system of associations in language can be an apt source of control, either in providing a plan for action or as an ongoing spine for nonverbal activity or routes of association.

Notice how all these developmental progressions depend on and utilize the dialectical laws of qualitative transformation and the interdependence of opposites. The stage model charts qualitative reorganization of functions overlaid on continously evolving strengths of the speech system. A double transformation, external to internal and impulsive to semantic, is proposed in which the form and source of regulation is qualitatively changed.

This general outline of Luria's work suggests two critical aspects of the model of verbal control to be examined in more detail. First, we shall consider why speech is so crucial for regulation; secondly, how control is effected. These are concerns in which the roles of reafference, orienting responses, inhibition, and the function of speech as a source of reafference must be considered.

In the cybernetic-based models for regulated voluntary action, the format for a central organizing plan is not always clearly specified. Bernstein describes the plan as a motor command or motor problem. Anohkin's acceptor of effect is unspecified as to format. Luria has wed these general schemes for planned activity to the tradition inherited from Vygotsky. Evolved control of behavior is verbal control (a view not restricted to Luria), and we may explore in greater detail why language or the speech system is so apt a choice for the regulatory or planning function.

Language, because it is a signal of signals and because it has a broad generalized character, has particular strength and facility in isolating stimuli and in allowing the individual a deeper analysis of objective and material reality. Luria's definition of voluntary activity is an activity whereby stimuli are identified and subordinated. In identifying and setting goals and in isolating relevant cues for orientation, language—by virtue of its specificity and associative links—has a clear capability to perform those functions.

Language is a rich and salient structural system, and the structural aspects of speech are particularly apt for planning. Syntactic structures permit both a temporal and spatial organization of activity. "If . . . then," or "when x, do y" constructions both embed commands to produce and to inhibit actions in a simple formalized scheme. It seems that Luria considers that some internalized form of speech is a suitable notational form for a central plan; he notes a developmental progression in the capacity to utilize for regulation the instructional, directive component of speech.

But language, however abstract and systematized, is grounded in motor activity. Luria treats this aspect of verbal behavior as an ontogenetically primitive factor in regulation. The initiation of speech activates a set of motor responses that can have an excitatory and impulsive impact on behavior. Here it appears that there is an implicit acceptance of the Pavlovian interpretations developed in studies of the first and second signal systems. Activation in one system holds consequences for activity arising in the other system.

Both in developmental and clinical work, the production of speech in the form of single words, instructions, comments, rhythms, counting or sequences of words can have a prosthetic function. Language as regulation appears in support of frailer or actually dysfunctional actions. In developmental work perseveration errors in the motor response can be counteracted by sequenced verbal commands either by experimenter or subject. Such commands appear to offer the subject some spine or ongoing structural support on which to hang sequences of motor acts. Similarly Luria notes that victims of stroke or paralysis can utilize counting aloud to perform sequenced motor activity otherwise beyond their powers of execution (Luria 1932, 1969). Luria, describing serial motor activity (tapping) among patients with motor damage, notes that the "spontaneous rhythmical pressure" timed to coordinate with verbal rhythms produced by the subjects increases regularity in the motor sphere.

One might question whether the function captured in these clinical and developmental studies is properly termed verbal regulation. Granted that speech is an accessible system (overlearned and receptive to rhythmic patterns), regulation in this instance may more appropriately be judged as motoric than as speech-specific.

Finally the speech system carries the primary weight of social and interpersonal communication. In Luria's use of interaction as a model for self-regulation, he is most dialectical and most distant from the treatment of language as a signal system. Control is initially transpersonal and in the end there is a dialogic internalization in which self-control is realized. This is consistent with Lenin's notion that mental functioning is the active reflection of objective material events. Since the format for social control is linguistic, it follows that the active reflection of that objective form, when internalized, will retain some linguistic character.

Having identified ways in which Luria considers the speech system central and necessary for regulation, we can consider how regulation and control are effected through the activation of the speech system. The concept of self-regulation seems to have undergone a somewhat subtle shift in Soviet research. For Pavlov and the tradition of researchers pursuing work on the first and second signal systems, regulation is identified with the interdependence and the interaction of verbal and motor response systems. Whether excitatory or inhibitory, the process of control is active. Language is assumed to have a positive power to orient, to direct the responding individual, and to forge connections between response systems. Within this treatment inhibition is often actualized in terms of competing active forces of excitation or increased activity of inhibitory or negative connections.

Cybernetic models of planned activity identify regulation with the organism's capacity to withhold responses and to time or change behavior acts through the use of information from prior events (external or internal). Here regulation centers on the concept of reafference. Luria interestingly has incorporated into his analysis of verbal regulation both the mechanisms of inhibition and of acceptor of effect for the maintenance of control in voluntary action. Wozniak (1972) has described in some detail how both mechanisms carry interpretive weight for Luria. Reafference can arise from extrinsic or intrinsic sources. In most of the experimental tasks set by Luria, reafference from exteroceptive and proprioceptive sources is available to the child. While not explictly identifying types of effective reafferance for the child, Luria implicitly assumes a developmental hierarchy with exteroceptive reafference as initially the sole powerful source or regulatory control. Control from proprioceptive reafference seems to arise first in nonspeech motor systems and finally in the speech system, where it is also coupled with exteroceptive auditory feedback. The final capacity of the child to execute silently and accurately an instruction suggests the evolution of feedback mechanisms to the level of an internal central plan independent of peripheral activity. This projected developmental history for feedback systems is similar to that proposed by Posner and Keele (1973) for the evolution of skilled motor performance.

Yet even while specifying types of reafference, the question of a mechanism for inhibition and control remains. Inhibition as a result of an orienting response may lead to the suppression of intersignal responses. Equally as plausible reafferent signals may, through reference to the acceptor of effect, permit correction and suppression of extra responses to conform to the planned action sequence. While these two mechanisms are theoretically separable, they are not clearly differentiated experimentally by Luria. Soviet researchers have identified distinctive physiological features of orienting responses, that is patterns of habituation and of cortical and subcortical excitation as studied by Sokolov (1963); Chuprikova (1972); Roger, Voronin, and Sokolov (1958). However these distinctions have not been applied to Soviet interpretations of Luria's work.

What one can conclude then is that Luria's model for verbal regulation retains the contradictory elements inherited from Pavlov; from the dialectical materialists, such as Vygotsky and Leont'ev; and from such cybernetic and dynamic modelers as Anohkin and Bernstein. Luria's interpretive scheme contains some of the reductionist aspects of the Pavlovian model, while his reliance on reafference betrays the influence of more dynamic models of regulation.

Luria's clinical work (1932, 1959, 1961, 1967, 1970) shows the same dual influences from Pavlovian models of interacting signal systems and dynamic conceptions of planned activity. In work begun in the 1920s and described in *The nature of human conflict* (1932), Luria draws connections between the developmental theory and his analysis of dysfunctional systems in adults with neurosis, aphasia, or some neurodynamic damage. Reactive processes in childhood are by nature diffuse and impulsive. Only with the appearance of a pragmatic and directive function for speech (as opposed to a significative one) can the child provide a functional barrier that mediates between analyzer activity (excitation from direct stimuli) and the motor sphere. Speech uniquely has the power to split reflexive action, separating preparation from execution. This view of a functional barrier created through speech is quite strikingly similar to Sechenev's treatment of the role of inhibition in the evolution of psychic reflexes.

The disorganization of planned action and the collapse of self-regulated behavior is the result of speech disorders which affect the maintenance of the functional barrier. Pathological conditions arise due to some change in the interaction of the direct system of analysis and the speech system. Luria pursues two possible outcomes at the loss of such a barrier. Damage to the speech system may affect performance negatively. In many empirical demonstrations Luria (1932, 1967) outlines the diffuse and perseverative motor performance of certain aphasics (retardates and hysterics) with frontal lobe lesions, comparing their performance to that of children not yet able to capitalize on the directive function of language.

Alternatively there are compensatory possibilities. If the two systems are dynamically interdependent, the ability of the regulatory power of the speech system may override other nonspeech neurodynamic disorders. Luria illustrates this possibility using both adult subjects suffering from Parkinson's disease (1932) and children with a cerebroasthenic syndrome (1967). Behavioral accounts of these children (they are exhaustible, unstable, restless, overexcited) suggest parallels with current North American categorization of hyperkinesis. In these studies formerly chaotic and error-filled motor responses to simple signals, discriminitive choices, and instructions for delayed movement gain regularity, precision, and control with the initiation of accompanying verbal signals.

Inversely Luria and Tzetlova (1969) report that in a study of verbal activity in aphasics, sustained verbal output was only possible when accompanied by some ongoing linear motor sequence. By way of explanation Luria notes the interdependence of first- and second-signal-system functioning, suggesting that the motor component of the speech act requires the aid of some concomitant act in the motor system. Such an explanation stays quite within the limits of the Pavlovian model of signal system interaction.

CONCLUSION

The intention in this chapter has been to trace the lines of research and theory which inform the contemporary Soviet model for self-regulation. Self-regulation, in the Soviet research tradition, is the hallmark of voluntary action and is characterized as the capacity to withhold, time, coordinate, or structure behavioral responses through the intervention and specialized action of the speech system. This chapter has traced the claim that speech has particular attributes arising ontogenetically, which are implicated in the appearance of controlled inhibition. It has noted that it is the incidence of inhibition which permits the accurate execution of complex voluntary serial actions.

In reviewing the model of self-regulation several outstanding problems arise. Most critically there is not yet a precise and experimentally verifiable analysis of how speech comes to regulate or direct behavior. It is conventional to think of human speech as a multilevel, hierarchical system which can therefore offer a variety of distinct mechanisms for regulation. Considering only the mechanism of reafference, human speech can provide feedback through a variety of its features: articulatory (proprioceptive), acoustic (exteroceptive), and semantic or syntactic (central). Such features may well affect self-regulation at different developmental stages and in different ways. Finally the Soviet claim that self-regulation is, perforce, verbal regulation requires a demonstration that the directive or planning functions of the speech system are unique and not transferable to some other response system or representational system in the individual. It would seem that experimentally based answers to the questions of regulatory mechanism and speech specificity will provide a necessary maturity to the analysis of self-regulation.

References

Aleksanian, A. M. The mechanism of internal inhibition. *Pavlov Journal,* 1958, *8,* 59-66.

Anohkin, P. K. Cybernetics and the integrative activity of the brain, in M. Cole and I. Maltzman, eds., *A handbook of contemporary Soviet psychology.* New York: Basic Books, 1969.

Asratyan, E. S. The causal conditioned reflex. *Soviet Psychology,* 1973, *11,* 112-129.

Badmayev, T., Materialist monism and the conceptual system. *Soviet Psychology,* 1966, *4,* 70-73.

Bernstein, N. *The coordination and regulation of movement.* New York: Pergamon, 1967.

Boyko, E. I. Modeling of higher forms of conditioning. *Soviet Psychology,* 1973, *9,* 36-46.

Briks, Z. N. Experimental study of typological characteristics of higher nervous activity of children of school age. *Works of the Institute of Higher Nervous Activity,* 1956, *2,* 177-206.

Brozek, J. Soviet psychology: Appendix B, in M. Marx and W. Hillix, eds., *Systems and theories in psychology,* 521-548, New York: McGraw Hill, 1963.

Chuprikova, N. I. The completion of temporary connections through speech. *Soviet Psychology,* 1972, *10,* 276-298.

Degtyar, E. N. The elaboration of associations in very young children. *Pavlov Journal,* 1961, *11,* 83-88.

Fuflygina, T. P. On the change in word reactions to word stimuli in children under the influence of external inhibition. *Works of the Institute of Higher Nervous Activity,* 1956*a,* *2,* 38-50.

______. On the irradiation of the inhibitory process from the second signalling system into the first." *Works of the Institute of Higher Nervous Activity,* 1956*b,* *2,* 122-127.

Gartsshtein, N. G. Associations between the disturbances of the interaction of the signal systems and certain autonomic disturbances in reactive depression. *Works of the Institute of Higher Nervous Activity,* 1955, *1,* 129-144.

Ivanov-Smolenskii, A. G. *Essays on the pathophysiology of higher nervous activity.* Moscow, 1954.

———. The basic paths from pathophysiology of the higher nervous activity to the psychiatric and neurosis clinic. *Works of the Institute of Higher Nervous Activity.* 1955, *1,* 1-10.

———. Developmental paths of experimental research into the work and interaction of the first and second signalling system. *Works of the Institute of Higher Nervous Activity,* 1956*a, 2,* 35-49.

———. New data from the study of neural mechanisms of the interaction of the cortical signalling system. *Works of the Institute of Higher Nervous Activity,* 1956*b, 2,* 1-29.

Ivaschenko, F. I. Examination of some verbal connections by the conditioned reflex method. *Pavlov Journal,* 1960, *10,* 502-508.

Kagan, J. and Kogan, N. Individual variation in cognitive processes, in P. Mussen, ed., *Carmichael's manual of child psychology,* vol. 1. New York: Wiley, 1970.

Kolitsova, M. M. Development of system as the basis of the process of generalization." *Pavlov Journal,* 1960, *10,* 179-184.

Kosilov, S. A. Interaction between the first and second signalling system in work processes. *Pavlov Journal,* 1960, *10,* 511-517.

Kostamarova, N. M. On differences in latent periods of reaction at the differentiation of verbal stimuli according to semantic (logical) features, in E. I. Boyko, ed., *Studies in higher neurodynamics as related to problems of psychology.* Washington, D.C.: Office of Technical Services, 1961.

Kostandov, Z. A. Defects of neurodynamics and particularly of interactivity of the cortical signalling systems in paranoic schizophrenia. *Works of the Institute of Higher Nervous Activity,* 1955, *1,* 34-61.

Kreindler, A. The theory of 'dynamic physiologic structures' and its application in the study of higher nervous activity in man." *Pavlov Journal,* 1960, *10,* 342-347.

Kupalov, P., Volokhov, A., and **Voronin, L.** Influence of Lenin's ideas on doctrine of higher nervous activity. *Pavlov Journal,* 1960, *10,* 173-179.

Kurbatov, B. M. Study of the dynamic transmission of a conditioned connection from one cortical signalling system into the other. *Works of the Institute of Higher Nervous Activity.* 1956, *2,* 92-99.

———. Certain conditions for the manifestation of dynamic transmission in children. *Pathophysiological Series.* Moscow: Akademeya nauk, 1958, *8,* 1-5.

Lenin, V. I. *Materialism and empirio-criticism.* Moscow: Progress Publishers, 1970.

Luria, A. R. *The nature of human conflicts.* London: Liveright, 1932.

———. The directive function of speech in development and dissolution. *Word,* 1959, *15,* 341-352.

______. Verbal regulation of behavior, in M. Brazier, ed., *The central nervous system and behavior.* New York: Josiah Macy Foundation, 1960.

______. *The role of speech in the regulation of normal and abnormal behavior.* New York: Liveright, 1961.

______. Brain and mind. *Soviet Psychology,* 1966*a, 4,* 62-69.

______. *Human Brain and psychological processes.* New York: Harper & Row, 1966*b.*

______. *Higher cortical functions in man.* New York: Basic Books, 1966*c.*

______. The regulative function of speech in its development and dissolution, in K. Salzinger and S. Salzinger, eds., *Research in verbal behavior and some neurophysiological implications.* New York: Academic, 1967.

______. Speech development and the formation of mental processes, in M. Cole and I Maltzman, eds. *A handbook of contemporary Soviet psychology.* New York: Basic Books, 1969.

______. *Traumatic aphasia.* The Hague: Mouton, 1970.

Luria, A. R., and **Yudovich.** *Speech in the development of mental processes in the child.* London: Staples, 1959.

Maraev, V. A. Effect of action of the second signal system on the skin galvanic reaction to a direct stimuli. *Pavlov Journal,* 1961, *10,* 2, 213-217.

Merlin, V. S. The dynamics of transfer of conditioned reflex connections from one signal system to another, in N. O'Connor, ed., *Recent Soviet Psychology.* London: Liveright, 1961.

Meleshko, S. D. Interaction mechanisms of the cortical signal system. *Pavlov Journal,* 1958, *8,* 333-338.

Meichenbaum, D., and **Goodman, J.** The developmental control of operant motor responding by verbal operants. *Journal of Experimental Child Psychology,* 1969*a, 7,* 553-565.

______. Reflection-impulsivity and verbal control of motor behavior. *Child Development,* 1969*b, 40,* 785-797.

Miller, S. A., Shelton, J., and **Flavell, J.** A test of Luria's hypothesis concerning the development of verbal regulation. *Child Development,* 1970, *41,* 651-665.

Pavlov, I. P. *Lectures on conditioned reflexes.* New York: International Publishers, 1928.

Payne, T. R. *S. L. Rubenstein and the philosophical foundations of Soviet psychology.* New York: Humanities Press, 1969.

Piaget, J. *The origins of intelligence in the child.* London: Routledge & Kegan Paul, 1952.

Posner, M., and **Keele, S. W.** Skill learning, in R. M. Travers, ed., *Second handbook of research on teaching.* Chicago: Rand McNally, 1973.

Rahmani, L. *Soviet psychology.* New York: Universities Press, 1973.

Raevna, S. N. Some disorders of the interactivity of the first and second signalling system in hysteria. *Works of the Institute of Higher Nervous Activity,* 1955, *1,* 62-87.

Ratner, K. S. Motor conditioned reactions to verbal stimuli in man. *Pavlov Journal,* 1960, *10*, 441-444.

Roger, A., Voronin, G., and **Sokolov, E. N.** An EEG investigation of the temporary connections during extinction of the OR. *Pavlov Journal,* 1958, *8,* 1-13.

Rubinstein, S. L. Questions of psychological theory. *Soviet Psychology,* 1955, *1,* 6-18.

Samsonova, V. G. Change in the accuracy of visual analysis on replacement of complex motor reactions by verbal responses. *Pavlov Journal,* 1960, *10*, 17-23.

Schniermann, A. Behkterev's reflexological school, in C. M. Murchison, ed., *Psychologies of 1930.* International University Series in Psychology, Worcester, Mass.: Clark University, 1930.

Sechenev, I. *Reflexes of the brain.* Cambridge, Mass.: MIT Press, 1963.

Seredina, M. I. Disturbances of the neurodynamics in obsessive neurosis. *Works of the Institute of Higher Nervous Activity,* 1955, *1*, 88-106.

Smirnov, A. A. On the fiftieth anniversary of Soviet psychology. *Soviet Psychology,* 1969, *6*, 19-39.

Sokolov, A. N. Speech motor afferentation and the problem of brain mechanisms of thought. *Soviet Psychology,* 1967, *6,* 3-12.

______. *Inner speech and thought.* New York: Plenum, 1972.

Sokolov, E. N. *Perception and the conditioned reflex.* New York: MacMillan, 1963.

Sokolova, M. V. Characteristics of age-dependent inhibition of verbal reactions in children. *Works of the Institute of Higher Nervous Activity,* Pathophysiological Series, 1962, *8*, 17-24.

Tikhomirov, O. K. The formation of voluntary movements in children of preschool age. *Problems of higher nervous activity in the normal and abnormal child,* vol. 2. Moscow: 1958.

Volosinov, V. N. *Marxism and the philosophy of language.* New York: Seminar Press, 1973.

Vygotsky, L. S. *Thought and language.* Cambridge, Mass.: MIT Press, 1962.

Wertsch, J. V. The regulation of human action and the given-new structure of private speech, in G. Zivin, ed., *The development of self-regulation through private speech.* New York: Wiley, 1979.

Wozniak, R. J. Verbal regulation of motor behavior: Soviet research and non-Soviet replications: A review and explication. *Human Development,* 1972, *15,* 13-57.

Yaroshevski, M. G. I. M. Sechenev, the founder of objective psychology, in B. B. Wolman, ed., *Historical roots of contemporary psychology.* New York: Harper & Row, 1968.

CHAPTER 3

The Regulation of Human Action and the Given-New Organization of Private Speech

JAMES V. WERTSCH
Northwestern University

One of Vygotsky's most important contributions to the study of the relationship between speaking and thinking was in the area of private speech.[1] He described it as speech in which, "the child talks only about himself, takes no interest in his interlocutor, does not try to communicate, expects no answers, and often does not even care whether anyone listens to him." (1962, p. 15) Due to his early death Vygotsky did not have the chance to develop all the implications of his ideas for developmental and cognitive psychology. The few studies he conducted on private speech supported his basic notions that it arises out of social speech and that it has a cognitive function.

In addition to these two properties, Vygotsky made other claims about the characteristics of private speech. These characteristics, primarily concerned with its content and structure, allowed Vygotsky to outline a theory in which private speech is the precursor of inner speech. He pointed out in several places that the structure and content of inner speech should differ in fundamental ways from that of external, socially oriented speech. Inner speech could not fulfill the cognitive planning the directing roles in the way Vygotsky outlined if it were simply a subvocal version of full-fledged external speech. Therefore he developed several ideas about the properties of inner speech and predicted that they would begin to appear in the child's private speech. He hypothesized that inner speech possesses three semantic characteristics: agglutination, the preponderance of sense over menaing, and the influx of sense. While these three characteristics are certainly of interest in a complete analysis of his ideas, we shall focus our attention here on Vygotsky's notions about what he called the main syntactic characteristic of private

[1]The term, private speech, will be used here rather than egocentric speech (Vygotsky's term). By using the term, private speech, rather than egocentric speech we hope to avoid confusing it with speech that is intended to be used in communication, but is egocentric. Also for the purposes of this paper, private speech will not be used for inner speech. The term is only concerned with vocalized speech.

and inner speech: its predicative structure. The greater part of this paper will be concerned with analyzing: (1) what Vygotsky had in mind when he said that private speech is predicative and (2) what this means for understanding how private speech is related to cognitive functioning. Much of the material for this analysis, whether Vygotsky's or that of other Soviet researchers, is not yet available in English.

THE GIVEN-NEW ORGANIZATION OF PRIVATE AND SOCIAL SPEECH

Although Vygotsky was interested in making predictions about the content and structure of inner speech, his work in this area was limited to hypotheses and insightful analogies. The only actual evidence he used in his work came from private speech. Since inner speech is by definition not accessible for analysis, this is the only kind of directly observable evidence we *can* have for such studies.[2]

In connection with his claim that the predicative syntax of inner speech begins to manifest itself in private speech, Vygotsky said that as private speech develops:

> It shows a tendency toward an altogether specific form of abbreviation: namely, omitting the subject of a sentence and all words connected with it, while preserving the predicate. This tendency toward predication appears in all our experiments with such regularity that we must assume it to be the basic syntactic form of inner speech [1962, p. 139]

When trying to understand Vygotsky's ideas about the syntax of private and inner speech, it quickly becomes evident that he was concerned more with a functional than a structural linguistic analysis of predicativity. While it is true that the best translation of the term he used in Russian *(predikativnost')* is predicativity, he was actually concerned with notions that have subsequently been developed in functional linguistics, such as given and new information, topic and comment, and theme and rheme, rather than with the syntactic or grammatical subject and predicate. In this regard it is important to note that Vygotsky said nothing about nouns and verbs when speaking of predicativity.

Besides the fact that Vygotsky consistently analyzed predicativity in private and inner speech by using notions similar to those used in functional linguistics, there is additional evidence that he had a functional definition in

[2]While inner speech is not directly observable, Vygotsky's notions on this topic have had a strong influence in the USSR on psycholinguistics (A. A. Leont'ev 1969) and neurolinguistics (Akhutina 1974, Luria 1975). It is included as a theoretical construct in many models of speech production and comprehension. Attempts to measure its presence (not its content or structure) are not uncommon in Soviet work (see Sokolov, 1968/1972).

mind. Specifically he recognized the difference between grammatical subject and predicate on the one hand and what he called psychological subject and predicate on the other. One should not be surprised that he included the psychological subject and predicate in his analysis, since Russian and Soviet linguists have traditionally been very concerned with psychological and social factors.

In order to understand how Vygotsky's notions of psychological subject and predicate play a role in private speech we need to distinguish them clearly from their grammatical counterparts. The notions of grammatical subject and predicate have usually been interpreted strictly in terms of surface syntax. For example factors, such as gender, number, and case agreement between a noun phrase and a verb, are generally accepted as means for identifying the grammatical subject. Although Chafe (1976) has recently suggested that the notion of subject of a sentence might also play an important cognitive role, we shall identify grammatical subject and predicate strictly on syntactic grounds, since this is what Vygotsky seems to have in mind.

On this basis we can say that in the case of English, the subject is a noun phrase that occurs before the verb phrase in declarative clauses and immediately after the auxiliary or operator in interrogative clauses, and has number and person agreement, where applicable, with the verb phrase. As Quirk, et al., (1972) point out it is difficult to define the grammatical predicate of a sentence, because it is a more complex and heterogeneous unit. For our purposes it will suffice to note that the predicate traditionally consists of units such as the verb (including auxiliaries), complement, object, and adverb.

Although several problems with these definitions arise if one pushes them far enough, for purposes of contrast with psychological subject and predicate they work tolerably well:

1. "John repaired the rocking chairs."
2. "He repaired the rocking chairs."
3. "John did it."
4. "The rocking chairs were repaired by John."

On the basis of these definitions we can say that "John" serves as the grammatical subject in (1) and (3), whereas "He" does in (2). Note that our definition of grammatical subject and predicate should not be confused with semantic notions like agent, since in sentence (4) "John" still is the agent—as in (1) and (3)—but "rocking chairs" is the grammatical subject. Whatever their weaknesses may be, our descriptions of grammatical subject and predicate will suffice, since their only purpose is to identify a distinction that Vygotsky was *not* using when he referred to predicativity in private and inner speech.

One fact to keep in mind when trying to distinguish psychological from grammatical subject and predicate is that the grammatical subject and predicate of a sentence remain constant regardless of the communicative context. A change in how a particular sentence is used by a speaker does not result in a change in its grammatical subject and predicate. We shall see that communicative-context factors can determine which words in an utterance will be the psychological subject and predicate.

What did Vygotsky have in mind when he used the notions of psychological subject and predicate? When dealing with the psychological subject, he said it is what the sentence "is about" and what is "in the listener's consciousness first." His examples indicate that when he talked about what is in the listener's consciousness first, he was referring to information that was in the listener's consciousness before hearing a particular utterance that adds to the information. With regard to the psychological predicate, he said it is "what is new, what is said about the (psychological) subject." (1956, p. 324)

It turns out that this distinction between psychological subject and predicate is very similar to the type of distinction first introduced into modern linguistic analysis by the Prague School linguists, such as Firbas (1966). Subsequently many of these ideas have been analyzed more closely and redefined. This has resulted in a proliferation of terms and distinctions. One of these distinctions, which is now widely accepted, is that between given and new information (Halliday 1967; Chafe 1974, 1976). Chafe defines it as follows:

> Given (or old) information is that knowledge which the speaker assumes to be in the consciousness of the addressee at the time of the utterance. So-called new information is what the speaker assumes he is introducing into the addressee's consciousness by what he says. [1976, p.30]

Note that like Vygotsky, Chafe uses the notion of consciousness in his definition of this distinction. In fact Chafe says that "They key to this distinction is the notion of consciousness" (1976, p. 30). Both in Vygotsky's and Chafe's analysis the state of a listener's consciousness can only be determined on the basis of the facts about a particular commuicative context. These striking similarities lead us to conclude that Vygotsky's distinction between psychological subject and predicate is essentially the same distinction that Chafe made between given and new information.

In addition to the distinction between given and new, Chafe outlines several other ways of analyzing the packaging of a sentence. Some of these correlate in great degree with the given-new distinction. But Chafe has shown that they should not be confused with it, since they can occur independently. He points out that in particular, contrastiveness has often been confused with new information, but is a separate phenomenon. This is evident from the fact that a contrastive item can carry given, rather than new, information.

Chafe points out that the portion of an utterance which conveys given information is characterized by lower pitch, weaker stress, and a tendency for nouns to be pronominalized. These properties, in addition to an analysis of the communicative situation, can often be used to identify which part of a sentence is being used in each of the two capacities. The way in which the sentence fits into the communicative context determines which parts of a sentence will be associated with the given and new information. This means that the parts of a sentence assigned to these two categories may not always be the same. One and the same sentence with a single assignment of grammatical subject and predicate can be broken down into different segments of given and new information when it is used to make different utterances.

For example if we return to our original sentence—(1) "John repaired the rocking chairs."—we see that either the grammatical subject or the grammatical predicate can convey the given or new information.

If two people are talking about John, we can assume that the notion of John is in the consciousness of both people. Therefore it is the given information. In this case if A uses (1) in an utterance to B, then repairing the rocking chairs would probably be the new information about John for B.[3] Under these circumstances, the grammatical and psychological organizations coincide. In such a communicative context "John" would normally receive relatively low pitch and weak stress. It also could be pronominalized as in (2).

On the other hand if A and B are discussing rocking chairs that have been repaired, and if A utters (1) to B, then "John" would probably carry the new information. It is the information introduced into B's consciousness. In this situation it would be reasonable for A to assume that the notion of repairing rocking chairs is already present in B's consciousness. The grammatical subject contains the new information (that is, Vygotsky's psychological predicate), and the grammatical predicate contains the given information (that is, Vygotsky's psychological subject). Although Chafe points out that pitch and stress for given and new information is more difficult to analyze in the case of verbs than of nouns, one would expect that the segment, "repaired the rocking chairs," in (1) would receive less emphasis on both these counts than in the first communicative context outlined above. Conversely that part of the sentence which conveys new information ("John") would receive higher pitch and greater stress. Although Chafe did not deal with substitution for

[3]As Chafe has pointed out the term, "new," is often misleading since it implies that the listener has never had access to the information. Actually it is concerned with information that is being introduced into the speaker's consciousness. In some cases this listener may have had access to the information before. The point is that it is being reintroduced into his consciousness in a particular speech context and that is why we are calling it "new." Due to the widespread acceptance of this term, we shall use it here, but Chafe suggests a better description might be "newly activated."

verbs, as he did with pronominalization in the case of nouns, we can safely conclude that because of the given-new organization of the information, (3) would be an acceptable sentence to use in the second communicative setting, but not in the first.[4]

So far this chapter has dealt with the notions of given and new information and grammatical subjects and predicates as they are analyzed in communicative interchanges involving at least two people. For instance Chafe's analysis of what is new involves what one person (the speaker) is introducing into the consciousness of another person (the listener). When Vygotsky speaks about private speech becoming abbreviated by dropping psychological subjects (that is given information), we are faced with a different situation. We are now trying to apply a distinction developed on the basis of two-person communicative interaction to a problem in which only one person is involved. It is no longer the case that one party (the speaker) can introduce new information into the consciousness of another (the listener). While it is true that in Vygotsky's theoretical framework that planning and directing function of private speech is formerly carried out with the help of a second person (usually and adult), this function later is taken over by the child. In Vygotsky's words, "This planning and directing function has moved from the interpsychological to the intrapsychological plane of functioning." At the point where the child is using private speech to carry out planning, are we to assume that there must be a speaker and a listener with two separate consciousnesses?

Kohlberg, Yaeger, and Hjertholm (1968) suggest that at one point in the developmental hierarchy of private speech "Questions answered by the self" we could expect to find some form of interpersonal discourse. Their hypothesis was based on Mead's (1934) notions about how the self emerges out of social interaction. However they found very few instances of this type of private speech in their data. Even if utterances of this type were more frequent, we are still left with the problem that at some point the development of private and inner speech will supposedly reach a stage where interpersonal discourse no longer should be the prevalent form of private speech. This means that we are once again in a position of analyzing the predicativity of private and inner speech where there is only one person's consciousness involved. Unlike the case that Chafe outlines where a speaker packages sentences on the basis of what he assumes to be given in the listener's consciousness, we are faced with private speech where some other factors must determine what is in the speaker's consciousness and what is to be introduced into it as new information.

[4]It should be noted that it is not necessarily the case that the entire grammatical subject or the entire grammatical predicate serves as either the given or the new information. It is often the case that parts of the grammatical subject or predicate will serve as new information, and so on.

How are we to analyze the predicative nature of private speech if we no longer can rely on what is in the consciousness of two separate individuals—a speaker and a listener? What I propose is that in trying to understand the given-new organization in children's private speech, we should base our analysis on the child's action rather than on social interaction with another person. When trying to understand how this will work, it is important to keep in mind that we have already determined that the given-new organization of an utterance in social speech is governed by contextual factors. It is not inherent in the sentence structure used. I am claiming that the given-new organization of private speech is also contextually determined. However the factors used to assign what is given and what is new information are different than in the case of social speech.

ACTION AND THE SOVIET THEORY OF ACTIVITY

Before going on to analyze the relationship between action and the given-new organization of private speech, we need to understand what we mean by action. This term has a special meaning in Soviet psychology—especially in the Vygotskian School. In developing a Marxist psychology Vygotsky laid the foundations for the notion of action, but his ideas have since been consolidated and developed further by other Soviet investigators, especially A. N. Leont'ev (1959, 1975).[5] Leont'ev, who was one of Vygotsky's students and early collaborators, has developed what is known as the theory of activity (*deyatel'nost'*) in Soviet psychology. While it is certainly the case that other viable schools exist, for the past two decades or so Leont'ev's ideas have provided the major theoretical underpinnings for psychology in the USSR.

Although the theory of activity was not fully elaborated until after Vygotsky's death, it is legitimate to use it in an analysis of Vygotsky's ideas on private speech because he provided the foundations for its main tenets. One should be aware of the original contributions Leont'ev has made to this theory, but he is the first to point out the great debt he owes to Vygotksy.

Leont'ev's account of activity involves three levels of abstraction. The first level is concerned with activity *(deyatel'nost')* and its associated motive *(motiv).* The fact that Leont'ev uses the term, activity, in two different ways can be confusing at times: on the one hand it refers to the theory of activity as a whole; on the other hand it can refer to one of the items at the first level of abstraction within this theory. When using activity in the first sense, I shall

[5]See Chapter 2 by Harris for details of the history of the Soviet view of self-regulation. That review emphasizes the conjunction of Marxist thinking and Pavlovian theorizing on neurophysiology and conditioning. Nevertheless the same assumptions about self-regulation are found in all Soviet work and are in agreement with those presented in this chapter.

always use the full phrase, theory of activity. When using the second sense, I shall refer to an activity or activities.

In his explication of an activity, Leont'ev often uses hunger as an example of a motive. This provides the energizing force behind an organism's activity, but at this level of abstraction nothing is said about the goals or ends toward which the organism is directed—it is primarily concerned with the motivating or energizing force behind behavior. While Soviet theorists have done very little research on problems at this level of abstraction in the theory of activity, they see the inclusion of their concept of a motive as a very important step in building a viable psychological model. This notion often plays an important explicit role in the formulation of psychological problems (for example Luria's 1975 model of speech production), and it is a part of the set of implicit assumptions underlying the work of other investigators.

The second level of abstraction in the theory of activity involves what Leont'ev calls an action *(deistvie)* and its goal *(tsel')*. The notion of an action has provided the impetus for a great deal of psychological research in the USSR, and it will be the level of abstraction that interests most of us. An action is a segment of human functioning directed toward a conscious goal. It may be a segment of behavior that is readily observable, such as going from point A to point B; or it may be a covert cognitive process, such as solving an arithmetic problem, which will have very few measurable external manifestations. One of the main tenets of the theory of activity at this level of abstraction is that actions that are executed internally have their precursors in external actions. This notion of the internalization of actions plays an important role in Leont'ev's theory and has been developed further, from a developmental standpoint, by Gal'perin and his colleagues.

The notion of internalization as used in the Vygotskian School involves one aspect that sets it apart from most other current ideas on this process. When Soviet developmental theorists speak of internalization, they are primarily concerned with the internalization of *social* processes. The Marxist foundations of Vygotsky's theory led him to stress that social interaction is the key to understanding individual cognitive processes. Therefore, when dealing with the issue of internalization, he claimed that this social interaction provided the content of what was to be internalized. We shall see that this general assumption plays an important role in the Soviet analysis of the origins of private speech.

According to Leont'ev the main criterion for defining an action is its goal. As external observers, we often can understand an action only when we understand the goal that the person had. In the case of the person carrying out the action, the goal was consciously realized before its inception.

Western psychologists are usually quite wary about utilizing notions like that of a goal in developing their psychological models. However, recent work in the philosophy of action in the West (here the meaning of the term, action, is not synonymous with Leont'ev's use of the word) indicates that is possible to provide viable accounts of teleologically based explanations, which avoid the pitfalls of earlier attempts. For example Bennett (1976) has developed a mode of explanation based on teleological laws. His approach deals directly with the problems in teleology raised by Spinoza. A key to Bennett's analysis is his treatment of the problem of representation. He distinguishes between two main levels of representation that may be involved in teleological laws. Leont'ev's account also has taken this problem into consideration since an action involves the agent's consciously recognizing the goal before undertaking an action. This aspect of his theory avoids one of the major problems of earlier teleological theories in psychology, the problem of representation in a goal-directed organism.

When dealing with action as a level of abstraction in the theory of activity, Leont'ev is concerned with an abstract entity defined in terms of its goal. The same action may be carried out in a variety of ways and in a variety of environments. For example in analyzing the action of getting from point A to point B, one must recognize that a variety of different routes may be equally effective. In analyzing the action of constructing a building in accordance with a plan, there are also a variety of approaches. We can account for a part of this diversity by analyzing the various subgoals that are involved. The agent not only must recognize the fact that identifiable subgoals exist; he must also recognize that they must be embedded and placed in a sequence in accordance with an overall goal. In his theory of activity, Leont'ev deals with some of these problems of structuring at the level of action.

However there are further questions about the execution of an action which cannot be answered at this level of abstraction. It is often the case that certain conditions in the environment influence the way an action is carried out without giving rise to consciously recognized goals or subgoals. The agent certainly deals with these factors in carrying out an action, but not in such a way that they are properly a part of the analysis at this level. By definition, an agent carries out his action on the basis of goals and subgoals, but in doing so he also unconsciously manipulates various aspects of the environment. One and the same goal or subgoal can be executed under a variety of different environmental conditions. These facts led Leont'ev to propose a third level of abstraction in his theory of activity.

This third level involves what he calls an operation (*operatsiya*) and its associated conditions (*usloviya*). This level is concerned with how actions are carried out in a particular context (that is under a specific set of conditions). It is often the case that several different operations are involved in a single action, but it is also possible for an action to be carried out using a single operation. In other words, the fact that several operations are normally involved in a single action is not necessarily a part of the relationship between these two levels of abstraction. Rather the distinction between them has to do with the fact that an action involves a conscious goal, whereas an operation does not.

The difference between actions and operations has provided the foundation for many studies in Soviet psychology. One can cite P. I. Zinchenko's (forthcoming) research on involuntary memory. He has reported several findings that support the notion that human memory is heavily influenced by the way in which materials are presented in terms of actions and operations. While recognizing the importance of structural factors in the material to be remembered, Zinchenko has focused his attention on problems arising out of notions like actions and operations. For example he has demonstrated that by carrying out different actions (that is, different types of processing defined in terms of different goals) with the same passage, subjects' recall of a passage can vary widely. He found that information about those aspects of the task not directly involved in carrying out the goal-directed action (that is, those aspects concerned with the operations and conditions of the action) were poorly retained. However by asking subjects to carry out a new action on the same material and thereby changing the organization of actions and operations, he found that memory for various aspects of the text changed. Specifically it changed in accordance with his hypothesis about the retention of material tied to an action, as opposed to material tied to an operation.

The theory of activity posits an important developmental relationship between actions and operations. Operations, which are unconsciously triggered by the contextual conditions of a task, often make their initial appearance as actions and are later routinized to the point where they properly fall under the definition of an operation. Leont'ev uses the example of shifting gears in an automobile to illustrate this point. When first learning to manipulate the lever to shift into first gear, the process may involve consciously goal-directed behavior, that is, an action. However after a period of time, the shifting of gears becomes automatic and routinized. Since the whole process no longer involves a conscious, goal-directed effort, it has become downgraded to the level of the abstraction of an operation. At this point if we were to analyze the actions that an agent is carrying out while driving, we might speak of things like driving to the store. Shifting gears would only be one of the operations involved and would depend on the conditions under which the action was carried out. If a problem should arise at any point in carrying out this operation (for example, if some difficulty should arise in shifting gears), the agent may once again focus on the problem, and the shifting may be temporarily converted back into a conscious, goal-directed process—an action.

This very abbreviated account of the levels of abstraction of Leont'ev's theory points out that the distinction between actions and operations is functional in nature. While there are certainly ontogenetic regularities in this theory, it is not the case that children at a specific age necessarily convert a certain set of actions into operations once and for all. In learning how to deal with the social and physical environment, the child must learn how to establish goals and to carry out the steps necessary to reach them, but there is no sense in which we would want to say that the child must "acquire" a set of goals at a certain age.

One of the major challenges posed by the Vygotskian school of Soviet psychology has been understanding how children develop the capacity to carry out goal-directed actions. Adults interact with children in such a way as to lead them through the processes needed to carry out an action. At this stage the child often will not understand the overall structure of the action while being led through it by the adult. Indeed in some cases the child may complete an "action" by means of following an adult's directions without ever realizing that an "action" or a "goal" was involved. We need to put "*action*" in quotation marks here since, by definition, the child is not carrying out a true action at the intrapsychological plane of functioning. He is not striving toward a goal that he has consciously identified. Rather he is being led through the steps of what the adult perceives to be the goal. At this stage we are dealing with an action that can only be carried out on the interpsychological plane of functioning. The child is incapable of formulating and executing most actions independently because he is unable to represent a goal that is not directly suggested by the environment; that is, the child can independently carry out only those actions that are directed toward goals not requiring a decontextualized representation. If the child at this early age is to carry out actions directed toward goals requiring this abstract form of representation, his attempts will have to be mediated and regulated by an adult capable of such representation. Otherwise the child is almost certain to be distracted and drawn off the task by irrelevant environmental stimuli.

As Vygotsky (1956) and his followers (for example Levina, forthcoming) point out, the child takes one of the major steps toward the ability to carry out goal-directed actions when he begins to use the means that adults have used to regulate him in order to regulate himself; that is, the child begins to carry out a process on the intrapsychological plane that formerly could only be executed at the interpsychological plane. The most important means by which others regulate the child is directive speech. According to Vygotsky the most important means for self-regulation is self-directed speech. This speech form grows out of the child's social speech and first appears as egocentric speech (which we call "private speech" here). Later it goes underground to become inner speech.

It is this speech form that allows the child independently to begin to formulate goals that require an abstract representation. Earlier the child's action had to be anchored in the environment or directed by an adult. When the child's action is regulated by the physical environment, we have an instance of a true action at the intraphychological plane of functioning because the goal is consciously recognized through constant reminders from surrounding stimuli. When the child's execution of an action requires adult intervention, we have an instance of an action that can only exist at the interpsychological plane of functioning. There is no question that young children can focus their attention for a period of time on carrying out a particular goal-directed task. However at this early stage there must be physically present objects in the task situation that attract and maintain the child's attention. The other side of this coin is that the child is easily distracted by environmental stimuli in such a way that unless the task-relevant stimili are more salient, it is often very difficult to remain on a task until it is finished.

During the time before the child begins to use private speech for self-regulation, we can say that in most cases independent behavior, appearing to be directed toward a goal, does not really constitute an action whose goal requires an abstract representation. The behavior is being guided by phenomena in the physical environment, which attract the child's attention. At this stage most of the child's behavior has not been organized into actions. Behavioral sequences, which may appear to be actions, are either guided by other-regulation or by object-regulation, rather than self-regulation. With the appearance of private speech, the child has a means for representing goals. This representation eventually will be independent of any perceptually present phenomena and therefore provides the means for focusing on an abstract goal and ignoring perceptually salient, but task irrelevant, aspects of the environment.

ACTION AND THE GIVEN-NEW STRUCTURE OF PRIVATE SPEECH

Once it becomes clear that when we speak of the regulatory function of private speech we are speaking of how this speech aids in the formulation and execution of goal-directed actions, we can begin to understand its given-new structure in a different light. Vygotsky and Levina have argued that there are several transitional stages in the form and function of private speech as it becomes differentiated from social speech and acquires its own functional capacities. At first private speech seems to be an integral part of a stream of motor behavior that results from regulation by adults or from nonsocial environmental factors. At this level private speech utterances seem to be comments about the ongoing behavior. Although this behavior may outwardly appear to constitute an action, it is not a self-regulated action as long as the agent's behavior is not guided by a conscious goal. In cases where the goal is indexed in the environment, the young child can carry out an action, but in all those cases where a decontextualized representation of the goal is necessary, the early forms of private speech will not be capable of supporting the execution of a self-regulated action.

Later, private speech will become more concerned with formulating and carrying out actions whose execution requires decontextualized representation. At this stage the form and function of private speech will change.

As private speech becomes more and more capable of supporting the execution of actions, its relationship with those actions will change, and the factors that determine its given-new structure will change. In this chapter, I shall examine only the first stage in this process, but it should be noted that the given-new analysis of private speech at other stages will also be determined primarily by the action the agent is carrying out, rather than by the social factors which Chafe has outlined in his analysis of the given-new distinction.

On the basis of this change from a social-oriented to an action-oriented analysis of the given-new distinction, the first thing we need to do is to develop a new version of Chafe's definitions of given and new information, one that will be applicable to private speech. This definition might read:

> In the case of private speech, given information is knowledge that is in the speaker's consciousness at the time of the utterance. So-called new information is what is being introduced into the speaker's consciousness.

We might label this the agnostic definition since we have modified Chafe's definition mainly by removing any mention of what contextual factors will be responsible for introducing new information into consciousness. By examining certain aspects of the structure and function of private speech, we shall be able to reintroduce the contextual factors that govern its given-new organization.

Before going on to analyze these factors, we should take a moment to examine the surface form of private speech. Chafe claims that in social speech the part of the utterance that conveys given information receives low pitch, weak stress, and may be pronominalized, but the part of the utterance that conveys new information is treated in the opposite manner. This tendency toward greater emphasis on those parts of the utterance conveying new information and less emphasis on those parts of the utterance conveying given information may be carried to its logical extreme in private speech. In this case the only thing to be vocalized is new information, and the parts of an utterance which would have conveyed given information are dropped entirely. In Vygotsky's terms the external form of private speech is reduced to the point where the psychological subject (given information) is omitted and only the psychological predicate (new information) is preserved.

As we shall see private speech does not have to reach its most mature level to be abbreviated in the way Vygotsky proposed. Even when it is still at the level of describing one's own behavior and has not yet taken on a truly directive function, it may consist of abbreviated utterances. Furthermore even at this early stage the principles of abbreviation are similar to the given-new distinction outlined above in connection with social speech.

There are two things to keep in mind when analyzing this early form of private speech: (1) It does not seem to be intended to be social. The child can often be playing by himself and not be addressing his descriptive remarks to anyone else. Indeed he may be so thoroughly engaged in acting and speaking that he will not notice social speech addressed to him.[6] This means that we should not try to analyze the given-new organization in the child's private speech on the basis of a speaker's input to a listener as Chafe is able to do in the case of social speech; (2) In its early stages private speech is inextricably linked with the child's action. Saying that it describes one's own behavior is somewhat misleading since it implies that there is behavior on the one hand and an optional description of it on the other. Rather it is the case that speech and behavior seem to be bound together as two aspects of a single phenomenon at the early stages of private speech.

We are now left with two facts about early forms of private speech that can lead us to a new basis for analyzing its given-new organization. On the one hand, since there is no interlocutor involved, we can hardly want to say that the given-new organization or private speech is based on the factors Chafe has outlined. On the other hand, the early forms of private speech are inextricably bound up with the child's action. Therefore it is logical to examine how the child's action could influence the given-new organization of private speech. It is this close relationship between action and private speech that should be at the heart of our explanation.

The private-speech data[7] to be used in this analysis from two 2-year-olds who were putting together a puzzle. The puzzle contained animal figures and was to be constructed in accordance with a model that the experimenter gave the child. Each of the two children worked on this task alone. Some relevant segments of private speech that were recorded and transcribed are:

Child A: 1. "Oh!"
2. "And a horse, horsie. And a foot, and a foot, and a foot . . ."
3. "Four cats (uninterpretable) And a dog, he goes here."

[6]Of course as Vygotsky pointed out, the incidence of all forms of private speech will be much greater when the child is in a context where social communication is possible. This is because private speech develops out of social speech and is not yet completely separated from it. The two functions are confused by the child at this point.

[7]The author is grateful to Karen Fuson whose data are used in this paper.

Child B: 4. "Hmm? Oh wh-oh, me got duck. Snake. Snake. Brreak."
5. "Puppy."
6. "Ta goo do. This snake, snake. Hey brak. Oh. Snake."
7. "Ooh. Waa. Owass. Eee-Eee. Ja open. Simmin. He go out. Hey monkey."

At first it may strike the reader that what we have here is a hodgepodge of uninterpretable and accidental utterances. No doubt the factor of interest to us is only one of several that influenced the speech in these cases. For example these private-speech utterances contain several instances of what Kohlberg, Yaeger, and Hjertholm (1968) called word play, for example (4) "Snake. Snake. Brreak."; (6) "Ta goo do."; (7) "Ooh. Waa. Owass. Eee-Eee."

However for our purposes it is important to note that many of the utterances are concerned with parts of the puzzle, for example (2) "And a horse, horsie. And a foot, and a foot, and a foot. . . . "; (3) "Four cats . . . And a dog, he goes here."; (4) "Oh wh-oh, me got duck. Snake. Snake."; (5) "Puppy." In (3) we see that the child not only mentions the piece of the puzzle; he also mentions where it goes. The utterances of other children in this study also contain both the name of the piece and the place in the puzzle frame into which it fits. As we shall presently see the important point is that the child may drop the name of the position in the puzzle frame into which a piece is to go, but he does not drop the name of the piece.

In analyzing the surface form of private speech, one can expect to find certain parts of the utterance dropped as outlined above, but it is more difficult to make predictions about other forms of attenuation as Chafe did in the case of social speech. This is so because children's private speech utterances are often concerned with objects in the speech situation. In such cases it is possible to use what Jakobson (1957/1962) calls shifters. These are often in the form of pronouns that are not used (as in social speech) to refer to information given in the listener's consciousness. Rather they are used to refer to some object which is in the actual physical context of the private-speech situation. For example we could expect to see utterances in private speech, such as: "This one goes in this place, and now this one." In these cases pronominalization does not necessarily mark given information.

The private speech of these two-year-olds undoubtedly reflects an early stage in the development of private speech, that is it is more concerned with describing and naming certain aspects of the action and the environment than with planning and directing action. We may consider this puzzle task to involve object regulation. After becoming acustomed to the general nature of a puzzle task, the child arrives at a point where the physical objects in the environment draw him into it. The child may be able to stay on the task as long as there are empty spaces in the puzzle frame and extra pieces At this point in the child's development of puzzle-building skills there is no longer a need for adult regulation of this particular task on the one hand. There is no need for abstract, decontextualized representation of the goal and subgoals on the other hand, since each step is indexed by the frame and the pieces in the task situation. There is a built-in self-corrective mechanism and hence, object regulation.

We are now in a position to begin to see that with regard to the analysis of these samples of private speech: (1) there is a given-new information organization based on what is already present and what is introduced into the child's consciousness and (2) this organization is based on the child's action.

In the case of completing a puzzle, we can see that the action, as well as the private speech, have a sort of given-new organization. Putting together a puzzle involves carrying out the same basic action on several different objects, that is the pieces. For each piece the child must select it and then put it in its position in the puzzle frame. Of course the process can be much more difficult with a complex jigsaw puzzle for example. But in the case of the materials used here, it was possible to select a piece first and then look for its proper placement. There was no need to identify what piece would be needed to complete the next step in a complex plan before making a selection. The process of completing puzzles was familiar to these 2-year-olds in this analysis. For this particular puzzle there was no need for the experimenter to do anything beyond presenting the materials and saying that the child could make the puzzle. No explanation of the type of action necessary for carrying out the task was required. In such cases we can assume that when presented with the materials, the type of action required is in the consciousness of the child and should be associated with the given information in the private-speech utterance. The unfamiliar aspect of the task is concerned with the particular materials used. This is the new information introduced into the child's consciousness and is treated as such in the private-speech utterances. In this case we are not dealing with one individual (the speaker) introducing new information into the consciousness of another (the listener). Rather we are dealing with how the structure of a task carried out by one person involves given information and how it causes new information to be introduced into the child's consciousness. Usually the only part of the situation vocalized in private speech is that part concerned with new information. The given information often is attenuated to the point of being dropped entirely from the child's utterance.

It is important to note that while it is true that what is vocalized as new information is connected with external objects, it is not these objects in and of themselves that determine what is new information. Rather we can only identify new information on the basis of *how objects fit into a goal-directed action.* In principle it should be possible to use similar objects in a different action in such a way that the organization of given and new information would be changed (perhaps reversed) and the child's private-speech utterances would reflect this. This would be done by changing the goal and hence the action.

For example let us assume that one puzzle piece could fit into some, but not all, of several different puzzle frames. If the child's goal was to identify those frames into which the piece fits, we would expect him to try to carry out the action; information about the puzzle frames into which it would, or would not, fit would be introduced into consciousness as the child attended to the various possibilities. Accordingly we would expect the child's private speech to reflect this. The given information would now be concerned with the piece involved; the new information would be concerned with the puzzle frame. Here we would not expect the content expressed in private speech to be about the piece, as was the case with the utterances we examined above. Rather we would expect little or no mention of the pieces involved and the verbalization to be about where the piece fits. For example if we had puzzle frames of different colors, we might expect to hear private speech utterances ("The green one." or "Now the red one."), as opposed to the utterances about the pieces as in the first task. I am not claiming that the part of the utterance concerned with given information will always be neatly deleted and the part concerned with new information will remain. Rather the claim is that if any part is deleted, it will be that segment concerned with given information. In some cases it may remain; and in some cases there may be no verbalization at all. We are a long way from being in a position to predict all aspects of a private-speech utterance on the basis of an action.

What our analysis of this alternative task situation indicates is that if we say that the given-new organization of private speech is determined by the child's action, we really are talking about the *action* involved and not the objects used in it. There is nothing about the objects when considered apart from the goal-directed action in which they are embedded that can tell us which aspect of a situation will be concerned with given information and which aspect will be concerned with new information. This notion of an action has not played a very important role in American psychology, but it turns out to be an integral part of many analyses we may eventually want to make.

We can now amend our definition of given and new information in private speech to read:

> In the case of private speech, given information is that knowledge that is in the speaker's consciousness at the time of the utterance. So-called new information is what is being introduced into the speaker's consciousness as a result of the action he is carrying out.

It should not be assumed that we are claiming that the child consciously realizes what is given and new. It may be possible for an observer to determine the given-new organization of information on the basis of the structure of the test involved and the child's verbalization, but this guarantees nothing about the child's awareness of how this information is organized. This is also true of the given-new organization of information is social speech.

The nature of the action being carried out in the young child's play will often be determined by the type of objects he is using, and these objects are often games or tasks which have been developed by adults and become loaded with cultural meaning over a period of many years. This typical social-cultural fact suggests that when dealing with such common objects we have a mixed case of other regulation and object regulation, that is adults (sometimes adults from a much earlier period of history) have structured the object environment in such a way that the child is regulated by it. This is different from cases where the object regulation is based on environmental objects that were not intentionally structured by others.

Studies of private speech in the past have usually been concerned with whether or not it occurs in children at certain developmental levels and under certain conditions. Little has been done in the way of examining its form and content. If, as Vygotsky proposed, it is a sign system that ultimately allows humans to plan and guide actions, it would be very useful to know more about the factors that allow it to fulfill this function. In particular we need to know more about the rules for its abbreviation.

In this chapter we have dealt with how abbreviation takes place in only one early form of private speech. As private speech develops its forms and functions will change. Rather than being a part or a description of an ongoing action, it will ultimately be distinguished from action and take on a genuine planning and regulatory function. Levina (forthcoming) has described these later stages in the evolution of the planning function of private speech. The main point for us to remember is that at all stages in the development of private speech, the analysis of its abbreviated form will have to be based on its given-new organization. The basis for understanding this given-new organization will be the goal-directed action being carried out by the agent. Although the ideas developed about this abbreviation may eventually need to be revised, there is every reason to believe that the given-new organization of private speech can provide clues about the ways in which it can fulfill its function.

One of the most important problems for investigators of private speech has to do with how it develops. It should not be viewed as a single, undifferentiated phenomenon that appears and remains in its original form. Rather it undoubtedly passes through a developmental hierarchy from a structural point of view. By understanding the stages in this development, we shall be in a better position to understand not only the speech involved, but also the nature of the cognitive processes it accompanies and then guides. Furthermore we should not overlook the possibility that certain aspects in the development of private speech may influence other areas of language development. It would be very strange indeed if private speech were a separate function that had no influence on the development of social speech.

References

Akhutina, T. V. *Neirolingvisticheskii analiz dinamicheskoi afazii.* [The neurolinguistic analysis of dynamic aphasia.] Moscow: Izdatel'stvo MGU, 1974.

Bennett, J. *Linguistic behavior.* Cambridge: Cambridge University Press, 1976.

Chafe, W. L. Language and consciousness. *Language,* 1974, *50,* 111-113.

———. Givenness, contrastiveness, definiteness, subjects, topics, and point of view, in C.N. Li, ed., *Subject and topic.* New York: Academic, 1976.

Firbas, C. J. On defining the theme in functional sentence analysis. *Travaux linguistiques de Prague,* 1966, *1,* 267-280.

Halliday, M. A. K. Notes on transitivity and theme in English, II. *Journal of Linguistics,* 1967, *3,* 199-244.

Harris, A. Historical development of the Soviet theory of self-regulation, in G. Zivin, ed., *The development of self-regulation through private speech.* New York: Wiley, 1979.

Jakobson, R. Shifters, verbal categories, and the Russian verb, in *Roman Jakobson: Selected writings, vol. 2.* The Hague: Mouton, 1962. [Originally published, 1957]

Kohlberg, L., Yaeger, J., and **Hjertholm, E.** Private speech: four studies and a review of theories. *Child Development,* 1968, *39,* 691-736.

Leont'ev, A. A. *Yazyk, rech' i rechevaya deyatel'nost'.* [Language, speech and speech activity.] Moscow: Nauka, 1969.

Leont'ev, A. N. *Problemy razvitiya psikhiki.* [Problems in the development of mind.] Moscow: Izdatel'stvo MGU, 1959.

———. *Deyatel'nost', soznanie, lichnost'.* [Activity, consciousness, and the personality.] Leningrad: Izdatel'stvo politicheskoi literaturi, 1975.

Levina, R. E., L. S. Vygotsky's ideas about the planning function of speech in children, in J. V. Wertsch, ed., *The concept of activity in Soviet psychology,* forthcoming.

Luria, A. R. *Osnovnye problemy neirolingvistiki.* [Basic problems of neurolinguistics.] Moscow: Nauka, 1975.

Mead, G. H. *Mind, self, and society.* Chicago: University of Chicago Press, 1934.

Quirk, R., Greenbaum, S., Leech, G., and **Svartvik, J.** *A grammar of contemporary English.* New York: Seminar Press, 1972.

Sokolov, A. N. *Inner speech and thought.* G. T. Onischenko, trans. New York: Plenum, 1972. [Originally published, 1968.]

Vygotsky, L. S. *Izbrannye psikohologicheskie issledovaniya.* [Selected psychological investigations.] Moscow: Nauka, 1956.

______. *Thought and Language.* E. Hanfmann and G. Vakar, eds. and trans. Cambridge, Mass.: MIT. Press, 1962. [Originally published, 1934.]

Zinchenko, P. I. Involuntary memory and goal-directed nature of activity, in J. V. Wertsch, ed., *The concept of activity in Soviet psychology,* forthcoming.

CHAPTER 4

The Piagetian Concept of Representation and the Soviet-Inspired View of Self-Regulation

JEAN-PAUL BRONCKART AND
MADELEINE VENTOURAS-SPYCHER

Université de Genève

Luria's conception (1961) of language as a regulator of motor activity brings out the more general problem of the relationships between language and thought or, more precisely, the problem of the relationship between language and cognition. In order to analyze this conception in detail, it seems useful to place it in the broader context of Vygotsky's developmental theory (1934/1962), and then to compare it with Piaget's ideas on the relation between thought and language. The aim of this chapter will be therefore twofold: (1) to analyze in depth the theoretical and experimental foundations underlying these two positons and (2) to use this analysis to formulate certain hypotheses about the significance of both Luria's findings and the data of those who have repeated his experiments concerning the effect of vocal rhythm on the control of motor behavior. More attention will be paid to the analysis of the Piagetian position than to Vygotsky's. This disproportion has nothing to do with any theoretical choice on our part, but simply reflects the availability of the writings of each author: whereas Piaget has written and published a great deal, Vygotsky's works are scarce and difficult to find.[1]

The intervention of language as a behavior-regulator can only be conceived once speech has been acquired or is in the process of being acquired by the child, that is at about age two. However, the problem of the interaction of speech with cognition is already evident at an earlier phase in the child's development, the phase of prespeech. The questions pertinent at each period are of a different nature: the prespeech period of development raises the problem of the origin of language and in what way it is different from other behavioral forms; the later period poses the question of the role language (once learned) plays in cognitive development.

[1]Not a single text by Vygotsky has been translated into French. Also note: the authors of this chapter have translated into English the specific Piagetian citations, page numbers are to the original works written in French.

THE CHILD'S ACQUISITION OF LANGUAGE

Piaget's Position

The problem of the genesis of language was first treated in what is one of Piaget's most remarkable books, *La Formation du Symbole Chez l'Enfant* (1946/1951). The ideas set forth in this work have been frequently defended by Piaget himself in a number of articles and popular works (especially 1963, 1964/1967, 1967/1971), but particularly by his followers, among whom H. Sinclair figures prominently (1971, 1973, 1974). The Piagetian position on language is often stated by a number of principles, which can sometimes seem like recipes. They cover three main themes:

1. Speech, only one of several manifestations of the symbolic function, is elaborated by man in the context of his interactions with his surroundings:

    > Since Saussure and others, we know that verbal signs are only one of the aspects of the semiotic function . . . in addition to speech, this function extends to imitation in its representational forms, . . . gestural mimicry, symbolic play, mental images, etc., . . . and too often we forget that the development of representation and thought . . . is linked to all of this semiotic function and not only to speech. [Piaget, 1968 pp. 78-79].[2]

2. The appearance of speech, at the end of the second year, is linked to the emergence of the symbolic function, which in turn appears at the end of the sensorimotor evolution. This second theme demands further development. In Piaget's works the appearance of the first words seems to depend on the concept of object permanence and on the mechanism of imitation.

    As far as object permanence in children is concerned, it is not considered present if a child can find an object only partially hidden from his view or if he can reproduce a movement made by the experimenter; he must be able to find an object which is hidden in different places before his eyes (cf. Sinclair, 1974, p. 2). Object permanence refers to what Bronckart calls[3] "a structural condition for content stability." Children are not able to produce these signs, that is to find a correspondence between a sound sequence and a content, unless the content has a certain stability. It must be noted however that those who have emphasized the role of object permanence in the acquisition of language are Piaget's successors (e.g., Inhelder, et al., 1971). Piaget is often satisfied simply to call attention to the fact that permanence coincides with the acquisition of speech (1937/1954, 1946/1951, 1967/1971).

[2]See Sinclair, 1974a, p. 38, for an identical formulation.

[3]Bronckart (1976), the phrase here is translated by the authors.

Piaget sees imitation as the explanation of the process of representation, that is, the establishment of a relationship between a word and its meaning. Here also Piaget's formulations seem to be more nuanced than those of his followers. In most of his writing the Genevan psychologist presents the role of imitation in the following terms,

> [It] marks the point where sensorimotor meets representational. [1946, p. 294] it is . . . one of the possible transition points between sensorimotor behavior and representational behavior. [1964, p. 104]

In certain texts however more radical affirmations seem to suggest that Piaget conceives of imitation not as a transitional "point" on the way towards representation, but as the cause itself of representation,

> Imitative accommodation explains the formation of the signifiers needed for representational activity. [1946, p. 295]

These sorts of statements have been taken up by his successors and particularly by Sinclair, who does not hesitate to say that,

> Imitation is the source of all representation. [1974*b*, p. 4]

3. Language always comes behind cognition or intelligence, as much on the level of children's acquisition as in its emergence in the human race,

> Intelligence precedes language, not only ontogenetically . . . but phylogenetically, as numerous experiments dealing with intelligence in the higher orders of monkeys have proven. [Piaget, 1968, p. 79]

Surely for Piaget verbal behavior is a characteristic particular to the human species; but he also holds against most philosophers and linguists that language is not the cause of the emergence of thought but rather one of its consequences. In the Piagetian perspective what characterizes the human species is a sort of superior cognitive power, made possible by a special neurobiological apparatus,

> The operations of thought and logico-mathematical structures, in the broadest sense, are due to the general coordinations of actions . . . and not to language or to specifically social transmissions; these general coordinations of actions themselves come from the nervous and organic coordinations which have nothing to do with social interactions. [Piaget, 1970, p. 177][4]

This theme has been frequently picked up by Sinclair,

[4]This quotation brings out the difference between the notions of an innate structure as proposed by Chomsky (1965) and Piaget's innate function (to be discussed later).

> In a certain sense, something like a basic schema of human language *does* exist, and so does a set of basic assumptions permitting an oriented approach to the input. Both derive from fundamental properties of the human mind and therefore, in a sense, from neurological coordinations. [1974*a*, p. 40][5]

To appreciate the full significance of these three affirmations, it is necessary to analyze the Piagetian explanation of language acquisition in greater detail and discover its epistemological and psychological implications.

In the various works concerning the symbolic (or semiotic) function, the central concept for Piaget seems to be that of representation. This term can have two different meanings: (1) in the broad sense, representation is thought, "all intelligence which no longer depends simply on perceptions and movements ... but rather on a system of concepts and mental schemes" (1946, p. 68); (2) in the more limited sense used by Piaget—and thus ours as well—representation is conceived as a function, which connects a given content (an object or a concept) with something that becomes its substitute or representative. In voluntarily keeping this discussion on an elementary level (which Piaget himself is sometimes obliged to do to simplify certain demonstrations) we can say that representation is, in reality, the psychological mechanism that permits the setting up of sign or signal systems as described by semiologists.[6] Thus between a landscape drawing and the real landscape, between the word "book" or "livre" and the concept of a book, between the gestures miming an act and the act itself, there exists a link, a relation—that of representation. In the etymological sense of the term, it is a question of "presenting something again"—an object, a characteristic, a behavior, or a concept. Using the terms of Saussure (1916) in their most popular sense, Piaget speaks of *signifier* to designate the word, gesture, or painting—in other words, the substitute; and he speaks of *signified* to designate the content that is represented by the signifier. Whence his classical definition of representation as the association of a signifier with a signified.

In the Piagetian analysis of language acquisition, three aspects of the symbolic function are discussed: (1) the content or signified, (2) the substitute or signifier, and (3) the mechanism which acts as go-between. The references for these aspects are to be found in the classical works of Piaget (1936/1952, 1937/1954, 1946/1951, 1964/1967) and are reorganized in the more recent writings (1961/1969 and especially 1968/1970).

[5]For other statements of this type, see Piaget (1977, p. 42) and Sinclair (1972, p. 223; 1975, p. 318.)

[6]Cf. Barthes (1953). Note the hybrid character of the expression, "semiotic function," at the same time functional and structural.

The Classical Analysis of Representation

The content of representational activity is an object or a behavior or one of their characteristics. Knowledge of objects and behavior is not however innate, that is, "given" to a child at birth; the child must come to know them through the various stages Piaget describes in most of his work on psychology (for the developmental period with which this chapter is concerned see *La Naissance de l'Intelligence Chez l'Enfant* (1936/1952), and *La Construction du Reel Chez l'Enfant,* (1937/1954). Referring to an assumption already established a good bit earlier (Baldwin, 1915), Piaget emphasizes that the newborn child is not able to distinguish between what is "given" by the outside world and his own "inner self." This distinction begins during the sensorimotor stage; by a progressive coordination of actions a progressively increasing objectivity slowly takes the place of primitive egocentricity. At the moment when representation appears, between 18 and 24 months according to Piaget, this cognitive evolution is far from being completed. In a way it never is finished even at the highest levels of formal intelligence. Object permanence, mentioned earlier, cannot be considered as a concept that works according to the law of all-or-nothing within the logical framework of the Piagetian system. There are degrees of object permanence, and the specific test developed by Piaget and his successors covers only one instance in a continuous evolution. Other psychologists (for example Klein, 1948) have mentioned that at as early as 8 months, babies recognize their mother's face. This is undeniably a form of object permanence. Piaget himself has written of more subtle permanences using the term, conservation.

The substitutes or signifiers of representational activity have been the object of several types of classifications made by Piaget and his many collaborators. The essential hypothesis underlying the classifications, which we shall analyze later, is that of a progressive passage from representation (in its broad sense) leading to representation (in its strict sense), that is to the symbolic function. For Piaget all knowledge consists of giving a meaning, a signification to objects and events. In the broad sense of the term all knowledge is representational,

> Every perception and every cognitive adaptation consists in assigning a significance (forms, ends or means, etc. . . .). [1964, p. 104]

Knowledge becomes symbolic when its general assigning function develops into a specific assigning activity that uses substitutes or differentiated signifiers. In the classical works (1936/1952, 1937/1954, 1946/1951, 1964/1967), Piaget maintains that the sensorimotor period is characterized by representation in the broad sense: it uses cues and signals that are undifferentiated signifiers. The Piagetian notion of a cue is analogous to the notion proposed by semiologists who say: smoke is a sign of fire, footprints in the snow are a sign that someone has been there, a hiccup is a sign of drunkenness, and so on. According to Piaget sensorimotor representational signs are internal translations (that are inside the subject) of certain characteristics of the object. These signs become organized progressively during development until they form mental images. The real symbolic stage begins when these images enable the subject to evoke (that is, to make a new presentation which necessarily *is* symbolic) of an object or an activity. Examples are putting a stuffed bear or doll to sleep, making believe that stones are trains, saying a word, and so on. In this new sort of activity the child uses signifiers that are differentiated, that is distinct from their signifieds. These signifiers are outside the subject (stones for trains or words for objects). These particular signifiers are symbols or signs and their presence attests to the fact that representation in its strict sense is at work. The appearance of the symbolic function is essentially characterized then not only by the use of undifferentiated signifiers (cues or signals), but also by the use of differentiated signifiers (symbols or signs).

The mechanism which determines the passage toward representation in its strict sense of evocation, that is, the possibility of making an object or event which is objectively absent, present by representing it somehow. The capacity to evoke, according to Piaget, is derived from the process of imitation. During the sensorimotor stage, imitations are made only in the presence of a model; then progressively the child becomes capable of imitating, with considerable time lapses, between the original activity he witnesses and his own imitation of that behavior. Finally imitation becomes an activity in its own right, an activity which presupposes that there is a mental trace or image of the model. It is not easy to know if, for Piaget, imitation explains the creation of images or if it merely makes the passage to representation possible.

The Modern Analysis of Representation

In the classical position representation constitutes a function that permits the evocation of a content or signified by means of substitutes or signifiers. If these signifiers are not clearly dissociated from their content, it is a question of representation in the broad sense; if they are clearly differentiated, then it is a question of representation in the strict sense. It was from about 1960 (see particularly 1961/1969 and 1968/1970) that Piaget's analysis of representation was more fully elaborated in the light of the principles and findings of genetic epistemology. As Piaget and his colleagues began to put more emphasis on the constructive, interactive character of all thinking, the notions of signifiers and signifieds, inherited from linguistics, proved to be too simple. All thinking was seen as being elaborated by an active interaction of the individual with his surroundings; the signifieds and signifiers therefore had to be redefined as the constructions of the subject.

The signified or content is known only inasmuch as the subject assimilates it which, in turn, is only possible through the schemes at the subject's disposition. Piaget maintained then that "the signifieds . . . [are] the schemes at all levels constituting the organism's schematization" (1968, p. 13)—or rather that signifieds are composed of schemes and their contents. To put it simply, signifieds correspond to what the subject is able to construct with his operatory structures; the individual's signifieds taken together constitute what Piaget calls the "*operative*" domain.

As far as signifiers are concerned, the picture is a bit more complicated since Piaget distinguishes between three levels of signifiers. The most elementary level is, according to the classical view, that of perceptual cues. A cue is not a faithful copy of an object; it is the figuration of one of its states inside the subject. In order to describe these perceptual cues, Piaget also speaks about the figurative apparatus as opposed to the operative status of the signifieds. At a more complex level words in natural languages make up a category of signifiers differentiated from their signifieds to which they also have an arbitrary relationship: there is no natural link between the words, "horse," "cheval." "Pferd," nor do they look like their content /horse/. While the figurative apparatus, which gives the perceptual cues, is clearly limited by a dependence on content (it is smoke that indicates a fire and not footprints in the snow), the verbal signifier is for its part purely a matter of convention; Piaget calls it a "real semiotic instrument." Between these two opposing levels (figurative and semiotic) there is an intermediate group of signifiers composed of nonverbal symbols, gestural language, mental images, and so on. These signifiers are distinct from their contents; they are also autonomous with respect to their signifieds, but they are not completely independent. For example when in symbolic play a child uses a book to represent a plate and some leaves to represent food, the signifiers (the book and the leaves) are not chosen arbitrarily: they have a certain resemblance (in terms of size especially) with their signifieds (the plate and the food), and in this respect they are figurative tools. Still these signifiers are not simply a part of the signified, and the subject can choose them from a relatively vast range of objects (he can take a book, an ashtray, a cloth, or even a piece of wood to represent the plate); the symbolism is in the choice. Piaget considers signifiers which are both figurative and semiotic to be in an intermediate category.

Piaget's Conception of Development

In these two versions of the Piagetian analysis of representation, the same hypotheses are formulated about the nature and origin of language. The first hypothesis is that of an absolute dependence of the figurative domain on the operational one: individual cognitive development means the development of operatory structures which, in turn, bring about the evolution of figurative structures. Piaget writes:

> Whereas operatory structures, operational intelligence included, are rooted in sensori-motor activities in one long continuous developmental

> process, the contrary is true of figurative structures which are always subordinate to the operatory structures, developing not by direct filiation, where one structure leads to the next, but by gradual additions from operatory structures and from interaction with the data of experience. [1961, p. 353]

The second hypothesis is but a corollary of the first. It assumes that *there is functional continuity, without any particular gap, between the different sorts of signifiers.* A subject, his development governed by the evolution of his operative apparatus, first of all constructs perceptual cues (that is undifferentiated and purely figurative signifiers), which he can then use to elaborate mental images and symbols, (that is differentiated signifiers), partly figurative and partly semiotic. Finally he produces the first signs of speech, which are pure semiotic instruments:

> First of all, there exists a figurative apparatus which has no semiotic function. Perception, for instance, is a system of signifiers, but the cues are not differentiated from the perceptual given. Then, there are mechanisms which are both figurative and semiotic, such as mental images, symbolic play, "deferred imitation", gestural language, etc. Finally, there is a category of semiotic instruments which themselves are not figurative, but belong to systems of signs. Natural languages belong to this category. [Piaget, 1968, p. 15]

Inasmuch as they adhere to these two hypotheses, the followers of Piaget can contend that representation in the strict sense is simply the evolutionary result of representation in the broad sense. On this basis as well, they can claim that language is only one tool of symbolic function and as such is dependent on cognitive structures. This position is based on epistemological considerations which will now be briefly examined.

The Epistemological Foundations of the Piagetian Position

The principles underlying the Piagetian position on language acquisition are presented in great detail in three recent works by Piaget: *Biologie et Connaissance* (1967) *Epistémologie des Sciences Humaines* (1970), and *Adaptation Vitale et Psychologie de l'Intelligence* (1974). These principles are quite original and bear little resemblance to the ideas predominant in current theory; those of neo-Darwinian biological theory (for example, J. Monod) on the one hand, and those of transformational linguistics (for example, N. Chomsky) on the other.

Biology plays a major role in these theories. According to Monod the human species is the product of a succession of mutations and selections by the environment. Of all these mutations the emergence of deoxyribunucleic acid (DNA) is of capital importance. It is DNA, the species' biological code, that makes the creation of a very elaborate communicative code—language—possible; language for Monod is synonymous with thought or the "noosphere." Chomsky takes a similar stand: language competence relies upon and is explained by a specific genetic apparatus. During language acquisition, only a few stimulations are enough to enable this competence to "emerge." Roughly, the dominant view of language in Western thought is one of a phenomenon based on biological apparatus particular to the species that makes the development of thought and intelligence possible.

For Piaget the subject's structures, whether they be intellectual or linguistic, cannot be considered as already given. They must be constructed. In addition, and in opposition to Monod's and Chomsky's contentions, thought precedes language both on the ontogenetic and phylogenetic levels. However Piaget clearly sees a direct relation between biological processes and thinking, as the title of his very important work, *Biologie et Connaissance* (1967) indicates, but the link between the two is made on the level of functional mechanisms. For him, at each level of living organization, the organism and surroundings are in interaction. Their relationships are defined as regulations that apply until a satisfactory equilibrium has been attained. This permanent dialogue between the organism and its surroundings seems to have two poles: (1) assimilation by which the organism makes sense of his surroundings and (2) accommodation which is a modification of the organism's structure as a result of contact with this same environment. According to Piaget, from the sea anemone to man, the same biological mechanisms are at work, and their recursive application results in the construction of more and more complex structures. Human intelligence is only the culmination, the crystallization at a given moment, of these general cognitive mechanisms, and language is merely a particular aspect of human intelligence.

Thus one can see why in order to defend this epistemological position, Piaget must treat language as one behavior among others, a result of the same cognitive mechanisms. In the same way that he analyzes the appearance of speech in children as a continuous process, he tries to demonstrate the continuity of the passage from the first signal system to the second at the level of the species (Piaget 1970, p. 343 ff.). He argues in particular that the elements of the first system, the cues that trigger certain behavior, are to be found on every level of biological life; at every level of animal behavior; and in children they are the only signifiers functioning until the age of sixteen months. (These signifiers remain at the child's disposition after that time as well). A second system of signifiers is to be found in certain superior primates and in man; it is the symbolic function that includes two types of signifiers: (1) symbols, used by both animals and human beings and (2) signs, used only by man. These language signs give man an unquestionable advantage, that is,

> The sign system has an undeniably exceptional advantage because of its constructive mobility and the considerable number of meanings that it is able to transmit. [1970, pp. 345-346]

Nevertheless, for Piaget they are only the result of an underlying cognitive evolution, that of the operative apparatus which has attained a level of development in man definitely superior to that in other species. This cognitive superiority is linked to a specific neurological apparatus.

Several points should be made with respect to the Piagetian epistemology. The first, which we merely mention, concerns the opposition between innate structures and innate functions. Piaget in all his writings defends the hypothesis of functional innateness against Chomsky and the neo-Darwinians who present claims for structural innateness (cf. Piaget's *Structuralism* 1968/1970). However he is indeed obliged to admit that the human species is different from others. Inasmuch as he rejects language as the reason for that difference, he must *de facto* also uphold a structural innateness, precisely that of a particular neurological apparatus.

The second point concerns the implicit consequences of the Piagetian position. The hypothesis of a functional continuity from biological processes to intelligence leads to the reduction of language to a tool for individual representation, systematically leaving out its social and communicative aspects. It is striking to note that the entire discussion above only looks at the organism as an individual interacting with its environment, making figurative tools and then making semiotic tools, which help to represent reality. Never are social contingencies nor the necessity nor the desire to communicate mentioned as contributing to the appearance of language. The arguments made by Vygotsky and the Soviets, as well as by Western theoreticians, like Wallon (1941), differ radically from Piaget on this point; for them language is in fact considered to be a social tool for communication and representation.

The Social Origin of Language

It is in *Thought and Language* (1934/1962) that Vygotsky clearly takes a stand against Piagetian conceptions regarding the acquisition of thought and language. The arguments he develops are generally well known, therefore they will be treated here briefly in spite of their importance.

One of the major theses of this work is presented in the chapter, "The Genetic Roots of Thought and Speech." For Vygotsky, rational language, specific to the human species phylogenetically and ontogenetically, has two distinct roots: (1) purely intellectual and (2) purely vocal.

Using Koehler's (1921), Wundt's (1900), and Yerkes' (1916) analyses, the Soviet psychologist first of all demonstrates that higher-order monkeys possess capacities that are undeniably intellectual (according to Yerkes, a degree of ideation equivalent to that of a 3½-year-old child). He also notes that these animals use a relatively rich language, but a very affective one, and that it works in the same way as instincts do. What seems essential to him is that these two functions are independent of each other,

> The similarity points once more to the independence of chimpanzee 'communication' from any intellectual activity. [Vygotsky, 1962, p. 41]

On the ontogenetic level, using the works of Buehler (1928) and Stern (1914) as references, Vygotsky argues that during the first year of life there exist intelligent, nonverbalized behaviors and vocal productions that have an unquestionably social function, but no intellectual role. At a certain point in development these two roots merge, thought becomes verbal and language becomes intellectual. It is this merging, not observable in animals, that is the essential characteristic of man. Once this meeting of functions has occured, the child uses the words of his social environment to designate various things. At the outset however the child does not always manage to make the correct correspondences. Only progressively does the child really grasp language and internalize it.

It seems possible to state Vygotsky's position by substituting the notions *representation, communication,* and *language* for what he calls respectively *thought, speech,* and *rational speech.* By "representation" we mean an individual process by which an organism structures the knowledge he constructs in his interactions with his surroundings; this is done in the form of substitutes, either internal (cues, images) or external (symbols, signals, words). We understand "communication" as a social phenomenon of exchange between two or more members of a group in the context of those global finalities that ensure the group's survival and cohesion. As for "language," it can be defined as one system that is both communicative and representational; it is composed of representational substitutes linked by social convention as to their meanings. This conventional association is responsible for denotation, the representative aspect of language. Elaborated in a context where individuals interact and have reciprocal expectations, language functions moreover as a system of values; these values make up the communicative (intentional) aspect of language.

Given this new terminology, the differences between the positions of Vygotsky and Piaget are clearer. For Piaget language comes exclusively from representation, which is but an individual mechanism with a biological origin; for Vygotsky language results from both a representative root *and* a communicative root, that of social exchanges through which socio-historical determinisms manifest themselves. This first difference involves a second. Piaget insists on a functional continuity of the processes of cognitive development; Vygotsky, on the contrary, emphasizes the revolution produced when the two roots of development merge,

> *The nature of development itself changes,* from biological to socio-historical. [1962, p. 51]

The themes essential to Vygotsky's thought present obvious analogies to those developed by the French psychologist, Wallon. In *L'Evolution Psychologique de l'Enfant* (1941), Wallon stresses the prolonged immaturity of human children,

> A child remains virtually helpless for a long time in front of the most elementary necessities of life. [p. 46][7]

Because of this inability to confront the outside world directly, the child must always rely upon his family, and most of his activity is mediated by his social entourage:

> Whereas the young animal, sometimes due to example and being forced by his mother, adjusts his reactions directly to the situations of his physical world, the child remains for months and years unable to satisfy his desires unless assisted by others. The only way of expressing [these desires] is by putting himself in contact with his entourage, that is with those of his reactions which arouse behaviors in others that are to his advantage, and those reactions in others which indicate his behavior should continue or change. As early as the first weeks or first days, the sequences for the first foundations of what will serve as interpersonal relationships are laid down. Expressive functions are way ahead of functions of realization. As a prelude to language, strictly speaking, they are the first to leave their mark upon man, essentially a social animal. [Wallon, 1941, pp. 46-47]

This passage seems to illustrate fairly clearly the need to postulate a communicative root as a fundamental social precedent of language.

Wallon also emphasizes the functional discontinuity of child development; he clearly indicates that,

> development in children does not proceed by simple additions of progress which always work in the same direction. [1941, p. 103]

Development is seen rather in terms of fluctuations or alternations (with phases of rapid development and others of apparent regression), in which maturation of nervous and muscular support, motor activity development, and emotional interactions all have an influence.

[7]This and the following quotations from Wallon, like those from untranslated works by Piaget, were translated by the authors.

Towards a New Conception of Language Acquisition

In this section the Piagetian and the social positions will be integrated in a conception of language acquisition that Bronckart (1976,1977) has been working on for the last several years.

What Must Be Explained in Language Acquisition

The Piagetian analysis of signs is in line with a popular conception held by a number of linguists and semiologists and usually associated with Saussure (1916). According to this conception the sign is made up of: (1) a conceptual content that is called the signified and (2) a sound substitute called the signifier. Between the two there exists a conventional or arbitrary relationsship. During the last 10 years, however, some important critical works, particularly by Engler (1968) and de Mauro (1972), have brought out the superficiality of this conception. The Saussurian sign notion is much more complex than Piaget seems to believe.[8]

One of the first tenets of the Saussurian analysis is that in order to construct a sign every speaker must deal with two areas of reality: (1) the material substance, or the meaning or content to be expressed and (2) the sound substance of the language that expresses the content. Between these two areas there exists no natural relationship of resemblance; they simply happen to be simultaneously present in a communicative context (for example the word "pipe" pronounced in the presence of the object / pipe /). Given these two material realities, the subject elaborates two images: one which Saussure (1916) calls the *sound image*, the other which he calls the *concept*, which we shall call the *meaning image.*

The point that we find of capital importance in the Saussurian demonstration is that the contrast between sound image and meaning image is not at all synonymous with the opposition between signifier and signified. For Saussure (1916), images are in fact individual constructions, whereas signifiers and signifieds are elaborations of a social nature. The passage from individual to social is accomplished by establishing a conventional correspondence between certain aspects or certain groups of sound images and certain aspects or certain groups of meaning images. The images or individual representations are reorganized by social convention; the results of this reorganization are called signifieds and signifiers. To take a simple example, the pair of English words "ox" and "beef" can be compared with the single French word "boeuf," if we limit ourselves to the content level. Every individual in Western

[8]The Piagetian position is understandable; up until 1968 almost all linguists adhered to this "superficial" conception of signs (see Bronckart, 1977, Chap. 4).

society, whatever his native language, has the chance to construct for himself various representations of oxen in its different states: big or small when alive, in the form of steak or corned beef when dead. These representations are the meaning images constructed by an individual subject.[9] The intervention of language, or rather of the social convention that is its basis, makes a restructurization (a reorganization) of these individual images necessary. For English speakers the language proposes two signifiers, "ox" and "beef." To these words two groups of meaning images correspond—those designated by "ox" and those designated by "beef." These are the reorganizations of images that are the signifieds in English. In French, convention supplies only one word. Thus, the signified necessarily has a wider field of application than the two English signifieds to which it corresponds.

The Saussurian conception of signs implies therefore that in a first stage, subjects construct personal images of the two material substances of sound and content, and that, in a second stage, language reorganizes these images in the form of signifiers and signfieds. In the light of this analysis we would like to take a new look at the problem of the acquisition of signs in children.

When at about 18 months a child produces the utterance "allgone" each time his mother leaves, an object falls to the ground, or to accompany play in which things are made to disappear and reappear, psycholinguists refer to these utterances as word-phrases or as holophrases (see Brown, 1973). For us this sort of production constitutes a sign in every sense of the word. The child in fact has constructed a sound image ("allgone") on the basis of the sound used in adult productions like "She is gone.", "The book is gone.", and so on. He has also constructed a meaning image that includes various events characterized by the disappearance of something. This is the first step in the elaboration of a sign, according to Saussure (1916). Besides these two individual constructions, the child has also made the association suggested by social convention: although there is no natural connection between these two types of image, he uses one to represent the other. Thus he reproduces approximately, of course, the meaning relationship belonging to his native language, which is the second step for Saussure.

For us every interpretation of language acquisition must give a satisfactory explanation of these two steps; that is why the Piagetian conception seems insufficient. It must be remembered that for Piaget human language is a tool used for interacting with the environment, constructed by the continuous working of general, essentially biological, mechanisms. Let us briefly examine the steps of this construction again. From birth on, a baby constructs various cues. These represent certain aspects of his environment and permit him to

[9]These images obviously depend on a social context, but this context does not impose the way in which the images are constructed.

identify certain stimulations. Later on these cues are organized into configurations or images, making deferred imitation and evocation possible. Up to this level Piaget's functional continuity seems plausible. With symbolic play something new appears: the subject represents an object (the car of a train) by *another* object (a stone). This new representative activity can be analyzed in the following manner: starting with an initial object O_1 (a railroad car), the subject constructs a mental image that can itself be represented by another object O_2 (a stone), on the condition that the two objects O_1 and O_2 bear a physical resemblance to each other. In this analysis symbolic play calls for the elaboration of only one mental image that takes the place of two physical objects, one of which stands for the other, on the condition that their relation is motivated,[10] that is that they share obvious characteristics. Symbolic activity remains quite similar then to the simple elaboration of mental images. Here functional continuity is therefore still likely. The case is completely different as far as verbal signs are concerned. When the first of these signs appear, the child (as has been shown) has to construct *two* separate mental images in radically different areas of reality, sound and meaning, and relate these images by means of the conventional rules of his mother tongue. This construction of a verbal sign is a real jump, a rupture in the single thread of development, inexplicable within the simple framework of the development of individual representation.

In short the Piagetian hypothesis of functional continuity which sees language as exclusively representational in origin, does not seem to hold up under scrutiny. Development in children, on the contrary, seems characterized by breaks, reorganizations, if not revolutions, as suggested by Wallon (1941) and especially by Mounoud (1971,1977). On the linguistic level, what remains to be explained is how one goes from the first Saussurian stage (individual images) to the social stage of signifiers and signifieds. In other words the transition from natural substitutes, requiring only a mental image (cues, images, and symbolic play), to artificial and social substitutes, which demand two images and the establishment of a relationship between then (verbal signs, mathematical symbols, highway codes, and so on),[11] remains to be explained.

The Theoretical Bases of an Explanation

The problem of language acquisition is one of the oldest problems that has interested psychologists. It is also a very timely problem in that it continually challenges the existence of the borderline that most social science specialists

[10]In the Saussurian sense of the term.

[11]Here we run into a distinction proposed by von Glaserfeld between "natural signs" and "artificial signs" (1974).

try to draw between the domains of the cognitive-psychological-individual and that of the social-relational-affective. Psychology, sociology, and psychoanalysis have the status of separate domains, since each has developed its own methods and conceptual apparatus, but each has to come to grips with the same object of study, *language,* the real social and individual interface. Each scientific conception of language reveals a deep epistemological position. Piaget, who with Chomsky (1968) and Monod (1970), follows the "biology is everything" tradition, reduces language to an essentially representational phenomenon, explaining its emergence as a progressive growth in complexity in the ways in which the individual interacts with his environment, physically and asocially. According to other theories, language is considered to be essentially communicative and social (see especially Sapir, 1969 and Whorf, 1964), and the need for an individual construction is not emphasized. Looking at language's hybrid status, it seems to us that these two positions need to be reconciled, and it is towards this end that we maintain a position similar to that of Vygotsky, whose hypotheses are similar to Wallon's (1941) conception of development.

In our opinion what remains to be analyzed and explained during the prelinguistic period is: (1) the preparation for the construction of mental images and (2) the preparation for the social convention which connects the two types of specific images—those formed from sound and those elaborated from content.

Image-making can be described as a process of individual construction. The best description of this process is, to our knowledge, the Piagetian one. The conventional correspondence between sound images and their content on the other hand requires something else. It is no longer a question of elaborating a knowledge of the physical world, but rather of the social and relational world. Obviously society is not introduced here abruptly as something which imposes itself brutally on the subject. Social knowledge as well must construct itself: it is the fruit of a permanent dialectic between partners.

To differentiate these two aspects of prelinguistic development, Bronckart has suggested a distinction between *representational schemes*—worked out on contact with the physical environment, inert and nonresponsive—and *communicative schemes*—constructed in interaction between social partners, active and autonomous—(1976, forthcoming). Representational schemes (what Vygotsky calls the "nonverbal intellectual root") having been analyzed in detail, we shall now say something about communicative schemes.

Communicative Schemes in Children

As indicated by the etymology of the French term, "enfant" (from the Latin "in-fari"—unable to speak), the child is a member of the species who does not share its principal means of communication, speech. More precisely, the child is confronted by his family members who, unlike him, have ways of making elaborate representations. They can also use a certain system of communication and representation—language. The study of communicative schemes is really the study of the interactions taking place between two unequal partners,the baby and the people around him. Wallon (1941) gives an admirable introduction to this study in a chapter dealing with affectivity and emotions:

> . . . emotions, due to their psychogenetic orientation, are what create the connections which prepare the way for intention and discrimination. The attitudes which characterize them, the sound and visual effects which they produce, are for others extremely interesting stimulations, which have the power to provoke similar, complementary or reciprocal reactions, depending on the situation for which they are the effect and the cue. A kind of consonance, either of harmony or disharmony, sets in very early between emotional attitudes which coincide in the same area of perception and action. [1941, p. 133]

As we have seen, this type of cognition differs utterly from that analyzed by Piaget. Here we are dealing with interactions that are essentially anticipatory, with expectations and with intentions.

Up-to-date data on this type of scheme is scattered among the available literature. Nonetheless we shall comment on some work done in this area. Condon and Sander (1974) have shown that newborn infants move head, shoulders, legs, and feet in synchronization with rhythmic and syntactic segments of words adults say to them. In this very early period of development, unconscious modes of interaction thus become established between the baby and his surroundings by means of the sound canal. Better known studies have revealed that at the age of about two months another type of communication appears. When the baby finds himself in a disagreeable situation, his muscular tensions increase, and his cries become high-pitched and nasal. When he is comfortable and relaxed however the noises he makes are low-pitched and not nasal because the muscles used for vocalizing are relaxed. This first differentiation in vocalizing is quickly discriminated by the people familiar with the baby, so that a rudimentary communication system operating on cries becomes established. Some months later, as the baby starts staying awake for longer stretches of time, long acoustic sequences develop, these are called vocalizations. More and more, the duration and the triggering of both these phonatory games as well as their characteristics depend on the nature of interactions with the milieu, especially with the mother. The third kind of communicative exchange—prosodic images, then phonological images and, finally, the lexical images proper to speech—structures itself progressively on these sorts of interactions.

The development of speech from vocalizations does not however exclude nonlinguistic vocalizations from the process of communication. Ricks (1975) has shown that exchanges by means of cries, far from disappearing, tend to increase. In an experiment as clever as it is simple, he asked mothers to listen to tape recordings of cries (made by babies in certain situations) and to try to identify their own child's cries as well as the context in which they were made. His results showed that the mothers had no trouble recognizing the situation in which the cries were made for *all* the babies. Thus certain infant vocalizations have universal acoustic characteristics and form a system of communications with those around them. Montagner (1972) and Montagner, et al., (1974) examined another kind of communication. He showed that there is a system of communication that works on mimicry and gestures between children ranging in age from 18 months to 4 years. This type of communication uses ritualized acts, that is, behavioral sequences of postural, gestural, and mimicking elements that, in a precise context, communicate an unambiguous meaning for children of that age.

Available findings like these can be summed up in this way:

1. Starting from the moment of birth there is an initial type of communicative interaction going on between mother and child: a rhythmic exchange governed by the mother's voice, which seems to play an important role in the child's emotional development.
2. Little by little the infant develops types of behavior which the adult interprets and to which the adult reacts, either by something he does or something he says. The infant's behavior operates with *signals,* whether they are cries, gestures, mimicry, or vocalizations (Weir, 1962).
3. The adults around the baby, who speak to him in a certain way, usually without cries or gestures, reinforce the vocal productions he makes that seem nearest to their own productions, that is his vocalizations. Aided by this feedback infant vocalizations develop a great deal and, at the moment when imitation starts, it is with these vocalizations that the child constructs his first phonological oppositions and his first verbal signifiers.

The Appearance of Speech

Between the ages of 12 and 16 months (approximately), the number of acoustic images at the child's disposal for communicating increases, and they become associated with his needs being satisfied, as do the vocal productions of the people around him. His voice now works as a means of satisfying some of his expectations. At the same time, on a strictly representational level, the child is busy elaborating a certain way of understanding the world. He is developing the ability to stabilize contents and he can evoke absent realities by using permanent images.

Speech appears in children, as Vygotsky has said, as the result of the merging of these two evolutions: representative constructions (for example the idea of /dog/) are incorporated in communicative schemes. The child finds a correspondence between the acoustic images elaborated from adult speech and the content images (like/dog/); that is he applies to his own individual representations a sound-context correspondence that previously he had been making only on a communicative level. Adults around him reinforce the correspondences he makes, thus the child gradually leaves personal evocation behind for social evocation. He becomes aware not only that he can evoke something that is not there, but also that an adult can do it too. It is this sharing of evocations that permits the child to adopt the social conventions on which language is founded.

THE ROLE OF LANGUAGE IN THE CHILD'S LATER DEVELOPMENT

The Different Positions

The Piagetian position does not give language a privileged status. Human beings are seen as distinctive basically due to their cognitive equipment, which enables them to construct successive levels of operatory structures and systems of signifiers that correspond to them. Language is only one system of signifiers among others. For Piaget language is neither necessary nor sufficient for the development of thought. (The point commonly brought up in this respect is that in many areas the deaf have a level of cognitive development that is the same as that of those who can hear).

In the Piagetian perspective it makes no sense to talk about interactions between language and other types of behavior. More precisely, the ideas of self-regulation through one's own speech is necessarily circuitous or senseless. Constructionists maintain that language cannot influence either development or actions. The evolution of language follows that of the operatory structures; symbols and signs simply happen to be particularly good for representing the highly elaborate operations of formal thought (see especially Piaget, 1964/1967; Sinclair, 1971; and Duckworth, 1973).

For Wallon (1941) not only the intellectual aspects, but also the emotional and sociocommunicative sides of development, must be taken into consideration in order to explain language completely. Social structures act on the child, not by creating ready-made attitudes and feelings, but by gradually integrating the subject's structures of thought. As Wallon puts it, "the social amalgamates the organic" (1941, p. 134). Thus when speech appears, it is the result of both intellectual and social development, and it uses them both. Wallon continues:

> To tell the truth, it [language] is not the cause of thought, but its instrument and support, without which thought cannot develop. If one sometimes falls behind the other, their reciprocal action quickly reestablishes the balance. [1941, p. 172]

Vygotsky's position is even more explicit. When language appears, the nature of development undergoes a radical transformation:

> Verbal thought is not an innate, natural form of behavior but is determined by an historical-cultural process and has specific properties and laws that cannot be found in the natural forms of thought and speech. Once we acknowledge the historical character of verbal thought, we must consider it subject to all the premises of historical materialism, which are valid for any historical phenomenon in human society. It is only to be expected that on this level the development of behavior will be governed essentially by the general laws of the historical development of human society. [1962, p. 51]

In the Vygotskian perspective language plays a decisive role. It takes control of the individual little by little in a three-step process. First the child reproduces the verbal forms of adult language without really understanding them. Later he uses vocal productions with other means (such as counting on his fingers) to solve different types of problems. This is what Piaget calls egocentric language. Finally the child internalizes language, which takes on the role of an organizer of behavior. It must be noted that the development of verbal thought for Vygotsky does not rule out nonverbal thought nor irrational vocal productions. On the contrary these two types of activity continue to develop,

> Nonverbal thought and non-intellectual speech . . . are affected only indirectly by the process of verbal thought. [1962, p. 48]

Language as Regulator

Luria tried to verify and illustrate Vygotsky's position that language organizes behavior by longitudinal studies (1959), by devising diagnostic and rehabilitation techniques (1963), and by studying language as a regulator of motor behavior under experimental conditions (1961). In this research Luria tried to locate the three steps in Vygotsky's hypothesis on the development of a progressively greater control of language on individual motor development. During the first stage, this control is supposed to be exercised exclusively by adult speech. Later the subject himself takes over control, with the help of the impulsive aspects of the utterances he emits. At last, in the third stage, all the characteristics of the subject's language (particularly its semantic aspects) are at work in determining his behavior. What we can call the

Vygotsky-Luria position then assumes an initial state E_1 in which adult speech exercises (by its impulse and meaning) a control on the subject's behavior. This state is followed by two others. First E_2 develops from E_1, that is, an initially external regulation gives way to regulations made by the impulse aspect of the vocal characteristics of children's productions. This is the first transfer of regulation (T_1). Next, internal control (E_2) is replaced by a regulation made by the semantic aspects of the subject's language (E_3). This second transfer (T_2) coincides with language's internalization.

Luria put together a good amount of experimental data to support these hypotheses. In a first series of research projects, he showed that adult language exercised an influence on motor behavior in children at a very early age. From the age of about 18 months on, vocal productions made around children had the effect of reducing certain stereotyped kinds of behavior or certain perseverative actions (see Lyublinskaya's experiments in particular, 1957). A second kind of experiment has also confirmed the existence of this initial E_1 stage by means of a technique perfected by Ivanov-Smolenskii. A young child is given a rubber bulb that is designed to record all presses. Each time an adult tells the child to press he is supposed to do so. The youngest subjects however press regardless of whether the order is "Press." or "Don't press." This negative understanding of certain orders lasts only up to the age of around 2½ years. At this point adult language-control on children's behavior seems to be well established. To examine the transfer from external control (E_1) to internal regulation (E_2 and E_3), a more complex experimental situation is necessary. Using a verbal order, like "Press when you see a light go on.", the experimenter asks the child to do something simple (one reaction for one stimulus) or complex (several reactions for a single stimulus or even one reaction for only certain subcategories of the stimulus). According to Luria a 3-year-old is incapable of doing such tasks, for even simple coordinations between stimulus and reaction break down rapidly. To maintain these coordinations the subject himself must say something. Thus if children aged 3½ years or more give the pertinent verbal orders themselves ("Press." "Press, press." and so on) each time the stimulus occurs, they manage to coordinate their motor reaction with the stimulus. It is indeed an intervention made by the child's language that insures success in performance on the task, but this intervention is not semantic. Whether the verbal reactions are positive or negative ("Press." or "Don't press."), they always provoke a motor reaction. In Luria's description, state E_2 is characterized by this regulation of behavior by the impulse aspect of the motor or vocal feature of language. The final stage (E_3) is not observed until age 5 or later. Here the verbal reactions play a semantic role. Discrimination tasks are executed perfectly (for example pushing when a green light goes on, not pushing when a blue one goes on).

Luria, like a good many other Russian psychologists, is frequently vague about his experimental techniques, his methodology, and sometimes even about the theoretical references made in his interpretations. Analyzing and redoing his experiments is thus no easy task. The first experiments done to repeat his work (Joynt and Cambourne, 1968; Miller, Shelton, and Flavell, 1970; Wilder, 1969) led to mostly negative results. However Wozniak (1972) questioned them on methodological and theoretical grounds. To put it briefly: the phenomenon of regulation did not belong to the area of verbal mediation as the persons who repeated the experiments thought, but rather were a kind of inhibition. At the same time other results were published (Bronckart, 1970; Rondal, 1973, 1975; and Beaudichon, Legros, and Oleron 1973), which confirmed beyond a doubt Luria's description of the existence of a regulator of the impulsive (motor or vocal) aspects of speech between the ages of 3½ and 5 years.

What Luria's Experiments Show

It seems to us that Luria's findings cannot be interpreted without checking certain elementary facts about his experiments. The analysis that Luria put forth in 1961 is based on several implicit hypotheses that need to be tested and made explicit. The most important hypothesis of Luria's implicit ones has to do with the verbal orders given to the children. Luria apparently did not see any problem in the children's understanding a sentence like "Press the bulb when you see the red light go on." As Bronckart (1973) stressed earlier, this hypothesis is, at best, open to argument. Even if one admits that a 3-year-old can understand such an order, one runs into a situation where an order is understood but not followed. Luria in his study tries to show that the successful performance does not stem from the order given by the experimenter, but from the vocal productions of the child himself. This sort of analysis, in our eyes, demands some basic experimental control: for each task a silent experiment must be made in order to see at what moment the adult order is understood and acted upon without the children saying anything.

Luria's second implicit hypothesis can be formulated as follows: between the ages of 3 and 6, the coordination of visual stimulus with verbal reaction appears before the coordination of visual stimulus and motor reaction. The children's verbal productions ("Press." "Go on." "Don't press." and so on) actually have a regulatory effect on motor reactions in that they are themselves shaped by the stimulus. This second implicit hypothesis is extremely daring and must be interpreted very carefully. A second experimental control study is then necessary to check the subject's capacities for coordinating visual stimulus and verbal reactions systematically for each experiment.

Experiments carried out between 1967 and 1969 notably used the two controls just mentioned (Bronckart, 1969, 1970, 1973). The technique developed for this series of experiments was adopted by Rondal (1973, 1975). Four important points issued from these studies:

1. Adult language (E_1) definitely has a regulatory role. It can elicit a simple motor reaction from the age of 1½ on, inhibit it from the age of 2½ on, and regulate a motor reaction to a visual stimulus from the age of about 3½ on. These regulations however depend on the semantic aspects of adult speech.
2. There was no evidence that the semantic aspects of children's speech (E_3) regulate their motor behavior. At the period where their verbal reactions ("I'm going to press twice." "I don't press it.") are followed by the right motor reactions, the children did better under silent conditions. An order given by the adult is therefore enough to explain good performances.
3. Luria's technique, which was to ask the subject to make both a verbal reaction and a motor reaction when the stimulus appeared, complicated an already complex task. This had the general effect of worsening the motor performance (Bronckart, 1970). Between the ages of 3½ and 4½, however, in certain experimental paradigms, the coordination of the visual stimulus and the verbal reaction preceded that of the visual stimulus and the motor reaction. In this case the verbal reaction had a positive effect on motor performance.
4. The effect the verbal reaction can have on the motor reaction is particularly of a rhythmic nature (Cf. Zivin, 1976; Harris, 1976).

What can be concluded from these findings? Luria's attempts to validate his position are a failure inasmuch as the existence of the two later stages of transfer of regulations was not proved. As far as T_1 is concerned, it is certain that the state E_2 (regulation by nonsemantic aspects of language) exists, but Luria himself has stressed (1961, 1963) that this is not the only or the most efficient mode of nonsemantic regulation; there is also no evidence that it develops directly from external regulation. As for T_2, there is no data pointing to the existence of the final state E_3.

In our opinion this lack of proof does not jeopardize Vygotsky's developmental hypothesis, which is without a doubt one of the most important ones in contemporary psychology and one to which we adhere. Our reservations concern Luria's interpretation of Vygotsky's position and the choice of the technique of pressing a rubber bulb. As Luria has reformulated Vygotsky on the transfer of regulations, it seems that during its first transfer, language loses its semantic characteristics. According to Luria, when the adult exercises control on the child's motor behavior, he does so by meanings that are understood by the child (at least after the age of 2): "Press." "Press when you see the light." "Don't press." and so on. When the child takes over the regulation of his actions by himself, the meaning of the words spoken no longer plays any role. This disappearance of meaning seems quite unlikely from the theoretical point of view. It also makes us skeptical about the possibility of establishing any relation (and thus a connection) between external regulation by the meaning and internal regulation by the impulse side of speech.

From a methodological point of view, the choice of the rubber bulb technique seems to us unfortunate. Let us cite, as an example of the problem it poses, the simplest possible experimental paradigm. The experimenter asks the child to keep his hand on the rubber bulb and to press each time the light appears. Three- and 4-year-olds manage to press on the bulb right from the first stimuli but, very quickly, perseverative pressures show up which finally completely disturb the stimulus-reaction coordination. The child's production of verbal reactions ("I press." or "Go on.") at the appearance of each stimulus eliminates these perseverative reactions, and that is why we talk about regulation by speech.

The problem here is to know what the status of the intermediary reactions is. According to Wozniak, they are explained by "certain other compelling classes of non-verbal signals, such as tactile stimulation of the palm" (1972, p.17). Have we here a general characteristic of motor development? Or at least a characteristic that can be generalized? Or is it simply an incidental effect due to the type of material used? These are the questions we shall now examine.

Rhythm and Language

While Luria's approach is open to criticism, there unquestionably exist certain phenomena of regulation by the impulsive aspects of speech. Three types of results serve to prove this point:

1. When children are asked to press twice when they receive the stimulus and are also asked to make any verbal response at all—not only "Press-press", but also "Bam-bam", "Sing-sing", or "Tou-tou." (Bronckart, 1970; Tikhomirov, 1958/1975)—their motor performance between the ages of 3 and 4 is better than when no such instructions are given.
2. In the same situation when children are asked to give a long verbal response (like "I shall press twice."), this utterance has no regulating effect at all. The subjects either press just once or several times (Tikhomirov, 1958/1975).
3. Many times this verbal order elicited three motor reactions instead of two; in this case the verbal response was broken up into three parts ("two/times/press." or "I/press/twice.") (Bronckart, 1970; Tikhomirov, 1958/1975).

These effects of the introduction of speech have been interpreted in different ways. Luria, from the viewpoint of neurodynamics that he develops, sometimes maintains that, "regulatory influence in our experiments proceeds . . . from the direct impellant or initiating action of the speech itself" (1961, p. 95). Still he usually sees verbal stimuli rather as having an inhibitory effect, a view that is shared by Wozniak in his discussion of the disappearance of persevering reactions.

Most western authors who have carried out replication experiments stress the correspondance between the number of verbal responses and the number of motor reactions; they maintain that vocal emissions reinforce motor behavior that has the same rhythm (Bronckart, 1970). Wozniak (1976), Zivin (1976), Harris (1976), and others emphasize this rhythmic coordination and consider it the basic mechanism involved in regulation. For them the rhythm of vocal productions has a special role as an integrator from the moment the processes of autoregulation set in, thus permitting a reinterpretation of most of Luria's findings.

How then do these authors define rhythm? Wozniak talks about a "mechanism of structural regulation" and of "temporal organization" (1976). Harris uses the term of rhythm "for the general case to describe the organization of particular sequences or pulses or beats in ongoing activity" (1976). Martin (1972) defines rhythmic patterns as "event sequences in which some events (elements) are marked from others; for example loud . . . sound . . . versus soft . . . sound. . . ." He calls the marked elements "accents." The accents occur with some regularity, regardless of tempo. Zivin (1976) sees rhythm as "patterns of onsets and durations."

A comparison of these definitions show that some speak of a mechanism while others talk about an organization, a pattern, or a series of separate events. Thus in certain cases rhythm is considered as a process; in others as a structure resulting from the working of a process. We think that it is important to know what role rhythm is considered to play in human development by psychologists not particularly interested in language, but interested in rhythm.

There is a huge literature on rhythm extending over several centuries. It includes phenomena outside the sphere of human activity, such as seasonal and diurnal rhythms. To narrow down the problem however, we shall concentrate on psychological rhythm. Philosophers were the first to examine the idea of rhythm. Plato offered an interesting definition of it as, "order in movement" (Laloy, 1904). A century ago Meumann (1894) thought of it as, "an emotion which discharges itself in ordered movements." With the birth of experimental psychology, Wundt (1911) and Pavlov (1927) became interested in the subject. For the Gestaltists rhythm was a privileged subject of investigation, since it was considered a good form, or "Gestaltverkettung" (Werner, 1919). More recently Fraisse has done long studies on the "periodicity and structure" of rhythm, where periodicity is considered to be a "succession of appearances and disappearances of a stimulation" (1956).

Psychologists have mainly studied physiological rhythm, like cardiac and respiratory rhythm. Using these models they have stressed the importance of parameters like repetition, periodicity, accent, and the regularity of separate events. It is the product or result of a rhythmic movement that has more often held their attention, not so much the movement itself. Rhythm is necessarily related to some kind of movement. Movement implies activity, which is essential to an organism. It is also where psychological behavior begins.

In order to say whether or not rhythm is a fundamental mechanism for behavioral organization, let us first look at where the phenomenon exists outside physiological rhythms. Starting from birth, movements begin organizing themselves in children, first as reflexes. All bodily activity organizes itself according to what Piaget calls the circulatory reflex: the fact that a movement repeats itself explains why it becomes stable. In this way too, very simple structures, like seizing an object or walking, develop. In addition organizations much more complex are similarly elaborated in 4- or 5-year-olds, (for example tying shoelaces). Piaget describes this development as initial sensorimotor schemes that are "made up of rhythmical structures" and are observable in all organisms as spontaneous, global movements.

If it is true that rhythm underlies all movement organized temporarily, it can also be an activity in itself which has its own development. Thus at the age of 2 children can imitate a regular pattern like . . . . . , beating time with two sticks, at the age of 3 children can imitate this kind of rhythm: ... ... ; at the age of 4: .. . . ; and at the age of 5: ˇ.. ˇ.. ˇ.. (one strong beat and one weak one) (Leibold 1936). Making rhythm is the purpose of the activity in such imitative behavior, whereas it is the apparent byproduct or form in the spontaneous sensorimotor behavior mentioned earlier.

From a rhythmical point of view, everything related to the organs of speech at a very early stage becomes functional for language sharing. Beginning with the first cries, a rhythm basically related to that of the baby's respiration can be observed. The first sounds, phonemes, and syllables develop by circular reaction. Very early, before the age of 2, stresses in intonation can be observed, although the same sort of variation in manual manipulation can be observed only at a much later date.

All rhythmic variations are closely related to the physiological and muscular rhythms of all the organs involved in phonation (tongue, glottis, lips, and so on). Harris (1976) distinguishes between four levels of rhythm in speech: pace, stress, intonation, and meter. But rhythmic productions at the speech level are even richer in variation. (One could also mention, for example quality of tone and duration.) Thus, at the level of speech, we are faced with a complex interweaving of different phonetic activities that have wide variations. One function of rhythm, so developed at the level of speech, is for the sake of communication. Vocal language has a great range of different rhythmic nuances.

Another common phenomenon in the regulatory role rhythm plays is its imposing the movement of one activity on another activity. Everyday examples can be found in music which makes people dance the work songs to whose rhythm slaves worked in pre-Civil-War America. This type of synchronization however is not natural and is the result of learning. Thus children of 3 cannot yet keep time to music.

It is our opinion that autoregulation can occur only between two motor systems, one of which is more developed than the other. The overdevelopment of speech might explain the effect of rhythmic regulation observed by Luria (as he implied in 1961) insofar as the more developed system (speech) took over for the less developed one (manual dexterity). There are numerous illustrations of this phenomenon in child development research.

Nevertheless the situations in which this autoregulation can take place are very rare. First of all, the rhythm must be extremely simple or else the task will be too difficult. What is more, as Zivin notes (1976), "speech can organize motor acts, not [that] it must." Finally it must be observed that language is only one among several means of regulation. In certain of his experiments, Tikhomirov (1958/1975) replaced verbal responses by sound stimuli, serving as a kind of orienting reinforcement. He observed that the sound signals or an exteroceptive afferentation, had an effect identical to impulsive speech signals. In certain other experiments he even concluded that "this kind of regulation is often more developed than that effected by means of supplementary speech impulses" (1975). The regulation of an activity by the rhythmic aspects of another activity is thus a rather universal, but infrequent, phenomenon. The intervention of language, which has the effect of doing away with perseverating responses, must be seen in the context of this general development of motor interactions. There is no way it can be used to test the validity of Vygotsky's general developmental theory.

CONCLUSION

In this chapter we have tried first of all to compare Piaget's and Vygotsky's positions on the nature of language, how children acquire it, and the general role it plays in development. We have shown that the central concept underlying the Piagetian position in this area is that of representation or symbolic function. The ability to make representations is only one stage in a subject's operatory development, a process characterized essentially by its functional continuity, that is, by the recursive working of certain cognitive mechanisms whose roots are biological. Following the unfolding of his evolution, the individual constructs mental images first, then symbols, and finally verbal signs. The creation of these signifiers cannot be separated from cognitive activity itself and thus language can have no special influence on other intellectual or motor functions. According to this view speech is basically an individual representative construction and only secondarily a social and communicative one. It is not at all a mechanism for regulating one's own motor behavior, such regulation comes from general cognitive activity.

As Vygotsky shows in his book, *Thought and Language*, his differences from Piaget are of an epistemological nature. Like Wallon, Vygotsky refuses to see man as the result of an evolution which is primarily biological and only secondarily social. On an ontogenetic level he suggests that there are two developmental roots, one representative, the other communicative. Language then results when the two merge. In this same perspective we analyzed communicative as well as representative schemes in the period which precedes the appearance of speech. The data on communicative schemes that we cited seem to bring out the importance of rhythmic and vocal factors in the establishment of the first interpersonal relations. For Vygotsky when language appears, it immediately conveys the group's social and historical meanings; the individual child internalizes these meanings with time, and verbalizable thought comes out of this progressive internalization. We take the liberty of emphasizing that there is no place in this conception for nonsemantic speech and that the onset of speech in no way does away with the evolution of representative and communicative schemes (or to be more precise, of strictly representative and strictly communicative schemes). They continue to develop and interact with each other.

This analysis comparing Piaget's and Vygotsky's positions has shown certain things missing in the Piagetian conception, which is centered too exclusively on representation. It has also allowed us to reinterpret results found by Luria and those who have replicated his experiments in the area of verbal regulation.

As soon as the child can reproduce adult speech, a certain type of conventional exchange is established (see Figure 1) by the connection of AL and CL through CC. By developing these exchanges, the child can enlarge his processes of verbal comprehension (CR) and make sense of orders given by the experimenter. The good performances observed in the experiments made with a silent control resulted from this understanding of adult language.

The two transitions imagined by Luria consist in going from the intervention by adult language (understanding AL) first to a regulation by the child's communicative schemes (CC) and then to a regulation by the child's own speech (CL). This return to the communicative schemes, seen as a necessary transitional step between intervention by adult speech and then by children's speech, seems to us incompatible with Vygotsky's view of development, particularly with this idea that language is semantic the instant it makes its appearance in the child.

Phenomenon of self-regulation by rhythm cannot be used as proof for the general hypothesis of an evolution from adult meanings to children's meanings in the development of thought. For us the explanation for these phenomena lies in the context of one single communicative strand

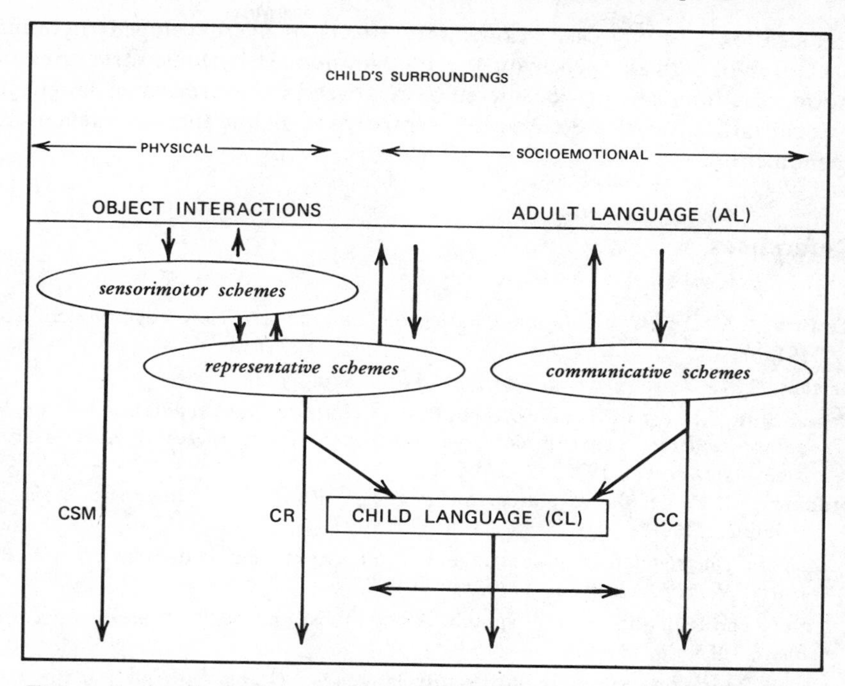

Figure 1. A schematic conception of child development, inspired by Vygotsky's hypothesis. CSM stands for the level of the child's sensorimotor development, CR for the level of his representational development, CL for the level of his spoken language and CC for the level of his communicative capacity.

that evolves with time. Indeed from birth onwards vocal interactions, especially their rhythmic characteristics, play an important part in the baby's emotional and social development. First one can see that adult productions control some of the baby's behavior. Later as vocalizatons develop, the baby's vocal and rhythmic productions greatly increase and diversify. It is very likely that the rhythmic structuralization of vocal productions is much more developed than that of delicate movements in young children. The noticeable difference from ages 3 to 4 between the coordination of visual stimulus and verbal reaction and that of visual stimulus and motor reaction (see particularly Bronckart 1970) argues for this likelihood. This difference would explain how, when sounds are organized rhythmically, they "bring about" rhythmically organized motor activity.

Results obtained on rhythmic activity by Luria and confirmed by Thikomirov (1958/1975), Harris (1976), Zivin (1976), and Bronckart (1970) have to be analyzed in the light of interactions among rhythmic structures on the communicative strand and rhythmic structures of certain sensorimotor organizations. In any case, momentary effects of overdeveloped rhythmic structures of human speech on the less developed rhythmic structures of motor reactions can be considered as a phase in the process of language internalization, which we see as an essentially social, and therefore semantic, phenomenon.

References

Baldwin, J. M. *Mental development in the child and the race.* New York: Macmillan, 1915.

Barthes, R. *Le degré zéro de l'écriture.* Paris: Seuil, 1953.

Beaudichon, J., Legros, S., and **Oleron, P.** Les debuts de l'auto-regulation verbale du comportement: Nouveau controle experimental des theses d'A. R. Luria. *Neuropsychologia,* 1973, *11,* 337-341.

Bronckart, J. P. Le rôle régulateur du language. (Ph.D. diss., University of Liege, Belgium, 1969).

______. Le rôle régulateur du language: Critique expérimentale des travaux d'A. R. Luria. *Neuropsychologia,* 1970, *8,* 451-463.

______. The regulating role of speech. A cognitivist approach. *Human Development,* 1973, *16,* 417-439.

______. Représentation et acquisition du language. (Paper presented at the 21st International Congress of Psychology, Paris, 1976.)

______. *Théories du langage: Une introduction critique.* Brussels: Dessart & Mardaga, 1977.

______. Les conditions de base de l'acquisition du language, in F. Löwenthal, ed., *Language and language acquistion,* Mons: Presses Universitaires, forthcoming(*a*).

______. Les fonctions de representation et de communication chez l'enfant, in J. Piaget, P. Mounoud, and J. P. Bronckart, eds., *La psychologie.* Paris: Gallimard, forthcoming(*b*).

Brown, R. *A first language.* London: Allen & Unwin, 1973.

Buehler, K. *Abriss der geistigen entwicklung des kindes.* Leipzig: Quelle & Meyer, 1928.

Chomsky, N. *Aspects of the theory of syntax.* Cambridge, Mass: MIT Press, 1965.

______. *Language and mind.* New York: Harcourt Brace & World, 1968.

Condon, W. S., and **Sander, L. W.** Synchrony demonstrated between movements of the neonate and adult speech. *Child Development,* 1974, *45,* 456-462.

Duckworth, E. The language and thought of Piaget, in M. Schwebel and J. Raph, eds., *Piaget in the classroom.* New York: Basic Books, 1973.

Engler, R. *Cours de linguistique générale de F. de Saussure.* Wiesbaden: Otto Harrassowitz, 1968.

Ferreiro, E. *Les relations temporelles dans le langage de l'enfant.* Paris: Droz, 1971.

Fraisse, P. *Les structures rythmiques.* Paris: Erasme, 1956.

Glaserfeld, E. von. Signs, communication and language. *Journal of Human Evolution,* 1974, *3,* 465-474.

Harris, A. E. The function of speech rhythms in the regulation of non-speech activity, in K. Riegel and J. Meacham, eds., *The developing individual in a changing world,* vol. I. The Hague: Mouton, 1976. (Originally presented at the Biennial Meeting of the International Society for the Study of Behavioral Development, Ann Arbor, 1973.

Inhelder, B., et al., Les débuts de la fonction symbolique. *Archives de Psychologie,* 1972, *41,* 187-243.

Joynt, D. and **Cambourne, D.** Psycholinguistic development and the control of behavior. *British Journal of Educational Psychology,* 1968, *38,* 249-260.

Klein, M. *Contributions to psychoanalysis.* London: Hogarth, 1948.

Koehler, W. Zür psychologie des schimpansen. *Psychologie Forschung,* 1921, *1.*

Laloy, L. *Aristoxème de Trente et la musique de l'antiquité.* Paris: 1904.

Leibold, R. *Akustisch motorischen rhythmus in früher kindheit.* Munich: Beeksche Verlagbuchandlung, 1936.

Lenneberg, E. H. *Biological foundations of language.* New York: Wiley, 1967.

Luria, A. R. The directive function of speech. I: Its development in early childhood; II: Its dissolution in pathological states of the brain. *Word,* 1959, *15,* 341-352, 453-464.

———. *The role of speech in the regulation of normal and abnormal behavior.* J. Tizard, trans. Oxford: Pergamon, 1961.

———. *Restoration of function after brain injury.* London: Pergamon, 1963.

Luria, A. R., and **Yudovich, F. Y.** *Speech and the development of mental process in the child.* London: Staples, 1959.

Lyublinskaya, A. A. Le développement du language et de la pensée chez l'enfant, in B. Simon, ed., *Psychology in the Soviet Union.* Stanford, Cal.: Stanford Univeristy Press, 1957.

Martin, J. Rhythmic (hierarchical) versus serial structure in speech and other behavior. *Psychological Review,* 1972, *79,* 487-509.

Mauro, T. de, *Cours de linguistique générale de F. de Saussure.* [Edition critique.] Paris: Payot, 1972.

Meichenbaum, D., and **Goodman, J.** The developmental control of operant motor responding by verbal operant. *Journal Experimental Child Psychology,* 1969, *7,* 553-565.

Meumann, E. Untersuchungen zür psychologie and aesthetic des rhythmus. *Philosophical Studies,* 1894, 10.

Miller, S. A., Shelton, J., and **Flavell, J. H.** A test of Luria's hypothesis concerning the development of verbal self-regulation. *Child Development,* 1970, *41,* 651-665.

Monod, J. Lecon inaugurale au College de France. *Le Monde,* November 30, 1967.

———. *Le hasard et la nécessité.* Paris: Seuil, 1970.

Montagner, H. Approche éthologique des communications non-verbales du jeune enfant à la crêche. *Actes du 1er colloque international de la société française d'éducation et de rééducation psychomotrice.* Tours: Chalmeil, 1972.

Montagner, H. et al. Approche étholophysiologique des communications non-verbales chez le jeune enfant. *Bulletin d'Audiophonologie,* 1974, *4,* 211-242.

Monoud, P. Développement des systemes de représentation et de traitement chez l'enfant. *Bulletin de Psychologie*, 1971, *25*, 261-272.

______. Nouvelles directions et nouvelles approches dans la théorie Piagétienne. (Paper presented at the 7th Annual Symposium of the Piaget Society, Philadelphia, 1977.)

Pavlov, I. P. Sur l'origine du sens du rythme. *Journal de Psychologie Normale et Pathologique*, 1927, *24*, 719-730.

Piaget, J., *La naissance de l'intelligence chez l'enfant*. Neuchatel: Delachaux & Niestlé, 1936. [*The origins of intelligence in children.* New York: International Universities Press 1952.]

______. *La construction du réel chez l'enfant.* Neuchatel: Delachaux & Niestlé, 1937. [*The construction of reality in the child.* New York: Basic Books, 1954.]

______. *La psychologie de l'intelligence.* Paris: A. Colin, 1941. [*The psychology of intelligence.* London: Routledge & Kagan Paul, 1950.]

______. *La formation du symbole chez l'enfant.* Neuchatel: Delachaux & Niestle, 1946. [*Play, dreams and imitation in childhood.* London: Heinemann, 1951.]

______. *Les mécanismes perceptifs.* Paris: P.U.F., 1961. [*The mechanisms of perception.* London: Routledge & Kegan Paul, 1969.]

______. *Le langage et les opérations intellectuelles: Problemes de psycholinguistique.* Paris: P.U.F., 1963.

______. *Six études de psychologie.* Geneva: Gonthier, 1964. [*Six psychological studies.* New York: Random House, 1967.]

______. *Biologie et connaissance.* Paris: Gallimard, 1967. [*Biology and knowledge.* Chicago: University of Chicago Press, 1971.]

______. *Le structuralisme.* Paris: P.U.F., 1968. [*Structuralism.* New York: Basic Books, 1970.]

______. *Epistémologie des sciences de l'homme.* Paris: Gallimard, 1970.

______. *Adaptation vitale et psychologie de l'intelligence.* Paris: Hermann, 1974.

______. *Jean Piaget. The man and his ideas.* New York: Dutton, 1973.

Piaget, J. and **Inhelder, B.** *Mémoire et intelligence.* Paris: P.U.F. 1968. [*Memory and intelligence.* London: Routledge & Kegan Paul, 1973.]

Ricks, M. S. Vocal signals in pre-verbal autistic and normal children, in N. O'Connor, ed., *Language, cognitive deficits and retardation.* London: Butterworths, 1975.

Rondal, J. A. Le rôle du language dans la régulation du comportement moteur. *Journal de Psychologie Normale et Pathologique,* 1973, *3,* 307-324.

______. Contrôle de la latence des réponses dans certaines tâches motrices avec et sans auto-accompagnement verbal. *Revue Belge du Psychologie Pédagogique,* 1975, *37,* 29-42.

Sapir, E. *Linguistique.* Paris: Editions de Minuit, 1969.

Saussure, F. de. *Cours de linguistique générale.* Paris: Payot, 1916.

Sinclair, H. Sensorimotor action patterns as a condition for the acquisition of syntax, in R. Huxley and E. Ingram, eds., *Language acquisition: Models and methods.* New York: Academic, 1971.

———. Some comments on Fodor's reflections on L. S. Vygotsky's 'Thought and language'. *Cognition,* 1972, *1,* 317-318.

———. Language acquisition and cognitive development, in T. E. Moore, ed., *Cognitive development and the acquisition of language.* New York: Academic 1973.

———. Epistemology and the study of language, in *Problèmes actuels de psycholinguistique.* Paris: CNRS, 1974*a.*

———. L'acquisition du langage d'un point de vue Piagétien. *Folia Phoniatrica,* 1974, *26,* 1-12*b.*

———. The role of cognitive structures in language acquisition, in E. H. Lenneberg and L. Lenneberg, eds., *Foundations of language development,* I. New York: Academic, 1975.

Stern, W. *Psychologie der fruehen kindheit.* Leipzig: Quelle & Meyer, 1914.

Tikhomirov, O. K. [The formation of voluntary movements in children of preschool age.] *Soviet Psychology,* 1975, *14,* 48-135. [Originally published, 1958.]

Vygotsky, L. S. *Thought and language.* E. Haufman and G. Vakar, eds. and trans. Cambridge, Mass.: MIT Press, 1962. [Originally published, 1934.]

Wallon, H. *L'évolution psychologique de l'enfant.* Paris: A. Colin, 1941.

Weir, R. *Language in the crib.* The Hague: Mouton, 1962.

Werner, R. Rhythmus, eine mehrwertige Gestaltverkettung. *Zeitschrift fur Psychologie,* 1919, *82,* 198-218.

Wilder, L. The role of speech and other extra-signal feedback in the regulation of the child's sensorimotor behavior. *Speech Monographs,* 1969, *36,* 425-434.

Whorf, B. L. *Language, thought and reality.* Cambridge, Mass.: MIT. Press, 1964.

Wozniak, R. H. Verbal regulation of motor behavior: Soviet research and non-Soviet replications. *Human Development,* 1972, *15,* 13-57.

———. Speech-for-self as a multiply reafferent human action system, in K. Riegel and J. Meacham, eds., *The developing individual in a changing world,* vol. I. The Hague: Mouton, 1976. (Originally presented at the Biennial Meeting of the Society for the Study of Behavioral Development, Ann Arbor, 1973.)

Wundt, W. *Volkerpsychologie, I: Die sprache.* Leipzig: Engleman, 1900.

———. *Grundzuge des Physiologischen Psychologie.* Leipzig: Engelman, 1911.

Yerkes, R. M. The mental life of monkeys and apes. *Behavior Monographs,* 1916, *3.*

Zivin, G. Developmental aspects of rhythm in self-regulation, in K. Riegel and J. Meacham, eds., *The developing individual in a changing world,* vol. I. The Hague: Mouton, 1976. (Originally presented at the Biennial Meeting of the Society for the Study of Behavioral Development, Ann Arbor, 1973.)

PART II

CONTEMPORARY EMPIRICAL EXTENSIONS

CHAPTER 5

The Development of Self-Regulating Aspects of Speech: A Review

KAREN C. FUSON
Northwestern University

Other chapters in this book review in some depth specific areas of self-regulating speech, present new data, and analyze different theoretical terms and perspectives. This chapter[1] will present a methodological framework within which the literature on the development of self-regulating speech in children will be reviewed. Research on relationships between speech and motor acts and between speech and nonmotor acts will be discussed rather briefly within that framework; in these sections ways in which, or mechanisms by which, speech affects behavior will be identified. Issues concerning how children learn self-regulating speech will also be treated. Limitations of present research will be pointed out and fruitful areas of future research indicated.

Five dimensions along which studies on self-regulating speech can vary seem particularly important. The first three involve environmental conditions in the data collection situation: (1) the familiarity or unfamiliarity of the setting in which the self-regulating speech is emitted, (2) the naturalness or artificiality to the subject of the type of task he is doing, and (3) the source of the goals set during the data collecting period. The familiarity of the setting to the subject would seem to influence the types and amount of speech that might be emitted. Extreme anxiety might inhibit all speech, extreme comfort and security might lead to more playful or imaginative use of speech. Intermediate

[1]I would like to express thanks to: James V. Wertsch for unpublished Soviet material related to self-regulating speech and for informative conversations; Michael Pressley for helpful comments on the first draft of this paper; Gail Zivin for a very detailed and substantive response to the first draft; and especially to James W. Hall for his ever-ready critical, constructive, and incisive reactions to the seemingly endless pages of writing and rewriting. Special thanks to Adrienne and Erica for letting me see and hear self-regulating speech in action so often and for going to bed promptly at 8:00 night after night so "Mommy can do her work tonight." Thanks also to the undergraduate and graduate students who have worked on parts of my self-regulating research, to the questions they raised, and to the insights they have contributed to my thinking.

CHAPTER CONTENTS

degrees of familiarity would of course lead to more muted effects. The naturalness to the subject of the type of task used in a study affects the subject's comprehension of the task, the types of strategies the subject brings to bear on the task (including the use of speech), and the degree of involvement in the task. Whether or not the goal of the child's action is set by the experimenter or by the child might influence both the motivational level of the child and the emission of certain types of self-regulating speech that might accompany or facilitate the choice of a goal (that is, goal setting by the experimenter might eliminate some types of self-regulating speech). There is little direct evidence on any of these points, for studies which vary any of them systematically do not exist. Rather studies seem to fall into groups of certain constellations of these three parameters, and the possible effects of any of these characteristics on the results of a particular study are often ignored.

The remaining two dimensions along which we will divide studies are the source and the content of the speech. The speaker of the words can be the child or another person, and the content of the speech can be determined by the child or by another person. Studies in which the speech comes from another rather from the self might seem inappropriate to a review of self-regulating speech. However, the fact that speech from another person can direct and control the behavior of young children before they can even speak seems to indicate that the precursors to the development of self-regulating speech lie in the considerable amount of experience a very young child has with the regulation of his or her behavior via the speech of others. This basic assumption of Soviety psychology, articulated originally by Vygotsky, is that the child's speech moves from the interpsychological to the intrapsychological plane, that is, that various cognitive functions are developed through interactions with other people (primarily adults) and then become internalized.

The content of the speech, the words themselves, can also come from the child or from another person. Providing children with certain words to say and then assessing the self-regulating effect of these words is a much more efficient way to gather data than waiting until the child spontaneously emits self-regulating speech. Unfortunately this technique possibly both overestimates the self-regulating abilities of children (by assessing what they can do, but not what they actually do ordinarily) and also underestimates such abilities by providing words that may fail to function as well as would words provided by the child herself. Thus studies in which the content of the speech comes from the child are clearly needed. Relative advantages of each type of research will be described when each type is reviewed.

Table 1 displays the possibilities created by variance along these five dimensions. Each of the dimensions is of course actually continuous (for example situations can range from very unfamiliar to very familiar), but for the sake of simplicity they will be regarded as dichotomous. The familiarity to the child of the exact research setting rather than the overall setting was used;

TABLE 1. An Organizational Scheme for Self-Regulating Speech Studies.

Source of Regulating Speech		Environmental Conditions			
		Goal of action set by E		Goal of action set by S	
		Unfamiliar setting artificial task	Unfamiliar setting natural task	Unfamiliar setting natural task	Unfamiliar setting natural task
S not the speaker (studies not reviewed here)		(1)		(3)	(4)
S is the speaker	Content of Speech not from S	(5) a. speech and motor acts (23 studies) b. speech and non-motor acts (65 studies) c. self-instruction training studies (12 studies)	(6) Meacham, 1972, 1979	(7)	(8)

Content of speech from S	Beauchidon, 1973 (9) Zivin, 1972, 1973	Berner, 1971 (10) Deutsch and Stein, 1973 Dickie, 1973 Fuson, Householder and Ubraska, forthcoming Goodman, 1977, 1978 Hjertholm, 1968 Kleiman, 1974 Klein, 1964 Kohlberg, Yaeger, and Hjertholm, 1968 Roberts, 1977 Roberts and Tharp, forthcoming Yaeger, 1968	Dickie, 1973 (11) Rubin, Hultsch and Peters, 1971	Pechman, 1978 (12) Rubin, 1979

Notes: E = experimenter; S = subject. Each unit (1-12) is called a cell.

thus a home, classroom, or playground was familiar, while a room in the school in which a child seldom played was regarded as (relatively) unfamiliar.

However Table 1 does not contain all of the logical possibilities of combinations of the task and setting dimensions. Two of these possibilities seem impossible to attain consistently in real life: the goal of action set by S in using artificial tasks in either a familiar or an unfamiliar setting. Though one can envision some intriguing, self-explanatory tasks put around a home or nursery school setting (familiar ones) or in a testing room (unfamiliar), many of the artificial tasks used by researchers are not self-explanatory and the task has to be explained to the child and thus the task goals set by the experimenter. Another omitted possibility is the task goal set by the experimenter in familiar settings with artificial tasks. It seems likely that any researcher concerned enough about the internal state of the child to venture into the field would use tasks familiar to the child.

The rows of Table 1 serve an organizing function for this paper. Each row of Table 1 poses a different related question with respect to self-regulating speech. These questions are as follows:

> *Top row:* "What kinds of child behavior (at what ages) can words emitted by others affect?"
> *Middle row:* "What kinds of child behavior can words selected by another and emitted by the child affect?"
> *Bottom row:* "What self-regulating speech do children produce and what does this speech affect?"

The extent to which the research answers each of these questions is obviously limited by the kinds of behaviors that researchers have examined. As we shall see later, in some areas our knowledge is quite limited.

Studies in the bottom row focus on the spontaneous use of self-regulating speech, while those in the middle row examine the effects of induced speech on the performance of various types of tasks. Studies regarding spontaneous use of self-regulating speech will be discussed first, followed by a review of studies from the middle row. The latter review will be divided into two major sections: the effects of speech on motor acts and the effects of verbalizations on nonmotor acts. Only a few studies examining the effects of words emitted by others (top row) will be discussed; these relate to the Soviet interpsychological hypothesis concerning self-regulating speech.

When considering research on speech, it is useful to keep in mind the following four different aspects of speech which can affect behavior:

1. The speech sounds (nonsemantic qualities).
2. The motor act of speaking.
3. The meaning of the spoken words (semantic qualities).
4. The process of choosing words to speak.

Wozniak (1976) differentiated the first three aspects and discussed possible mechanisms that might be related to them. Such possible mechanisms will be discussed here in the review of studies from the middle row.

Aspects 1 and 3 can be operative in studies located in the top row; 1, 2, and 3 can be operating in research in the middle row; and all four can be affecting outcomes in research in the bottom row. Though distinctions among these aspects have been made by some authors, research designs have often confounded them. As various studies are described, the reader should attempt to keep in mind these various possible acoustic, motor, semantic, and word-selection aspects of speaking.

STUDIES IN WHICH SPEECH CONTENT IS DETERMINED BY THE CHILD

The studies located in the bottom row of Table 1 are those in which the content of the speech uttered by a child is determined by the child rather than being provided to him by the experimenter. In most of these studies no instructions at all about speaking are given to the child. The child is simply brought into a room, given some tasks to do, and the speech spontaneously uttered by him during the completion of the tasks is recorded. The researcher is then faced with trying to make some determination of the varying types and functions of such speech. Most studies have also tried to determine the effects of subject or task variables on such spontaneous speech.

The results of both types of study pivot around the categories of speech that the researcher employs. Comparisons across studies are often difficult because researchers use: (1) entirely different categories or (2) use similar categories, but different operational definitions of them. A clear understanding of the results of this group of studies on spontaneously uttered speech is further hampered by the incomplete or haphazard reporting in many of these studies. In order to make comparisons across studies for this review, some reported statistics were recomputed from other data and some new statistics were computed for the first time.

In this paper no attempt will be made to discuss the theoretical and verbal tangle involved in the uses and meanings of the words (egocentric speech, inner speech, private speech, speech-for-self) that are used to describe this spontaneous speech to or for self. See Zivin (Chapter 1) for an analysis of the uses and meaning of those words. In that chapter private speech is the broadest category; it includes speech which is and speech which is not assumed to be self-directed by the child in his own speaking. Speech-for-self is that subset which is easily assumed to be directed to self. For ease of reviewing studies that do not make this distinction, along with ones that do, this chapter will refer to all of the studies that gathered data on the utterances of children to or for themselves as *the private speech studies* and to the speech itself as *private speech.* Thus *private speech* will usually be used throughout this review, although *speech-for-self* may often be the more precise label.

The speech recorded in these studies is of varying kinds, some of which are self-regulating and some of which are not. This paper will concentrate on the self-regulating aspects of private speech in these studies.

Most of the studies to be reviewed have employed tasks that are natural for the child — puzzles, coloring, making pictures with stickers, and so on. Thus the type of speech that the child emits during these tasks would seem to correspond fairly closely to that which he might emit in the course of his normal daily life. We have almost no data on how much and what kind of speech children actually do emit in their normal day-to-day life. Kohlberg, Yaeger, and Hjertholm (1968) reported coefficients of egocentrism (percent of nonsocial speech) for speech that preschool children emitted at school, but this statistic gives no indication of *how* children used speech that was categorized as being egocentric (nonsocial) speech. Three recent studies on the private speech of elementary-school children doing school tasks (Roberts, 1977; Roberts and Tharp, forthcoming; Pechman, 1978) are the only exceptions.[2] However these studies focus largely on children's vocalizations during the decoding process of reading. At this point we simply do not know how much children talk to and for themselves, nor do we know how much or in what ways they actually use speech to regulate their own behavior. Difficulties in finding these answers are compounded by the apparent phenomenon that much speech-for-self becomes covert around the age of six or seven, though Pechman (1978) found some external evidence of speech-for-self as late as 10 years of age. Naturalistic studies on the content of speech-for-self may have to concentrate on children younger than 8 years however.

Studies in an Unfamiliar Setting Using Artificial Tasks

Zivin (1972) reported results for spontaneously uttered speech by 4-year-olds while doing finger mazes. The number of children who did not vocalize at all during this task was half the sample (39 of 80), and the number of vocalizations was quite small (a mean of 1.6 per child, or 3.4 per vocalizing children on all four mazes). Silent children were faster and more accurate than were vocalizers. Most (about 75%) of the vocalizations were task irrelevant or inarticulate, reflecting an emotional reaction to errors rather than self-regulating speech. Three different strategies seemed to be used to solve the mazes. Zivin analyzed the data with respect to differences in vocalization among strategy groups (1972, 1973). The number of subjects within each

[2]Note two additional studies on preschoolers that do examine how spontaneous speech is used: Goodman (1978) and Rubin (Chapter 8). Goodman sets the task goals; Rubin does not. These works became available after this chapter was completed.

group was small, and the relationships involved are too complex to review adequately. The reader is referred to those papers for an example of the kind of detailed matching of specific types of behaviors with specific kinds of vocalization that may be useful in self-regulating research. Though the results do not form an easily interpretable pattern, two tentative conclusions might serve as hypotheses for future research: (1) in this type of task self-regulating speech is predominantly associated with a particularly well-organized approach and (2) semantic vocalizers seem to be more reflective than nonsemantic vocalizers.

The other study in Cell 9 of Table 1 (Beaudichon, 1973) will be discussed in the later sections on task performance and task difficulty.

Studies in an Unfamiliar Setting Using Natural Tasks

Most of the private speech studies fall within Cell 10: the goal of the action is set by the experimenter (through the selection and presentation of certain tasks), the tasks are natural ones for the children (they have done similar tasks before), and the setting is relatively unfamiliar to the child (it may range from totally unfamiliar to only somewhat unfamiliar — the small room used may be in a university setting or in the child's school). Because the bulk of the studies fall within Cell 10, the general issues involved in all the private speech studies will be discussed here; other studies from the bottom row will be included where they are relevant.

Amount of Private Speech

The most striking result from the private speech studies, and at the same time a result that becomes clear only after one has examined these studies in some detail, is that the amount of private speech emitted in most of the study situations is very small. Many children do not emit any private speech at all in these situations. The actual small magnitude of private speech emitted is not immediately clear from many studies because researchers often report and discuss the relative distribution (that is, percent) of speech utterances in various categories rather than giving any rates of such emissions. Most also fail to report the number of children who did not use any private speech at all, and those few studies that do give this data find many such children.

Table 2 describes certain summary characteristics of the private speech studies: age of subjects, task and person situations, the percentage of subjects emitting private speech, and the mean number of private speech utterances per minute. The percent figures are taken from the texts of several studies; some researchers reported such a figure somewhere in the text, while most omitted it entirely. Less than half the studies reported any rate of speech statistic, such as the mean number of private speech utterances per minute. Where possible this was calculated from the data given in each study. Researchers often focused so

TABLE 2. Characteristics of and Amounts of Private Speech in Private Speech Studies.

Studies	Characteristics			Private Speech	
	Age of subjects	Task situation	Person situation	% of Ss exhibiting any private speech	Mean number of private speech utterances per minute
Beauchidon (1973)	5.6 to 6 7.6 to 8	ordering and classifying cards easy and difficult tasks noninstructed/told to think aloud[a]	alone	CND	0.60 to 4.3
Berner (1971)	3, 4, 5	different puzzles and/or stickers	1. E across table coding S behavior 2. alone	1. 95% 2. 60%	1. 2 2. 0.66
Deutsch and Stein (1973)	4.0 to 5.2	Six puzzles; three conditions[a] for puzzles 2, 3, and 4 1. personal failure—stopped before completion 2. faulty materials—two pieces removed from puzzle 3. success—child permitted to complete puzzles	E present in room; to questions during puzzle, reminded children she could not help or talk	CND	[d] before conditions: 0.25 1. 0.72 2. 0.11 3. 0.14
Dickie (1973)	2.6 to 8	1. puzzles and coloring 2. free play	1. familiar peer doing some task at a separate table 2. mother filling out a questionnaire at a separate table	CND	[d] 1.6 to 2

Fuson Householder and Urbanska (forthcoming)	2, 3, 4, 5	1. building a block tower 2. easy puzzle 3. different puzzle 4. attribute people (fantasy play)	alone	1. 59% 2. 57% 3. 39% 4. 72%	1. 0.91 2. 1.55 3. 1.16 4. 3.41
Goodman (1977)	3.6 to 5	Six puzzles	E in room to give puzzles	CND	1.75
Hjertholm (1968)	4.6 to 5.0	1. stringing beads 2. easy and difficult puzzles 3. block tower 4. difficult puzzle	E for all tasks, mother also for first two	CND	1. 0.10 2. 0.91 3. 0.34 4. 0.9 [d]
Kleiman (1974)	4.0 to 4.11	three Porteus mazes involving driving a car through the "town" three puzzles (two of Yaeger's)	alone (additional activities with E were alternated to alleviate anxiety at being left alone over several tasks)	CND	4.97 [d]
Klein (1964)	3.6 to 7	1. puzzles with an impossible piece 2. coloring	alone	53%	2 to 3 (?) [c, d]
Kohlberg, Yaeger, and Hjertholm (1968)					
Study 1:	4 to 9	normal school environment	peers, teachers	50%	CND
Studies 2 and 3:	4 to 10	making a sticker picture	E doing parallel task sitting beside S	50%	0.8
Study 4:	4.6 to 5	stringing beads, block tower, two puzzles	E for all tasks; mother for some	CND	0.12 to 1.0

TABLE 2. (continued)

Studies	Characteristics			Private Speech	
	Age of subjects	Task situation	Person situation	% of Ss exhibiting any private speech	Mean number of private speech utterances per minute
Roberts (1977) Roberts and Tharp (forthcoming)		selecting words to fill in sentences; known and new words	alone	CND	0.27[e] 3.52[f]
Rubin, Hultsch, and Peters (1971)	4.6	free play	1. alone 2. with a peer 3. with the familiar E	1. 59%[b] 2. CND 3. CND	CND
Yaeger (1968)	N, K, First-graders	1. three puzzles, encouraged to talk 2. one puzzle, instructed not to talk	E present, told when wrong praised when right	CND	1. 2.99[d] 2. 1.54
Zivin (1972, 1973)	3.6 to 4.6	finger mazes	E in room, back turned	51%	1.68[d]

Notes: CND: can not determine from data given in the study

a: each child given only one condition; in all nonmarked cases, each child was given all conditions
b: Kenneth Rubin, personal communication
c: taks referring—contained some communication speech
d: calculated by author from data given in the study
e: task relevant, not reading aloud
f: sounding out of words or reading words aloud

on the questions of group differences within their own studies that they did not seem even to have considered the question of "How much private speech is there?" This question is important if we are to have any understanding of the role speech-for-self does play in the self-regulation of behavior on a day-to-day basis.

The figures in Table 2, where known, indicate that the percent of children who exhibited no private speech in the task situation varied from 50 to 40%. Data from two studies on speech and cognitive processes concur with these figures. Kuenne (1946) reported that about half the 2½- to 6-year-old children who had generalized a rule for size transposition tasks spontaneously verbalized this rule during the trials; Conrad (1971) reported that about half of his sample of 4-year-old children spontaneously verbalized such phrases as, "Cat goes with cat." or "Cat here." on a picture-sorting task.

It may be that the spontaneous use of speech for self-regulation is not a characteristic of all children. Although this suggestion is contrary to the original Soviet hypothesis about the developmental necessity of some stage of verbal self-regulation, the low spontaneous appearance of speech-for-self suggests that self-regulation by speech may not be a more mature aspect of self-regulation through which all children eventually pass. It may be one of several possible ways to regulate oneself, and it may be employed to greater and lesser extents by different children. Unfortunately, although the studies have examined the effects of various task and subject characteristics on speech-for-self, none of them (except Klein, 1964, and Zivin, 1972) separated for analysis the children who emitted no speech-for-self from those who emitted some such speech. Thus we do not know important characteristics that might be associated with either group.

The mean number of utterances[3] of private speech per minute varies from 0.10 to 4.97, with most studies reporting below two utterances per minute for conditions in which no instruction about speaking were given. Not all of these utterances serve self-regulating functions; many are affect, nonsense, or irrelevant vocalizations. Thus the amount of self-regulating speech actually emitted spontaneously is fairly small. This small magnitude may be a fairly good measure of the amount of speech-for-self used in natural task situations or it may have been depressed by task, setting, or situation sampling characteristics.

Puzzles, mazes, and sensorimotor tasks have predominated in these studies. It may be that such tasks are susceptible to solution by perceptual strategies that are not facilitated by speech. Blank (1974) suggested that speech might be more valuable for tasks in which the components are separated in time.

[3]Researchers used different definitions of "utterance." Some defined it by form (for example as a sentence or a part of a sentence); others used a time criterion, such as a three-second pause in speaking. Some researchers did not state their definition of an utterance.

Beauchidon (1973) used tasks that seem to meet this criterion because they involve ideas of sequence: children had to place pictures in a sequence according to various criteria. However the mean for each age group (5½ to 6 and 7½ to 8) was only 0.74 self-regulating utterances per minute on the easy tasks; on the difficult task, in which the child had to order the pictures and then draw the one that was missing, children aged 5.6 to 6 increased to 1.75 self-regulating utterances per minute. But the older children (7½ to 8) did not increase (though possibly these children used covert speech). Thus these tasks do not seem to elicit a great deal of speech, possibly because the cards were all perceptually present. Tasks which involve planning a sequence of actions might have more need for the sequential function of language. However, as seen in Zivin's (1972) study, when the sequence can be done very quickly and all the visual stimuli are simultaneously present (as in finger mazes), vocalization by 4-year-olds does not seem to aid performance and is infrequent. This point concerning segmental sequencing will be discussed again at the end of the chapter when self-regulating speech is discussed with respect to goal-directed action.

In these situations setting characteristics may also be responsible for depressing private speech to a level below what it would be in more natural situations. Kleiman (1974) described the experimental private-speech situation as in some ways a measure of ego strength, for many of her 4-year-old children found being left alone very difficult. She found it necessary to intersperse tasks done with the experimenter in order for the children to deal with the alone situation. In the study reported in Fuson, Honseholder, and Urbaska (forthcoming), we found that some of the 2- and 3-year-old children cried (or almost cried) at the beginning of the alone situation, though most of them overcame these feelings by becoming involved, at least temporarily, in the task. The effect of this affective state on the production of speech is unclear however. Klein (1964) reported a biserial coefficient correlation of 0.29 between difficulty of separation from parent in the testing situation and more talking in the private-speech situation (chi square was not significant). Though Klein separated talk into task-relevant and irrelevant, he unfortunately did not report whether the speech produced by the children who had had difficulty separating from a parent was more in the task-relevant or irrelevant categories. An opposite description of high-private-speech talkers is reported by Kleiman (1974): children judged to be independent by their teachers produced significantly more self-directive speech than nonindependent children. The results of these two studies do not conflict if one hypothesizes that anxiety both increases affective and task-irrelevant speech and depresses self-directive speech. However, low-anxiety situations do not necessarily result in a large amount of private speech. Hjertholm (1964) also briefly reported in Kohlberg, Yaeger, and Hjertholm, (1968) had her subjects do tasks in their homes with the mother present for the first two tasks and the experimenter for all four—a seemingly minimally anxiety-producing situation. She reported less than one private speech utterance per minute (see Table 2). In summary, it seems that we do not at present know what the effects might be of situation-produced states such as anxiety on the production of private speech in testing situations.

Presence of Other Persons in Private Speech Situations

The person situation column in Table 2 indicates another difficulty in the private speech studies: in less than half of the studies was the child alone when the speech samples were produced. The presence of another person creates two kinds of problems: it may change the type and/or amount of speech produced and it introduces the necessity of separating social from private speech. Only one study (Berner, 1971) has data for children alone and with another person in a similar situation. Berner found that fewer children spoke at all in the alone situation (60% rather than 95%) and those who did emitted only one-third as many mean number of utterances (0.66 rather than 2). Unfortunately the quality of Berner's tapes of children alone did not permit her to categorize their utterances, so we have no data on any differences in the types of speech produced while alone nor in the presence of another person.

The amount of private speech may be inflated not only by the presence of another person, but also by the criteria used for differentiating private and social speech. Those studies which describe these criteria clearly (Berner, 1971; Dickie, 1973; and Goodman, 1977) use such rigorous criteria for social speech (eye contact with the other person, explicit reference to the other person, or repetition of a comment) that their private-speech utterances were probably inflated. Dickie noted that, even with these criteria, raters had difficulty differentiating outward-directed private speech from social speech, especially for her younger subjects (2½ to 5).

Even the identity of the person in the room with the child can affect the type of speech produced according to Dickie's (1973) data. Children aged 2½ to 8 produced more private speech in all categories in the presence of a friend than in the presence of the mother. Age affected the differences in self-guiding speech considerably, with the youngest (2½ to 4) children making slightly more self-guiding statements in the presence of the mother than with a friend (9.5 versus 8.5), and the two older groups, 4- to 5½- and 6- to 8-year-olds, producing considerably more such statements in the presence of a friend (6.3 versus 12.3 and 3.9 versus 15.5). A similar age-related pattern existed for social speech, so two possible interpretations exist for the self-guiding results. The older children may simply have talked more to their friend than to their mother, and the strict criteria for social speech may have placed a good deal of this quasi-social speech in the private speech category. Or the presence of a friend may have been much more distracting for the older children than the presence of their mother, and they needed to emit more self-guiding speech to remain task-focused (this was Dickie's interpretation). Regardless of the reason, these data indicate that an important situation variable that affects amount of speech has been ignored by most studies.

Categories of Private Speech

The only set of categories that has been used by several researchers is the set outlined in the Kohlberg, Yaeger, and Hjertholm (1968) paper. These categories are hypothesized to be developmentally ordered as follows:

Level I. Presocial Self-Stimulating Language

1. Word play and repetition.

Level II. Outward-Directed Private Speech

2. Remarks addressed to nonhuman subjects.
3. Describing own activity.

Level III. Inward-Directed or Self-Guiding Private Speech

4. Questions answered by the self.
5. Self-Guiding comments.

Level IV. External Manifestations of Inner Speech

6. Inaudible muttering.

Level V. Silent Speech or Inner Thought

Each level represents a stage in the development of private speech moving from early practice with word sounds and words (*Level I*) to inner speech (*Level V*). These categories are based on theoretical notions of Vygotsky and Mead (1934). The Kohlberg, Yaeger, and Hjertholm (1968) paper discusses these ideas (and those of Piaget) at some length and then outlines the above categories. Three different theoretical ideas of Vygotsky (1934/1962) are reflected in these categories: (1) internalization of egocentric or private speech (as seen in the titles and order of the levels II through V), (2) the emphasis on self-guiding speech (category 5), and (3) the notion that egocentric or private speech is initially outer-directed because it has not yet been sufficiently differentiated from social speech (the location and nature of Level II). The influence of ideas of George Herbert Mead (1934) appear in the emphasis upon an internal dialogue with oneself (Level III and especially category 4).

These categories are interesting and involve some central issues in private speech. Unfortunately they possess methodological and conceptual problems. These will be briefly outlined and two additional sets of categories will be described. See Fuson, Householder, and Urbaska (forthcoming) for a more detailed description of the methodological and conceptual issues involved in these categories.

The chief methodological problem with the Kohlberg categories is the reliability of the classification of uttterances into the categories. The Kohlberg, Yaeger, and Hjertholm (1968) paper reported four studies, two major ones and two smaller ones. For the two major studies, only the percent of egocentric (nonsocial) speech was reported. The Kohlberg categories were actually employed in the analysis of only the last two small studies. For neither of these analyses were inter-rater reliabilities reported, and in the fourth study there appeared to be a considerable difference between the two raters on the main two self-regulating categories: describing activity and self-guidance. Early studies which used the Kohlberg categories reported low inter-rater agreement (Berner, 1971; and Rubin, Hultsch, and Peters, 1971), while two more recent studies (Dickie, 1973 and Deutsch and Stein, 1972) reported reliabilities of 0.85 and above. None of these studies reported their operational definitions of the categories, so it is difficult to judge what is the source of these different reliabilities.

Another problem with these categories is that they do not seem to describe satisfactorily all private speech. More recent users (Goodman, 1977; Yaeger, 1968, and Kleiman, 1974) have found it necessary to add additional categories. Two obvious kinds of speech that occur when a child is alone that are not included in the Kohlberg categories are fantasy play and expressions of affect. Kleiman (1974) rearranged and extended Kohlberg's categories to the following twelve:

Task-Related

Self-Directive
- Analytic statements
- Directions to self
- Feedback
- Comments and describing activity
- Questions and conditional statements
- Repetition of task-related speech

Nontask comments

Feeling statements

Fantasy or play

Sound play

Exclamations and fill-in phrases

Incomprehensible utterances

These categories seem much more comprehensive and they offer a more detailed division of categories which might be regarded as self-regulating ones. In particular, the effort to differentiate ways in which speech might function during task solution (analytic, feedback, directions to self) is noteworthy.

Unfortunately the more detailed descriptions of what Kleiman (1974) included in each of the categories do not always match the name of the category and some categories contain puzzling combinations of kinds of speech. *Feedback* includes statements in which "the child labels a part of the puzzle or maze, describes an attribute of the puzzle or maze, or guesses what the puzzle will look like when finished." The first two would seem sometimes to be serving as *Analytic statements* ("The child reasons out what is required in order to do the task."), while the last one might be either an *Analytic statement* or assisting the *Feedback* function ("The child assesses his progress in completing the task."). *Repetition of task-related speech* is included as a task-related category although it is sound play of the most primitive kind ("He repeats the same words over and over."). Such speech does not obviously serve a regulating function and is not *task-related speech* in the usually intended meaning of speech whose meaning is related to the ongoing solution of the task. Reasons for the inclusion of questions and conditional statements in the same category are not evident. *Feeling statements* include task-related evaluations of how well the child is doing on the task. *Exclamations and fill-in phrases* turns out to be a catch-all category that includes affective expressions as well as phrases describing activity, both of which belong to other categories. In short the titles of these categories show considerable thought and insight, but the operational definitions of them require further effort.

The chief conceptual difficulty in the Kohlberg categories — see Fuson, Householder, and Urbaska, (forthcoming) for a detailed discussion—and one which is repeated in the Kleiman categories, is in regarding *Describing own activity* statements as neither self-guiding nor self-directive. This distinction proved difficult to make operational, for confusions between categories 3 and 5 largely created low reliabilities (Kohlberg, Yaeger, and Hjertholm, 1968; Rubin, Hultsch, and Peters 1971). A child's statements describing his own activity seem in context to be serving self-guiding functions, for an experimenter observing such comments judged them so, while one listening only to tapes coded the same utterances as *Describing own activity* (Kohlberg, Yaeger, and Hjertholm, 1968). Vygotsky argued that a child uses words first to represent his actions (that is, to describe them and thus to accumulate experience) and then later uses words to anticipate his actions (that is, to plan them). This transition is necessarily a gradual one, and descriptions of actions will increasingly become separated from the stream of ongoing behavior and subordinated to some end-goal, that is, they will increasingly serve self-regulating functions.[4] Levina (1978) describes the mechanism by which speech increasingly comes to serve this regulating function:

> Vygotsky attached great importance to the notion that the verbal formula is concerned with what is basic and essential (from the standpoint of meaning). Vygotsky thought that one can use this to find the means and paths of further transformations in the use of the word for cognitive purposes. This is the means for *liberating* the child from the concrete visual situation with all the details which are not essential to the basic direction of the action. Vygotsky stated that it is as if *speech separates an ongoing action* from its concrete circumstances. By representing what is basic, speech becomes the means for freeing the agent from the immediate field which prevails over the limited possibilities of visual cognition. It is no accident that speech turns out to be used first as a means for accumulating experience and later as a means for liberating the agent from concrete conditions so that is possible to focus on the conditions necessary for carrying out an action. [p. 8]

Thus what is needed are categories that are connected by the same overall description (and therefore reflect this conceptual continuity), but somehow identify speech that is definitely serving a planning function. Detailed analysis (for example frame by frame evaluation) of the relationship between the emission of an utterance describing an activity and the engagement in that activity is possible but complex, costly, and fraught with definitional problems. For example, can an utterance serve a planning function only before a puzzle piece is selected, or when it is in mid-air, or when it is placed? A simpler conservative method is to let the utterance itself determine this; describing one's activity in the future tense, commanding oneself, or describing one's own mental internal state ("I want . . .", "I think that . . . ", "I need to . . .") all clearly seem to indicate planning. Their different forms may also indicate nuances in function or in ontogeny, so they should perhaps be separated rather than lumped into one regulating category.

An additional Vygotsky assertion has not been tested by any previous set of categories. This is that, "The child's speech becomes less concerned with the surrounding world and more concerned with the child's own action" (Levina, 1978, p. 7). In order to test this assertion categories which differentiate descriptions of things and of actions are required.

A set of categories that meets the above two criteria and in addition encompasses the range of speech utterances that the Kleiman categories

[4]Such after-action speech can be seen as self-regulating in a different way than before-action or during-action speech which is interpreted as planning. Zivin and Meacham (Chapter 1 and Chapter 7 respectively) present a regulating interpretation of, respectively, Vygotsky's earliest regulatory speech and memory-aiding speech.

included is described in Fuson, Householder, and Urbaska (forthcoming). These categories were constructed to include types of speech-for-self emitted by 2- through 5-year olds alone in a room doing four structured tasks. They then were extended to samples of children speaking while playing alone in their own homes. Inter-rater reliabilities for these categories ranged from .85 to .99. Kohlberg's categories 3 and 5 are included in IA (Regulating Statement Form), and categories 2 and 4 are parts of IB (Regulating Social Form).

These categories were used to classify private speech utterances from forty-eight 2- through 5-year-olds while along in a room in their school doing four tasks (building a tower, two puzzles, playing with six plastic people). The four major categories are Regulating, Affective, Fantasy/Role Playing, and Incomprehensible. The category system is as follows:

I. Regulating

A. Statement Form

1. Present/past *or* 2. Future tense

a. Describing the surrounding world.

(i) Describing a thing (sentence using verb *to be*, noun, adjective).

(ii) Describing one's own external state ("I have . . .", "Me got duck").

b. Describing actions (sentence, adverb).

c. Describing one's own mental internal state ("I need to . . .", "I want . . .", "I think that . . .").

B. Social Form

1. Command.

2. Question (that does not get answered).

3. Question and its answer.

4. Responding form (for example "OK", "Yes", "No").

II. Affective

A. Play

1. Word play: nonsense words, rhyming words and jingles.

2. Singing.

B. Emotional expressive (for example "Oooh", "Damn", a sigh, "uhm").

III. Fantasy/Role Playing

A. Imitating persons.

B. Imitating objects, sound effects.

IV. Incomprehensible/Inaudible

The chief difference between the Kohlberg and Fuson category systems is in their assumptions about the functional unity of private speech. Kohlberg assumes that "private speech is a relatively unitary category with a common functional meaning" and "that . . . the various forms of private speech represent different developmental levels of behavior with a common self-communicative functional significance" (p. 732). The Fuson category system assumes instead that private speech serves three main functions: a regulating function, an emotional/expressive function, and a fantasy/role playing function. Each main category is proposed to be a type of speech-for-self that appears early and remains throughout life. Developmental changes are hypothesized to be reflected in differences in distributions within categories. For example the Vygotskian hypothesis concerning a shift from a child's describing of his environment to describing his own activity would be reflected in shifts from IAIa to IAIb. The amounts of speech within each main category are hypothesized to vary considerably with the child's setting (for example task situations would elicit more regulating speech, while free play would elicit more affective and fantasy-role playing). The fourth category (IV. Incomprehensible) is at the present time a category that will contain inarticulate or whispered speech by quite young children, muttered speech from older children, and any speech whose content cannot be distinguished because of limitations of the equipment being used in the research. These quite different sources will of course need to be sorted before any meaningful interpretations of speech from this category can be made.

What is the present evidence concerning the functional unity of private speech and the developmental sequence proposed by Kohlberg? This evidence is reviewed in some detail in Fuson, Householder, and Urbaska (forthcoming). At the present time the percent of speech in category 1 (self-stimulating) seems to be more a function of setting (for example task, free play) than of age, and results for categories 2 through 5 are difficult to interpret because of reliability problems with 3 and 5. The internalization hypothesis of Vygotsky seems to be upheld, though the percent of muttering varies with the setting (for example 20 to 40% in a task situation: Kohlberg, Yaeger, and Hjertholm, 1968; and 7% in free play: Dickie, 1973) and the onset of internal speech seems to be related to Piagetian operativity in 6½- to 10-year-olds (Pechman, 1978). In addition the decline in self-guiding speech noted in Kohlberg, Yaeger, and Hjertholm stops around age 6½ or so, and self-guiding and muttering are used interchangably and about equally through the period of early concrete operational thought (about age 9). The variance in percent of category 1. (Word play and repetition) in different task settings (for example 5% in a task situation: Kohlberg, Yaeger, and Hjertholm, 1968: 30% in a free play situation; Rubin Hultsch, and Peters, 1971) is probably partly due to the failure of the Kohlberg categories to include a place for expressions of affective states (for example a happily playful state, anger, frustration) in any but a primitive repetitive word-play manner.

In the only two studies that include an age range young enough to test assertions concerning the lower Kohlberg categories, Dickie (1973) and Berner (1971) found no change in percents of speech in categories 2 through 5 for 2½- through 5-year-olds, and Dickie reported small (4% and 7%) significant decreases for 6- to 8-year-olds in categories 2 (Commanding objects) and 3 (Describing own activity), no change for this age group in 4 (Self-answered questions), and an insignificant increase in 5 (Self-Guiding). These studies vary considerably in the proportions in each of these categories. Again setting (task or free play) seems to be a more important influence than age.

In summary the internalization of private speech is the only developmental aspect of Kohlberg's categories that seems to be strongly upheld. Speech in other categories seems to be as influenced by setting as by age; because most studies using older children also used tasks rather than free play, some evidence that was interpreted by individual authors to support the developmental aspects of Kohlberg's categories can now be seen to be just as likely to have been due to the task setting.

It thus seems timely to examine an alternative hypothesis: that private speech, or speech-for-self, serves several different functions, that these functions remain invariant throughout life, and that different patterns might exist within each type of function (that is, a particular developmental change might cause a change of form or content in one function but not necessarily in another). Our own pilot data from college students indicate that regulating, affective, and fantasy-role playing speech-for-self are all used by college students; different students report different concentrations of such usage. These hypotheses would then suggest a reversal of the present research strategy: that instead of focusing on the internalization of speech-for-self, we turn some attention to the conditions under which adults externalize speech-for-self. Answers to this may help us understand better the functions speech-for-self serves for children or help us pinpoint differences for children and adults. I, for example frequently find myself commanding garage doors, syrup lids, and boot zippers—all utterances that belong in Kohlberg's category 2 (Remarks addressed to nonhuman objects). I do this when my nonverbal strategies have failed. Do young children similarly resort to a verbal strategy, or do they possess fewer nonverbal strategies than I and more frequently employ a verbal strategy (which, after all is very frequently a powerful strategy in helping them achieve their aims) as their first choice?

Thus it seems that the Kohlberg categories raised many fundamental issues and contained bold insights, but their omission of important kinds of speech-for-self (fantasy, affective speech), their problems with lack of reliability, and the failure of evidence to support their suggested developmental sequence (except for Vygotsky's internalization hypothesis) suggest that a new set of categories building on what we now know be devised. The Fuson categories are offered here as a first draft of such a new set.

The question of the reliability and the consistency of the use of a category system across studies is crucial when results of different studies are compared. One of the causes of the differing findings in private speech studies (to be detailed below) is that researchers used different defintions of even the same category system. More detailed reporting of the operational definitions used for a category system would be quite helpful in avoiding this problem in future research.

Effects of Spontaneous Private Speech on Task Performance

A central issue in the development of self-regulating speech is *when* such speech *is* in fact helpful in regulating behavior. Unfortunately few of the researchers who recorded spontaneous private speech as a function of various conditions (for example age, task difficulty) systematically recorded performance that may have been affected by that speech. Such data, although correlational in nature, would be a useful supplement to experimental studies.

One study, described in more detail in a later section, reported strong correlations between self-guiding speech emitted during work on ordinary school tasks within the classroom and school reading (.87) and mathematics (.62) achievement (Pechman, 1978); this was true only for children in the early transitional period of concrete operations (about 6½ to 7½).

Five additional studies report data concerning relationships between speech and task performance, Beaudichon (1973); Dickie (1973); Klein (1964); Roberts (1977); and Yaeger (1968). Dickie (1973) found low nonsignificant correlations between success on puzzles and private speech; Beaudichon (1973) reported small positive nonsignificant correlations between performance on ordering tasks and total number of utterances; and Yaeger (1968) reported significant positive correlations (.65 and .58) between time to solution and amount of task-related speech (more speech indicated a longer solution time) for preschoolers and kindergarteners, but a negative correlation of minus 0.32 that approached significance for first graders.

These results included nonregulating private speech. When speech that is almost exclusively regulating is considered, consistently positive relationships between speech and performance are found. Children aged 3½ to 7 who completed a puzzle had twice as many task-related utterances and a higher proportion (70% versus 48%) of task-related speech than did children who failed to complete the puzzles (Klein, 1964). In Beaudichon's (1973) study task-related speech was positively related to performance, although some of the correlations involved were not significant. In particular, on difficult problems, correlations between performance and speech describing the task materials were significant and fairly large (.45 for the 5½- to 6-year-olds and .59 for the 6½- to 7-year-olds). Roberts (1977) found that the highly specific task-relevant speech of reading aloud was, on harder tasks, more frequent for successful than for unsuccessful first-graders in a read-and-answer task. (Definitional difficulties for his less specific categories are discussed later.)

In addition to the usual conditions, Beaudichon included one in which children were instructed to think aloud as they worked. This is an interesting condition and should probably be used more often in studies on self-regulatory speech, though one should not assume that the resulting overt speech necessarily represents the type or quantity of covert speech that would have been used. Unfortunately this condition was used only for the difficult task. In addition the same subjects who had completed the easy task were used in this instructed condition; comparisons were then made between the instructed-difficult and the noninstructed-difficult groups. For example the young 5½ to 6 instructed children spoke only half as much as the young noninstructed children (1.25 versus 2.67 mean utterances per minute) while the older 6½ to 7 instructed children spoke four times as much as the noninstructed children (4.3 versus 1.04 mean utterances per minute). The percent of speech in the two regulatory categories (long-term and describing task materials) increased from 65% in the noninstructed condition to 80% in the instructed condition for the younger children, but was the same (80%) for both older groups. The younger, but not the older, instructed children also did considerably and significantly better on the difficult task than did the younger noninstructed children. Because of the basic design error, one cannot of course tell how the instructions to think aloud are interacting with the child's having already done the easy task; the performance difference in particular could be a practice effect rather than an effect of a higher percentage of regulatory speech. A replication correcting this design problem would be a contribution toward the use of externalization of self-regulatory speech as a window to the function of such speech.

Variables Which Affect the Production of Self-Regulating Speech

Task Difficulty. • Vygotsky (1934/1962) proposed that the amount of self-guiding speech increased when the task was made more difficult. Results do not unambigously support this assertion and such an increase seems to vary both with age and type of difficulty. Kohlberg, Yaeger, and Hjertholm (1968) reported that the mean number of egocentric comments per six minutes was two higher (5.3 versus 3.4) for a difficult puzzle than for an easy puzzle and that the distribution of these comments in the Kohlberg categories was similar for the two puzzles. However Yaeger, in another paper (1968), reported that the actual working time for each child had been unavailable and that their data had been computed by dividing the mean number of comments by the total time allowed for each task. Because many of the children had completed the easy puzzle early and had stopped work (and speech) early, the figures had underreported the rate of comments for the easy puzzle.

Yaeger (1968) gave to preschool, kindergarten, and first-grade children three puzzles which varied in difficulty. She found no significant differences in the amount of task-related speech for puzzles of varying difficulty, but instead reported a significant effect of task order which varied by age: the mean number of task-referring comments increased significantly for preschoolers and first-graders (from 2.65 to 3.81 and 2.55 to 4.33) and decreased for kindergarteners (from 3.04 to 2.44). However because her method gave praise when children put in a puzzle piece correctly, her effect may be an age-related differential reaction to praised performance or to some other aspect of her situation rather than a characteristic of self-guiding speech.

An order effect in opposite directions depending upon conditions was reported by Deutsch and Stein (1972) for 4-year-olds. The mean total private speech utterances decreased over six puzzles for the success (child allowed to finish puzzle) and task interruption (pieces missing from the puzzle) conditions, while they increased for the personal failure condition (session always ended before the child could complete the puzzle). Thus nonpraised ordinary puzzle performance seems to lead to a decrease in private speech. These results indicate that it is not just difficulty, but the type of difficulty imposed that is important. If the task seems difficult to the child because his efforts do not solve it (the personal failure condition), private speech increases. If however the source of the difficulty is external, in this case the repeated omission by the experimenter of two pieces of the puzzle, private speech will decrease.

One might expect two different kinds of speech to increase with task difficulty — affective, emotional expressions of frustration or discouragement and self-regulating comments. Two studies distinguish these types of speech clearly enough to provide some evidence about these two effects. Zivin (1972) found more spontaneous vocalization of all types by 4-year-olds on difficult than on easy finger mazes; most of these vocalizations were affective expressions following errors. Beaudichon's (1973) data indicate that affective expressions increase with task difficulty for younger children (5½ to 6) from 0.16 to 0.92 mean utterances per minute, while they decrease for older (6½ to

7) children from 0.27 to 0.18 utterances per minute (numbers computed from Beauchidon's data, data which were somewhat misleadingly reported per subject by task, each of which varied in total time).

For Beaudichon (1973) the mean number of utterances per minute in the category correlated with performance (describing task materials) increased from 0.22 to 1.03 for the younger children and from 0.59 to 0.79 for the older children. The distributions of speech did not vary for the younger children with task difficulty (the percent of speech in the describing task materials was about 37%), but for the older children it increased from 46 to 76% on the difficult task. Somewhat inexplicably however, though speech in this category was correlated with task performance and older children did considerably better than did younger children, younger children on the difficult task emitted more speech in this category than did older children (1.03 versis 0.79 mean utterances per minute). A refinement of this category might be required to determine whether there is a quality difference in such statements. In uninstructed conditions more difficult problems (ordering and completion) elicited from 5½- to 6-year-olds more private speech of all kinds (an increase from 0.60 to 2.67 utterances per minute), with an increase in self-guiding utterances from .43 to 1.75 per minute. However 6½- to 7-year-olds exhibited a slight decrease in private speech of all kinds (from 1.32 to 1.04 utterances per minute) and in self-guiding speech in particular (from 1.09 to 0.84). The reason for the older children's shift to less overt speech for the difficult task is not obvious, although it may be possible that covert speech is more efficient for the older children and they may prefer to use it for difficult tasks. More covert speech by 7-year-olds is surely in line with Soviet hypotheses, but the differential age effect for the easy versus hard tasks is not.

Age. • Berner (1971) and Klein (1964) reported that the *number* of 3-, 4-, and 5-year-olds and 3½- to 7-year-olds, respectively, who talked at all while doing puzzles in a room alone was not correlated with age. It is fairly clear however that the *amount* of external private speech produced decreased from about age 4 or 5 to age 8 (Dickie, 1973; Beaudichon, 1973; Kohlberg, Yaeger, and Hjertholm, 1968). Four studies indicate that the pattern is not so clear for children 5 and under: Fuson, Householder, and Urbaska (forthcoming) found significantly higher numbers of utterances for 2-year-olds than for 3-, 4-, and 5-year-olds; this effect was mainly due to the regulatory category. Berner (1971) reported a lower number of private-speech utterances for 4-year-olds, mostly as a result of differences in the describing activity category. Yaeger (1968) found that the describing activity category showed a slight linear drop from preschool to first grade, but that kindergarten children produced fewer directions to self than did preschoolers and first-grade children. Dickie (1973) found a small positive correlation (.22) between scores on the Peabody Picture Vocabulary test and inner-directed speech (questions and selfguiding) for 2½- to 5-year-olds and a small negative correlation (minus .24) for children aged 5 to 8. The latter may indicate more covert speech in the high verbal children.

Figures for the percent of total speech which is nonsocial indicate a rise from age 3 to ages 4 and 5 (from 58 to 67% and 70%: Berner, 1971) and a drop after age 5 or 5½ (from 81% at 4 to 5½ to 73% at age 6 to 8; Dickie, 1973; from 31% at age 4 to 11% at age 6 in the school situation and from 15% at age 4 to 7% at age 10 in the sticker situation: Kohlberg, Yaeger, and Hjertholm, 1968).

There is some evidence that, although the absolute amount of private speech decreases, the proportion of private speech that is self-regulating in nature increases with age. Klein (1964) found a significant correlation of 0.37 between age and task-relevant speech, and Beaudichon (1973) reported that the proportion of self-regulating speech rose from 68% for 5½- to 6-year-olds to 81% for 6½- to 7-year-olds. This latter effect however, was confounded with task difficulty, for this difference was due almost entirely to differences on difficult tasks.

Thus the developmental pattern for the appearance of private speech seems to be more complex than the simple inverted U proposed by Vygotsky (1934/1962). At the present time the evidence suggests an initial high level of production of such speech by 2-year-olds, a drop in production when such speech becomes differentiated from other motor activity, a rise to a high around age 4 and 5, some irregularities in production around 5 to 6, with continued use during school tasks about 40% of the time for 7-, 8- and 9-yearolds and 30% for 10-year-olds. The irregularities around 5 and 6 remain to be verified and clarified; the present evidence for this possibility is: (1) the drop and subsequent rise in certain categories reported for kindergarteners by Yaeger (1968), who also indicates that Kohlberg, Yaeger, and Hjertholm (1968) found a similar phenomenon though it was discounted in that paper as a socioeconomic status (SES) sampling effect; (2) the decrease in all categories of private speech that 5½- to 6-year-olds exhibit when instructed to think aloud (Beaudichon, 1973); and (3) the slope change at age 5 noted by Dickie (1973). Possibly speech is undergoing some consolidation process around this age that affects various aspects of self-regulating speech.

Verbal and Communication Ability and IQ. • High verbal ability seems both to increase the quantity and to change the quality of private speech emitted. Kleiman (1974) split her 4-year-old sample on their median score on the Wechsler Preschool and Primary Scale of Intelligence (WPPSI). The high WPPSI group had higher average mean rates per minute of total private speech (6.3 years versus 3.5), task-related speech (2.6 versus 1.3), self-directive speech (1.7 versus .8), and feeling statement (.7 versus .3) than did the lower group. Measures of verbal flexibility and fluency had no significant relation to private speech. This whole sample was a very verbally effective one—its mean score on the WPPSI was one standard deviation above the

WPPSI mean. This sample produced by far the highest mean rate of private speech in the private-speech studies (escept for Roberts, 1977, and Roberts and Tharp, forthcoming, who used a reading task which elicited a great deal of sounding-out of words). This high mean rate may be in itself an indication of the positive effect of verbal ability on the production of private speech. Deutsch and Stein (1972) found that children above their sample median on the Peabody Picture Vocabulary test produced significantly more private speech and had a higher mean score on the Kohlberg private speech categories (recall that Deutsch and Stein viewed the Kohlberg categories as a six-point scale and reported a mean-level score rather than amounts of speech within categories). Most of this effect was due to the personal failure condition (child interrupted before she or he could finish the puzzle).

Listening to speech, as well as understanding it, also seems to be associated with a higher rate of overall private and of self-regulating speech. Three-, 4-, and 5-year-old children wearing earphones were classified as listeners or nonlisteners depending on the amount of disruption in the child's speech when the feedback sound of his own voice was delayed a fraction of a second. Later, listeners produced a higher percentage of self-guiding speech (19% versus 12%) and more private speech (40 versus 25 utterances) when solving puzzles than did nonlisteners (Berner, 1971).

General communicative performance as measured by amounts of social speech may be related to frequency of private speech. Kohlberg, Yaeger, and Hjertholm (1968) reported a correlation of 0.68 between the amounts of social speech and private speech (as collected over a two-hour period in the child's school) of 4- and 6-year-old children. However Pechman (1978) reported no association between social speech and private speech by 6½- to 10½-year-olds in elementary-school classrooms. The difference between these two results may be an effect of the type of private speech emitted. Most of the private speech in the Pechman study consisted of children reading aloud (to themselves) parts of the instructions to their school tasks; the private speech of the Kohlberg, Yaeger, and Hjertholm children was not of this type. The relationship between social and regulatory speech should be examined earlier with special attention paid to the age of the child and the type of regulatory speech emitted.

The main effect of higher IQ seems to be to make young high-IQ children produce amounts of private speech equivalent to that for average slightly older children (Kohlberg, Yaeger, and Hjertholm, 1968; Yaeger, 1968). In addition IQ is positively related to task performance for children who talk while solving a puzzle, but is unrelated to task performance for those children who do not talk (Klein, 1964). Finally, on sentence-completion tasks, which required the correct choice from a pair of words, high-IQ first-graders concentrated their task-irrelevant speech utterances after they had finished the task while low-IQ children distributed these task-irrelevant utterances throughout the task (Roberts and Tharp, forthcoming). This finding is consistent with one interpretation of the Beaudichon data proposed earlier: a good performance may be due more to the lack of distracting, task-irrelevant speech than to the presence of self-regulating speech.

Roberts and Tharp (forthcoming) and Roberts (1977) report some additional IQ-related data that are, in the view of this author, misleading. They report that "lower IQ children, who were also less successful in the tasks, employed more self-instructions than high IQ students, calling into question the efficacy of self-instructional training in this type of task" (Roberts and Tharp, forthcoming p.1). First the difference was very small (2.32 versus 2.11 utterances out of a mean total of 37 utterances). More importantly "self-instruction" is a misnomer. Statements to self ("a statement referring to speaker's behavior") comprised only 6% of the task-relevant speech. Most of these statements were from their Evaluation category (for example "This is fun." "I can't do this.") These statements were largely uttered after a word had been filled in or when a child had given up on a particular item. Thus these statements did not serve as self-instructions. The category which by its definition would seem to deserve the name self-instructions is Strategies: "any statements which included or indicated planful behavior, or involved a direction for the child or another to perform task related behavior." There were twelve such statements out of 1898 task-related utterances (1760 of these were Reading Aloud). These strategic statements were emitted by low- and high-IQ children (the authors do not indicate how many of the twenty-five children emitted such statements). Thus a more accurate statement of the findings of these studies is that lower-IQ children emit more (negative) evaluation statements concerning themselves and the task than do higher-IQ children, and these statements are distributed throughout the task period rather than being concentrated after task completion as for higher IQ children. These authors also report that the amount of "task-directed private speech" is negatively correlated with reading competence and number of correctly completed sentences and that low-IQ but not high-IQ children emitted more "task-directed private speech" during the hard task. However this speech was not regulatory; it was (predominantly) negatively evaluative and probably served more of an affective/expressive function than any other. The authors' statements indicating that their findings call into serious question assumptions about the function of self-directive private speech should be evaluated in light of the above information. What does deserve more discussion is that these authors found virtually no regulatory speech. The predominant strategy used was Reading aloud. This strategy undoubtedly is the most effective one for their task.

Sex. • Although most researchers have balanced their samples by sex and several have reported their data separately by sex, few have examined sex differences in private speech. The results of the few who have done so can be briefly summarized. Yaeger (1968) reported no sex differences on task-related speech among preschoolers, kindergarteners, and first-graders while solving puzzles. Dickie (1973) found sex differences in only two of the Kohlberg categories for 2½- through 8-year-olds doing puzzles, coloring, and free choice play with toys. These two categories were: more presocial self-stimulating speech by the boys (7.9 versus 5.8 mean utterances) and more outward-directed commands of objects by the girls (5.4 versus 3.8 mean utterances). Finally 4-year-old boys doing enlarged Porteus mazes and puzzles produced a higher rate of feeling statements (.68 versus .37 per minute) than did girls (Kleiman, 1974). Kleiman does not report a significant effect of sex on overall rate of private speech and does not report rates separately by sex. However, in reporting data concerning the effects of verbal ability, she reports mean rates of total private speech for high- and low-verbal-ability boys as 7.2 and 4.3, while the comparable rates for girls are 5.8 and 2.3. Thus boys in her sample generally seemed to produce a considerably higher total rate of private speech than did girls. Thus researchers have found few sex differences, and the ones that exist usually have been confined to specific private speech categories that have involved some interactions with verbal ability.

Reflective/Impulsive Dimensions. • Dickie (1973) reported that the lower levels of the Kohlberg categories were related to impulsivity as measured by errors and number correct on the Picture Absurdities subtest of the Detroit Test of Learning Aptitude. Impulsive 2½- to 8-year-olds were more likely to use presocial self-stimulating and outward-directed private speech during tasks than were reflective children. Kleiman (1974) found that reflective 4-year-olds who were slow and accurate on the Matching Familiar Figures test (MFF), produced significantly and considerably more total private speech than impulsive (fast and inaccurate) children (86 versus 40 mean utterances). Their higher rate of total private speech (6.2 versus 4.4 per minute) was largely the result of a higher rate (1.6 versus 4 utterances per minute) of sound-play (singing, humming, or making car sounds). Zivin (1972) found more task-relevant speech produced while doing finger mazes for 4-year-olds who had performance characteristics that made them look reflective than did 4-year-olds who looked impulsive. She did not however use the standard MFF to test impulsivity/reflectivity.

Kleiman (1974) also made a division of the sample on MFF errors alone (with vocabulary score as a covariate). Accurate children (below the mean on errors) had significantly higher rates of total private speech (6.3 versus 3.9 utterances), task-related speech (2.4 versus 1.5), self-directive speech (1.6

versus 1.1), and feeling statements (.7 versus .4) than did inaccurate children.

A similar analysis, using MFF response time rather than errors, showed only one significant effect: children with shorter response times had a significantly higher rate of self-directive speech than children with longer response times (1.6 versus 1.0). Thus the ability to respond quickly (perhaps reflecting an ability to process information quickly) may increase the likelihood that speech can be used for self-regulation.

More of the accurate children produced some fantasy statements (53% versus 38%), and they produced a higher mean number of such statements (2.6 versus 0.9). Kleiman hypothesized that the much higher use of fantasy statements (some quite imaginative) and sound-play by accurate children served to release frustration and so on, and was an index of resilient ego strength in that the child could operate in both advanced and regressive modes of speaking. An alternative explanation is that the high-fantasy, accurate children were just very accomplished and could do the assigned tasks while being playful and creative; that is, playfulness in this situation is a result of feelings of competence and is an advanced mode rather than a primitive one.

A description of attentional strategies used by accurate children may be pertinent to the above findings on private speech. Welch (1975) reported that accurate 4-year-olds in a free-play situation are differentiable by their ability to do two things at once, for example they can remain involved in a task while scanning the room or looking at the behavior of other people. This ability is independent of age and of IQ. The use of this attentional strategy—doing two things simultaneously (or at least alternating very quickly and effectively between them)—may contribute to the higher rate of self-directive speech for accurate children; they may be better able to speak while acting and also to listen (to themselves) while speaking. These results suggest that the MFF scores might be a good variable to use in future studies on speech and motor acts as well as in private speech studies.

Self-Regulating Speech When the Goal of the Action Is Set by the Child

Some few studies provide data on spontaneous speech of children who are engaging in tasks chosen by themselves (though usually from some restricted set of tasks provided by the experimenter). The first of these is the only study that has gathered data on children's use of self-regulating speech in the elementary school classroom (Pechman, 1978). Forty 6½- to 10½-year-olds were observed in two types of schools (structured and open) for 60 minutes; each was observed in 3- to 10-minute intervals as they worked in their classroom on teacher-assigned tasks. The groups were equated by chronological and mental age, achievement, and Piagetian developmental stage. Amount of task-focused private speech was not affected by type of classroom, but more such speech occured during individualized and small-group assignments. About 40% of the observations of 7-, 8-, and 9-year-olds and 30% of those of 10-year-olds contained self-guiding speech or muttering. Much of the self-guiding speech involved the saying of words or numbers in the school task. During the early transitional operational period, amount of self-guiding speech in the classroom was strongly correlated with reading (.83) and mathematics (.62) achievement. Performance on Piagetian concrete operational tasks was the major predictor of the decline of private speech when mental and chronological age, achievement, classroom style, and sex were controlled. Results with respect to the Kohlberg private-speech categories were discussed earlier.

Some methodological problems still remain to be worked out in this type of field study. Inter-rater reliabilities for the Kohlberg categories ranged from 75 to 86%. The low figure is from the lip/tongue movement and inaudible-muttering category, a relatively difficult one to observe. The self-guiding speech was coded on the spot rather than being recorded, so more refined analyses of its content are not possible. Nevertheless this study was carefully done. It used important controls and demonstrates that research on selfregulating speech can be done in wholly natural settings.

In addition such research may uncover new aspects of self-regulating speech. For example one informal observation of Pechman (personal communication) that might be examined in future research bears on the key question of what determines whether self-regulating speech is overt or covert. Pechman noted that children seemed not to be vocalizing short or simple words, but only those which were longer or more difficult. The following example from mathematics indicated that this phenomenon had something to do with the level of understanding of the word content rather than simply indicating a difference in reading decoding difficulty: one child silently mouthed almost all the numbers on her mathematics paper (these were 1 to 20), but she consistently voiced loudly those over 20. While care must be taken that field research not be reduced to the level of demonstration by anecdote, such informal observations can contribute to the formulation of hypotheses to be examined in future research.

Two studies placed children in a small room with a selection of toys and activities from which the child could choose. The Rubin, Hultsch, and Peters study (1971) varied the person situation of the child (alone, with a peer, and with a familiar male adult). The Dickie study (1973) varied the person situation (with a friend and with mother) and the task (puzzles/coloring and free play). Both of these studies categorized speech using the Kohlberg categories. They found a much higher proportion of presocial self-stimulating speech (repetition and word play) than did any other study using the Kohlberg categories (30% and 18%, respectively, with all other studies reporting 7% or less). There was both a significantly greater amount (8.2

versus 5.5 mean utterances) and a higher proportion (21% versus 16%) of presocial self-stimulating speech in the free play than in the task situation (Dickie, 1973). These two results seem to indicate that a free-play situation and the presence of a familiar person in a task situation (all other studies used an unfamiliar experimenter) each contribute to a greater amount of presocial self-stimulating speech. Dickie also found for the free-play situation significantly more utterances of outer-directed speech (commanding objects: 6:1 versus 3.1; describing activity: 11.9 versus 10.3) and significantly fewer utterances of inner-directed speech (dialogue: 3.3 versus 4.1; selfguiding: 8.1 versus 10.5) than for the task situation. Thus though one might expect some self-guiding speech to occur in the selection of goals in a free-play situation, any increase is more than offset either by a smaller overall proportion of goal-directed behavior in a free-play than in a task situation or by an occupation in free-play activities requiring less self-directed speech (such as some types of pretend play). Studies that both use categories of different types of self-regulating speech and that connect types and amounts of self-regulating speech to different types of activites are needed in order to understand the various ways in which speech-for-self regulates behavior.

Several verbal conditioning studies have examined factors that affect the amount of control over some naturalistic behaviors one can gain by conditioning verbal descriptions of these behaviors. Most of these studies are limited by their small sample sizes and restricted population (low SES children), but they do represent the only data we have concerning the ability of a verbalized goal to regulate behavior over a delay period of as long as 24 hours.

In an early series of studies, Lovaas (1961, 1964) and Sherman (1964) established that modification of the verbal behavior of young children changes the related nonverbal (food choices, toy choices) behavior only in some children and only to a somewhat limited extent. Risley and Hart (1968) found that with 4-year-old, low SES black children, differential snack rewards for reporting the use of a particular toy earlier in the day had little effect on the children's use of toys. After children had been rewarded only for reports that corresponded to their actual use on that day (that is, reports corresponded to behavior), rewards only for the use of a particular toy resulted in all six children in the group using that toy subsequently. After the reinforcement of the verbal and then of the corresponding verbal and nonverbal behavior had been repeated over several materials, reinforcement of a verbal report only resulted in the use of that toy on the following day. Thus these 4-year-olds could set a goal, remember it, and act on it 24 hours later. The precise role of verbalization in each of these steps, however, is not clear. Conditioning with a different group of six children indicated that unless a high level of reporting was maintained, neither of the procedures was effective, and the level of doing dropped to the level of reporting rather than vice versa. Thus in this population, talking about what one had done was not a natural behavior, and such talk decreased if it was not rewarded.

Israel and O'Leary (1973) argued that the self-regulating potential of speech would indicate that a training procedure in which the verbal behavior preceded the nonverbal behavior would be more successful than the reverse (as was done in Risley and Hart, 1968). With low SES 4-year-olds, they found that correspondence between children's descriptions of what they played with and their actual play developed only when reinforcement was contingent upon both verbal and nonverbal behaviors and when the training was in a say-do order. Reinforcement of a verbal behavior alone or of a do-say sequence did not produce high levels of correspondence between verbal and nonverbal behavior. Because Israel and O'Leary were examining a self regulating hypothesis, systematic data gathered on spontaneous self-regulations emitted by children during the play period would have helped to answer questions concerning the various roles of verbalization. They did report that more children in the say-do than in the do-say condition emitted, in the play situation, vocalizations, such as "I'm going to play with the beads." or "I'm playing with the beads;" but gave no details concerning such spontaneous vocalizations.

The small group of studies just described are the only ones in which the child is free to set his own action goals. Moreover the first three are the only ones in which this action goal is not subject to experimenter manipulation. Although one would want to understand the ways in which self-speech can regulate behavior when the action goals are set by others (such as in schools), most of a child's action goals in his day-to-day living are set by himself. We have almost no understanding of how speech is used or can be used by the child in setting or in carrying out his daily life tasks; of whether such overt verbalizations as are emitted by a child do in fact regulate his behavior; or of to what extent covert verbalizations are used by children in regulating their actions. Data gathered in homes, yards, playgrounds, and in schools are required in order to answer these questions.

Summary of Results on Spontaneous Self-Regulating Speech

Naturalistic data on children's use of self-regulating speech are sparse. Most of our knowledge about spontaneously produced speech to, or for, self is from experimental situations in which tasks (mostly puzzles) have been given to children. The tasks used have been fairly limited in nature, and their largely spatial/visual nature may not be tapping some kinds of self-regulating speech nor determining the true extent of self-regulating capabilities in children. In most studies an experimenter, a peer, or a familiar adult has been present (though usually noninteractive) in the room; this has necessitated differentiating social speech from speech-for-self, a problem that still has not been solved satisfactorily. We know that the absence of another person in the room decreased the amount of speech emitted, but we do not know how or to what extent person presence affects regulatory speech.

Even with the above restrictions the evidence seems to indicate some general results. The amount of private speech for, or to, the self seems to be rather small—on the order of less than two utterances per minute. Verbal ability, accuracy on the Matching Familiar Figures test (MFF), a task rather than a free-play situation, instructions to think aloud, listening to one's own speech, presence of a friend rather than mother, task failure if it is the child's fault, and (perhaps) task difficulty tend to result in larger amounts or a higher proportion of self-regulating speech. The developmental course of spontaneous self-regulating speech is not yet clear, but it seems to be a complicated one with peaks for 2-year-olds and 4- to 5-year-olds, with perhaps some type of complex qualitative change around age 5. Self-guiding speech and muttering is still being used during school tasks by children in the early transition stage of concrete operations (6½ to 7½). Some self-guiding speech (for example reading directions aloud) and muttering are used in the classroom as late as age 10½. Spontaneously uttered self-regulating speech probably aids performance; more work needs to be done in this area, for interpreting present results is complicated by some failures to separate distracting nonself-regulating utterances from regulating utterances and to deal adequately with the possible presence of covert verbalizations.

There are still difficult theoretical and methodological problems in this area of research. Conceptual frameworks for discussing self-regulating speech are quite fuzzy, and operational definitions and categorizations of such speech differ from study to study. In addition no one has successfully dealt empirically or theoretically with covert regulatory speech. The common developmental picture is of overt regulatory speech becoming covert around the ages of 5 to 7. This picture has resulted in research on young children focusing on overt regulatory speech and research on older children focusing on or assuming covert regulatory speech. However the results of Locke and Fehr (1970) and Pechman (1978) taken together suggest that 4-year-olds covertly label pictures and that even 10½-year-olds use regulatory vocalizations in school tasks. The latter result may be largely a result of the nature of the reading task or of doing tasks involving reading in a room with other people doing other things, but it does suggest that there are untapped areas of regulatory vocalizations in the everyday lives of elementary school children which should be examined if we are to have a complete picture of the development of regulatory speech.

STUDIES IN WHICH THE WORDS ARE SUPPLIED TO THE CHILD

Cell 5 from Table 1 contains by far the largest number of studies. Each of the studies is an attempt to ascertain the effect of self-speaking on some small aspect of a child's behavior. For the purposes of discussion, these studies have been divided into three large groups. The first group will be those studies examining the relation between vocalization and simple motor acts. Soviet theory and methodology in this area will be outlined. Then a set of five different kinds of vocal-motor interactions are proposed, and possible mechanisms for each of these are discussed. Western replications of the Soviet research are discussed with respect to each of these mechanisms. The second large group of studies are those concerning vocalizations and nonmotor tasks. Some general considerations in this area are presented, and then six specific effects of verbalizations are discussed. The third and smallest group of studies in Cell 5 is discussed in the section on learning self-regulating speech.

These two main groups of studies have different roots. The first group comes from Soviet research and includes American replications of Soviet studies and new studies designed to answer questions raised by the Soviet research. The second group of studies are a subset of work from the main stream of American research on verbal learning, memory, perception, and behavior modification; this subset includes samples from those designs in which children say aloud or to themselves the words supplied by the experimenter.

Vocalization and Simple Motor Acts

Soviet Theory and Methodology

Essential to an understanding of the Soviet and Soviet-inspired research on the relationship between speaking and other motor acts is some awareness both of Soviet methodology and reporting style and of two Soviet theoretical principles. Research in the Soviet Union is done primarily within research laboratories, each headed by a prominent person. Some of this research (especially theses) is published in journals, but much of it exists only in laboratory manual form. The head of a given laboratory will then deliver papers which summarize results (but often not details of the methods) of several of these studies. Some of the summary papers by Luria on the relationship between speech and other motor acts translated into English in the late 1950s and early 1960s were the source of American knowledge of Luria's work. The sample sizes involved in this research were quite small and the methodological details were often incomplete; this made it difficult to ascertain exactly what children of different ages had in fact been able to do. This uncertainty made it difficult to judge whether a replication of a Luria study had in fact been a replication, and therefore just what might account for contradictory results.

This situation unfortunately led to a concentration of efforts on Lurian methodology—on studies which tried to delineate and determine the effects of small differences in Lurian experiments. In retrospect a more productive use of this time and energy might have been to focus on the conclusions Luria drew from his experiments concerning the relation between speech and other motor acts and to design new and different experiments that would have tested these conclusions rather than to focus so narrowly on the paradigms and equipment used by Luria.

The theoretical principles that provide the context for the Lurian work concern the function and development of language. The first, enunciated by Pavlov, is the idea of language as a second signal system, a second order system of symbols which can control certain aspects of the lower systems of nonsymbolic signals. For example verbal instructions can permit human subjects to make almost instantaneously connections between two formerly unconnected things, a process that must be done slowly by conditioning with animals.

The second theoretical principle is one discussed first by Vygotsky: the passage from the interpsychological plane to the intrapsychological plane; this principle indicates that children form certain complex mental operations through social interactions with adults. Thus any developments in self-regulating speech would be expected to occur first in interactions with adults and then to become internalized.

A considerable amount of physiological research concerning the effect of the second signal system on orienting responses has been done in the Soviet Union; more recently the idea of an orienting response has been used in a more general way by Gal′perin to mean what we might call a "mental set." These uses of the principle will be discussed later. Readers interested in further methodological and theoretical perspectives on Soviet self-regulating speech might read Luria (1969), Harris (Chapter 2, particularly on the second signal system), Wertsch (Chapter 3) and Wozniak (1972).

Soviet Research

Luria's research (1932, 1955/1957, 1959, 1957/1961*a*, 1961*b*, 1969; Luria and Yudovich, 1959) focused on the ability of words to initiate and to inhibit discrete actions by the squeezing of a rubber ball in response to various kinds of visual or auditory signals (colored lights or a bell). The complexity of the relationships between the signals and the desired responses varied in several steps: from a simple "When the light goes on, press the bulb once." to a more complex "When the red light is on, press the bulb once. When the green light is on, press the bulb twice." Inhibition of a response included the total inhibition of any response ("When the green light is on, don't press."), the inhibition of intersignal perseverative responses, and the truncation of a potentially longer response (for example pressing once, for a short time, to a long stimulus light can be viewed as requiring the inhibition of the pressing response once it is made). In some experiments the pressing responses were made without speech accompaniment; in others the child vocalized using words supplied by the experimenter. Various experiments with differing instructions and children of different ages were reported in a somewhat diffuse way so that clear comparisons were and are still sometimes difficult to make. The recently published translations of work by Tikhomirov (1975-1976) and Yakovleva (1975-1976) are the only presently translated long and detailed accounts of specific experiments done under Luria's supervision; the following outline of Luria's results will rely fairly heavily on these reports.

Luria outlines three stages in the relationship between speech and other motor acts. *Stage 1* has children from about age 1½ to about 3 years of age. The focus in this stage is on the control of a child's behavior by the speech emitted by others (adults). A child in this stage can carry out direct adult instructions only immediately after the instruction. A child looks at the light when he hears "When you see the light . . .", and he presses when he hears the subsequent part of the instruction ". . . press the ballon." He is not able to store the "When—then" instruction and wait for the first signal. Young children can be conditioned to make such pressing responses to the light, but this conditioning process works much as it does for animals, with little obvious benefit from language. In addition, for children in this stage neither speech from an adult nor from the child is able to inhibit an ongoing motor act. Pressing the bulb at this age apparently creates tactile-kinesthetic stimulation that tends to make the pressing response of the child perseverate: the child makes many intersignal pressing responses.

Luria and his coworkers were unsuccessful in inhibiting these intersignal responses through verbal instructions without additional nonverbal stimulation. They were successful in extinguishing the intersignal squeezes in this stage by adding a new initiating instruction ("Touch your knee.") immediately after the child had pressed the bulb initially and then by gradually fading this second response. These intersignal pressing responses also were eliminated in eight of the seventeen 1½- to 2-year-olds and in thirteen of the sixteen 2- to 3-year-olds by creating or emphasizing the existence of a causal relationship between the child's press and the turning off of the light (Yakovleva, 1975/1976). Children who had been conditioned to press the bulb when the light was turned on were then told, "When you see the light, press the balloon and thereby put out the light." Tikhomirov reports similar results with five 3-year-olds using the ringing of a bell as signal that the child had completed the motor response of squeezing the bulb (as usual the squeeze was in response to a light). If this bell-ringing was not mediated by adult language (that is if the child was not warned in advance that such a bell would ring), the sound served to increase rather than decrease the number of intersignal presses. When the child had been given an advance instruction ("Ring the bell and ring it only when the light comes on."), the bell sound resulted in a sharp drop in intersignal presses. However the specific instructions given do not let us determine whether it is the simple visual (or audio) feedback about the press or the causal relationship established by the words and carried out by the child that was responsible for this effect.

Adult instructions during this stage also do not seem able to redirect an ongoing motor act (for example an instruction, "Take the stockings off.", while the child was putting them on merely intensified his ongoing act). However Luria's examples of this phenomenon from the Shchelovanov Laboratory are all of instructions exactly opposite to what the child was doing. If all the test situations were of this type, Luria's claim that adult language cannot "switch the child from one action to another" is too strong; it should be only that language cannot switch a child from one action to its opposite. In addition, without a detailed report of the actual experiments, it is not clear whether the child understood that he was to change actions rather than that he was to follow the new instruction after he had completed the old (after all, one ordinarily only takes stockings off after one has them on).

Stage 2 has children (age 2½ and beyond) who are capable of storing a "When—then" instruction from an adult and waiting for the first light before pressing. The stored instruction does not inhibit perseverative responses however; children continue to emit a substantial number of intersignal presses, that is, they are initially unable to inhibit extra presses. At this stage the child's emissions of vocalizations are largely coordinated with his motor actions. The effect of the child's vocalizations at this stage is described by the Soviets as coming from the "impulsive" aspect of speech rather than the semantic aspect. The impulsive aspect of speech is seen to be due to the "innervating verbal impulse, the innervation of definite speech organs which create a center of excitation in the motor speech area of the cerebral cortex" (Luria, 1961, p. 51). Several experiments indicate quite clearly that semantic effects of the child's own speech are not yet operative. If the child is told to say "Go." and to squeeze each time he sees the light, the intersignal responses decrease considerably. Tikhomirov (1958/1975-1976) reported that for children in this stage who were instructed to squeeze twice and say "Two.", the impulsive structure of the verbal act predominated and the child consistently pressed only once. In another such experiment the child was instructed to press the bulb twice when he saw the light and to say "Go. Go." as he did so. Other children were instructed to say "I shall press twice." while so doing. The structure of the verbal act determines the motor response: children who say "Go. Go." are able to press twice; children who say "I shall press twice." give a single long press lasting the duration of the sentence. Tikhomirov also reported that saying the nonsense syllable "tu" or "tu tu" respectively, aided 4 out of 12 children. The semantic aspect was also somewhat operative in this experiment however, for saying "Once." and "Once-twice." was helpful to more than 4 children. A further experiment with 3- and 4-year-olds indicates that the impulsive, excitatory effect of speech overcomes the semantic effect (Luria, 1961). If a child is instructed to press when he sees the red light and to refrain from pressing when he sees the green light, he is able to press correctly most of the time and to inhibit correctly about 58% of the time. This indicates that a stored instruction is able to effect inhibition of action to some extent at this stage. But if the child is then instructed to say "Press." and to press to the red light and to say "Don't press." and not to press to the green light, the number of incorrect presses to the green light rises from 42% to 70%. Thus the impulsive effect of vocalizing overrides the semantic content of the vocalization.

Two additional experiments by Tikhomirov indicate impulsive effects of the Stage-2 child's speech. Children in the nonverbalization condition who are told to give a short squeeze to a long light are unable to inhibit their squeeze and continue to squeeze until the light goes off. Those children who are instructed to say "tu" to each light are able to inhibit this longer squeeze and give only one short squeeze to each long-light stimulus. The second experiment indicates that for children in Stage 2, saying "must not." to a light stimulus does not enable them to inhibit a squeeze to that stimulus (that is the impulsive aspect cannot be inhibited by the content of the words.)

Though in Stage 2 the child's own language is not able to inhibit his motor responses due to the impulsive effect of his speech, adult language at this stage can inhibit such responses. An adult saying "Don't." between the light signals is now able to reduce greatly the number of intersignal presses.

In *Stage 3* (beginning about 4½ to 5 years of age) children become capable of storing and acting upon rather more complicated "When—then" statements and their speech becomes able to inhibit motor movements. Children in Stage 3 can successfully follow instructions of "Press to the red light and don't press to the green light.", needing at first to say the "Don't press." direction aloud. Thus speech at the third stage affects behavior through its semantic aspect, through the "system of elective significative connexions which are produced by speech" (Luria, 1961, p. 59). Children at this stage can be forced to regress to second stage impulsive types of functioning if the rate of signal emission is increased.

Luria, following Vygotsky, describes a fourth stage, that of the self-regulating speech becoming internal, covert speech. In some of his writings (for example Luria, 1961, p. 59) inner speech is a part of the third stage, while in other writings (for example Luria, 1961, p. 61) it is described as following the third stage. Luria does not describe experiments with respect to the timing involved in this fourth and final internal stage of speech; knowledge of its existence is necessary however for any accurate understanding of the Soviet position on self-regulating speech. Sokolov (1968/1972) discusses experiments that relate to this inner-speech stage.

In summary, in the first stage (1½ to 3) the child's speech is not capable of regulating his behavior at all; the adult's speech is capable of initiating immediately following child actions, but not of inhibiting ongoing or preseverating actions. In the second stage (2½ to 4½ or 5) adult speech can inhibit ongoing child actions; children can use their own speech to initiate immediately following actions, but not to inhibit them; and they can store adult "When—then" instructions of a fairly simple type and use these instructions to produce the necessary initiating speech signals. The effect of speech at this stage comes from the sounds or from the act of speaking, but not from the meaning of the words. In the third stage (4½ on) children can use their own speech both to initiate and to inhibit actions and can produce these speech acts from stored, somewhat complicated instructions from an adult. The meaning of the words rather than the speaking act or the sound is more influential here, and the self-regulating speech gradually becomes internalized and functions as inner speech.

Possible Mechanisms for Verbal-Motor Interactions

Interpretation of the Western replications of the Soviet research is difficult, for these replications form a complex tangle of foci on different parts of the Lurian work, of different assumptions about the underlying mechanisms between speech and motor acts, and of different methodologies. Moreover keeping in mind the varying foci of the Lurian work requires constant vigilance by the reader, for researchers do not often separate these out (and some are seemingly unaware of them). Making inferences about mechanistic assumptions in various studies is also difficult, for these often consist only of vague references to some sort of "verbal mediation" process or to some sort of "impulsive" effect. Ascertaining methodological differences requires extremely careful and detailed reading of reports; this is further complicated by the fact that vital information is sometimes omitted (for example no details of warmup or training procedures). A complete dissection of the present work with respect to all of these dimensions is beyond the scope of this paper. What we shall do instead is to try to specify the different foci of the Lurian work and to present mechanisms that could account for results in that area; research bearing on these mechanisms will be discussed. Some important methodological problems will also be described.

The Lurian research bears on the following different effects of vocalization:

I. Initiation of Actions

II. Inhibition of Actions

A. Not emitting a response at all:

1. Correctly not emitting a response to a negative stimulus.
2. Not emitting a response in the absence of a stimulus (inhibiting responses independent of any signal).

B. Inhibiting an ongoing response:

1. Not emitting continued responses to one stimulus (perseveration).
2. Ending a response while still sensing the stimulus (for example emitting a short squeeze to a long light).

These various effects of vocalization are not clearly differentiated in the reports of the Lurian research. Sorting them out is made more difficult by the fact that some experiments concern stored instructions and some concern vocalizations (some involve both). The vocalizations may come from the adult or from the child, the vocalizations may be meaningful or not. These different aspects are not varied systematically across the impulsive and inhibitory effects. Each Lurian stage describes some combination of some of these conditions and some of the effects.

The effects are also not differentiated in most Western replications. In particular, most Western researchers seem not to consider the difference between initiation and inhibition. Their theoretical discussions and instructions reflect a verbal-motor, temporal bias which resulted in their focusing only on the initiation effect. In order for speech to initiate an action, it must precede it. But, as we shall see, mechanisms in which speech follows the act can account for effects B 2. Wozniak (1972) pointed out the Lurian focus on inhibiting responses (especially II B 1) and proposed the orienting response mechanism for that effect (to be discussed later). The American focus only on initiation is particularly ironic because most researchers used error measures (omissions, extra pushes, and pushes to a negative signal) which would have allowed them to differentiate initiating and inhibiting effects.

Vocalization and the Initiation of Motor Acts. • No one is very clear about the details of mechanisms connecting vocalization and initiation of motor acts. Presumably different mechanisms govern impulsive and semantic aspects. The impulsive mechanism hypothesized by the Soviets is the nonlocalization of the effects of verbal impulses described earlier: a spoken word evokes a center of excitation in the speech part of the cortex, and this serves as a supplementary center of excitation for the motor act. This mechanism implies that it is the motor act of speaking rather than the sounds that is responsible for the initiative impulsive effect. The Soviet evidence for this impulsive effect has been presented earlier. Particularly telling seems to be the data indicating that vocalizing seems to create motor acts reflecting the rhythm of the vocalization rather than the semantic content of the vocalization.

Western replications of the initiative impulsive effect of speech have generally supported the existence of such an effect. Rondal (1976) reported the most thorough set of experiments examining this particular effect. Rondal found that vocalization of "Press." aided the performance of children aged 3½ to 5 on the simple press-to-light task and on the simple discrimination task. In addition he found with a series of more difficult tasks (for example "Press three times for the single light and not at all for the double light.", "Press once every third light.") with older children, aged 5 to 8, that the impulsive rhythmic initiating effect was still functioning to aid performance. Moreover after a task in which vocalization had been required, 65% of the children manifested external signs (for example lip movements) indicating inner verbalizations at least once. These verbalizations seemed to correspond rhythmically rather than semantically to the motor behavior. The most difficult of these tasks were repeated with adults, with covert verbalization indexed by self-report in one study and by labial electroactivity in another. Inner verbalizations were indicated by both types of measures in many of the adult subjects. These verbalizations often seemed to occur at the beginning of the task and to reappear when something unexpected or confusing occurred.

Some studies have reported negative results with respect to an impulsive initiating effect. Bronckart (1973) reported no difference between a vocalize and nonvocalize condition for performance on the task of "When you see a red light, squeeze." for children from 2½ to 5 years. Rondal (1976) reported only a slight difference due to a decrease in preseverating responses (continued or added brief presses after the initial press at light onset). That saying "Don't press." increases the number of presses to a negative signal also does not seem certain. Bronckart (1973) and Miller, Shelton and Flavell (1970) found only a slight increase in the number of erroneous squeezes to the negative light. Wilder (1968) and Jarvis (1964) found no such significant effect, though Wilder's sample might have been the wrong age to show this effect (ages 3 and 5). Jarvis did find some rhythmic evidence for 4-year-olds: the "Push." condition resulted in one-third as many pushes to the negative signal as did the silent and "Don't Push." conditions. The sequence of conditions was counterbalanced, and Jarvis reported the above effect only for treatments when given in the Luria sequence (silent, "Push.", and "Don't Push."); for all other sequences there were no differences due to conditions. Jarvis's concern about order effects apparently was justified and raises questions about all studies in which subjects were administered the conditions in only one sequence. However one might question whether a silent treatment can really involve no verbalization with children this old if it follows a treatment requiring a verbalization. The solution to the problem of sequence effects lies in the use of between-subject rather than within-subject designs. In addition Luria sets Stage 3 as early as 4½ years, so one would really expect most of Jarvis's subjects to respond to the treatments with no differences.

Bronckart and Rondal replicated the "When you see the light, press twice." experiment (Bronckart, 1973). They found 20 to 30% correct responses for 3½- to 4-year-olds; 40 to 60% for 4- to 5-year-olds; and 80% or more for 5-year-olds and older children. When the child's verbal self-regulations were added ("Squeeze. Squeeze."), responses improved slightly between 3 and 5 years. Verbalizations of "I squeeze twice." created multiple motor responses and of "Twice." created single-motor responses. These results are not of the magnitude reported by Luria, but they do support the impulsive, excitatory, initiating function of speech.

A study by Joynt and Cambourne (1968) is often cited as the single Western replication that unequivocably supports Luria's results. Most of their tasks bear on the impulsive initiative effect. Ironically, though this study was very thorough in its approach and used three tasks and four speech conditions, the results are not maximally informative due to limitations in data analysis and reporting. In particular, errors of commission, omission, and intersignal errors were not separated, so the effects within each paradigm of speech on motor initiation and on motor inhibition cannot be disentangled. In addition (and perhaps as a result) some of the results do not agree with Luria's findings. The error score differences for the speech conditions strongly support the Luria results only in the simplest task ("Squeeze when you see the light."). However in the two-color discrimination task there is only a slightly higher error score for the incongruent verbalization condition, ("Say don't squeeze. and do not squeeze."); in the squeeze-once-or-twice task ("Squeeze once for a red light and twice for a green light.") there are essentially no differences among verbalization conditions. The chief contribution of this study is to focus on a child's language ability rather than on his chronological age as the criterion for inclusion in a particular stage. Correlations between age and motor performance were consistently higher for language age (as measured by the score on the Illinois Test of Psycholinguistic Abilities—ITPA) than for chronological age.

The Soviet initiative impulse mechanism and Rondal's (1976) experiments with older children both indicate a rhythmic relationship between speech and motor acts. There is some recent American work seeking to ascertain the relationships between vocal and motor acts with a repeated sequence of components. These studies have focused on rhythmic aspects of this relationship. Such work is still largely in the hypothesis-generating stage and has produced few results. One of the main questions in this area is whether there is a central timing mechanism that coordinates vocal and other motor responses or whether certain aspects of the vocal system can regulate by way of rhythm sequences of motor acts. Harris (1976) proposes several rhythmic aspects of speech that might be involved in regulating motor actions: stress, intonation, and meter. She suggests that these rhythmic aspects of speech are particularly helpful for "immature and developing organisms, in situations of stress, or situations where disease, organic deficits, and interference of some speech function is suspected" (Harris, 1976, p. 178). The only study reported to date concerning this conjecture foundered on methodological difficulties; the rhyme chosen ("One potato, two potato") was not appropriate to the task (pressing the correctly colored panel in a self-paced sequence of presentations) and hindered rather than aided performance (Meacham, Harris, and Blaschko, 1973). Zivin (1976) analyzed some of the Tikhomirov (1958/1975-1976) and Luria bulb-press and vocal records for rhythmic patterns and found repeated patterns of stressed presses (the particular patterns vary from child to child). She also reported data indicating that spontaneous rhythmic coordination between vocal and manual activity in a free-play situation dropped from 17.3% for 5-year-olds to 8.6% for 6-year-olds. She thus speculated that younger children may use vocal rhythm to help organize and effect motor acts while older children seem less likely to do this.

Both Harris's notion and Luria's notion of the impulsive initiative function of speech implicates a fairly primitive mechanism which is replaced or superseded by more complex ones involving semantic features. Rondal's (1976) experiments with older children and adults suggest a different interpretation and a slightly different mechanism than a general excitatory function. The form of the vocalization (for example none, one, or two discrete vocalizations or long short, short long) seems to help define the task; its rhythmic aspects seem to model the motor action, to serve as a middle step (mediator) between the semantic aspect of the instructions ("Push twice when you see the light.") and the rhythm the motor act requires. Preliminary results reported by Wozniak (n.d.) for both the double squeeze response and for a pounding board task ("Pound once." or "Pound four times." with and without accompanying counting) support this notion. One would expect this defining task aspect of vocalization to be required more when instructions are given verbally than when they are given nonverbally (for example by the manual modeling of the correct response). The Soviet excitatory mechanism would predict that vocalization would aid motor performance regardless of how the task instructions are given. Such experiments differentiating these instructions might easily be done.

The verbal response also may be easier to remember than the motor response. Its use may facilitate the motor response initially while the motor response is being learned and maintain it at times of confusion—as Rondal's (1976) data indicates adults spontaneously do—and over time—Birch (1966) indicates that children younger than 4½ have difficulty in maintaining a motor response to an initial verbal command over a period of minutes and

Meacham, Chapter 7, suggests that speech aids preschoolers' memory of action goals. These three memory functions might operate independently of those mechanisms (defining-task or excitatory) that are responsible for the effect. Experiments in which the onset of the vocalizations is varied might be useful in exploring memory effects.

Early Lack of Coordination of Vocal and Motor Responses. • In all of the above discussion of initiating impulsive effects, vocal and motor responses were coordinated. For simple tasks these effects seem to be operating primarily for 4-year-olds, while they are exhibited overtly for increasingly older children and covertly for adults as tasks become more and more difficult. However for each kind of task there is an earlier period during which children seem to have difficulty with coordinated vocal and motor responses. Children respond to the requirement of a vocal and a manual task as if these were two separate acts; the two emissions are either considerably delayed or only one response is given. These results have been found with a wide range of tasks, including: pressing a button for 3-year-olds (Birch, 1971); bulb-squeezing twice for 3- and 4-year-olds (Bronckart, 1973); doing a reverse discrimination task for 3- and 4-year-olds (Van Duyne, 1972); squeezing a clown's nose for 3-year-olds (Wilder, 1968); pushing a button for 4-year-olds (Jarvis, 1964); squeezing a bulb for 3- and 4-year-olds (Miller, Shelton and Flavell, 1970); riding a tricycle forward, backward or stopping it for 3-year-olds (Meacham, 1972*b*); and completing a finger maze for 3- and 4-year-olds (Zivin, 1972). McCabe, Levin, and Wolff (1974) and McCabe (1979) examined the effects of motor acts on speech content. They found that for 4-year-olds, but not for 7-year-olds, manipulation of toys while producing sentences about the manipulations decreased the quality of the sentences relative to those produced in the no-manipulation situation.

Thus it seems quite clear that there is a period during which self-speech is not only not regulating, but is in fact detrimental to some types of motor performance and vice versa. During this period speaking is "just another thing to do," which adds to the task complexity rather than facilitating the motor response. Near the end of this period (which varies by task), vocal and manual responses begin to become coordinated.

Two possible mechanisms have been suggested to account for this early data on noncoordination. Wozniak (1972) suggested that a child's vocalizations create an "orienting reflex," the Soviet label for a generalized nonmodality specific sensitization of the sensory apparatus. This orienting reflex sets the organism to react to incoming sensations and makes it impossible to emit the required motor response. The functioning of this mechanism requires that the verbal response be emitted before the motor response. Some American researchers have found that in younger children the order of response is predominantly motor-verbal, even when instructions stress the opposite order, and that 40% of the verbal responses are omitted, while only about 10% of the motor responses are (Miller, Shelton and Flavell 1970). The orienting reflex mechanism would not be functioning in cases such as these. However Wilder (1968), for example, found that for 3-year-olds the verbal response replaced the motor act. Though most researchers report mean numbers of omitted motor responses and some report at least some figure for omitted vocal responses, practically no one has specifically reported data for the number of trials on which vocal or motor responses alone were given. These are necessary because low mean scores could come from trials in which both responses were omitted. Data reported in the above manner could enable Wozniak's orienting reflex hypothesis to be evaluated. Because the orienting reflex becomes habituated over time, this hypothesis would predict more motor omissions in early trials than in later ones. Thus data should also be reported by time of trial.

The other mechanism proposed to account for this lack of coordination of vocal and manual response, and the frequent omission of one or the other, is an intuitively simple model that Bloor (1977) calls a "limited channel capacity." He argues that the verbal and motor systems should be considered as acting quite independent of each other and as competing for limited channel capacity. Such a mechanism was hinted at by Bronckart when he spoke of a competition between the vocal and manual motor systems (1973, p.434). Such a competition could occur at the control or at the outlet level. The word "channel" implies that Bloor means outlet, that is, a sort of queueing effect in which the responses must take turns in being emitted. Such a notion is in general agreement with the pattern in the preoperational period of centration and alternation rather than simultaneity of actions and thoughts. However a careful reading indicates that Bloor is instead hypothesizing a capacity allocation for each system that involves attention, memory, and decision-making resources. Bloor tests this hypothesis by a two-color light experiment with 7-year-olds, using various combinations of the vocal response (saying "Blue." or "Red.") and the manual response (pushing a blue or a red button). His theory predicts that in the case where the manual and vocal responses disagree, the response not in agreement with the stimulus will require more processing capacity and thus will lead to more errors. This did in fact occur. The problem with this experiment is that the vocal response was ambiguous; a response of "Push blue." would have clearly indicated whether the vocalized color referred to the stimulus light or to the button to be pushed. This experiment also involves a semantic effect with older children, and one might wish for an experiment with the much younger age group in which the lack of coordination is generally found. The notion of a limited processing capacity, if developed further (as Bloor evidently is doing), may prove valuable in understanding the early lack of coordination of the vocal and manual systems.

Mechanisms regarding this early lack of coordination will require evidence concerning the relative speed, strength, and stability of vocal and of manual responses. Present evidence is a bit unclear. A stable system of vocal responses alone seems to be established relatively early. Bronckart (1973) reported that vocal responses showed no perseveration earlier than did bulbpressing responses, and Tikhomirov (1958/1975-1976) reported fewer intersignal vocal than motor responses.

The evidence on the relative speed of vocal and motor responses is contradictory and may depend on the motor response involved. Birch (1971) found vocal responses faster than a manual response of pressing a button five inches from the starting hand position (differences ranged from .3 to 1.5 seconds), while Tikhomirov (1958/1975-1976) reported faster manual bulb presses than vocal responses (differences of .5 and .6 seconds). Wilder and Fogel (1974) failed to report vocal and manual (pressing a telegraph key) times, but reported slower response times on the second block of five trials. In contrast Birch (1971) found equal or faster response times across his three blocks of three trials each; children seemed to improve on his button pressing task. He also found an order effect for the separate vocal and manual responses. When the vocal trials were first, the manual responses were from 1.3 to .6 seconds faster than when the manual trials occurred before the vocal trials; the vocal trials seemed to aid the initiation of a motor response. Future research in this area is required, but it is clear that it will have to be done most carefully, for results are extraordinarily susceptible to procedural influences.

Thus at the present time the results concerning an early lack of coordination of the vocal and manual systems require additional theoretical and empirical work. Even if Wozniak's orienting reflex hypothesis is supported, that will only account for the cases (most likely a minority) in which the vocal response precedes the manual one. We must await further data concerning the specific nature of the order of emission of vocal and manual responses and of patterns of response omission.

Vocalization and the Inhibition of Motor Acts. • Four possible ways in which the Lurian work explicitly or implicitly indicated that speech could inhibit motor acts were outlined earlier. The first of these is one of the two ways involving not emitting a response at all: correctly not emitting a response to a negative stimulus. This necessarily seems to involve some type of semantic control. Moreover as the earlier evidence indicated a rhythmic initiating effect of vocalization for young children, such inhibition possibly requires at younger ages no vocalization at all. Rondal's (1976) finding that a vocalized response of "No." decreased rather than increased responses to the negative stimulus in the critical age range of 3.6 to 4.6 might be taken to indicate the contrary: that a strong semantic content in a vocalization even at a young age can permit the semantic aspect to override the impulsive initiating effect. However "No." is a peculiar—perhaps unique—case of a word that has been paired *so often* with aversive stimuli that it elicits a sort of startle or hesitation as no other word(s) probably can. Thus this result cannot tell us much about general effects of verbalization in this age range.

Children seem to be able to exercise some inhibitory control from stored "When—then" instructions even at a fairly young age. Beiswenger (1968) with a lever press (rather than a more traditional bulb squeeze) and with no selfverbalizations found 59% correct for 3½- to 4½-year-olds, 89% for 4½- to 5½-year-olds and 96% for 5½- to 6½-year-olds. He also found that children responded to a single new instruction reversing the positive and negative lights with the same high level of performance as on the original command. As described earlier Luria reported a 58% inhibitory rate for 3- and 4-year-olds. Miller, Shelton, and Flavell (1970) reported a similiar figure in the silent condition for 3-year-olds (about 85%). Their subjects were pretrained, however, so these figures may be unusually high. In any case even children as young as 3 years seem to be able to exercise some considerable inhibitory control over the emission of motor acts without overt self-verbalization.

Both speech reinforcement from an adult with each trial and practice on a ten-second delay task can enable children who were unable to inhibit responses on a verbal instruction to do so. Paramonova (reported in Yakovleva, 1975-1976, and Tikhomirov, 1958/1975-1976) accompanied each positive and negative signal with the proper verbalization ("Squeeze." and "Don't squeeze."). This enabled 3- and 4-year-olds who could not previously respond regularly to respond correctly very quickly (usually in two or three positive responses and three or four negative responses). Golden, Montare, and Bridge (1977) used tasks that required a response to a delayed signal (that is, a temporary inhibition of the initiation of a motor act). They found that a five-minute training period involving practicing waiting to get a block until the children heard a whistle (after a 10-second delay) increased the extent to which 24- and 30-month-old boys followed verbal instructions.

The one mechanism that would seem to account for the inhibition to a negative stimulus of motor acts is Bloor's (1977) very clear explication of a mechanism postulated by Luria in an early work (1932) and one which, Bloor argues, still shows itself implicitly in some of Luria's work. This mechanism is the "functional barrier" which controls, by the opening and closing of "gates," the expression of diffuse excitation from the sensory system that has been diverted into the verbal system. As noted earlier, the verbalization of the instruction (as opposed to instruction by physical modeling for example) may also serve to maintain in memory the conditions under which the response should be inhibited. It is unclear just how useful the "functional barrier " is in understanding verbal control over inhibition of motor acts. What it does imply is that some decision point can be inserted prior to the emission of a motor act. This decision point is less effective if the cues are non-existent or if contradictory information is perceptually present, such as in a game of "Simon Says" where the non-cued actions are modeled by the leader (Strommen, 1973). The existence of such a decision point does have considerable import for the possibilities of helping young children learn to emit vocalizations that can help them inhibit certain motor behaviors. Many parents have seen 2-year-olds spontaneously self-instruct themselves "No." as they reach for a light cord or some other forbidden fruit. My daughter avoided many accidents between the ages of 3½ and 4½ by instructing herself intently as she went tearing through the house toward the bathroom, "Don't go. Don't go." Such potential uses of self-verbalizations in the inhibition of motor responses have gone unresearched. The training research on impulsive children (reviewed in another section) is an exception, but even there the potential of self-verbalizations is examined only with a special population. The potential of self-regulating speech for ordinary children in their ordinary home, play, and school lives has not really been tapped.

Type II A 2, (see p. 176) "Not emitting a response in the absence of a stimulus (inhibiting responses independent of any signal)" has not been systematically investigated. Intersignal intervals have been so short that either there is virtually no time for such independent responses or such responses are so close to the signal that they are interpreted as perseverative responses. Operational definitions differentiating these independent responses from perseverative ones would probably be fairly difficult to make, though one or two responses considerably after the signal and during a long intersignal interval would probably fit this case. In any case, this category of response is likely to remain more a logical possiblity than a phenomenon of important developmental significance.

The second major type of inhibition is the inhibition of an ongoing response. The most frequently discussed type is "Not emitting continued responses to one stimulus (preservation)". The Lurian work places a major emphasis on perseverating responses. Several different experiments examine alternative ways of eliminating perseverative responses. These include speech from the experimenter, speech from the child, the signal light going off with the bulb press, a bell that rings when the bulb is pressed, and adding a motor task (putting the hand on the knee) immediately after the bulb is pressed. This emphasis on perseverative responses and the tone in which they are discussed leads one to believe that perseverative responses are a general developmental phenomenon and that most children exhibit them. Western researchers have found a much lower rate of perseverations (Bronckart, 1973; Wilder, 1968), with Rondal (1976) and Wozniak (in a personal communication) finding about a rate of 20%. Because data are reported by trial rather than by child, it is not clear whether all children emit a few perseverative responses or whether there are perseverators and nonperseverators. Wozniak seems to have found the latter (in a personal communication). Miller, Shelton and Flavell (1970) report an even lower initial rate under the silent condition (15% for 3-yearolds and 5% for 4-year-olds), but these data are from subjects who had already undergone a training/practice period. The difference in perseveration figures may come from two sources. Much of the Lurian work was done at the Institute of Defectology. The backgrounds of the subjects are never described, though Yakovleva (1975-1976) does describe her subjects as coming from a day-care center. Thus the Soviet subjects may have included more than an average number of children with neurological problems. The Soviets also focused on younger children (including age 1½ and 2) than have the Western studies. One would expect more perseverative responders in this younger age group.

Whatever the "normal" rate of perseveration is at different age levels, it seems likely that the continuous tactile-kinaesthetic stimulation from the bulb makes the number of perseverations higher than that for experiments that use a button or foot press, for example. Thus a substantial proportion of even the lower amount of perseveration reported in Western replications may be largely due to the particular motor response involved. Experiments which compare the number of perseverators (a more important developmental measure than number of perseverations) at various age levels on tasks that provide continuous tactile-kinaesthetic contact with the subject and those which do not, would help to establish the general developmental importance of the perseverative response for theorists who (unlike the Soviets) do not hold a primary belief in the developmental need to refine diffuse neurological irradiations (supposedly reflected in perseverations) in order for motor actions to be mastered.

There are at least four mechanisms that could account for data on the elimination of perseverative responses. Because these mechanisms may bear somewhat more generally on the development of other aspects of self-regulating speech, they will be outlined briefly. In general there is some evidence to support each mechanism, but no definitive work corroborating one to the exclusion of others; it is quite possible that each operates to eliminate perseverative responses only under particular circumstances.

The first mechanism is one involving external "feedback" afferentiation, or an "auxiliary afferent impulse" (Tikhomirov, 1975-1976 p. 55). Wozniak (1972) describes this mechanism more clearly than do either Luria or Tokhomirov. This mechanism depends on what Anokhin (1961) called the "acceptor-of-effect," a stored representation of the desired response against which the emitted response is checked. If the emitted response matches the desired response, further responses are inhibited. Below a certain age, the emitted response of a press on the bulb is not sufficiently specific to match the desired response, and some additional external response is required for the child to *know* that the desired response was emitted. Speech from experimenter, speech from the child, the extinguishing of a light, and the ringing of a bell—all function to provide such external afferentiation (Yakovleva, 1975-1976; Tikhomirov, 1958/1975-1976). The barking of a toy dog can also function successfully in this manner (Rondal, 1976). Thus either audio or visual feedback will do. This implies that it is the audio portion of a child's vocalizations rather than the motor act of speaking that is responsible for this self-regulation (elimination of perseverative responses). This feedback mechanism requires that the child understand the desired response, that is that he be able to store some representation of this response and that this representation be remembered over time.

A second mechanism that may be operating in some of these experiments is one described earlier with respect to vocalizations and impulsive effects: the vocalizations, light going off, and bell-ringing may serve to model and define the desired response "Press once to each signal." The young child may not understand "once" or he may not understand "to each signal;" the external responses may model each of these. An additional means of adding meaning to the pressing act may be operating in the light experiment: children are told to "Press the bulb and put out the light" (Yakovleva, 1975-1976). By imbedding the pressing act in a meaningful activity, both understanding and motivation may be raised. Experiments that use imaginative stories in which the pressing act is made both meaningful and also the cause of an effect without external feedback could determine whether meaning or the acceptor-of-effect is primarily operating in these experiments.

The third mechanism emphasizes the role of the orienting reflex. Wozniak (1972) argues that the vocalizations, the bell ringing, and the visual stimulus of the light going off create an orienting reflex (defined earlier) that is responsible for the elimination of perseverative responses. Evidently both the speaking act and the audio portion of the vocalization can create such an orienting reflex. Alterations in skin conductance and digital vasoconstriction indicated that adult females (males were not tested) who, after hearing a tone, counted silently to twenty and then mouthed, said silently, or said aloud "Go." gave orienting responses to both the mouthed and the spoken word, but not to the covertly produced word (Wozniak, Acredolo, and Peterson, 1973). The median number of trials to habituation was 7 for the mouthing condition and 17.5 for the vocalization condition, indicating two different orienting mechanisms—one stemming from the movement (mouthing) alone and the other stemming from the acoustic effect of actual verbalization. Preliminary results indicate the same two effects in 7-year-old girls (Wozniak, 1976). Wozniak's argument that the orienting reflex eliminates perseverative responses is fairly convincing. As before, because the orienting reflex habituates, experiments that report the course of perseverations over trials are needed. Because perseverations only on later trials might also be due to forgetting of the desired response, some control over this factor should be included in the design.

The fourth mechanism (also described by Wozniak, 1972) applies to the experiments in which a child is told to put his hand on his knee immediately after his squeeze. This second response is gradually faded until the child merely squeezes the bulb. This method is successful in eliminating perseverative responses. The mechanism is a Pavlovian one: the excitation from the second motor response is a competing sensation for the motor pathway and thus results in the inhibition of the further responses of the first kind. Presumably the force of a direct instruction to emit the second response is stronger than the perseverative effect stemming from the first response. The effect of vocalizations by the child may also be due to this mechanism, particularly if responses are frequently emitted in the motor-vocal (that is squeeze precedes words) order as American researchers seem to report.

This mechanism may have considerable practical import for helping children learn to regulate their behavior through their own speech. For example on a foot-press task with kindergarten children, Meichenbaum and Goodman (1969) reported that overt repetition of "Don't push." for impulsive children and both overt and covert repetition for reflective children were equally successful in inhibiting foot presses, but covert repetition of "Don't push." by impulsive children resulted in a higher number of pushes to the negative stimulus. That the impulsive children actually produced the covert responses is uncertain, but impulsive 5-year-olds do seem to require either the speaking or the hearing of the words for their meaning to be effective in this situation. That it was the motor act of vocalization that inhibited the foot seems likely. This procedure will not work with children who are able to coordinate their motor and vocal responses, but it may prove quite powerful with young or with developmentally delayed children. This mechanism also reflects a phenomenon of which many parent are aware, that it is easier to redirect a child to a new desired activity than to get him simply to stop an undesirable one. A study that verified this phenomenon with respect to a child's own speech was done by Meacham (1972*b*). He found that for 3-, 4- and 5-year-old children who followed "Go forward.", "Go backward." and "Stop." commands from a tape (or repeated the command as well as executing it), intervals containing verbal activity contained more appropriate motor activity and contained more changes from inappropriate to appropriate activity. More to the present point, he found that it was easier for a child to shift from doing an old activity to doing a new activity than it was to simply stop the old activity.

The final type of inhibition in the Lurian work is II B b: "Ending a response while still sensing the stimulus (for example emitting a short squeeze to a long light.)" Vocalizations by children seem to enable them to accomplish this type of inhibition (Tikhomirov, 1958/1975-1976). The acceptor-of-effect, the orienting reflex, or the defining-task mechanisms described earlier, all would seem to account for this phenomenon. Bronckart

(1973) has reported the most detailed research on this phenomenon and reports data and an explanation differing from the Soviet ones. He found that vocalization enabled only the younger subjects (3- and young 4-year-olds) to emit a short squeeze, while for children 5 years and older, even vocalizers emitted a squeeze of the same length as the stimulus light. Bronckart's explanation was that the vocalization condition was more difficult than the silent condition for the younger children, and their squeeze was delayed until the stimulus light had gone off; thus there was no reason for them to emit a long squeeze. Simultaneous squeezing and vocalizing was easier for the 5-year-olds, however, and the squeeze was emitted at the beginning of the stimulus and continued until the light went off. Bronckart's explanation of the Lurian phenomenon may prove to be correct but may not be very helpful in explaining performance on other tasks. Further data with varied kinds of stimuli are needed to determine under what conditions and to what extent self-speech can regulate motor behaviors which are at variance with the stimulus. Some of Rondal's (1976) more difficult tasks might provide a good starting point for such experiments.

A Methodological Note

A detailed methodological analysis of the Lurian work and the germane Western research is beyond the scope of this paper (see Wozniak, 1972; Bronckart, 1973; and Bloor, 1977). The single point to be made here concerns the utility of American studies in evaluating the validity of the Soviet findings and hypotheses. That utility has been limited both by methodological variations that reduce the comparability of the studies and by a failure to report certain details that would increase the information gained from these studies.

First, in the Western studies in which the subjects received pretraining or practice trials, performance on such practice trials typically is not reported, even though this data is of potential interest: if one is interested in the selfregulating abilities of speech, then one is certainly interested in how difficult it is for a child to learn to perform correctly in various vocalizing conditions in addition to how well a child continues this accurate performance over trials. For example the 3- and 4-year-old subjects in Miller, Shelton and Flavell (1970) had from 6 to 21 practice trials. Certain distributions of low and of high numbers of trials over the vocalizing conditions would support parts of the Lurian effects, while other distributions would not. Results of all trials should be reported in future research, even if researchers wish to differentiate between trials in which subjects are learning the response (that is in which they may not have understood it or may not have been able to emit it).

Second , the distribution of different kinds of errors by trial across *all* trials needs to be reported, for different distributions will support different mechanisms. For example a silent condition and a condition in which the vocalization is rhythmically isomorphic to the motor response might both have the same number of omitted motor responses, but the silent omissions might fall heavily near the end of the trials, while the vocalizing omissions might fall near the beginning. Such a pattern, undetectable from a single mean statistic, would imply that the motor act alone is simpler to learn but more susceptible to forgetting, relative to the vocalizing condition. Knowing this kind of information about various kinds of motor tasks at various ages would enable training procedures to be used that were geared to the conditions of the motor response desired. The Western papers typically report neither condition differences during training nor trial by trial data. Thus the reported disconfirmations of the Soviet work are as unconvincing as most of these investigators evidently find the Soviet work to be.

Conclusion

The overall developmental picture provided by this research is one of an initial lack of coordination of the vocal and motor systems, with speech being an extra thing to do. When the speaking and motor systems become coordinated (around 4 or 5 years of age), vocalization that is rhythmically isomorphic to the desired motor response can aid motor performance. A year or so later the semantic content of words begins to become more powerful than their rhythmic patterns; vocalization and motor actions again diverge, with the semantic content of the words rather than the rhythmic aspect being more able to regulate the motor act.

Semantic control of motor acts has been little studied. An example of a study on this transition period is Meichenbaum and Goodman (1969). They found that when children spoke the word "Faster." and "Slower." while emitting hand taps, the rate varied with the meaning of the word. Impulsive kindergarten children demonstrated an impulsive-motoric relationship between the words and taps, saying one word with each tap; reflective children exhibited a more semantic relationship, saying one word every several taps. More studies of the semantic potential for regulation of motor acts would be useful, particularly if these motor acts are ordinary and not laboratory ones. However Rondal's (1976) more difficult experiments indicate that older children and even adults use the rhythmic aspects of speech to regulate their motor behavior. Thus, as is true for many other developmental patterns, the ages at which the divergence-convergence-divergence pattern (that is, no control/divergence rhythmic control/semantic control) described above seem to vary with specific tasks. Moreover the final divergence (semantic control) refers to the potential ability of speech at that time and does not indicate that the earlier patterns will not occur (one can think of fiendishly difficult vocalizations and motor acts that would push adults back to the first divergent state). In particular it may be that the rhythmic aspects of speech are particularly suited for the regulation of motor acts, while semantic regulating effects occur predominantly in cognitive rather than motor acts. Tasks which involve both motor and cognitive action might be a particularly fruitful area to research. This author has observed that some school tasks, such as printing letters ("Up-down-up." for an N) and adding large numbers ("Bring down the 2 and carry the 1.") elicit spontaneous self-regulating speech. Teaching children self-regulating speech for some of these tasks might better help them learn and remember these sequences of motor acts.

On the negative side one is struck by the lack of articulated theoretical perspectives, by the nonanalytical examination of general rather than specific regulatory effects of vocalization, and by the extraordinary narrowness of the tasks used in the research on relationships between speech and motor acts. The best this body of research has to offer empirically at present is some fairly uniform evidence concerning both the positive rhythmic initiating effect of vocalization, particularly in somewhat difficult tasks, and the positive effect of vocalization (as well as of nonvocal means) in eliminating perseverative responses. A number of different mechanisms have been identified that may be responsible for different self-regulating effects. These have been described above, and some experiments which might support the existence of particular mechanisms have been suggested. If future research on the relationships between speech and motor acts is to have any theoretical import, any generalizable significance, it must stem from a specified theoretical perspective and focus on specific effects.

A second major attribute of this body of research, in which regulating words are supplied to the child, is its almost complete remove from motor acts children ordinarily (or even occasionally) do. Meacham's (1972*b*) research on the effects of a child's speech on following commands while riding a bicycle is a notable exception. Future research that uses tasks more familiar and natural to children might find different, and probably more important or central, effects of self-regulating speech. It would certainly prevent the generation of a whole body of research on effects that are largely a result only of specific characteristics of some laboratory task, such as the bulb press.

Self-Regulating Speech in Nonmotor Tasks

The motor task research reviewed above was done within the context of self-regulating speech, that is, it was designed explicitly to determine the effects of speech on motor behavior. There is a very large body of developmental research in other areas (for example memory and verbal learning, perception, motivation) that contains some results pertinent to self-regulating speech, but in which the question of effects of verbalization or of vocalization is ordinarily not a directly addressed central issue. In some of these areas (for example memory and verbal learning) the role of verbalization is assumed to be large, but its exact nature is usually inferred rather than directly examined. Thus a thorough discussion of possible roles of verbalization in nonmotor tasks would entail descriptions of current theoretical explications of these roles in order to supplement the often sparse amounts of empirical evidence concerning these roles.

The relative lack of data that directly concern the role of verbalization is not simply a matter of neglect. Studying these roles is made enormously difficult by the fact that just as the semantic aspect of vocalization begins to exercise considerable control over behavior, speaking becomes internalized as covert speech. Thus it is difficult to create a no-verbalization condition, for one cannot control covert speech processes; moreover the semantic content of covert speech cannot be measured, so one also can only rarely be confident that a covert-verbalization condition was in fact such a condition.

Because a thorough theoretical, empirical, and methodological discussion in this area is beyond the scope of this paper, this section will be limited to two parts. In the first part some issues involved in the spontaneous production and effectiveness of verbalizations will be discussed and some illustrative examples given. In the second part some ways in which verbalization seems to affect behavior will be outlined and then briefly related to natural self-regulating speech. The reader should keep in mind that the effects of verbalizations in this research vary greatly with the particular task and particular type of verbalization. There is no single effect of verbalization or effect of vocalization. Most of the examples will be from the area of verbal learning and memory, for this area contains the broadest range of effects. Examples from other areas will be brought in where they seem useful.

Issues in the Effectiveness of and Production of Verbalizations

Three deficiencies of young children with respect to effectiveness or production of verbalizations have been discussed in the literature. These are a mediational deficiency, a production deficiency, and what we shall call a continued-use deficiency. A mediational deficiency is inferred whenever a verbal response does not mediate between external stimuli and overt responses. A production deficiency refers to occurences in which a child has available a potentially effective verbalization, but fails to produce it in a situation in which it would be helpful to do so. A continued-use deficiency occurs when a child has been successfully instructed or trained to produce a verbalization that is effective and then fails to continue to produce the verbalization when no longer constrained to do so.

Mediational deficiencies have been noted for years, and as long ago as 1946 Kuenne proposed that there was a developmental stage in which a verbalization did not control or influence a child's overt choice behavior on transposition tasks. In studies in which verbalizations were required, such verbalizations were at times at variance with the child's behavior. For example some 3- and 4-year-olds trained to say "White wins, black loses." on an initial discrimination task continued with the (now incorrect) verbalization on the subsequent reversal task while performing correctly on the reversal task (Kendler, 1964). This effect seems very similar to that found with motor acts: there is a period during which the verbal and motor streams are independent. However Reese (1962) reviewed much of the early evidence with respect to the existence of this developmental level, which he termed the "mediational deficiency hypothesis" He suggested that this deficiency might characterize an early stage of concept formation rather than a distinct developmental stage. That is, with a verbal concept that is not well established, a mediational deficiency may occur at any age. The subsequent findings that the effectiveness of a verbalization is strongly task-and-verbalization-dependent (for a review see Stevenson,1972) support Reese's view. This view also has certain face validity: the semantic content of a verbalization can only be expected to influence behavior if that content is understood. Young children possess fewer well-understood concepts than older children; thus one would expect to find verbalizations that are effective for older children and not for younger ones. Thus in research on self-regulating speech one would expect that there might be experimenter—provided speech that would not regulate the child's behavior and there may even be some spontaneously uttered speech that is relatively ineffective as well.

The term production dificiency was first used in a paper by Flavell, Beach, and Chinsky (1966). In that study spontaneous rehearsals of picture labels were recorded during an interval between presentation and test. Of 20 children at each grade level, 18 kindergarten children, compared to 8 second-graders and 3 fifth-graders, exhibited no verbalization at all. These results, combined with those from a later study (Keeney, Cannizzo, and Flavell, 1967) which indicated that 6- and 7-year-olds can easily be trained to rehearse in this task and that such rehearsal increases their recall scores to a level equal to that of spontaneous rehearsers, ruled out a mediation deficiency in favor of a production deficiency for the younger children.

The notion of a production deficiency changed the interpretation of some of the early literature on the mediational deficiency. Many early researchers did not require verbalizations on test trials, but did assume that children were verbalizing. They interpreted age differences as indicating a mediational deficiency. This was true, for example, in the early reversal-nonreversal shift studies, such as Kendler and Kendler (1959). Silverman (1966) had children aged 3 to 4 and 7 to 8 label the dimension relevant to the shift on the reversal trials and found no age differences in performance. The poorer reversal performance of younger children in some of the earlier literature probably reflected production rather than mediational deficiencies. As Flavell, Beach and Chindey (1966) pointed out, one needs to know that a verbalization was actually produced before one can infer its ineffectiveness as a mediator.

The simple view of the developmental relationship between verbal mediation and production is that a verbalization is at first not effective; then it becomes effective; but not produced appropriately; and then it becomes produced appropriately as well. This description may be accurate for simple verbal strategies or for ones which become very effective quite rapidly (as verbal rehearsal seems to do, for example). However a Kendler study (1972) indicates that for strategies that more gradually reach a high level of effectiveness, mediational and production deficiencies are likely to coexist for a long time, and each will follow its own path to extinction. Kendler used a mediated transfer paradigm that examined whether verbal labels associated with particular patterns would elicit the motor responses which had previously been paired with those labels in two other patterns. Kindergarten, second-grade, fourth-grade, and college subjects did this task under either an overt-label condition or a no-overt-label condition. Performance at all ages was superior in the overt-label condition. Her results indicated that the mediational deficiency in this task dropped rapidly from kindergarten (40%) to second grade (20%) and disappeared by fourth grade, but that the production deficiency was operative at the 50% level through fourth grade and dropped to the 20% level at college. Future research on either of these deficiencies should include designs and analyses that are capable of considering this type of more complex relationship.

Research on a delay-of-gratification task indicates that providing a cue as to when to produce a verbalization will increase the effective use of the verbalization. Patterson, et al., (forthcoming) found when preschoolers were given a temptation-inhibiting verbalization, those given either an external cue ("When Mr. Clown Box tries to distract you.") or an internal cue ("When you think to look at Mr. Clown Box.") for when to emit this verbalization displayed greater self-control than children given the verbalization, but no such cues. The superiority of a task-continuing verbalization plus a cue was repeated in a boring marble-dropping task (Patterson, et al., forthcoming). Thus research on self-regulating speech might examine the power of providing children with cues as well as with regulating verbalizations and might explore the effectiveness of providing or of helping children to determine cues which children might use with their own self-generated regulating verbalizations. In naturalistic situations, such as the home or school, production deficiencies may be avoided to some extent by the presence of an observant mother who will know the strategies of which the child is capable and who will cue him by questions, reminders, and so on, to produce the strategy that he possesses.

Results concerning the continued-use deficiency have implications for training children in the use of regulating verbalizations, for they indicate that a successful use of a verbalization is not necessarily enough to indicate that a child will voluntarily continue to use the verbalization. In the study described in the section on the production deficiency (Keeney Cannizzo, and Flavell, 1967), 6- and 7-year-olds who did not spontaneously rehearse picture names were trained to do so; their recall scores rose to match those of the spontaneous rehearsers. After the 10 induced-rehearsal trials, 3 trials were given in which the children were no longer explicitly instructed to rehearse. Ten of the seventeen induced-rehearsal subjects failed to rehearse on these trials, that is though the strategy was effective, children did not continue to use it—they failed to reproduce the strategy in the same situation in which they had been using it.

Belmont and Butterfield (1977) discuss continued-use deficiencies (they do not use this term) in the context of the durability of instructional effects. They review studies in which such deficiencies occurred with retarded subjects (Brown, Campione, and Murphy, 1974; Butterfield and Belmont, 1972; Wanschura and Borkowski, 1975). Butterfield and Belmont (1972) found that only the subjects who continued to use the strategy at the post-test had had their performance improved during training (when all subjects were using the strategy); that is, very sensibly, those for whom the strategy improved their performance continued to use it while others did not. Whether or not this simple explanation applies more generally is at present unclear. Other researchers report only group data, so one is unable to separate characteristics of those who did and those who did not continue to use the verbalization. It is clear that within-subject comparisons are obviously required in future studies on continued-use deficiencies.

The research regarding these three types of deficiencies raises some interesting research questions for spontaneous self-regulating speech. The mediational deficiency raises the question of whether private speech uttered by young children is truly regulating or whether it is merely epiphenomenal, that is, a relatively functionless accompaniment to activity. In contrast, the production and continued-use deficiencies create the possibility that children could use speech for self-regulation earlier and to a greater extent than they spontaneously do.

Some Effects of Verbalizations

Several effects of verbalizations will be discussed briefly. They are presented as distinct effects for the purpose of discussion. In actuality they frequently occur together, and measuring the existence of, or controlling for, undesired effects from each of them presents difficult methodological problems.

A General Attentional Effect. • Vocalization seems to improve the performance of young children on some kinds of tasks even when the semantic content of the vocalization is incongruent with the referent of the vocalization. For example Bush and Cohen (1970) found recall of colored cards by preschoolers when either relevant (color names) or irrelevant (animal names) labels were applied to the color patches. Brooks (1971) found improved performance for children as young as 3½ years with either congruous or incongruous phrases in a task requiring the recognition of pictures as old or new. Researchers describe these effects of vocalization as a general attentional effect. It is clear that the effect is not a semantic one. But the source of this increase in attending to the task is not clear. It might be due to the motor act of speaking or to an orienting reflex to the vocalization (that is to the sound of the vocalization). If it is the latter, one would expect the improvement in performance to extinguish over trials or one might expect a similar effect from another acoustic stimulus (a bell or the experimenter's vocalization). The separate sources of this attention effect might be examined in future research. This attentional effect of vocalization (whatever its mechanism is) may be the crucial advantage of overt rather than covert self-regulating speech in adults as well as in children.

An Indicative Effect. • The semantic content of a verbalization can direct attention to certain stimuli and away from others. This effect is similar to the act of pointing. It is an effect that operates frequently during communicative speech when one is trying to regulate the behavior of others. This effect presumably is operating in most studies when a child stores and then acts upon the initial instructions of the experimenter. Its role in self-regulation has been less studied. This effect has been demonstrated in experiments in which children labeled the central stimulus; such labeling reduced the amount of incidental learning (Dusek, 1978; Hagen and Hale, 1973; Wheeler and Dusek, 1973). Dusek (1978) found that this labeling effect on incidental learning was similar to the effect of pointing to the central stimulus.

Determining Relevant Attributes. • One of the chief semantic effects of verbalization is in facilitating identification of the attributes of a problem situation that are relevant to the problem solution. This positive effect of experimenter-provided and subject-emitted labels has been observed in many different kinds of tasks. Soviet researchers have found that verbal labels enable young preschool children to make discriminations among complex patterns (for example on butterfly wings) that older preschool children without such labels could only rarely distinguish (Liublinskaya, 1964). Positive effects of labels have been reported by American researchers in enabling preschoolers to recall color patches difficult to describe (Bernbach,

1967); for modifying first-graders' attention to particular elements of pictures (Bacharach, Carr, and Mehner, 1976); for kindergarten children's performance on the initial discrimination and later reversal shift (Kendler, 1964); for picture recognition performance by 4-year-olds (Ward and Legant, 1971); for visual-temporal discrimination—one light flash versus two light flashes—(Blank, 1974); and for discriminating, remembering, and classifying by shape by 3- and 5-year-olds (Nelson, 1976). This effect may be operating to a considerable extent in spontaneous self-regulating speech also. The large amount of spontaneously uttered speech, which described task materials and details of the task solution (Beaudichon, 1973; Fuson, Householder, and Urbaska, forthcoming), might well be a part of the child's process of determining the relevant attributes of the task situation.

Modifying Cognitions about, or Representations of, a Task or Task Situation. • Covert or overt use of verbalizations can prolong both the length of time a child is willing to work on a simple task as well as to wait for a promised reward. Instructions to self-induce positive affect states ("Think fun thoughts.", "Repeat your happy statement whenever the lights go out.") enable 3- through 8-year-olds to wait for a preferred reward, to work longer on a repetitive task, and to increase their resistance to a forbidden toy (Fry, 1975; Mischel, Ebbesen, and Zeiss, 1972; Masters and Santrock, 1976; Moore, Clyburn, and Underwood, 1976; Santrock, 1976). Other types of verbalizations by children in delay-of-gratification situations can shorten or lengthen the delay period, probably as a result of a combination of modification of the child's representation of the task situation, of attention, and of memory for the task goal. The use of temptation-inhibiting or reward-oriented verbalizations by preschoolers enabled them to resist the lure and task-distraction of a talking toy longer than children who gave task-oriented or no verbalizations (Mischel and Patterson, 1976, forthcoming; Patterson and Mischel, 1975, 1976). Verbalizations which emphasize the immediacy or the reinforcing characteristics of rewards shorten the delay period (Mischel and Baker, 1975; Mischel and Moore, 1973; Mischel and Underwood, 1974; Mischel and Patterson, 1976; Moore, Mischel, and Zeiss, 1976; Toner and Smith, 1977). A study by Kanfer and Zich (1974) indicates that it is the hearing of the semantic content of the verbalizations that is probably responsible for the above effects, for hearing a tape recording either of their own voice or the experimenter's voice emphasizing the positive consequences of nontransgression was equally effective in delaying 5- and 6-year-olds from looking at a surprise.

Somewhat surprisingly, instructions to think about the experimental conditions in certain ways can over-ride the actual conditions. Preschoolers instructed to think about absent rewards had a significantly shorter delay period than control subjects (Mischel and Moore, 1973), a result similar to that for behavior in the actual presence of rewards. In an experiment resulting from the finding that the presence of a picture of a reward increases rather than decreases the delay period (Mischel and Moore, 1973), preschoolers were assigned to one of four conditions involving all possibilities of reward-present/picture-present and think-of-the-stimulus-as-a-picture (Moore, Mischel, and Zeiss, 1976). The think instructions superseded the actual experimental condition, with thinking of the picture as the actual reward decreasing the delay period. For more details of the above studies and of other studies having to do with the effects of verbalization on children's self-control, see Pressley (forthcoming).

Verbalization can aid in representing the end state or the desired solution to a problem. Bem (1970) called this possessing an adequate understanding of the "problem as solved." Some types of experiments with children use verbal instructions that implicitly (and sometimes explicitly) contain a verbalization concerning the "problem as solved." Usually however the child must make this inference for himself. Using a condition in which children were asked to describe their end-goal, this is their view of their problem as solved, would be one way to examine possible facilitative effects of such a verbal representation. Such a representation might be provided to those children who could not describe it themselves. With younger children the form of this verbal representation will probably be important. In the section on verbalization and motor acts, it was pointed out that the rhythmic form of the vocalization can serve as a representation of the desired motor act. The order of the words is also important to young children. With respect to semantic content 3- and 4year-olds apparently can follow verbal instructions only if the order of the words parallels the order of the required action sequence (Beiswenger, 1969). Five-, 7-, and 9-year-olds can place an object representing the grammatical subject of a statement more easily than one for the grammatical object (Huttenlocher and Strauss, 1968), and fourth-graders could place the logical subject of the sentence more easily even though it was the grammatical object (Huttenlocher, Eisenberg, and Strauss, 1968).

Spontaneous utterances which modify cognitions about or representations of a situation were frequently found in Fuson, Householder, and Urbaska, forthcoming). These utterances occurred in fantasy play with plastic people and served as perceptual supports for objects or actions which did not fully or unambiguously represent what the child had decided they would represent (for example "This is the mother.", "They are sisters.", "They're playing ball.", "They're going to school."). This type of regulation of fantasy play is extremely common and may be one of the most important regulating functions that speech serves in early childhood. "Saying it, makes it so." may be more true of this period than of any other period of life. Sometimes speech may actually not regulate a child's behavior by adapting it to fit the constraints of the world, but may instead adapt the world to fit the behavior of the child.

Rehearsing to Aid Memory. • A major way in which verbalization aids memory is by rehearsal of to-be-remembered items. One presumed function of this rehearsal is to keep items in short-term memory (Atkinson and Shiffrin, 1968). This is a useful function both for brief retention of a few items and for maintaining the items so that more elaborate processing for long retention is facilitated (Craik and Lockhart, 1972).

There seems to be a fairly clear developmental pattern in rehearsal. Children aged 4 and 5 spontaneously and overtly produce picture labels (Locke and Fehr, 1970). In fact children as young as 3 years evidently produce (covertly) verbal associative responses to words presented for memory (Hall and Halperin, 1972); such verbalizations are presumed to occur more or less automatically. However preschool children evidently do not deliberately engage in item repetition to enhance their memory, and even many 6- and 7-year-olds do not spontaneously rehearse items (Locke and Fehr, 1970; Keeney, Cannizzo, and Flavell, 1967; Flavell, Beach and Chinsky, 1966; Daehler, et al., 1969; Kingsley and Hagen, 1969; Hagen, Hargrave, and Ross, 1973). When spontaneous rehearsal does begin, it moves with age from repetition of only the given stimulus item to a serial repetition of previously presented items along with the given stimulus item. For example on a recall task of 18 unrelated items, third-graders rehearsed only a mean of 2.5 items together, while sixth- and eighth-graders rehearsed between 4.0 and 4.5 items together (Orenstein, Naus, and Liberty, 1975). This developmental progression means that an instruction to verbalize in a particular way may facilitate performance (for children who have a production deficiency for that verbalization) or may hinder performance (if that verbalization prevents the use of a more effective verbalization).

The use of overt or covert rehearsal to aid memory would seem to be one way in which children and adults spontaneously regulate themselves. The laboratory nature of most memory tasks may underestimate the ability of young children to use speech in this way. Istomina (1975) for example reported that recall by 3- and 4-year-olds who went to buy items at a pretend store was double that of children in the standard laboratory recall situation.

Aiding Encoding and Retrieval Processes in Memory. • Verbalizations of various kinds seem to aid encoding and retrieval processes in memory. As with rehearsal, different verbalizations seem to be effective at different ages. Separating the effects of verbalization on encoding from those on retrieval is a difficult problem, and there is at present little research that indicates clear-cut effects of verbalization on one as opposed to the other.

Simple naming or labeling a stimulus item seems to have a facilitative effect. Labeling the central stimulus facilitated central learning for third through seventh-graders, while simply pointing to it did not (Dusek, 1978). Naming the target pictures facilitated memory performance for nursery school children on a delayed (20 sec.) picture recognition task in which rehearsal was made impossible by a conversation with the experimenter (Ward and Legant, 1971). Naming items in a serial recall task increases performance on the recency positions, but this effect is assumed to be an effect on short-term memory alone (Hagen and Kingsley, 1968).

As children become capable of using more sophisticated verbalizations and verbal relations in the aid of memory, simple naming decreases rather than increases performance, for it interferes with the use of these more powerful types of verbalizations. Examples of these more sophisticated verbal effects are verbal elaboration and the use of category labels. Verbal elaboration in the form of a sentence about the interaction of two unrelated stimulus words enhances paired-associate learning in children 6 years and older (Rohwer, 1973). The use of category labels either before presentation of a word list containing categorizable items or before recall seems to aid the recall only of children above about age 10 (Kobasigawa and Middleton, 1972; Nelson, 1969; Rossi, 1964; Williams and Goulet, 1975).

The relatively late effectiveness of category labels seems to be related to difficulties younger children have with category organization rather than to the use of labels per se. Presenting category names as retrieval cues seems to have a positive effect on recall, though in most studies the effect of being given the category name is confounded with that of exhaustive search of category, which also aids recall (Eysenck and Baron, 1974; Hall and Madsen, 1978; Halperin, 1974; Kobasigawa, 1974; Lange, 1973; and Scribner and Cole, 1972).

The facilitative effect on memory of naming or labeling may be one of the chief impetuses for, or benefits of, that fairly considerable portion of spontaneously uttered self-regulating speech in young children that consists of labeling or describing things. The more sophisticated verbal strategies may be used by older elementary-school-aged children to aid them in the considerable demands on memory placed by many school tasks.

ISSUES IN LEARNING SELF-REGULATING SPEECH

This paper has reviewed a substantial amount of data and theory on the amount and type of self-regulating speech that children produce spontaneously and a large amount of literature on the relationships between verbalization and both motor and nonmotor acts. This section considers questions concerning the origins of self-regulating speech. There is very little research on how children learn self-regulating speech. Most of the research that does exist is with special populations of children.

The Soviets—especially Vygotsky, (1934/1962; forthcoming)—hypothesize that the development of self-regulating speech moves from the interpsychological plane to the intrapsychological plane. This movement is modeled in Table 1 (p. 138) by a movement from the top row (source of regulating speech not from the child) through the middle row (child the speaker but content of speech from another) to the bottom row (child the speaker and the source of the content of the speech). Ordinarily this movement takes place over a period of years. However a small group of training studies on children's use of self-regulating speech indicates that the movement from the top row to the middle row can be compressed into fairly short periods under certain conditions (see Meichenbaum, 1977, and Pressley, forthcoming for more extensive reviews).

The subjects in these training experiments were children with specific behavioral problems such as impulsivity, hyperactivity, or agression. In one such study Meichenbaum and Goodman (1971) were able to improve the performance of 8-year-old impulsive children on the Porteus Maze, the performance subtests of The Wechsler Intelligence Scale for Children (WISC), and the MFF. The training procedure was carried out in four halfhour sessions and included fading from experimenter speech to child overt speech to child covert speech, particular solution strategies, self-praise, and practiced recovery from errors. The five children trained in this self-instruct fashion showed significantly greater improvement on the above measures than did either an attentional control group that had the same amount of exposure to the experimenters and test materials, but no self-instructional training, or than did untreated control children. This improvement held up on a one month follow-up. A second experiment that they reported tried to separate the effects of the various components of the self-instructional training. There were three training groups: cognitive modeling (modeling the experimenter's reflective solution of the MFF by successively eliminating all of the variants except one and by practicing dealing with errors); modeling plus self-instruction (the above modeling plus explicit use of the model's verbalizations, which were then faded to covert use by the child); and a control group (generally instructed to "Go slow.", but given no specific strategies). On two measures that differentiate reflective from impulsive children (MFF decision time and number of errors), the model plus self-instruction group performed significantly better; on decision time, the modeling group also performed significantly better than the control group. Three of the five model-plus-self-instruction children spontaneously verbalized the learned instructions to themselves on the post-test. (No information was given on whether the other two used, or reported using, covert verbalizations.) Thus it seems that children can be trained to emit self-regulating speech and this speech can regulate their behavior.

Superiority of a self-instruction-trained group over some type of control group has been reported for hyperactive 9-year-old boys on the Porteus Maze (Palkes, Steward, and Kaana, 1968); for institutionalized emotionally disturbed boys on the MFF (Finch et al., 1975); for impulsive first- and second-grade children on a range of tasks (Robertson and Keeley, 1974); for three hyperactive and aggressive 4-year-olds on a range of tasks and classroom behaviors (Bornstein and Quevillon, 1976); on the Porteus Maze for hyperactive 7- to 12-year-old boys who attributed performance differences to their own efforts—but not for those who attributed performance to the teacher's biases or to luck (Bugenthal, Whalen, and Henker, 1977); for impulsive fifth- and sixth-grade children on the MFF and on the Wide Range Achievement Test (Glenwick, 1976); for aggressive 6- to 8-year-old boys on Maze's subtest of the WISC and on the MFF (Camp, et al., 1977); for hyperactive children on the MFF, story completion tasks, the listening comprehension subtest of the Durrell, and the measure of time on the Bender-Gestalt (Douglas, et al., 1976).

However the above results are subject to a number of limitations. First, almost all of the treatments involved more than simple self-instruction (that is self-regulating) training. Many of them included training in specific strategies for solving particular types of problems (for example the MFF); self-reinforcement; and modeling of the desired behavior (including the self-verbalizing) which is followed by a fading procedure moving towards the child doing the desired behaviors alone. Some included components of operant conditioning. Needed now are more analytical studies, such as the second experiment of Meichenbaum and Goodman (1971), that systematically vary these components in order to determine which ones are responsible for the effects. It does seem fairly clear that general self-instructions to "Go slow." or "Stop and think." are not as effective as such self-instructions combined with those concerning a specific strategy (Meichenbaum and Goodman, 1971; Bender, 1976; Finch, et al., 1975; Burns, 1972). In addition verbal self-instruction plus modeling seems to be more effective than modeling alone (Meichenbaum and Goodman, 1971; Bender, 1976), and overt verbalization by the child is superior to reading instructions silently (Palkes, Steward, and Freedman, 1972). But effects of other components of these training methods have not yet been isolated.

A second major limitation is that so far the generalizability of such training seems to be fairly limited to the types of tasks used in the training. To the extent that the improved performances are due to particular strategies, this result is not surprising, and training on a broader range of tasks seems to lead to more generalizability of the training (Douglas, et al., 1976). Studies examining the duration of training effects also would be of interest.

The success of these training studies seems to be due to three kinds of effects: (1) inhibition of the first (impulsive) response that occurs to the child, (2) substitution of a response selected through some more strategic process, and (3) a tying of verbalizations to subsequent behavior. The inhibition may be due either to the sound of the verbalization (by way of one of the mechanisms discussed in the section on vocalization and simple motor acts) or to the semantic content of the verbalization (for example "Stop."). The more strategic response is obviously the result of the particular strategy taught; the general inhibition can eliminate incorrect responses, but it cannot by itself select correct ones. The third effect, a connecting of the semantic content or verbalizations to behavior, is an inference drawn from an observation Meichenbaum (1977) makes several times: children who serve as subjects in these studies often seem to emit verbalizations that are at variance with their behavior. They seem in this respect to be like the younger normal children described in both the motor and nonmotor research who displayed independent verbal and behavioral streams. One possible explanation for the success of training may be that verbalizations were linked to the desired behavioral responses. It may be fruitful to examine this possibility in future research.

A rather different kind of study illustrates another possible population that can benefit from training in self-regulating speech. This area also holds more promise for discovering something about the usual development of self-regulating speech in young children. Karnes, Teska, and Hodgins (1970) examined the effects of four different preschool programs on 4-year-old children from low-income and low-education homes. The experimental program lasted two hours a day for seven months. It involved three teachers, each of who had five children with whom they worked throughout the program. Manipulative and multisensory materials in preacademic areas were presented by the teachers for one hour each day in a game format that required concurrent verbal responses. The teachers initially modeled the desired kinds of verbal responses and gradually faded to child-repeated teacher responses and then to child-selected verbal responses. This emphasis on appropriate verbalizations by each child was continued throughout all of the other class activities (music, field trips, and so on). This program provided over seven months experiences that moved the children from behavior in the top row of Table 1 (p. 138) to that in the bottom row. Children in the program made impressive gains on standardized tests. The group mean gain on the Stanford-Binet was 14 points; every child in the program increased his IQ score. Gains were made on the Peabody Picture Vocabulary test (+10.3) and on the following subtests of the ITPA: verbal encoding (+11.2), auditory-vocal automatic (+10.7), auditory-vocal association (+6.7), motor encoding (+6.7), and visual-motor sequencing (+7.8). There were three other groups in the study. Children in one of them, the traditional preschool, made gains on some tests, while children in the other two made no gains or showed losses. These patterns seemed to be related to the amount of opportunity the children had for verbalization during and about their activities. In the two no-gain groups, the children did not verbalize frequently (for example pretend play was done largely nonverbally) and the programs did not require these verbalizations.

This study both underscores the importance of experiences in which a child's overt verbalization is related to his ongoing activity and supports the Soviet hypothesis concerning the steps through which this verbalization may be learned. Of course data on natural caretaker-child interactions in the home and on private speech of children in the home are needed to examine whether the movement from adult-modeled to child-chosen-and-emitted verbalizations is a naturally occurring one. One function of private speech as it is practiced in the home or other natural environments may be to insert utterances (statements, commands, and so on) that have been made by a parent or an older sibling into a child's own repertoire of self-regulating speech and to practice the use of such utterances over a period of time. That is, the child may use his own fading procedure. Of course the child also makes up some of his own self-regulating utterances. These different sources may possibly be at least partially identified by the form of the utterance. For example the category "Regulating — Social Form" in the Fuson private speech categories (p. 150) may come directly from others, while more of the "Regulating — Statement Form" may be made up by the child on the spot. Longitudinal studies in the homes of young children would be helpful in isolating these sources of self-regulating speech.

The training studies reviewed in this section have largely been successful in helping children learn to regulate their behavior by speech. This is not always true of training studies with young children. From such failures of training procedures are often inferred either developmental deficiencies (children this young just cannot do the task) or learning deficiencies (children this young cannot learn to do this task). These failures might, however, also indicate an experimenter deficiency: the experimenter was just not clever enough or creative enough to figure out a training procedure that would work. The successful self-regulating studies almost all had one common training characteristic. They used fading. Their success (and the success of Bem, 1967, with 3- and 4-year-olds on a verbal-motor task) indicates that fading might be a fairly powerful training method for young or developmentally delayed children.

The Soviet interpsychological to intrapsychological hypothesis concerning the development of self-regulating speech has been mentioned at several points during this review. Vygotsky's discussion of this hypothesis is quite vague. The notion of goal-directed activity and recent American research on mother-child interaction can provide some additional specificity to this hypothesis. We would suggest that it is useful to think of the adult and the young child as a single unit in accomplishing goal-directed activities. Each contributes to certain portions of the activity. The child, for example, may select the goal (a ring-stacking toy) and then may select and begin to execute a plan for reaching that goal (begin putting the rings on). He may experience difficulty in some stage of executing his plan and turn to the mother for help at that point. Or her participation may be needed at an earlier point, in selecting a goal ("Why don't you build a fort with your blocks?") or a plan ("Now that you've taken all of the rings off, you need to put them back on. Put the stick in this little hole, like this."). A child becomes able to complete simple or familiar activities without the participation of the mother and gradually throughout early childhood (to age 5 or so) he becomes capable of increasingly long and complicated sequences of goal-directed activities without any aid at all. Older siblings, other caretakers, and even peers also contribute needed steps in some goal-directed sequences. The support of these more capable people enable a child to use bits and pieces of actions in a more connected and integrated fashion than he would be capable of doing himself. This is the "teaching on the fly," the two or three minutes of showing and telling when the child needed it, which characterized mothers of children scoring high on a wide range of tests (White and Watts, 1973).

The attitude that characterizes this approach is that of Ainsworth's sensitive mothers (Ainsworth, Bell, and Stayton, 1974; Stayton, Hogan, and Ainsworth, 1971): the valuing of the child as a separate individual with his own desires, goals and so on. This attitude would lead the mother to leave as much of the sequence of goal-directed activity as possible up to the child and only enter in when required.

The mother (the teacher or other caretaker) is the possessor of a large number of strategies for solving all sorts of everyday problems and difficulties that occur in the life of a child. She knows how to button clothes, tie a Superman cape, use scissors, draw, read, throw a ball, pour juice, write letters, dress a doll, and spell. She daily and hourly acts as did the experimenter in the training studies on self-regulating speech: modeling, explaining, and gradually fading a particular strategy or skill until the child can do it. This process is accompanied by much verbalization by the mother. Objects are named, attributes described, actions anticipated and evaluated, choices proposed. As the child becomes more capable, directives may be replaced by leading questions and then by more indirect hints. The mother's regulating speech may be replaced by the child's self-regulating speech. In some pilot work with mothers asked to help their child solve a puzzle, this pattern of movement from mother-directed to child-initiated solution and from mother-regulating speech to self-regulating speech was seen with 4-year-olds (Wertsch, personal communication).

Although children can learn to do things by observation, the results of Karnes, Teska, and Hodgins (1970) and Clarke-Stewart (1973) indicate that verbalization during adult-child interactions is associated with superior cognitive growth (as measured by standardized tests). No one has yet looked at differences in the amount or kind of self-regulating speech exhibited by children who have had varying amounts of such positively directive speech from their mothers. But such interactions would seem to be the experience par excellence from which self-regulating speech might develop. Future research might well examine not only the differing verbal ability of such children (as is presently done), but the extent to which such children can and do regulate their behavior by their own speech.

CONCLUSION

Repeatedly during this review the limited nature and the artificiality of the tasks involved in the research has been pointed out. The fact that in almost all of the research the task goals were set by the experimenter has also been noted. Both of these types of restrictions bear on one of the chief differences between these research settings and the settings in which natural self-regulating speech occurs: that the activity is not a goal-directed activity selected by the child from a range of possible choices, all of which are set within a continuing stream of behavior. In the research settings the child does not have to select a goal from a range of attractive alternatives, there are no interruptions or distractions during his activity, the task is so well-defined that he does not have to decide when or if he has completed it (to his own satisfaction), and he does not really have much option to decide whether he wishes to continue this activity or select a new one. Each of the above seems to be a place where self-regulating speech would be useful and might well occur.

In addition to taking place in a restricted setting, most of the research focuses only on some part of "execute the next step of the plan" in the goal-directed activity. In addition to this important function, self-regulating speech might be used in selecting, storing, and recalling specific strategies; in analyzing features of a situation that might call for a strategy; in remembering the goal during the plan execution; in providing feedback on one's progress through a plan execution; in evaluating one's performance; and in directing one's attention outwards, towards some aspect of the external environment, or inwards, towards some aspect of a person's own internal state ("I want . . .," "I need . . . ," "I feel . . .).

Research is needed that focuses on some of these other possible functions of self-regulating speech. In a rare study of this sort forty-eight 3-, 4-, and 5-year-olds while riding a tricycle followed tape-recorded instructions to go, stop, up and back (Meacham, 1979). Half of the children repeated each instruction after it was heard; half did not. Children in the verbal condition were significantly more likely to change to an appropriate motor activity in intervals (analysed every 3 sec.) in which there was verbal activity (60%) than in intervals in which there was none (39%). Meacham discussed the possible functions of the semantic aspect of verbal activity when in the moderate proportion of cases it follows rather than precedes motor activity. His suggested functions are: describing the outcomes of motor behavior, aiding memory of the desired goal, and facilitating comparison of the desired goal with the present action. More naturalistic research tasks and more comprehensive analyses of the specific functions of self-regulating speech, such as Meacham's, seem to be fruitful and important areas for future research.

The final points in this conclusion concern the four different attributes of words (described earlier in the paper) that can affect behavior: (1) the speech sounds, (2) the physical act of speaking, (3) the meaning of the spoken words, and (4) the process of choosing words to speak. Research related to the first three has been reviewed. There is practically no research on the development of self-regulating speech that directly focuses on the fourth way — the process of choosing words to speak. However it may be very important. Olson (1970) noted the power of the psycholinguistic point that because words provide information, they "designate, signal, or specify an intended referent relative to the set of alternatives from which it must be differentiated" (p. 264). This choosing process generates more information than was there before the choice process occurred. This additional information is first available to the chooser of the words in the very act of choosing. Thus it is possible that some speech-for-self in young children may simply be externalizations of this word-choice process. As such it is not the utterance per se that may have the regulating effect, but may rather be the process of choosing the words. One of the main problems in all of the research in Cell 5—and one of the causes of the failure of much of it to find strong facilitative effect of words — is that the word choices made by the experimenter may not differentiate the referent from the set of alternatives that the child sees and so may not provide to him the information that the experimenter thinks it should.

The Olson paper is sometimes used to argue that speech-for-self is redundant, that it cannot contain any information. This argument is based on a confusion of Olson's terms, speaking and language, which Olson makes at the very end of his (1970) paper:

> First, notice that language is merely the specification of an intended referent relative to a set of alternatives. All of that information is perceptual and it was available to the speaker before he generated the utterance. Therefore, to the speaker there is no information in an utterance. Speaking is redundant. Hence, language does not restructure thought. (p. 272)

In the process of examining alternatives and choosing a set relative to which a referent will be specified, a person generates new information. That information was certainly potentially available to the person before he chose the words to speak (that is he possessed all of the perceptual and conceptual prerequisites for generating that information), but so was a very large number of other kinds of new information that would have been created if a different set of alternatives had been chosen. Thus there is a considerable difference between being potentially available but not yet generated and having actually been generated. Once the speaker has selected the words to speak, it is true that there is no new information in the actual overt utterance of these words. Saying already selected words aloud is redundant to the speaker. But this certainly does not imply that the covert or overt use of language does not restructure thought. As Olson has so clearly and persuasively described, the very choice of a word generates new information. This information can be used to regulate one's own behavior.

The relationships among the four aspects of speech (speech sounds, physical act of speaking, semantic meaning, process of choosing a word) that can regulate behavior are somewhat complex. Two different pairings of these four should be considered in future research. Understanding the semantic meaning (decoding) can be considered as a process which accompanies listening (hearing the speech sounds), and the process of choosing a word (encoding) as accompanying speaking. Dickson (1978) has found evidence with both adults and children that encoding and decoding abilities in referential communication tasks may be independent abilities, that is, it may be that some people are particularly good encoders (and/or speakers) while others are good decoders (and/or listeners). Thus some future research on self-regulating speech should assess encoding (or speaking) ability separately from decoding (or listening) ability.

Another pairing of the four aspects of speech involves the overtness of the act. The speech sounds and the physical act of speaking can be thought of as the two parts of an overt act of communication — listening and speaking. Understanding the meaning of spoken words and choosing words to speak can be considered as two parts of the internal cognitive processing involved in such communication acts, that is, as the decoding and encoding of information. Research literature on verbalization as a motor act has focused on the overt, while the verbal mediation literature has been more concerned with the covert processes. However, the distinction between overt and covert acts is not quite so clear-cut, for speaking and listening both have covert and counterparts—producing and hearing acoustic images. We have very little knowledge of the developmental course of these acoustic images or of their relative effectiveness. Fairly young children can produce them however. Children aged 4½ to 5½ spontaneously produced subvocal (not audible on a microphone clipped just beneath the chin; not visible to an observer) naming of pictured objects during presentation of the pictures for a recall task (Locke and Fehr, 1970). We shall have to invent very creative methods if we are to examine all of these kinds of covert activities involved in speech.

Untangling these separate effects of verbalization has presented and will continue to present difficult methodological problems. The problems will occur in research on both experimenter-provided and spontaneously produced self-regulating speech. Careful and creative work will be required in order to ascertain in specific situations *whether* speech is regulating behavior and *how* this regulation is being accomplished.

References

Ainsworth, M. D. S., Bell, S. M., and **Stayton, D. F.** Infant-mother attachment and social development: Socialization as a product of reciprocal responsiveness to signals, in Martin P. M. Richards, ed., *The integration of a child into a social world.* Cambridge: Cambridge University Press, 1974.

Anokhin, P. K. Features of the afferent apparatus of the conditioned reflex and their importance for psychology, in N. O'Connor, ed., *Recent Soviet psychology.* New York: Pergamon, 1961.

Atkinson, R. C., and **Shiffrin, R. M.** Human memory: A proposed system and its control processes, in K. W. Spence and J. T. Spence, eds., *The psychology of learning and motivation,* vol. 2, New York: Academic, 1968.

Bacharach, V. R., Carr, T. H., and **Mehner, D. S.** Interactive and independent contributions of verbal descriptions to children's picture memory. *Journal of Experimental Child Psychology,* 1976, *22,* 492-498.

Beaudichon, J. Nature and instrumental function of private speech in problem solving situations. *Merrill-Palmer Quarterly,* 1973, *19,* 117-135.

Beiswenger, H. Luria's model of the verbal control of behavior. *Merrill-Palmer Quarterly,* 1968, *14,* 267-284.

______. Linguistic and psychological factors in the speech regulation of behavior in very young children. *Dissertation Abstracts International,* 1969, *30* (1-B), 399-400; Ann Arbor, Mich: University Microfilms. No 69-12, 037.

Belmont, J. M., and **Butterfield, E. C.** The instructional approach to developmental cognitive research, in R. V. Kail, Jr., and J. W. Hagen, eds., *Perspectives on the development of memory and cognition.* Hillside, N.J.: Erlbaum, 1977.

Bem, S. L. Verbal self-control: The establishment of effective self-instruction. *Journal of Experimental Psychology,* 1967, *74,* 485-491.

Bem, S. L. The role of comprehension in children's problem solving. *Developmental Psychology,* 1970, *2,* 351-358.

Bender, N. Self-verbalization versus tutor verbalization in modifying impulsivity. *Journal of Educational Psychology,* 1976, *68,* 347-354.

Bernbach, H. A. The effect of labels on short-term memory for colors with nursery school children. *Psychonomic Science,* 1967, *7,* 149-150.

Berner, E. S. Private speech and role-taking abilities in preschool children. Unpublished doctoral dissertation, Harvard University, 1971.

Birch, D. Verbal control of nonverbal behavior. *Journal of Experimental Child Psychology*, 1966, *4*, 266-275.

———. Evidence for competition and coordination between vocal and manual responses in preschool children. *Journal of Experimental Child Psychology*, 1971, *12*, 10-26.

Blank, M. Cognitive functions of language in the preschool years. *Developmental Psychology*, 1974, *10*, 229-245.

Bloor, D. The regulatory function of language, in P.J. Morton and J. C. Marshall, eds., *Psycholinguistics, developmental and pathological.* Ithaca, N. Y.: Cornell University Press, 1977.

Bornstein, P. H., and **Quevillon, R. P.** The effects of a self-instructional package on overactive preschool boys. *Journal of Applied Behavior Analysis,* 1976, *9,* 179-188.

Bronckart, J. P. The regulating role of speech. *Human Development,* 1973, *16,* 417-439.

Brooks, L. R. The contribution of verbal descriptions to visual memory in nursery school children. Hamilton, Ontario: McMaster University. (Unpublished manuscript, 1971). [Cited by M. T. Chi. Short-term memory limitations in children: Capacity or processing deficits? *Memory and Cognition, 1976, 4*(5), 559-572.]

Brown, A. L., Campione, J. C., and **Murphy, M. D.** Keeping track of changing variables: Long-term retention of a trained rehearsal strategy by retarded adolescents. *American Journal of Mental Deficiency,* 1974, *78,* 446-453.

Bugenthal, D. B., Whalen, C. K., and **Henker, B.** Causal attributions of hyperactive children and motivational assumptions of two behavior-change approaches: Evidence for an interactionist position. *Child Development,* 1977, *48,* 874-884.

Burns, B. The effect of self-directed verbal comments on arithmetic performance and activity level of urban hyperactive children. Unpublished doctoral dissertation, Boston College, 1972.

Bush, E. S., and **Cohen, L. B.** The effects of relevant and irrelevant labels on short-term memory in nursery school children. *Psychonomic Science,* 1970, *18,* 228-229.

Butterfield, E. C., and **Belmont, J. M.** The role of verbal processes in short-term memory, in R. L. Schiefelbusch, ed., *Language research with the mentally retarded.* Baltimore: University Park Press, 1972.

Camp, B. W., Blom, G. E., Herbert, F., and **van Doorninck, W. J.** Think Aloud: A program for developing self-control in young aggressive boys. *Journal of Abnormal Child Psychology,* 1977, *5,* 157-169.

Clarke-Stewart, K. A. Interactions between mothers and their young children: Characteristics and consequences. *Monographs of the Society for Research in Child Development*, 1973, *38*, (6-7), 1-109.

Conrad, R. The chronology of the development of covert speech in children. *Developmental Psychology*, 1971, *5*, 398-405.

Craik, F. I. M., and **Lockhart, R. S.** Levels of processing: A framework for memory research. *Journal of Verbal Learning and Verbal Behavior,* 1972, *11,* 671-684.

Daehler, M. W., Horowitz, A. B., Wynns, F. C., and **Flavell, J. H.** Verbal and non-verbal rehearsal in children's recall. *Child Development,* 1969, *40,* 443-452.

Deutsch, F., and **Stein, A. H.** The effects of personal responsibility and task interruption on the private speech of preschoolers. *Human Development,* 1972, *15,* 310-324.

Dickie, J. R. Private speech: The effect of presence of others, task and intrapersonal variables. *Dissertation Abstracts International,* 1973,*34* (3-B), 1292; Ann Arbor, Mich: University Microfilms. No. 73-20, 329.

Dickson, W. P. Referential communication between teacher and child: Reliability andvalidity of measures of encoding and decoding effectiveness. (Paper presented at the American Educational Research Association, Toronto, April, 1978).

Douglas, V. I., Parry, P., Marton, P., and **Garson, C.** Assessment of a cognitive training program for hyperactive children. *Journal of Abnormal Child Psychology,* 1976, *4,* 389-410.

Dusek, J. B. The effects of labeling and pointing on children's selective attention. *Developmental Psychology*, 1978, *14*(1), 115-116.

Eysenck, M. W., and **Baron, C. R.** Effects of cuing on recall from categorized word lists. *Developmental Psychology,* 1974, *10,* 665-666.

Finch, A., Wilkinson, M., Nelson, W., and **Montgomery, L.** Modification of an impulsive cognitive tempo in emotionally disturbed boys. *Journal of Abnormal Child Psychology,* 1975, *3,* 45-52.

Flavell, J. H., Beach, D. R., and **Chinsky, J. M.** Spontaneous verbal rehearsal in a memory task as a function of age. *Child Development,* 1966, *37,* 283-299.

Fry, P. S. Affect and resistance to temptation. *Developmental Psychology*, 1975, *11,* 466-472.

Fuson, K. C., Householder, J., and **Urbaska, F.** *The use of private speech by two- through five-year-olds,* forthcoming.

Glenwick, D. S. Training impulsive children in verbal self-regulation by use of natural change agents. *Dissertation Abstracts International*, 1976, *37*, 459-b; Ann Arbor, Mich: University Microfilms. No. 76-14,758.

Golden, M., Montare, A., and **Bridger, W.** Verbal control of delay behavior in two-year-old boys as a function of social class. *Child Development,* 1977, *48,* 1107-1111.

Goodman S. A sequential functional analysis of preschool childen's private speech. (Paper presented at the meeting of the Society for Research in Child Development, New Orleans, March, 1977.)

———. The integration of verbal and motor behavior in preschool children. Unpublished doctoral disseration, University of Waterloo, Ontario, 1978.

Hagen, J. W., and **Hale, G. A.** The development of attention in children, in A. D. Pick, ed., *Minnesota Symposium on Child Psychology*. Minneapolis: University of Minnesota Press, 1973.

Hagen, J. W., Hargrave, S., and **Ross, W.** Prompting and rehearsal in short-term memory. *Child Development*, 1973, *44*, 201-204.

Hagen, J. W., and **Kingsley, P. R.** Labeling effects in short-term memory. *Child Development*, 1968, *39*, 113-121.

Hall, J. W., and **Halperin, M.** The development of memory-encoding processes in young children. *Developmental Psychology*, 1972, *6*, 181.

Hall, J. W., and **Madsen, S. C.** Modifying Children's Processing of Categorizable Information for Memory. *Bulletin of the Psychonomic Society*, 1978, *11*, 291-294.

Halperin, M. S. Developmental changes in the recall and recognition of categorized word lists. *Child Development*, 1974, *45*, 144-151.

———. The function of speech rhythms in the regulation of nonspeech activity, in K. Riegel and J. Meacham eds., *The developing individual in a changing world*, vol. 1, The Hague: Mouton, 1976

Harris, A. Historical development of the Soviet theory of self-regulation, in G. Zivin, ed., *The development of self-regulation through private speech*. New York: Wiley—Interscience, 1979.

Hjertholm, E. W. *Comparison of American and Norwegian nursery school children on independence behavior and training* (Project S-135, June 1964-September 1968). [Unpublished project report, University of Chicago.]

Huttenlocher, J., and **Strauss, S.** Comprehension and a statement's relation to the situation it describes. *Journal of Verbal Learning and Verbal Behavior*, 1968, *7*, 300-304.

Huttenlocher, J., Eisenberg, K., and **Strauss, S.** Comprehension: Relation between perceived actor and logical subject. *Journal of Verbal Learning and Verbal Behavior*, 1968, *7*, 527-530.

Israel, A. C., and **O'Leary, K. D.** Developing correspondence between children's words and deeds. *Child Development*, 1973, *44*, 575-581.

Istomina, Z. M. The development of voluntary memory in preschool-aged children. *Soviet Psychology*, 1975, *13*, 5-64.

Jarvis, P. The effect of self-administered verbal instructions on simple sensory-motor performance in children. *Dissertation Abstracts*, 1964, *25* (3), 201, Ann Arbor Mich.: University Microfilms. No. 64-09, 238.

Joynt, D., and **Cambourne, B.** Psycholinguistic development and the control of behaviour. *British Journal of Educational Psychology*, 1968, *38*, 249-260.

Kanfer, F., and **Zich, J.** Self-control training: The effects of external control on children's resistance to temptation. *Developmental Psychology,* 1974, *10,* 108-115.

Karnes, M., Teska, J., and **Hodgins, A.** The effects of four programs of classroom intervention on the intellectual and language development of 4-year-old disadvantaged children. *American Journal of Orthospsychiatry,* 1970, *40,* 58-76.

Keeney, T. J., Cannizzo, S. R., and **Flavell, J. H.** Spontaneous and induced verbal rehearsal in a recall task. *Child Development,* 1967, *38,* 953-966.

Kendler, T. S. Verbalization and optional reversal shifts among kindergarten children. *Journal of Verbal Learning and Verbal Behavior*, 1964, *3*, 428-436.

______. An ontogeny of mediational deficiency. *Child Development,* 1972, *43,* 1-17.

Kendler, T. S., and **Kendler, H. H.** Reversal and nonreversal shifts in kindergarten children. *Journal of Experimental Psychology,* 1959, *58,* 56-60.

Kingsley, P. R., and **Hagen, J. W.** Induced versus spontaneous rehearsal in short-term memory in nursery school children. *Developmental Psychology,* 1969, *1*, 40-46.

Kleiman, A. S. The use of private speech in young children and its relation to social speech. Unpublished doctoral dissertation, University of Chicago, 1974.

Klein, W. An investigation of the spontaneous speech of children during problem-solving. *Dissertation Abstracts*, 1964, *25* (3), 2031; Ann Arbor, Mich.: University Microfilms. No. 64-09, 240.

Kobasigawa, A. Utilization of retrieval cues by children in recall. *Child Development*, 1974, *45*, 127-134.

Kobasigawa, A., and **Middleton, D. B.** Free recall of categorized items by children at three grade levels. *Child Development,* 1972, *43,* 1067-1072.

Kohlberg, L., Yaeger, J., and **Hjertholm, E.** Private speech: Four studies and a review of theories. *Child Development,* 1968, *39,* 691-736.

Kuenne, M. R. Experimental investigation of the relation of language to transposition behavior in young children. *Journal of Experimental Psychology*, 1946, *36*, 471-490.

Lange, G. The development of conceptual and rote recall skills among school-age children. *Journal of Experimental Child Psychology*, 1973, *15*, 399-406.

Levina, R. E. L. S. Vygotsky's ideas on the planning function of children's speech, in J. V. Wertsch, ed., *The concept of activity in Soviet psychology,* forthcoming.

Liublinskaya, A. A. The development of children's speech and thought. [Originally: *Speeches at the Conference on Psychological Questions*, 1953, 124-138.] in B. Simon, ed., *Psychology in the Soviet Union*, 1957, London: Routledge and Kegan Paul, 1957.

Locke, J. L., and **Fehr, F. S.** Young children's use of the speech code in a recall task. *Journal of Experimental Child Psychology,* 1970 *10,* 367-373.

Lovaas, O. I. Interaction between verbal and nonverbal behavior. *Child Development*, 1961, *32*, 329-336.

———. Control of food intake in children by reinforcement of relevant verbal behavior. *Journal of Abnormal Social Psychology*, 1964, *68*, 672-678.

Luria, A. R. *The nature of human conflict.* New York: Liveright, 1932.

Luria, A. R. The role of language in formation of temporary connections, in B. Simon, ed., *Psychology in the Soviet Union*, London: Routledge & Kegan Paul, 1957. [Originally published in *Voprosy Psikhologii*, 1955, 73-87].

Luria, A. R. The directive function of speech in development and dissolution. Part I: Development of the directive function of speech in early childhood. *Word*, 1959, *15*, 341-351.

Luria, A. R. The genesis of voluntary movements, in N. O'Connor, ed., *Recent Soviet psychology*, Oxford: Pergamon, 1961*A*. [Originally published in *Voprosy Psikhologii, 1957, 6*, 3-19.]

Luria, A. R. The role of speech in the regulation of normal and abnormal behavior. J. Tizard, trans., Oxford: Pergamon, 1961*B*.

Luria, A. R. Speech development and the formation of mental processes, in M. Cole and I. Maltzman, eds., *A handbook of contemporary Soviet psychology*. New York: Basic Books, 1969.

Luria, A. R., and **Yugovich, F. I.** *Speech and the development of mental processes in the child.* London: Staples, 1959.

McCabe, A. E. A paradox of self-regulation in speech-motor interaction: semantic degradation and impulse segmentation, in G. Zivin, ed., *The development of self-regulation through private speech.* New York: Wiley, 1979.

McCabe, A. E., Levin, J. R., and **Wolff, P.** The role of overt activity in children's sentence production. *Journal of Experimental Child Psychology,* 1974, *17,* 107-114.

Masters, J. C., and **Santrock, J. W.** Studies in the self-regulation of behavior: Effects of contingent cognitive and affective events. *Developmental Psychology,* 1976, *12,* 344-348.

Meacham, J. A. The development of memory abilities in the individual and society. *Human Development,* 1972, *15,* 205-228*a*.

———.Verbal-motor interactions during sequences of motor activity. *Dissertation Abstracts International,* 1972, *33* (11-B) 5545; Ann Arbor, Mich.: University Microfilms, No. 73-11, 205*b*.

———. Integration of verbal and motor activities. (Paper presented at the Biennial Meeting of the Society for Research in Child Development, Philadelphia, March 1973.)

———. The role of verbal activity in remembering the goals of actions, in G. Zivin, ed., *Development of self-regulation through private speech.* New York: Wiley, 1979.

Meacham, J. A., Harris, A. E., and **Blaschko, T.** *Integration of verbal and motor activities.* (Paper presented at the Society for Research in Child Development, Philadelphia, March 1973.)

Mead, G. H. *Mind, self, and society.* Chicago: The University of Chicago Press, 1934.

Meichenbaum, D. *Cognitive-behavior modification.* New York and London: Plenum, 1977.

Meichenbaum, D., and **Goodman, J.** Reflection-impulsivity and verbal control of motor behavior. *Child Development,* 1969, *40,* 785-797.

Meichenbaum, D. H., and **Goodman, J.** Training impulsive children to talk to themselves: A means of developing self-control. *Journal of Abnormal Psychology,* 1971, *77,* 115-126.

Miller, S. A., Shelton, J., and **Flavell, J. H.** A test of Luria's hypotheses concerning the development of verbal self-regulation. *Child Development,* 1970, *40,* 651-665.

Mischel, W., and **Baker, N.** Cognitive transformations of reward objects through instructions. *Journal of Personality and Social Psychology,* 1975, *31,* 254-261.

Mischel, W., and **Moore, E. S.** Effects of attention to symbolically presented rewards upon self-control. *Journal of Personality and Social Psychology,* 1973, *28,* 172-179.

Mischel, W., and **Patterson, C. J.** Substantive and structural elements of effective plans for self-control. *Journal of Personality and Social Psychology,* 1976, *34,* 942-950.

______. Effective plans for self-control in children, in W. A. Collins, ed., *Minnesota Symposium on Child Psychology, vol. 11. Minneapolis: University of Minnesota Press, 1977.*

Mischel, W., and **Underwood, B.** Instrumental ideation in delay of gratification. *Child Development,* 1974, *45,* 1083-1088.

Mischel, W., Ebbesen, E. B., and **Zeiss, A.** Cognitive and attentional mechanisms in delay of gratification. *Journal of Personality and Social Psychology,* 1972, *21,* 204-218.

Moore, B., Clyburn, A., and **Underwood, B.** The role of affect in delay of gratification. *Child Development,* 1976, *47,* 273-276.

Moore, B., Mischel, W., and **Zeiss, A.** Comparative effects of the reward stimulus and its cognitive representation in voluntary delay. *Journal of Personality and Social Psychology,* 1976, *34,* 419-424.

Nelson, G. K. Concomitant effects of visual, motor, and verbal experiences in young children's concept development. *Journal of Educational Psychology,* 1976, *68*(4), 466-473.

Nelson, T. The effects of training in attention deployment on observing behavior in reflective and impulsive children. *Dissertation Abstracts* 1969, *29,* 2659.

Olson, D. R. Language and thought: Aspects of a cognitive theory of semantics. *Psychological Review,* 1970, *77,* 257-273.

Ornstein, P. A., Naus, M. J., and **Liberty, C.** Rehearsal and organizational processes in children's memory. *Child Development,* 1975, *46,* 818-830.

Palkes, H., Steward, M., and **Freedman, J.** Improvement in maze performance of hyperactive boys as a function of verbal training procedures. *Journal of Special Education,* 1972, *5,* 337-342.

Palkes, H., Steward, M., and **Kahana, B.** Porteus Maze performance of hyperactive boys after training in self-directed verbal commands. *Child Development,* 1968, *39,* 817-826.

Patterson, C. J., and **Mischel, W.** Plans to resist distraction. *Developmental Psychology,* 1975, *11,* 369-378.

———. Effects of temptation-inhibiting and task-facilitating plans on self-control. *Journal of Personality and Social Psychology,* 1976, *33,* 209-217.

Patterson, C. J., Mischel, W., Carter, D. B., and **Quasebarth, S. J.** *The role of cues in plans for children's self-control,* forthcoming.

Pechman, E. M. Spontaneous verbalization and motor accompaniment to children's task orientation in elementary classrooms. Unpublished doctoral dissertation, University of Michigan, 1978.

Pressley, M. Increasing children's self-control through cognitive interventions. *Review of Educational Research,* forthcoming.

Reese, H. W. Verbal mediation as a function of age level. *Psychological Bulletin,* 1962, *59,* 502-509.

Risley, T. R., and **Hart, B.** Developing correspondence between the non-verbal and verbal behavior of preschool children. *Journal of Applied Behavior Analysis,* 1968, *1,* 267-281.

Roberts, R. N. The competent academic problem solver: Toward an integrated model. Unpublished doctoral dissertation, University of Hawaii, 1977.

Roberts, R. N., and **Tharp, R. G.** A naturalistic study of school children's private speech in an academic problem solving task, forthcoming.

Robertson, D., and **Keeley, S.** Evaluation of a mediational training program for impulsive children by a multiple case study design. (Paper presented at the meeting of the American Psychological Association, New Orleans, August, 1974.)

Rohwer, W. D., Jr. Elaboration and learning in childhood and adolescence, in H. W. Reese, ed., *Advances in child development and behavior,* vol. 8. New York: Academic, 1973.

Rondal, J. A. Investigation of the regulatory power of the impulsive and meaningful aspects of speech. *Genetic Psychology monographs,* 1976, *94,* 3-33.

Rossi, E. L. Development of classificatory behavior. *Child Development,* 1964, *35,* 137-142.

Rubin, K. H. The impact of the natural setting on private speech, in G. Zivin, ed., *The development of self-regulation through private speech.* New York: Wiley, 1979.

Rubin, K. H., Hultsch, D. F., and **Peters, D. L.** Non-social speech in four-year-old children as a function of birth order and interpersonal situation. *Merrill-Palmer Quarterly,* 1971, *17,* 41-50.

Santrock, J. W. Affect and facilitative self-control: Influence of ecological setting, cognition, and social agent. *Journal of Educational Psychology,* 1976, *68,* 529-535.

Scribner, S., and **Cole, M.** Effects of constrained recall training on children's performance in a verbal memory task. *Child Development,* 1972, *43,* 845-857.

Sherman, J. A. Modification of nonverbal behavior through reinforcement of related verbal behavior. *Child Development,* 1964, *35,* 717-723.

Silverman, I. W. Effect of verbalization on reversal shifts in children: Additional data. *Journal of Experimental Child Psychology,* 1966, *4,* 1-8.

Sokolov, A. N. *Inner speech and thought.* G. T. Onischenko, trans., New York: Plenum, 1972. [Originally published, 1968.]

Stayton, D. M., Hogan, R., and **Ainsworth, M. D. S.** Infant obedience and maternal behavior: The origins of socialization reconsidered. *Child Development,* 1971, *42,* 1057-1069.

Stevenson, H. W. *Children's learning.* New York: Meredith, 1972.

Strommen, E. A. Verbal self-regulation in a children's game: Impulsive errors on 'Simon Says'. *Child Development,* 1973, *44,* 849-853.

Tikhomirov, O. K. The formation of voluntary movements in children of preschool age. *Soviet Psychology,* 1975-1976, *14,* (1-2), 48-135. [Originally published, 1958.]

Toner, I. J., and **Smith, R. A.** Age and overt verbalization in delay-maintenance behavior in children. *Journal of Experimental Child Psychology,* 1977, *24,* 123-128.

Van Duyne, H. J. The development of the control of adult instructions over nonverbal behavior. *The Journal of Genetic Psychology,* 1972, *120,* 295-302.

Vygotsky, L. S. *Thought and language,* E. Hanfmann and G. Vakar, eds., and trans., Cambridge, Mass.: MIT Press, 1962. [Originally published, 1934.]

Vygotsky, L. S. *Mind in society,* M. Cole, V. John-Steiner, S. Scribner, E. Souberman, eds., Cambridge, Mass.: MIT Press, forthcoming.

Wanschura, P. B., and **Borkowski, J. G.** Long-term transfer of a mediational strategy by moderately retarded children. *American Journal of Mental Deficiency,* 1975, *80,* 323-333.

Ward, W. C., and **Legant, P.** Naming and memory in nursery school children in the absence of rehearsal. *Developmental Psychology,* 1971, *5,* 174-175.

Weir, M. W., and **Stevenson, H. W.** The effect of verbalization in children's learning as a function of chronological age. *Child Development,* 1959, *30,* 143-149.

Welch, L. R. A re-evaluation of the concept of cognitive tempo: A naturalistic study of attention patterns. (Paper presented at the Society for Research in Child Development, Denver, March, 1975.)

Wertsch, J. V. The regulation of human action and the given-new structure of private speech, in G. Zivin, ed., *The development of self-regulation through private speech.* New York: Wiley, 1979.

Wheeler, R. J., and **Dusek, J. B.** The effects of attentional and cognitive factors on children's incidental learning. *Child Development,* 1973, *44,* 253-258.

White, B. L., and **Watts, J. C.** *Experience and environment: Major influences on the development of the young child.* Englewood, N.J.; 1973.

Wilder, L. The role of speech and other feedback signals in the regulation of the sensorimotor behavior of three- and five-year-old children. *Dissertation Abstracts International,* 1968, *30,* (3-A), 1262; Ann Arbor, Mich.: University Microfilms, No. 69-14, 587.

Wilder, L., and **Fogel, D. S.** The motor component of speech in the verbal regulation of behavior. (Paper presented at the Canadian Psychological Association, 1974.)

Williams, K. G., and **Goulet, L. R.** The effects of cueing and constraint instructions on children's free recall performance. *Journal of Experimental Child Psychology,* 1975, *19,* 464-475.

Wozniak, R. H. Verbal regulation of motor behavior — Soviet research and non-Soviet replications. *Human Development,* 1972, *15,* 13-57.

———. Speech-for-self as a multiply reafferent human action system, in **K. Riegel** and J. Meacham, eds., *The developing individual in a changing world,* vol I. The Hague: Mouton, 1976.

———. *The verbal regulation of motor activity — an interim report.* Institute of Child Development, University of Minnesota. (Unpublished report, no date.)

Wozniak, R. H., Acredolo, C., and **Peterson, R.** Effects of overt vocalization and silent articulation on elicitation of the orienting response. In preparation. [Cited by R. H. Wozniak. Speech-for-self as a multiply reafferent human action system. (Paper presented at the Society for Research in Child Development, Philadelphia, March 1973.)]

Yaeger, J. A. Self-directing speech and puzzle-solving in children. Unpublished doctoral dissertation, University of Chicago, 1968.

Yakovleva, S. V. Conditions for the formation of the simplest voluntary actions in very young children. *Soviet Psychology,* 1975-1976, *14* (1-2), 13-47.

Zaporozhets, A. V. The development of voluntary movements, in B. Simon, ed., *Psychology in the Soviet Union.* London: Routledge & Kegan Paul, 1957. [Originally published in *Voprosy Psikhologii,* 1955, 42-49.]

Zivin, G. L. Functions of private speech during problem-solving in preschool children. *Dissertation Abstracts International,* 1972, *33,* (4-B), 1834; Ann Arbor, Mich.: University Microfilms. No. 72-26, 224.

———. Speech-for-self as a function of individual styles of central organization. (Paper presented at the Society for Research in Child Development, Philadelphia, March 1973.)

CHAPTER 6

A Paradox of Self-Regulation in Speech-Motor Interaction: Semantic Degradation and Impulse Segmentation

ANN E. McCABE
University of Windsor

The question of how humans come to control their activities by telling themselves what to do has intrigued many investigators, as the various chapters in this book attest. Both in the Soviet Union (for example, Luria, 1961; Zaporozhets and Elkonin, 1964/1971) and the Western world (for example, Meichenbaum and Goodman, 1971; Wozniak and Nuechterlein, 1973), we have seen demonstrations of the modification of behaviors ranging from simple motor acts to complex problem-solving as a result of the introduction of an individual's speech for himself. It has, in general, proved to be an extremely useful ability.

In virtually all these studies there has been a rather singular focus on the behavioral effects of verbal intervention and little attention has been paid to the speech production itself. Questions have been framed in terms of verbal control, and as a result the verbalizations have been considered a "given." Recognizing that by 3 or 4 years of age the child has a rather well-developed language system, but does not yet exhibit marked control of his other actions through it (that is verbal control), it has been considered reasonable to question how and when this strong and flexible language system comes to be imposed on other weaker and less flexible systems. This view of the problem is at the heart of the other chapters of this volume.

This view is adequate to the problem only if the speech production itself is not affected by the combination. The purpose of this chapter is to examine the

A portion of the research reported here was funded by the Wisconsin Research and Development Center for Cognitive Learning supported in part as a research and development center by funds from the National Institute of Education, Center No. NE-C-00-30—65. The opinions expressed herein do not necessarily reflect the position or policy of the National Institute of Education and no official endorsement by the National Institute of Education should be inferred. Appreciation is expressed to Larry Waterman and Chris Gricksheit for assistance in data collection and to Mary Anne Martin for clerical assistance.

question of whether speech does, in fact, remain unaffected when it is combined with motor activity. The chapter will examine some previously reported data and present some new data in an effort to shed light on that question. To conclude, it will offer some speculations on the answers for interlocking facilitations in the development of verbal self-regulation by both semantic and impulse aspects of that private speech that is emitted for oneself.

There are three possibilities with respect to the effect on speech production of combining speech with another activity: (1) it is unaffected by the combination, (2) it is facilitated by the combination, or (3) it is interfered with by the combination. If the first is true, we can legitimately concern ourselves only with the impact of speech on other behavior. If the second or third exists, we must view the relationship between speech and other activity as one involving a bidirectional interaction. However it is only the third possibility that creates a problem for the traditional hypothesis of verbal self-control (Vygotsky, 1934/1962; Luria, 1960, 1961).

Certainly a minimum requirement for language to be able to provide a plan and a guide for behavior, is that the individual in question be capable of generating the relevant verbalization. A second requirement is apparent from considering that if combining the two activities results in a breakdown of the language itself, it is difficult to see how effective verbal self-control is possible. One cannot tell oneself what to do, if doing it makes it difficult or impossible to say anything reasonable to oneself. The data and discussion to be presented here suggest that the relevant quality of speech is in fact negatively affected when it is combined with motor activity, at least among children 2½ through 7½ years of age.

INCIDENTAL EVIDENCE FOR SPEECH DEGRADATION

Disruption in speech output has been reported by several investigators. Luria (1961) mentions that attempts to establish self-regulation by speech among 2½-year-old children failed because the "verbal reactions rapidly became extinct" (p. 41). Thus at the younger age levels employed in these studies, the child's speech was affected by the demand for the dual response. He was incapable of executing both responses; the result was a disruption of the verbal as well as the motor response.

A study by Meacham (1972 and expanded in Chapter 7 of this volume) also suggests that motor activity may affect speech production in 3½-year-olds. The task involved combining a verbal direction with an ongoing motor activity. His results distinguish three qualitatively different patterns of interaction. The first pattern, found among 3½-year-olds, involved a continuation of the motor activity at the expense of the speech; 4½-year-olds showed a hesitation in the motor activity, but no disruption of the speech;

finally, 5½-year-olds showed no difficulty in producing both. Although the children showing the speech disruption were a year older than children showing a similar pattern in Luria's studies, this might be attributed to a difference in task difficulty.

Some unexpected findings in a study the author reported several years ago (McCabe, Levin, and Wolff, 1974) suggested that verbal-motor interaction was not unidirectional for 4-year-olds. In this study 4-year-old children were asked to manipulate toys and/or to tell a story about them. I found that verbal responses were as much affected as were motor responses when they were combined, as compared to when they were produced singly. The significance of these findings lies in the fact that certain motor-verbalization combinations result not only in the failure of motor regulation through task-relevant speech but also in an actual disruption of the speech itself. Furthermore the verbalizations showed a decrement of speech quality. Thus, through age 4 on these tasks, language does not remain unaffected when combined with motor activity, and the effect is negative.

In noting a decrement in quality of verbal product (McCabe, Levin and Wolff, 1974) lower levels of syntactic complexity or well formedness are not suggested. The decrement appears rather as an impoverishment of semantic content. This demands some exploration. Why should the semantic content of the speech be negatively affected by combining it with a concurrent relevant motor activity?

Implications from Luria's Framework

Some insight into why concurrent motor behavior might impoverish semantic content may be gained from a closer examination of Luria's (1961) work. In discussing the development of the verbal regulation of behavior, he outlines a two-dimensional stage-like sequence whereby the verbal control of a bulb-press response becomes possible. One dimension of this development involves a gradual internalization of control beginning with control by an external agent (an adult speaking to the child), through control by the child's own overt speech, and reaching a mature stage when the child becomes capable of using his own internal or covert speech. The second dimension involves an actual change in the function served by speech: from serving first as an initiator, but not an inhibitor of a motor response, it begins to take on both these functions. This however is not yet the final state in this dimension of development. The instruction "Don't press." will initiate pressing just as will the instruction "Press." Luria implies (1960) that the child could as well have been uttering a nonsense syllable, and the effect would have been the same. Luria has termed this control the "impulse aspect" of speech (1961, p. 85): the motoric impulse in the speech carries over to create an impulse in the hand. The final stage in the sequence of development is reached when the "significative (or meaningful) aspect" becomes influential in initiating and inhibiting the concurrent motor act.

The finding that the impulsive or motor aspect and the significative or semantic aspect assume control during separate stages suggests that the functions of these two aspects, rather than being interdependent through developmental transmission of control from one to the other, may simply be independent. This independence is especially indicated by the fact that the significative aspect of speech eventually assumes the role of a true facilitator, whereas the impulse aspect does not. The significative aspect functions by concentrating attention on relevant dimensions and/or by providing a plan for a sequence of behaviors to be implemented. For example, in looking for a name in a telephone book, we might repeat the surname, "Jones," over and over until we find it; having found Jones, we might go through the list of Joneses repeating the first name, "John"; and then perhaps we might go through all the John Joneses repeating the initial or the street name, and so on. Here we are concentrating on what is relevant to the task of finding the telephone number. Having found the number, we are likely to repeat it as we are dialing it or writing it down. Repeating the number here serves as a guide for the sequence of dialing or writing.

The impulsive aspect on the other hand appears to help by hindering. The effectiveness of the task-relevant speech in regulating the bulb-press during this second phase depends on the conflict produced by the execution of both speech and hand responses. As Wozniak (1973) has phrased it, "Luria was discussing a feedback effect of speech on an already active and, in fact, perseverating motor response which reflected back on the response to conflict with it and inhibit it" (p. 6). The control comes through inhibition which, in turn, comes through interference of the nonspeech motor system by the speech system.

It is important to note that it is the significative aspect of the speech that is the weakest at this early stage, in that it is this component that fails in its influence. It should also be noted that this failure of control is not due to the child's lack of understanding of what he is saying. He can both understand the instruction for himself and can produce it appropriately to the stimuli when it is produced separately from the motor task. The difficulty comes about when he is asked to combine the two responses. He tells himself to do one thing, "Don't press.", and does something quite different: he presses.

Luria suggests that when the impulse and significative aspects of speech are in conflict, it is the impulse aspect that exerts control. Within the usual Lurian paradigms, however, the possibility of thoroughly examining effects on the quality of the significative component is rather limited. Since the child is told precisely what to say, he is simply repeating a statement that has already been formulated for him. Although some studies do test and guarantee comprehension of task instruction that the child will utter to himself (Meacham, 1972), one can rarely be sure this is true in most Soviet and Soviet-inspired studies in which children are told what to say to themselves. They might be considered similar to the case of a child reciting the "Pledge of Allegiance to the Flag" or a memorized poem without any understanding of the meaning of what is being uttered and, perhaps, without recognizing that this formulation of sounds has any meaning. In these cases the child is producing the motor component of the speech, but it is possible that he is not really producing a significative component. Luria's interpretation of his data implies that the significative component is there, but that its relative weakness with respect to the impulse component eliminates its effectiveness. An equally plausible explanation is that the child parrots the command for himself without the command's generating any meaning for him. This interpretation is similar to the mediation deficiency hypothesis (Flavell, Beach, and Chinsky, 1966) but is unique here in being applied to overt instructions for oneself.

In either case, the significative component of the speech appears to be the weakest element in the total production at an early developmental stage and therefore the one most susceptible to disruption. There is an unfortunate lack of corroborative evidence on this issue however. Providing the child with a specific instruction for him to say to himself has been the rule in studies of verbal control (for a review see Wozniak, 1972) and as long as this is the case, it is not possible to examine the aspects of the verbal response separately. It is only when it is left up to the child to generate an appropriate verbalization that we can assess his ability to produce the significative component.

Empirical Reports of Speech Degradation

Several investigators have reported qualitative differences in the child's spontaneous private speech, which corroborate the idea that motor tasks may degrade semantic quality. The McCabe, Levin, and Wolff (1974) findings suggest that spontaneous verbalization is difficult for the young child. Kohlberg, Yaeger, and Hjertholm (1968) ranked private speech in a hierarchy of maturational levels, each level increasing in quality for aiding behavior or thought. These authors report improvement in the guiding character of private speech as a function of age. They also report that less mature forms of such speech were associated with more difficult rather than easier tasks. Caution is required in accepting the latter result because task difficulty was determined to a large extent by the children's comments. Meichenbaum (1975) and Meichenbaum and Goodman (1971), using the Kohlberg, Yaeger, and Hjertholm (1968) hierarchical categories of private speech, report that children rated as operating with an impulsive cognitive style used more immature speech than did children rated reflective. Zivin (1972) found significantly more inarticulate speech on hard finger mazes than on easy ones.

The general conclusions that can be drawn from these observations are that: the less mature the child, the less likely he is to say anything that might be considered useful to him and the more difficult the task, the less mature the speech. The quality of the significative component of speech-for-self then does vary as a function of several factors, which are apparently related to task facility. We shall return to this issue later.

This chapter has so far been concerned with the nature of verbal-motor interaction, specifically the questions of if and how speech is affected. Having argued that it is affected, and qualitatively so, the next question concerns the source of the conflict.

EMPIRICAL SEARCHES FOR THE SOURCE OF SPEECH DEGRADATION

Study I

If we consider overt speech to be an activity consisting of at least two components, a motor component and a significative component—which are somewhat independent (that is, either can be produced without the other)—then overt self-guidance on a motor task demands three productions. These are the production of the two speech components and the production of the motor response to be guided. The child may experience difficulty in these situations because he cannot do so many things at once. Miller, Shelton, and Flavell (1970), in a simpler analysis of the problem, similarly suggested that too many simultaneous responses are a source of manual error in Lurian studies. If one of the components could be eliminated, that might eliminate the tested task difficulty. Since it is the significative aspect of the speech that is of most interest here, eliminating it would not be very informative. Instead it would be interesting to see the effects of manipulating either or both of the other components.

It is possible that the source of the difficulty lies in the need to produce two motor acts, the motor component of the speech and the accompanying motor activity. Even though the child succeeds in emitting both, his difficulty in doing so may be reflected in impoverished verbal content. We can examine this possibility by not requiring the nonverbal motor activity, as in McCabe, Levin, and Wolff (1974), or by eliminating the motor component of the speech. Combining manual manipulation with covert speech production would allow an assessment of (1) whether the child has difficulty in combining motor activity and speech in its totality or (2) whether the difficulty is more specific to the motor-motor character of overt speech and other motor production.

This latter approach presents two initial problems. Can children as young as 3 or 4 years produce covert speech? Even if they can, how can it be observed and measured? The common assumption (for example, Piaget, 1923/1955, 1962; Vygotsky, 1934/1962) seems to be that young children are not capable of covert speech. At the same time there is no reported evidence that young children have ever been instructed to produce covert speech. With the awareness that children do not always do all that they can do (Keeney, Cannizzo, and Flavell, 1967; McCabe, Levin and Wolff, 1974) some pilot testing was undertaken. Children were presented with two objects and asked to think of a story about them, but to keep the story secret. The children gave every evidence of being able and willing to comply with the instructions. When asked to tell the secret stories, they were obviously prepared. Incidental observations of facial expressions, such as furrowing of brow followed by a smile, also indicated ability to perform the task. Several children thought for a moment and then whispered, "I got one."

The problem of observing the covert sentences was a bit more difficult. Since sentence elaboration is a known facilitator of paired-associate learning (Davidson, 1964), such a paradigm seemed to be a good vehicle for examining the sentence-production ability. If the children could produce covert sentences, this should be reflected in their recall performance. Further evidence would be provided by requesting the children to reproduce the sentences later. Distortion and/or forgetting were a risk, but there was no reason to suspect that it would operate differentially for different production conditions: that it would be greater when covert sentences were produced with the nonverbal motor activity than when these sentences were produced alone.

Subjects

Children of two age levels were included. Children of the age of about 7 years would be expected to be more practiced in the use of self-guiding speech and therefore would have less difficulty producing the combinations of responses. Four-year-olds should have difficulty with some combinations.

Sixty children between approximately 3½ and 4½ years of age ($\overline{X}$ = 4 years, 2 months) served as subjects in the younger group and sixty children between approximately 6½ and 7½ years of age ($\overline{X}$ = 7 years, 1 month) served as subjects in the older group. Boys and girls were about equally represented in both groups. Within each group Ss were randomly assigned to the six treatment conditions described below.

Materials

Pairs of objects were formed from a collection of 24 common children's toys (a metal truck, a wooden rolling pin, a plastic bird). All toys were small (2 to 8 inches on the longest dimension) and easily labelable by children. Pairs (for example, pig and boat) were formed so that an interaction between them was possible but not obvious.

Since visual feedback from the manipulation of the objects might have been an interfering variable in the work of McCabe, Levin, and Wolff (1974), in this study the child's manipulations were hidden from his sight. For this purpose a cardboard box "stage" was constructed with a cloth curtain hung across the front of the stage. The child could then put his hands under the curtain and make the toys "act" on the stage without seeing the actual interaction. The back of the box was left open so that an observer could record the manipulations.

Procedures

The children were tested individually in a small experimental room. Upon entering the room the child was seated at a low table and told he was going to play a game with some toys which would be shown to him two at a time. Instructions as to what he was expected to do were then given according to the condition to which the child had been assigned:

Overt Story — Manipulation: Make one toy do something to the other toy and tell a story about what they are doing.

Overt Story—No Manipulation: Tell a story about one toy doing something to the other toy.

Covert Story — Manipulation: Make one toy do something to the other toy and think of a story about what they are doing, but keep the story secret.

Covert Story — No Manipulation: Think of a story about one toy doing something to the other toy, but keep the story secret.

Control — Manipulation: Make one toy do something to the other toy and think of the names of the two toys.

Control — No Manipulation: Think of the names of the two toys.

Subjects in each condition were then given three practice toy pairs to ensure that they knew what was expected. If a child failed to produce an appropriate sentence or manipulation, an example was provided by the experimenter. Following the example pairs, the 12 experimental pairs were begun. The instructions in each treatment group were repeated for each of the pairs of toys used. This step was undertaken to insure that a child would not fail to produce the requested interactions due to forgetting an instructional set. After the presentation of all 12 pairs, children were given a recall trial in which one member of the original pair was presented and the child was asked to recall the other member. Following the recall test, pairs were recreated and the child was asked to tell the story he had thought of earlier. (Children in the control conditions were asked to "make up a story" since they had been instructed only to think of the names of the toys earlier.)

Scoring Data

As a measure of the quality of the sentences and manipulations, transcripts of both kinds of productions were submitted to two independent "blind" judges. Productions in which the two toys were directly interacting in a manner that conformed reasonably well with the properties of both were scored as acceptable (1), all others were scored as not acceptable (0). Thus for a pair consisting of a plastic cowboy and a metal pitcher, sentences such as "He's pouring coffee." or "He's drinking out of it." were considered acceptable, while sentences such as, "The cowboy's sitting on it." or "He hit it." were considered not acceptable. Similar criteria were employed for the rating of manipulations. Interrater reliability for sentence ratings was .87 and for manipulation ratings .91. Scores for each child were obtained by averaging the ratings of the two judges.

Results

Recall test results yielded relatively little information and will not be dealt with in detail. Essentially the recall test proved too difficult for the 4-year-olds.

More interesting results were obtained with regard to the sentences and manipulations produced. As can be seen in Table 1, overt sentence production at both age levels appears to suffer when combined with manipulation. Covert sentence production also seemed to suffer, but only among 4-year-olds. For the 7-year-olds, eliminating the motor component of the speech appears to eliminate the difficulty in sentence production. In contrast to McCabe, Levin, and Wolff (1974), the manipulation ratings were unaffected by combination with sentence production, either overt or covert, at either age level.

The findings are interesting since they indicate the reliability of the effect on overt speech production and since they suggest that covert sentence production becomes more compatible with accompanying motor activity as a function of age.

There is a difficulty, however, concerning the validity of the sentence productions. It is possible that children in the covert-sentence conditions produced no sentences during the learning trial and only produced them on the spot when asked to repeat them aloud. Alternatively, the intervening recall trial may have interfered with remembering the sentences produced. Neither of these objections, however, can really account for the differential productions in the two covert conditions. In answer to the first objection, an observation of the sentences produced by the manipulation and no-manipulation control subjects who were asked to produce sentences on the spot during the post-recall trial revealed no differences between sentences produced by children who had previously manipulated the objects and those who had not. Nevertheless, the validity of the sentences for children in the

TABLE I Means and Standard Deviations of Sentence and Manipulation Ratings (Study I)

		Overt Sentences		*Covert Sentences*		*Control*	
		M	No M	M	No M	M	No M
4-year-olds:							
Sentences	$\overline{X}$	7.50	10.60	8.00	10.00	8.95	8.95
	SD.	2.90	1.00	2.46	2.16	2.07	3.25
Manipulations	$\overline{X}$	7.85	—	7.15	—	7.25	—
	SD.	1.84	—	3.45	—	2.82	—
7-year-olds:							
Sentences	$\overline{X}$	8.35	10.15	9.45	9.70	10.35	9.35
	SD.	2.72	1.13	1.90	.95	2.20	2.05
Manipulations	$\overline{X}$	9.10	—	9.85	—	9.50	—
	SD.	3.41	—	1.51		2.08	—
Both ages:							
Sentences	$\overline{X}$	7.92	10.37	8.72	9.85	9.65	9.15
Manipulations	$\overline{X}$	8.47	—	8.50	—	8.37	—

Note: M equals manipulation

covert conditions needed further documentation. In an effort to solve this problem and also to test the reliability of the covert sentence-motor interaction, a further study was undertaken.

Study II

If intervening recall trial in Study I distorted the memory and consequent reproduction of the sentences generated earlier, then giving the children an opportunity to repeat the sentences aloud immediately should eliminate the problem. In addition children in the manipulation conditions of Study I were touching the objects, while children in the no-manipulation conditions were not. It could be argued that touching (by producing additional stimulation) rather than the motor manipulations was responsible for the decrement in sentence performance in the manipulation conditions.

Birch (1974) has noted that when instructions emphasize one of the task components, there is a resultant decrement in performance on the other component. In Study I the order of instructions seems to emphasize the motor response. Although the order of instructions given before the presentation of each pair was randomly alternated across trial, if the original instructions emphasized the motor response, this may have been enough to produce the sentence decrements in the combined conditions. Since sentence production was the basic type of data, instructions for the combined conditions in Study II were reversed, thereby giving emphasis to the request for sentence production.

Subjects

A group of 30 children aged 2½ to 5 years ($\overline{X}$=4 years, 5 months)' served as subjects and were randomly assigned to the two treatment conditions. Boys and girls were approximately equally represented in both groups. Due to an equipment failure the sentences of one child were not recorded, leaving 29 children in all.

Procedure

The procedure was similar to that of Study I with the following exceptions:

1. Only two treatment conditions were employed: Covert Sentence — Manipulation and Covert Sentence — No Manipulation.
2. Children in the No-Manipulation condition held the objects inside the stage, but did not manipulate them.
3. After the presentation of each of the toy pairs, the toys were put out of the sight of the child and he was asked to tell the story he had just thought of.
4. No recall test was administered.
5. The order of instructions for children in the combined response condition was reversed so that they were told to make up a story about one toy doing something to the other toy and to make them do it. This instruction sequence may have emphasized sentence production.

Scoring of Data

Transcripts of sentences were scored in the same manner as for Study I. Interrater reliability was .93. Manipulations were scored by only one judge.

Results

Summary data for sentence and manipulation ratings are presented in Table 2. As is evident from the table, children asked to produce both responses produced poorer sentences than children asked to produce only the verbal responses. This is consistent with the results of Study I.

TABLE II Means and Standard Deviations of Sentence and Manipulation Ratings (Study II)

		M	No M
Sentence	$\overline{X}$	5.57	8.32
	SD.	3.83	3.58
Manipulations	$\overline{X}$	6.67	—
	SD.	2.74	—
	N	15	14

Note: M equals manipulation.

Discussion of Studies I and II

None of the procedural modifications appeared to have any substantial effect since both the direction and the degree of difference was approximately the same as that found in Study I. The intervening recall trial in Study I does not seem to have produced marked distortion or at least cannot be considered to account for the differing sentence performance of the manipulation and no manipulation groups. The variable of touching the objects also does not seem to matter. Altering the order of instructions did not produce any substantial change in the sentence and manipulation ratings. Although scores on both measures are somewhat lower than those in Study I the relationships among them remain the same.

The first conclusion drawn from these data is that the demand for simultaneous sentence production and motor activity indeed results in a decrement in sentence quality at the semantic level. Although the difference is not large, on the order of 15 to 20%, it is highly reliable.

The second conclusion is that with age this detrimental effect narrows from affecting both overt and covert speech to affecting only overt speech. For the younger children it does not seem to matter whether the verbalization requested is overt or covert, while for older children it does.

This lack of a difference under conditions of overt and covert sentence production for the younger children suggests two interpretations. Covert verbalization at this age may be very close to an overt verbalization. Even though there were no apparent lip movements or other speech motor involvements, the covert production may have carried with it enough of a motor component (see Sokolov, 1968/1972) to induce conflict between manipulation and speech production (that is, there may have been enough activation of the speech-motor apparatus to induce an efferent conflict, even though it was not sufficient to produce apparent movement). This interpretation assumes that the source of the difficulty in the task is the dual motor production.

Alternatively, it may be that for the younger child neither form of language is truly compatible with accompanying motor activity. Even though in covert language production the child has effectively eliminated speech-motor activity, the task is still too demanding and the language production suffers. The result is that the young child with either type speech is incapable of effectively integrating the language with the motor activity.

The fact that among older children the quality of overt sentence production is substantially decreased in the combined condition but that of covert sentence production is not, shows that the two forms of speech do not operate in the same way by age 7. The difference between overt and covert language production of course involves more than the elimination or reduction of speech-motor involvement. It is not possible to determine here which, if any, of the possible precise sources of conflict (for example auditory feedback, complexity of cortical activity for production, multiplicity of behavior monitoring) is involved in the evident conflict. Regardless of the precise source of the conflict, overt speech does appear to produce a conflict not produced by covert speech. While covert speech, it seems, can be easily integrated with accompanying motor activity, overt speech does not appear to be any more compatible than it was for the younger children. At age 5 overt or covert speech interferes with the processing that is behind the production of appropriate semantic content. At age 7 only overt speech interferes with this processing. One might tentatively expect even older persons to be similarly susceptible to such interference in overt speech quality.

The third conclusion is on the general relative weakness of the semantic rather than the motoric (or even the syntactic) component of speech. In these studies it was again the meaningful component of speech which proved to be the weakest and the first to be affected when the combination activity becomes difficult.

A DUAL ASPECT VIEW OF SPEECH FUNCTIONS IN MOTOR FACILITATION

A provocative contradiction appears when these semantic decrement results are contrasted with other findings. Despite the wide choice of what to say in these two studies, the child was not really given the option to produce speech or not. With concurrent motor activity, the quality of overt speech suffered. Observation of children in more natural settings reveals that, even when it is not demanded, they do often opt for speech accompaniment. Especially interesting is the common report (for example, Kohlberg, Yaeger, and Hjertholm, 1968; Meichenbaum, 1975; Vygotsky, 1934/1962; Roberts,

Chapter 9) that as the task becomes more difficult for the child, he begins to externalize speech as an aid. While the child might use covert speech in a less demanding situation, the increase in difficulty elicits overt private speech. This is somewhat paradoxical. If overt speech is less compatible with accompanying activity than is covert speech, one would expect less rather than more overt speech as task difficulty increases. For the child (or adult) to introduce a controlling activity that is not completely compatible with the task should serve only to increase further the difficulty. This increase in difficulty, furthermore, would express itself by diminishing the very characteristic of the speech, which might otherwise be facilitative.

When discussing the developmental internalization of self-guiding speech and its externalization during the performance of difficult tasks, it is usually implied that overt and covert self-guiding speech are on a qualitatively identical continuum of quantity. Overt speech is in some sense quantitatively "more speech," or at least "more speech-associated stimulation" than is covert speech. This is because they usually are seen as functionally equivalent, despite physical differences. The paradox can be constructively resolved by considering that the shift from covert to overt speech involves the introduction of a qualitatively different self-guiding function.

It is quite clear that among the 3½-year-old children in Luria's experiments, the impulse aspect of speech operates by conflicting with the motor activity. This has the facilitative effect for the child of segmenting his bulb-pressing. One does not generally consider that this impulse aspect of speech may continue to function usefully beyond this early childhood period. Furthermore, focusing on a verbal-regulation explanation of task improvement blinds one to the fact that with age (or practice) performance of the task becomes subjectively easier, completely apart from speech involvement. This increase in general proficiency with respect to the task reduces the need for the rudimentary form of verbal control provided by the impulse aspect of speech to further facilitate performance. With a more difficult task however we might see the child reverting to a dependence on the impulse aspect.

When self-guiding speech becomes overt, it may be due to a need for the control provided by the impulse aspect: an individual may be activating old strategies on a trial-and-error basis or the learning of many complex motor activities may be facilitated by initially breaking the activity down into smaller sequential units. Overt speech may provide a means for this kind of segmentation. As proficiency increases, the need for the simplification by segmentation no longer exists. The overt speech disappears and the performance of the activity becomes smoother.

Consider the following example. Suppose that I am teaching you to knit. You have never tried it before and so have no idea how to go about it. First I demonstrate to you the necessary sequence of movements. I put the right-hand needle through the loop of yarn on the left-hand needle, loop the string of loose yarn around the right-hand needle, and then pull this new loop through the previous one. If you watch someone who is experienced at the activity, you won't see this as a sequence of steps, but rather as one continuous smooth movement. As a beginner, however, you would not be able to achieve the same smoothness and continuity. What you would need to do is to take things one step at a time. You would see basically three steps and perform them one at a time. In the process of doing so, chances are, you will find that you are talking to yourself. If I have described the steps to you, you will probably utter some abbreviated version of what I said. If I have not provided such verbalization, you might utter "One, two, three." or There, there, there." It won't really matter what you say. You would be aided just as much by counting as you would be by describing the steps. The point is that saying something while you are working at it serves to segment the action and thereby facilitate it. It would be hard to argue that your counting is verbal direction in the sense of telling yourself what to do. There isn't any real information provided by such self-guiding speech. As you become more proficient you would find that you were no longer saying anything aloud and you would also find a greater continuity in the action sequence.

Again take a task that is less easily visualized. Suppose that you are learning a new dance. Very likely you would find that you would be counting as you performed the steps. Isn't the function of this counting to help keep time to the music? This would seem to be the case until you notice that the counting is present whether or not there is any music accompanying you, and also that the counting doesn't necessarily have a definite rhythm. What it does serve to do is to break down the complex movement into a series of smaller and more manageable units. As you become more practiced at the steps, the counting disappears and your movement becomes smoother.

At some point in learning the action sequence, facilitation is gained from segmentation. It is at this point that we are most likely to observe overt speech-for-self. What I have argued, is that it is the impulse aspect of this speech that serves here as the facilitator and that it does so by interfering with the motor activity. Once a level of proficiency is attained, the overt speech drops out, and we can assume that any further verbal control comes from covert speech. By age 7 it is covert speech which has a significative aspect not so fragile that meaning cannot exert a more stable aiding influence.

Thus the interaction between the speech and the motor activity is a two-way interaction whose direction oscillates according to age and task facility. In the initial learning stages the motor activity is aided by the impulse aspect of the speech, which gradually gives way as proficiency in performing the motor activity increases. This increase in proficiency, in turn, makes it possible for the significative aspect of covert speech to come into play and to further facilitate motor performance. (Increased motor proficiency appears particularly necessary to allow covert signification below age 7.) As the motor activity becomes better learned and more automatized, even the covert speech becomes unnecessary and disappears. The functions served by these two aspects of speech are at once different, in that they exert qualitatively different effects, and similar, in that they both serve to aid in the learning of the motor activity. Their usefulness is appropriate to the level of facility of the accompanying motor behavior, which increases with their alternate aid.

The arguments presented are admittedly speculative. They are an attempt to account for the fact that humans opt to employ a form of behavior that, from one perspective, does not appear particularly adaptive. Furthermore we can assume that this is only one of the functions served by overt in contrast to covert speech.

References

Birch, D. "Motivation sharing in vocal-motor interaction." (Paper presented at the meeting of the Canadian Psychological Association, Windsor, Ontario, June 1974.)

Davidson, R. E. "Mediation and ability in paired-associate learning." *Journal of Educational Psychology*, 1964, *55*, 6, 352-356.

Flavell, J. H., Beach, D. R., and **Chinsky, J. M.** Spontaneous verbal rehearsal in a memory task as a function of age. *Child Development,* 1966, *37,* 283-299.

Keeney, T. J., Cannizzo, S. R., Flavell, J. H. Spontaneous and induced verbal rehearsal in a recall task. *Child Development,* 1967, *38,* 953-966.

Kohlberg, L., Yaeger, J., and **Hjertholm, E.** Private speech: Four studies and a review of theories. *Child Development,* 1968, *39,* 691-736.

Luria, A. R. Verbal regulation of behavior in M. Brazier, ed., *The central nervous system and behavior.* N. Y.: Josiah Macy Foundation, 1960.

______. *The role of speech in the regulation of normal and abnormal behavior.* J. Tizard, trans., New York: Liveright, 1961.

McCabe, A. E., Levin, J. R., and **Wolff, P.** The role of overt activity in children's sentence production. *Journal of Experimental Psychology,* 1974, *17,* 107-114.

Meacham, J. A. "Verbal-motor interaction during sequences of motor activity." (Ph.D. diss., University of Michigan, 1972.)

Meacham, J. A. "The role of verbal activity in remembering the goals of actions," in G. Zivin, ed., *The development of self-regulation through private speech.* New York: Wiley-Interscience, 1979.

Meichenbaum, D. "Theoretical and treatment implications of developmental research on verbal control of behavior." *Canadian Psychological Review*, 1975, *16*, 22-27.

Meichenbaum, D., and **Goodman, J.** Training impulsive children to talk to themselves: A means of developing self-control. *Journal of Abnormal Psychology,* 1971, *77,* 115-126.

Miller, S. A., Shelton, J., and **Flavell, J. H.** A test of Luria's hypothesis concerning the development of verbal self-regulation. *Child Development,* 1970, *41,* 651-665.

Piaget, J. *The language and thought of the child,* M. Gabain, trans. New York: Meridian, 1955. [Originally published, 1923.]

———. *Play, dreams and imitation in childhood.* New York: Norton, 1962.

Sokolov, A. N. *Inner speech and thought,* G. T. Onischenko, trans. New York: Academic, 1972. [Originally published, 1968.]

Vygotsky, L. S. *Thought and language,* E. Hanfmann and G. Vakar, eds. and trans. Cambridge, Mass.: MIT Press, 1962. [Originally published, 1934.]

Wozniak, R. H. "Verbal self-regulation of certain cognitive operations: The nature and effects of speech as a multiply reafferent human action system." (Paper presented at the Biennial Meeting of the Society for Research in Child Development, Philadelphia, March 1973.)

Wozniak, R. H., and **Nuechterlein, P.** *Reading improvement through verbally self-guided looking and listening.* A Research Development, and Demonstration Centre in Education of Handicapped Children Teachers' Summary, University of Minnesota, 1973.

Zaporozhets, A. V., and **Elkonin, D. B.** *The psychology of preschool children,* J. Shybut and S. Simon, trans. Cambridge, Mass.: MIT Press, 1971. [Originally published, 1964.]

Zivin, G. "Functions of private speech during problem-solving in preschool children." (Ph.D. diss., Harvard University, 1972.)

CHAPTER 7

The Role of Verbal Activity in Remembering the Goals of Actions

JOHN A. MEACHAM
State University of New York at Buffalo

The purpose of this chapter is to discuss the role of the semantic aspect of verbal activity or speech in describing and remembering the goals of actions, so that the outcomes of these actions may be evaluated. This process will be illustrated by data that reflect sequences of changes in children's verbal and motor actions, including changes from initially inappropriate motor actions to appropriate actions. This role of verbal activity in remembering can be distinguished from interpretations of the role of verbal activity that emphasize either the impulsive or motoric aspects of verbal activity, or the mediational function of verbal activity in discrimination learning, remembering, planning and so on. Thus the role of verbal activity discussed is semantic in nature, but is not consistent with common interpretations of mediation theory.

IMPULSIVE AND MEDIATIONAL INTERPRETATIONS

Although developmental or age-related changes in the function of verbal activity or speech have implications for understanding the relationship between language and thought, in this chapter the sequence of changing relationships between language and *actions* will be emphasized. It is through the comprehension and translation of adults' verbal instructions into actions that the child's cognitive abilities are able to develop in their dependence on historical and cultural contexts (Wozniak, 1972, p. 23; Vygotsky, 1934/1962). Several examples may be given: Van Duyne (1974) has suggested that the ability to follow instructions is a prerequisite to achievement in the schools. The effectiveness of one's own verbal activity in providing self-rewards and self-instructions has been demonstrated also in numerous research and clinical applications (for example Israel and O'Leary, 1973; Meichenbaum and Goodman, 1971; Thoreson and Mahoney, 1974), and activities such

[1]Curt Acredolo and Egan Ringwall were quite helpful in suggesting improvements on an earlier version of this chapter.

as impulsiveness in hyperactive children (Meichenbaum and Goodman, 1971) and "craziness" in adult schizophrenics can be changed by training people to talk to themselves in appropriate ways (Meichenbaum and Cameron, 1973). Recently attention has been given to the role of self-instructional strategies in the performance of the elderly (Eisner, 1976; Katz, 1974; Meichenbaum, 1974). Verbal activity may also play a role in the development of planned or voluntary action (Wozniak, 1972; Eisner, 1976). Leithwood and Fowler (1971) have noted that the role of cognitive mediation in such motor actions as musical performance, car driving, and gymnastic activity has been considered insufficiently. Luria (1958/1960*A*) has presented evidence on verbal activity and abnormal motor development. Meichenbaum and Goodman (1969) have suggested that verbal activities may contribute to the individual's conceptual tempo or cognitive style.

The problem areas identified in the preceding paragraph have in common, in addition to an emphasis on relationships between language and action, an historical and theoretical tie to a series of investigations by Luria (1932, 1958/1960*A*, 1960*B*, 1957/1961*A*, 1961*B*, 1960/1963, 1959/1969; Luria & Yudovich, 1956/1959) on the importance of verbal activity in the development of voluntary control of motor actions in children. Luria suggests that between the ages of approximately 2 and 6, the relationship betwen verbal and motor actions passes through a series of stages. During the first stage the verbal activity of an adult is sufficient to initiate motor actions in the child, but not to cause a change if the child is already engaged in an ongoing motor activity. During the second stage the child is able to perform single, discrete motor acts if he engages also in a verbalization such as "Press" or "Go." During the third stage the semantic aspect of the verbal activity becomes important in guiding the course of the motor action. (A more complete description of these stages is available in Luria, 1959/1969; Wozniak, 1972; and Bronckart, 1973.)

Although Luria's investigations are cited frequently as being consistent with, and in support of, verbal mediation theory, there exist no solid replications of his basic demonstrations (Bronckart, 1973; Rondal, 1974; Wozniak, 1972 p. 35). Further, there is little agreement as to the best interpretation of the data that Luria does present. Wozniak (1972, 1976) has suggested that verbal regulation of motor activity may be brought about through the child's orienting responses to either kinesthetic feedback from the motoric aspect of verbal activity, or auditory feedback from the acoustic aspect of the verbal activity. Others have suggested that some sequences of motor activity may be organized or otherwise regulated by coordination with various rhythms that may be involved in the production of verbal activity (Harris, 1976; Meacham, Harris, and Blaschko, 1973; Zivin, 1976). A number of the phenomena described by Luria can be interpreted also in terms of changes in the ability of the child to engage simultaneously in two potentially incompatible activities, a verbal activity and some other motor activity (Birch, 1971; Bronckart, 1973; Meacham, 1972*b*).

It is questionable, however, whether such interactions of the impulsive or motoric aspects of verbal activity with other motor activities should be referred to as instances of "verbal control," "verbal regulation," or "voluntary action." The use of such terms as these suggests too easily that verbal activity plays a role in guiding motor activity. A guiding function, it should be noted, would require a foreknowledge of the course and outcome of the motor activity. That such foreknowledge is not always present is illustrated by a 3-year-old-boy who was asked to repeat a series of commands (Meacham, 1972*b*). While the experimenter was holding the boy by the hands in order to keep him near the microphone, the boy gave a squeeze of the hand with each command which he repeated. There had been no training or responding with manual activity previous to this observation, and the impulsive squeezing by the boy served no function in the immediate situation. This boy's hand-squeezing, as well as some of the basic phenomena that Luria describes in the bulb-press paradigm, may be better understood as an incidental and involuntary interaction between verbal and motor activities, rather than indicative of the development of control, regulation, or voluntary action in the child.

Researchers, because of their expectations concerning the guiding function of verbal activity later in development, may have assumed too readily that impulsive or motoric effects are necessarily the precursors of voluntary action, and so attention has been diverted from the effects of the semantic aspect of verbal activity on motor activity. As a result it has been assumed, but not directly verified, that the ability of the child to control his motor activity proceeds from an impulsive, nonsemantic control in Luria's second stage to a semantic control in Luria's third stage. In the face of questions on the meaning of the terms "control" and "regulation" as applied to impulsive effects, and the obvious comprehension by the child of the semantic aspect of verbal activity throughout the sequence of stages (Bronckart, 1973), it is clear that these assumptions ought to be suspended and greater efforts made to understand the development of the role that the semantic aspect of verbal activity may play in the guidance of motor activity.

The role of verbal activity in guiding motor activity has been considered generally within the framework of verbal mediation theory. However, as Wozniak (1972, 1976), Meacham (1972*b*), Wilder (1976), and others have noted, this framework is inappropriate for interpreting many of the phenomena which Luria describes. In particular, verbal mediation theory requires that verbal activity precede motor activity in order to play a guiding role. However, Wohlwill (1973, p. 186) implies that even the occurrence of a verbal-motor sequence does not confirm that the verbal activity is mediating the motor activity. Yet in several investigations with preschoolers the motor activity was found to precede the overt verbal activity. The distinction between mediation and guidance of motor acts will become more clear presently.

As examples of research inconsistent with the mediation framework, both Miller, Shelton, and Flavell (1970) and Birch (1971) found motor activity to precede verbal activity in a dual reaction-time task. In Miller, Shelton, and Flavell's investigation children had been instructed to respond in a motor-verbal sequence. Also Zaporozhets, Zinchenko, and Elkonin (1964/1971) report that for older preschoolers "at first glance . . . it seems that the child speaks and acts simultaneously; however . . . one can observe that the verbal expression is found always at the end of the activity" (p. 213). Other Soviet researchers have made similar observations. Kohlberg, Yaeger, and Hjertholm (1968) cite studies by Traugott (1959) and Gan Kova (1960) that "indicate that children aged 6-7 can use verbal planning and task solution before overt action in the task, whereas children aged 3-4 can only verbalize in accompaniment with or following overt task action" (p. 699).

The remainder of this chapter is concerned with the question of how a guiding function of the semantic aspects of verbal activity, as opposed to the impulsive or motoric aspect, can develop when verbal activity *follows* rather than precedes the motor activity. It will be argued that an important function of verbal activity for preschoolers is to describe the outcomes of completed motor activities.[2] Later in development, verbal activity assists in remembering the anticipated goals of motor activities, so that the actual outcome of a motor action may be evaluated relative to the anticipated goal. Thus at this later stage in development, the semantic aspect of verbal activity serves to guide motor activity, not through initiating or directing motor activity (that is, by mediating, or coming between, a stimulus and a response), but rather by facilitating the remembering of anticipated goals and thus making possible a continuing evaluation of both completed motor actions and activities in progress.

Data to support this role of verbal activity in remembering the goals of actions come from an investigation that permitted the recording of extended sequences of changes in children's verbal and motor activities, including changes from initially inappropriate to appropriate activities. Since previous research on the interaction of verbal and motor activities has not permitted the examination of such changes in children's motor activities following their

[2]Vygotsky (1934/1962) vaguely suggested a self-regulating function of the speech that preschoolers use to describe an activity after it is completed. This was his earliest stage of self-regulation, as outlined by Zivin (Chapter 1).

evaluation of the activities in which they initially engaged, the rationale, method, and results of this investigation will be described in some detail.

CHANGES DURING SEQUENCES OF MOTOR ACTIVITY

Rationale for the Investigation[3]

The present investigation (Meacham, 1972 *b*; 1978) introduces three fundamental changes in the experimental paradigm employed by Luria (1960/1963) and others to investigate verbal-motor interactions more appropriately: (1) The task for the child is structured so that the primary focus is on changes in the sequence of the child's ongoing activities. Continuous recording of the child's motor activity permits observation of whether or not the child engages in an appropriate motor action following an initially inappropriate motor action; (2) An ambiguity in the interpretation of the effects of verbal activity in previous studies is avoided through presentation of verbal commands (for example, "Go") rather than arbitrary stimuli to which meaning must be assigned ("Go when you see the blue light"); (3) High priority is given to procedures that are easy for the child to understand and to activites in which the child engages normally. Each of these three points is amplified below.

Changes in the Sequence of Activities

In previous studies of verbal-motor interactions, the conceptualization, experimental procedures, and the analysis of data have focused on discrete instances of motor activity, for example, the pressing of a rubber bulb. A more appropriate analysis of behavior, however, considers changes in the sequence of activities as the individual moves from one activity to another (Atkinson and Birch, 1970). Specifically, previous studies have required the child to wait patiently for the appearance of a stimulus and then to engage in various motor and verbal activities. The child's activity during the waiting period has been ignored entirely, however, to simplify conceptualization of the experimental paradigm and the child's performance. In fact the child is likely to be engaged during the waiting period in a variety of spontaneous motor activities, shifting position, touching the experimental apparatus, looking about the room, and so on.

When an individual engages in a particular activity, he simultaneously ceases to engage in an immediately preceding activity. The occurrence of such a change of activity depends on the relative strengths of the two activities. Consequently measures made on one (for example, latency of response)

[3]The author is indebted to David Birth for the significant role that his verbal activity played in guiding the course of this investigation.

depend on characteristics of the preceding activity. More generally it is necessary to consider each activity as it occurs within a continuous stream of activities in order to measure and interpret the frequency with which the child engages in the activity, the latency of response, the length of time spent in the activity, and so on (Atkinson and Birch, 1970). In previous studies of verbal-motor interaction, as in most traditional investigations of behavior, only the unit of behavior of immediate interest has been observed, and the importance of the surrounding sequence of activities has not been considered. The paradigm introduced in the present investigation, on the other hand, provides an activity in which the child can be engaged throughout each observational sequence, an activity whose nature can be determined at any time.

If the semantic aspect of verbal activity is important in guiding the changes in a sequence of motor activities, children engaging in verbal activity might follow instances of inappropriate motor activity by attempting to engage in the appropriate motor activity. Unfortunately Luria's bulb-press procedures and those of other investigators do not allow the observation of changes to appropriate motor activity, following initial inappropriate motor activity. Continuous recording of motor activity does, however, permit such observations to be made.

Mediation and Verbal Guidance

In certain of Luria's investigations and in those of Miller, Shelton, and Flavell (1970) and Meichenbaum and Goodman (1969), the child was required to respond with a press to the blue, but not to the yellow, light. It is not clear, however, whether the child's inappropriate responses to the negative stimulus are due to (1) failure to remember to which of the stimuli he has been instructed to press or (2) inefficiency in guiding his motor actions. When the child's verbal activity is found to be facilitating, it remains unclear whether the verbal activity is functioning as a mediator between the external stimuli and the appropriate actions that have been assigned to the stimuli or whether the verbal activity is contributing to the process by which the child guides his motor activities. Since the present investigation focuses upon the latter, that is, the interaction between concurrent verbal and motor activities, the child is presented with verbal commands (for example, "Go" and "Stop") rather than arbitrary stimuli such as lights.

Choice of Experimental Activities and Procedures

An attempt was made to create an experimental situation involving activities similar to those in which children are engaged routinely. In addition an effort was made to ensure that instructions to the child and the task in which the child engaged were as simple and straightforward as possible. Instructions used in previous investigations, suggesting semantically inconsistent verbal and motor actions (for example "When the light goes on say 'Don't push' and push"), were avoided. The training procedures were designed to avoid suggesting to the child through the instructions or in demonstrations of the motor activity anything regarding the sequencing or timing of the verbal and motor activities. Some investigators (for example, Miller, Shelton, and Flavell, 1970) have explicitly instructed the child to engage in a verbal and then a motor action.

In summary, the present investigation involves a simple and familiar situation for the child in which the sequence of changes from one motor activity to another can be recorded continuously. Among the important questions to be considered are (1) the appropriateness of the child's motor activity, particularly when the child engages in verbal activity during the same interval of observation and (2) the frequency of changes to appropriate motor activity following initially inappropriate motor activity.

Method

The method of investigation can be summarized briefly. Each of 48 children was instructed individually to ride a tricycle appropriately following each command ("Go," "Stop," "Up," and "Back") in two sequences presented by tape recorder. Half the children were instructed to repeat aloud each of the commands. A continuous record of the presentation of commands and each child's verbal and motor activity in three-second intervals following each command was obtained.

The 48 children, assigned to three age groups, were between the ages of 3 years 0 months and 6 years 1 month. Children were assigned in order of participation to either a verbal or a nonverbal condition and to one of two alternate sequences of commands. Equal numbers of boys and girls were assigned to each group. The means and ranges of ages of children in the three age groups are as follows: (1) Mean = 3 years 4 months, Range = 3 years 0 months to 4 years 0 months; (2) Mean = 4 years 5 months, Range = 4 years 0 months to 4 years 11 months; (3) Mean = 5 years 7 months, Range = 4 years 11 months to 6 years 1 month.

The main item of apparatus was a shiny red tricycle with bright red, white, and blue streamers on the handlebar grips. In order to record information regarding the rate and direction of movement of the tricycle, a small motor was positioned alongside the front wheel. Thus as the motor was turned by the front wheel of the tricycle a small current was generated. This current was conducted to a recorder through a cable 15 ft. long attached firmly to the rear of the tricycle. As the analog pen of the recorder indicated the amount of voltage generated by the motor, it also indicated the rate and direction in which the tricycle was moving.

A microphone was mounted at the center of the handlebars of the tricycle. If the child turned to one side, the handlebars were generally turned also, so that the microphone was always in the most efficient position for recording the child's verbal activity. The audio input was conducted through the cable to a tape recorder and to a relay, which activated an event pen on the recorder. Thus the onset and offset of commands presented and the child's verbal activity were displayed on the paper simultaneously with the record of motor activity in which the child was currently engaged.

The two main experimental conditions were: (1) a verbal condition in which children were instructed to engage in the appropriate motor activity following each command and to repeat each command aloud and (2) a nonverbal condition in which children were instructed only to engage in the appropriate motor activity. The purpose of these two conditions was to contrast the performance of children who accompanied their motor activity with verbal activity with that of children who did not.

Two different sets of tape recorded commands were presented to each child. The first of these sequences was analogous to the "Go/Don't go" or "Press/Don't press" paradigm for previous studies and thus presented only the commands "Go" and "Stop." Intervals of three seconds were provided between each command, in light of criticism that the intervals employed in previous studies were too brief (Wozniak, 1972). The number of commands in each sequence (eight) was determined by pilot-testing, and reflected both the length of time over which children continued to attend to the presentation of commands and the amount of space required for the "go" motor activity relative to the size of the room in which the testing was done.

The second set of sequences of commands presented the commands "Up," "Back," and "Stop." It was constructed primarily to contrast commands that, if the child responded appropriately, would lead the child either to disengage from an ongoing motor activity and stop, or to disengage from one ongoing motor activity and shift immediately to another motor activity. There were 10 commands in each of these sequences. "Up" and "Back" were chosen rather than, for example, "Forward" and "Backward," because they are, as are the commands "Go" and "Stop," words of one syllable and familiar to children between 3 and 6 years of age. Two sequences of each type were presented to each child.

Testing was done in a large room, 24 ft. long and 18 ft. wide, and bare except for a large table and chairs along the sides. As each child arrived at the room with a parent, the experimenter explained that he and the child would play some games together and that when they were finished the experimenter would have a surprise to give. Rather than risk having the child initiate a sequence of motor and verbal activity without fully understanding the instructions, the child was first instructed and trained using a small toy truck.

Then after getting on the tricycle, the child could be given quite brief instructions and told to do what had been done before with the truck. The instructions actually used were decided on after the experimenter had considered tape recordings obtained from pilot-testing. An effort was made to arrive at instructions that were natural sentence constructions for the experimenter and also easily understandable by the child.

The experimenter uncovered a blue and white dumptruck, 3 in. long, and after asking the child about the color of the truck and what it could be used for said: "Let's play a game with this truck. I'm making the truck go, go, and stop. Can you make the truck do what I say? Listen: Go, go, stop, stop, go, stop . . . Very good." As the experimenter said this he demonstrated the appropriate movements with the truck and then passed the truck to the child. This practice with the truck continued until the experimenter was satisfied that the child was not simply alternating between go and stop, but was in fact waiting to hear each command. For children in the verbal condition, the experimenter then said: "This time, say what I say: Go, go, stop, stop, go, stop . . . Very good." It should be noted at this point that the instructions have been arranged carefully not to imply any sequencing of the motor activity involved in pushing the truck and the verbal activity. For some children it was necessary to specify more directly the verbal activity that was required, for example "Say go . . . say stop . . . say stop," until the child engaged in verbal activity when presented only "Stop" or "Go." This procedure was continued until each child reached a criterion without coaching of three correct, but not necessarily sequential, repetitions of the commands presented. It was considerably more difficult to reach this criterion with younger children than with older children. The training for the up-back-stop sequences, later in the procedure, was similar. The experimenter demonstrated with the toy truck that "Up" was to indicate movement in the forward direction, and "Back" movement in the reverse direction.

The experimenter then told the child that he could ride the tricycle, and crouching in front of the tricycle said, "Now let's play a game on the tricycle. I want you to listen carefully and you'll hear 'go' and 'stop'. I want you to go and stop just like you did with the truck, okay?" For children in the verbal condition, the experimenter then added: "Remember, you must say each word, just like you did before." The experimenter then turned on a tape recorder, which he held in his hand. As the commands were presented, the child rode the tricycle toward the experimenter. Most children arrived at the end of the room just after presentation of the last command in the sequence.

The data for each child consist of a record showing the presentation of four sequences of verbal commands and a continuous record of the child's motor and verbal activity between presentation of one command and the next. The times from the onset of each command to each successive change in motor activity and to the onset of the child's verbal activity were measured to the nearest .1 sec. Reaction times were measured not only to the first change of motor activity within an interval of observation, but also to each successive change of motor activity. In general there were but one or two changes of activity within each interval of observation. The records of each child's motor activity were examined in order to determine: (1) whether or not the first change of activity within an interval was appropriate, that is, consistent with the implication of the command or (2) if the child was already engaging in the appropriate activity, whether or not the child continued to do so. However, if the child was engaged in an inappropriate activity, then the remainder of the three-second interval was examined for a change to an appropriate motor activity.

Results and Discussion

Although a number of findings emerge from this investigation (Meacham, 1972 *b*), only those few that are relevant to this discussion of the role of the semantic aspect of verbal activity will be presented. The frequency of changes to an appropriate motor action following an initially inappropriate motor action is greater for older children than for younger children. A ratio was computed of the number of changes from inappropriate to appropriate motor activity, relative to the total number of instances of inappropriate activity. As the ratios in Table 1 show, given that a child engages in an inappropriate motor activity, older children change to an appropriate motor activity more often than younger children. This age effect is significant for both the go-stop sequence, $F(2.36) = 4.89$, $p \leq .05$, and the up-back-stop sequence, $F(2.36) = 4.08$, $p < .05$.

TABLE 1. Mean Numbers of Intervals During Which Children Engaged in Inappropriate (I) or Inappropriate Followed by Appropriate (I + A) Motor Activity

	Go-Stop Sequence			Up-Back-Stop Sequence		
Age	I	I + A	$\frac{I + A}{I + (I + A)}$	I	I + A	$\frac{I + A}{I + (I + A)}$
3 years	1.81	.69	.28	3.56	1.56	.30
4 years	.56	1.06	.65	2.00	1.38	.41
5 years	.31	1.13	.78	1.06	1.00	.49

For children in the verbal condition, changing to an appropriate motor activity is more likely if there is verbal activity during the same interval (60%) than if there is not (39%). This association is significant, $X^2(1) = 5.07, p < .05$. It should be noted that the frequencies shown in Table 2 are observations and not children. Thus the hypothesis, tested and rejected, is that the distribution of observations is the same when verbalization occurs as when it does not. In order to evaluate the extent to which the finding can be generalized across different samples of children, observations were grouped according to the order in which children participated, as if the second half of the experiment were run as a replication. The distributions are similar for the two groups of children, and chi-square analysis indicates that the association between verbal activity and changing to an appropriate motor activity is not different for the "original" and "replication" groups, $X^2\ (1) = 2.72$, p greater than .05.

TABLE 2. Number and Proportion of Intervals During Which Inappropriate Motor Activity Was (I + A) or Was Not (I) Followed by Appropriate Motor Activity

	I		I + A	
Verbal activity	*n*	Proportion	*n*	Proportion
Present	17	.40	25	.60
Absent	57	.61	36	.39

Further evidence that verbal activity may play a role in guiding changes to an appropriate motor activity following an initially inappropriate activity is provided through an examination of verbal and motor reaction times. For 20 of the 25 instances of change accompanied by verbal activity, and for 9 of the 11 children making such changes, the appropriate verbal action preceded rather than followed the change. The mean reaction time from onset of command to verbal activity is 1.19 sec., and to an appropriate motor activity that follows an inappropriate motor activity is 1.77 sec., $t(10) = 3.41, p < .01$.

This finding of an association between the occurrence of verbal activity and changes to a more appropriate motor action following an initially inappropriate motor action (Table 2) is open to several interpretations. One possible interpretation, inconsistent with the hypothesis of verbal guidance of motor activity and with the reaction time data, is that changing from an inappropriate to the appropriate motor action leads to verbal activity. A second possible interpretation is that engaging in some additional covert activity (for example, perceiving that one has engaged in an inappropriate motor action) leads to engaging in both the appropriate motor action and verbal activity. This interpretation, however, leaves unclear what the function of such overt verbal activity might be. A third possible interpretation is that engaging in verbal activity serves to instigate or otherwise maintain covert activities, which in turn lead to subsequent changes in motor activity that otherwise may not have occurred. This is consistent with the obtained reaction time data, in which verbal activity preceded changes from an inappropriate to an appropriate motor activity. These covert activities may include remembering the anticipated goal of the motor activity and evaluating the outcome of the motor activity relative to this goal. This hypothesis is further explored later in this chapter.

When data from the verbal and the nonverbal conditions are compared, no differences are found in the frequency of inappropriate motor activities. One of several possible interpretations of this finding is that the initiation and direction of motor activity do not depend on verbal activity. This interpretation is consistent with the normality of motor coordination of deaf children, although alternative and equally viable developmental sequences for verbal and nonverbal children may be possible. Support is provided for Bronckart's (1973) conclusion, following a review of the literature, that "in the majority of cases the task is not less well done in the silent than in the verbal condition" (p. 433). A second interpretation, also consistent with Bronckart's conclusion, is that the 3-, 4-, and 5-year-old children in this investigation had already achieved Luria's third stage, according to which the semantic aspect of *covert* verbal activity, as well as overt verbal activity, may serve to guide motor activity. Thus the requirement to engage in overt verbal activity in the verbal condition would be coincidental with already ongoing covert verbal activities. This second interpretation, however, would require revising downward the approximate ages for Luria's stages. A third interpretation is that the motor activity, riding a tricycle, is so simple, familiar, or well practiced for preschoolers that the requirement that the child engage in verbal activity in the verbal condition could not be or was only minimally facilitative. If so, then an immediate task for researchers who wish to maintain the hypothesis of verbal initiation and direction of motor activity is to specify, according to dimensions of complexity, familiarity, and so on, those motor activities for which guidance by overt verbal activity is facilitative and those for which it is not. The construction of a general theory will await data from a variety of motor activities, including both laboratory and naturalistic investigations. The possibility that the processes under investigation are peculiar to certain response systems, for example, the hands as opposed to the feet, ought to be considered also (see Wolff, 1974). A fourth interpretation is that, although verbal activity facilitates motor activity, the quality, intensity, or frequency of verbal activity in the present investigation was not sufficient to demonstrate this.

The mean reaction times for the verbal activity of children in the verbal condition are slower than the reaction times for initiating the first motor action (which is not an action to which there has been a change from an inappropriate action). For the go-stop sequence, the mean motor reaction time is .89 sec., and the verbal reaction time is 1.18 sec., $F(1,18) = 22.17, p < .01$. For the up-back-stop sequence, the respective reaction times are 1.01 and 1.25 seconds, $F(1,18) = 13.77, p < .01$. When means for the two sequences are combined, verbal reaction times are faster than motor reaction times for only 4 children. For the remaining 20 children in the verbal condition, the motor reaction times are faster than the verbal reaction times. This finding of a motor-verbal sequence is consistent with the results of Miller, Shelton, and Flavell (1970), Birch (1971), and Zaporozhets, Zinchenko, and Elkonin (1964/1971). As others have noted, it is difficult within a verbal mediation theory framework to argue that verbal activity is initiating or directing motor activity, if the overt verbal action is found to follow rather than precede the motor action.

REMEMBERING THE GOALS OF ACTIONS

The general question in this section concerns whether or not the semantic aspect of verbal activity can have a guiding function for motor activity when verbal activity follows the motor activity. The hypothesis to be considered is that one function of the preschooler's verbal activity is to describe and facilitate remembering of the anticipated goals of motor activity, so that the outcomes of motor activities may be evaluated relative to the anticipated goals and a more appropriate motor activity may be subsequently engaged in if necessary. Thus verbal activity may be said to have a role in guiding motor activity, although an indirect role at this point in development and not an initiating or directing role. Among the aspects of this hypothesis which ought to be considered are the following: Do preschoolers forget the anticipated goals of their motor activity? If so, what might be the consequences? What is the developmental sequence by which children come to use verbal activity for remembering the anticipated goals of actions? Evidence can be drawn from a number of sources, including the investigation just described.

Consequences of Forgetting the Goals of Actions

Do preschoolers forget the anticipated goals of their motor activities? One purpose of the investigation described had been to eliminate the necessity for the child to remember arbitrary associations between colors and motor actions. Preschoolers may have difficulty also in remembering the goal specified by a verbal command long enough to consummate that goal in motor activity. This is not an assertion that preschoolers' motor activity is not goal-oriented; rather the goals may persist for only relatively brief durations before being replaced by other more immediate goals. To begin with a familiar example, it may happen that, although one has come to a restaurant with a particular dish in mind, consideration of the menu leads to substitution of a different entree. Assuming that the meal goes well, one is likely to consider afterwards that the anticipated goal had been fulfilled, although in fact the goal had changed in the course of being fulfilled. Similarly, in the case of a preschooler, engaging in a particular course of motor activity may lead to a substitution of the actual outcome for the anticipated goal. This would appear to be a more likely possibility for the preschooler than for an older child or adult, in the light of what is already known regarding the relatively limited remembering abilities of preschoolers as well as the characteristic dominance of perceptual over representational activities in the preoperational child.

A number of examples may be given. Evidence of forgetting the anticipated goals with a substitution of actual outcomes for those goals is found in a study by Strommen (1973), who investigated the development of the ability to play the game of "Simon Says." The study included preschool, kindergarten, first-, and third-grade children with approximately 40 children at each age. Eleven preschoolers, eight kindergartners, and four first-graders

> proceeded to err on every inhibition trial even though they "understood" the task as presented in the instructions. These children gave no indication of recognizing any discrepancy between their performance on example trials and on test trials, whereas other children frequently reacted to errors on test trials with expressions of dismay, sheepish grins or giggling, or body motions that appeared to serve as competing responses. [p. 852]

One interpretation of this observation is that in the course of engaging in the inappropriate motor activity, these children forgot the initial command to inhibit and consequently substituted the actual outcome of their motor activity for the anticipated goal.

A study by Trabasso and Foellinger (1975) illustrates that the modality in which commands are given may affect how well actions are understood, remembered, and carried out. Kindergarten, second-, fourth-, and sixth-grade children were presented with sequences of eight verbal or visual commands. The commands each consisted of an action and an object, for example, touch your nose, raise your hands, and so on. Performance was better for visual commands than for verbal commands, especially for the younger children. Visual commands may be remembered and performed better than verbal commands because they specify more concretely the goals of the motor activity.

Indirect evidence that preschoolers experience difficulty in remembering the goals of motor actions is provided by observations that young children engage in motor activity immediately on being presented with the goal of the motor activity. In other words the child must engage in activity toward the goal before it is forgotten. Lisina and Neverovich (1964/1971) report an investigation by Yendovitskaya in which children were asked to put construction materials into three boxes in a given sequence. Younger preschoolers performed the task by following only the instructions that related to the goal, but ignored instructions pertaining to the method for achieving the goal. How is this assertion of fixedness in preschoolers' activities towards a goal consistent with the general view of preschoolers as easily distracted? Perhaps the term distracted, referring to a state of conflict between two simultaneously competing goals, is inappropriate. For the preschooler a more appropriate characterization may be that goals are easily forgotten and thus the child ceases motor activity towards one goal and initiates motor activity towards an alternative goal.

What are the implications of the child's forgetting of the goals of actions for the quality of motor activity? One general schema for considering this question involves the principle of feedback, introduced into the psychological literature as the Test-Operate-Test-Exit or TOTE schema (Miller, Galanter, and Pribram, 1960). According to this schema motor activity is initiated or guided by the discrepancy between the anticipated state and the current state of the organism. Within such a schema evaluation of ongoing or completed motor activity requires both a memory of the anticipated goal of the motor activity and a perception of the current outcome of the motor activity (this second aspect will be discussed later). But how is an exit accomplished if the anticipated goal has been forgotten in the course of the motor activity? One means would be to substitute the actual outcome for the anticipated goal. Such a substitution would have no unfortunate consequences as long as the motor activity has been appropriate; but if the motor activity is inappropriate, such a substitution would lead to an exit with no further corrective or compensatory motor activity. In this manner the quality of motor activity is dependent on remembering what one anticipated doing. Verbal activity has been found to facilitate remembering (for example, Conrad, 1972). Thus verbal activity may play a role in remembering the goals of motor activities and consequently in testing or evaluating the outcomes of those motor activities relative to intended goals, but this is not the same as verbal activity playing a role in initiating or directing motor activity.

Some data to illustrate this role of verbal activity in remembering the goals of action are provided by the investigation described in the preceding section. In that investigation an association was found between the occurrence of verbal activity during an interval and changing to a more appropriate motor activity following an initially inappropriate motor activity. According to the present hypothesis the verbal activity facilitates the remembering of the anticipated goal, which is then available to be compared with the actual outcome of the motor activity. When a discrepancy is perceived, a change in motor activity occurs. Rondal (1974) has made a similar suggestion on the basis of recordings of electrical activity of lip muscles, as an indication of covert verbal activity, in adults and adolescents performing a bulb-press task. Errors in task performance are likely to be followed by verbal activities that "help the subject to signal to himself the defects in the performance and hence to concentrate his attention on them." Zivin (1973) also finds verbal activity to be associated with errors in performance. As 4-year-olds discover the correct paths through a series of finger mazes, "all the predominately task-relevant speech is in false paths, not choice points."

Indirect evidence is provided by Acredolo and Wozniak (1975), who used a procedure similar to that of Birch (1966). Preschoolers were instructed to push a lever all the way down and hold it down. The continuous record of lever depression showed that younger children shifted to alternative motor activities, such as partial depression or rapid manipulation of the lever, more often than older children. Nevertheless the younger children did correct their inappropriate activities by returning frequently to full depression of the lever, indicating that they were able to remember the required goal of the motor activity and that they were able to engage voluntarily in the required motor activity. Compensatory or corrective activities may follow from the perception of a lesser discrepancy in the case of older children than for younger children.

Describing the Outcomes of Motor Activity

An aspect of the TOTE schema is that, in order to test or evaluate the motor activity, the child must have available not only a memory of the anticipated goal, but also a perception of the actual outcome of the ongoing or completed motor activity. Verbal activity, occurring after the motor activity, may provide a means by which the child can describe the outcome of the motor activity to himself.

Is a child not able to perceive directly the outcome of his motor activity? One situation in which this may be the case is precisely the Luria bulb-press paradigm. Pressing a rubber balloon for a preschooler may be what pressing the accelerator and releasing the clutch are for an adolescent learning to drive. Initially the adolescent perceives how the motor activity is progressing not through tactile or kinesthetic feedback, but rather when the car jumps forward or stalls. Similarly the quality of the preschooler's bulb-pressing is increased when additional information on the outcome of the motor activity is provided. For example, Rondal (1974) found that the bulb-pressing of the 3-year-olds was improved when the bulb-press was followed by the barking of a mechanical dog. Luria (1961 *a*) reports that children are able to give a single, discrete press if the press turns off a light and the child has been instructed to press the bulb in order to turn off the light. In these examples the barking dog and the extinguishing of the light provide information to the child regarding the outcome of his motor activity. In the absence of information that can be used to test for whether or not the goal has been achieved, the child ought to continue pressing. The role of the external stimulation in these examples may be not to directly inhibit the ongoing motor activity but rather to provide information that, in conjunction with the memory of the anticipated goal, may be used to evaluate the continuing progress and the outcome of the motor activity.

The child's verbal activity can play a role in informing the child more completely of the outcome of his motor activity. Kohlberg, Yaeger, and Hjertholm (1968), expanding on Mead's (1934) theory of the development of language and thought, suggest that one function of collective monologue in private speech

> is communicating information to the self, is communicating the meaning or nature of the child's activity to the other, and hence is establishing the meaning for the self . . . From Mead's view . . . the young child does not have an awareness of his own action prior to communicating about it to others. [p. 704]

Kohlberg, Yaeger, and Hjertholm find that the proportion of private speech that can be included within the category of describing one's own activity declines steadily with increasing age, from approximately 35% at 5 years of age. This category includes "remarks about the self's activity which communicate no information to the listener not apparent from watching him" (p. 707). The function of such verbal activity for the child's perception of outcomes of motor activity is suggested by Luria and Yudovich (1956/1959):

> The word has a basic function not only because it indicates a corresponding object in the external world, but also because it abstracts, isolates, the necessary signal, generalizes perceived signals and relates them to certain categories; it is this systematization of direct experience that makes the role of the word in the formation of mental processes so exceptionally important. As the word influences the child, therefore, it deepens and immeasureably enriches his direct perception, forms his consciousness. [p. 23-24]

Lisina and Neverovich (1971), although describing the function of an adult's instructions rather than the child's own verbal activity, express a similar view of the role of verbal activity in enriching the perception of the outcome of motor activity: "Verbal directions isolate the most essential aspects of action for children, which may be difficult for the child to isolate out of the totality of circumstances from visual observation" (p. 345).

The Development of Verbal Guidance of Motor Activity

Leont'ev (1972/1974, p. 23; also see Meacham, 1977) has described actions as processes structured and directed by conscious goals. Consideration of actions within the TOTE schema, however, has shown the need to differentiate between anticipated goals of motor actions and actual outcomes of motor actions. Verbal activity may play a role in guiding the child's motor actions, both by facilitating the remembering of anticipated goals and by enriching and communicating to the child a perception of the outcomes of the motor activity.

The purpose of the present section is to place certain events within a possible developmental sequence. Four stages will be described, although it will be argued that there is considerable continuity in the function of verbal activity from one stage to the next.

The *first stage* may be characterized by the independence of the semantic aspect of verbal activity from motor activity and from covert activities or thought. Gal'perin (1953/1957; also see Gal'perin 1959/1969) suggests that in such a stage "the child can act correctly and with obvious understanding of objective relationships, yet he cannot give a comparable account of them and of his action" (Gal'perin, 1957, p. 220). Zaporozhets, Zinchenko, and Elkonin (1971) also describe an early stage characterized by "two independently ongoing types of activity: speech activity and intellectual activity" (p. 213). For example, Kendler (1964) observed that kindergarten children would continue to verbalize a rule learned prior to a reversal shift, even though the verbal rule conflicted with the correct choices that they were making. Thus, although the child in the first stage may accompany his motor activity with overt verbal activity, the two activities are independent, at least as far as the semantic aspect of the verbal activity is concerned.

In the *second stage* the child may engage in verbal activity to describe the outcomes of his motor activities, as Kohlberg, Yaeger and Hjertholm (1968) have suggested. Zaporozhets, Zinchenko, and Elkonin (1971) describe similarly an intermediate stage in which

> speech becomes a means for reflecting the situation. The experimenting child while executing a movement . . . immediately states it in his speech, thus describing what appears to be a verbal form of the activity, a copy of his behavior and the situation. [p. 213]

Because the verbal activity describes the outcome of the motor activity, it necessarily follows the motor activity (cf. the findings of Miller, Shelton, and Flavell, 1970; Birch, 1971). In this stage verbal activity "remains connected with the child's direct action in a particular situation" (Luria and Yudovich, 1959, p. 54), and so does not fulfill a guiding role, either to initiate or direct motor activity, or to facilitate the remembering of anticipated goals and thus aid the evaluation of the outcome of motor activity.

The *third stage* is characterized by the child's use of verbal activity to describe not the outcomes of motor activities, but rather the anticipated goals of motor activities. The transition from the second to the third stage may await the development, through practice at describing, of sufficient efficiency so that the verbal action may be subordinated as an operation to facilitate the action of remembering (in Soviet psychology operations and actions stand in a means-end relationship; see Meacham, 1972 *a*, 1977). In addition the transition may depend on covert activities or thought achieving a certain level of salience, in order that the content may be described in verbal activity. There is a continuity in the function of verbal activity from the second to the third stage—*describing* the products or outcomes of activities. Nevertheless this transition from describing actual outcomes to describing anticipated goals may be a critical one in development, for by describing anticipated goals the child is better able to remember them, and so it becomes possible to compare the remembered thought with the actual outcome.

Elkonin (1959/1969), in discussing an investigation by Manuilenko (1948/1975) in which the length of time children could engage in a particular pose was assessed, suggests that a qualitative change of behavior occurs when "for the first time behavior begins to be compared with an image, and the latter begins to emerge as a model" (Elkonin, 1969, p.203). Verbal activity is one means by which such an image may be retained in mind sufficiently long to be compared with the behavior. In the absence of verbal activity, the image may be overwhelmed by the perception of the actual behavior. Within this stage motor activity is still not initiated or directed by verbal activity; verbal activity plays a role in guiding the motor activity by facilitating the remembering of goals and the evaluating of outcomes. Data to illustrate this guiding function have been described earlier in this chapter, particularly the association between the occurrence of verbal activity and changes from an inappropriate to an appropriate motor activity. The achievement of this stage is summarized nicely by Luria and Yudovich (1959):

> . . . by comparison of the result obtained during the process of activity with that system of connections which underlay the project, the child ought to reach a position where he could objectively evaluate this product apart from his activity and consequently also take up a critical relation to it. [p. 84]

Through the second and third stages, verbal activity may follow rather than precede motor activity. Of course, the reaction time data of Miller, Shelton, and Flavell (1970), Birch (1971), and the investigation described in this chapter depend upon the observation of overt verbal activity rather than covert activities, and it would not be necessary that these activities be initiated centrally in the same sequence in which they appear peripherally. Nevertheless there may be some advantages for the preschooler to engage in verbal activity following the motor activity. First, for the child to engage simultaneously in verbal and motor activity would be to risk the disruption of either activity due to competition between the impulsive or motoric aspect of verbal activity and the required motor activity. The problem for the young child may be one of not being able to engage in two motor activities at the same time. Second, for the verbal activity that describes the anticipated goal to occur near the conclusion of the motor activity rather than before, would appear to be the optimal time for the testing or evaluating of the outcome relative to the anticipated goal. It may be, however, that the motor-verbal (in contrast to verbal-motor) sequence is of interest only as it helps us to understand the differentiation of this guiding role of verbal activity out of the descriptive role, but it is not critical in the actual process of remembering and evaluating. In short, the important developmental transition involves not whether verbal activity follows or precedes motor activity, but rather whether verbal activity describes the outcomes of motor activity or, later in development, the products of covert activities or thought.

The *fourth stage* is one in which verbal activity in conjunction with other covert activities may play a major role in planning and guiding the course of the child's motor activities. Zaporozhets, Zinchenko, and Elkonin (1971) describe this stage as one involving "greater and greater verbalization of intellect and intellectualization of speech . . . Speech here no longer follows the child's activity . . . but now dictates and determines the child's activity" (p. 214). The phenomena characteristic of this stage are those typically described in American research in terms of verbal mediation theory. As verbal mediation has been adequately reviewed elsewhere,[4] these phenomena are not discussed here. In summary, in this interpretation the descriptive role of verbal activity is emphasized: the child engages in verbal activity to describe first the outcome of this activity and later in development to describe the anticipated goals of his activity. The latter permits remembering the goals of action, the evaluation of outcomes, and the subsequent compensation or correction of motor activity.

[4]See Chapter 5 by Fuson.

CONCLUSION

Previous researchers have assumed that the impulsive and motoric aspects of verbal activity are the precursors of voluntary action. However, in this chapter it has been argued that many of the phenomena which Luria describes can be understood better as interactions of incompatible motor activities, and thus greater attention ought to be given to the role that the semantic aspect of verbal activity can play in the guidance of motor activity. The general question that is raised is how verbal activity can guide motor activity when it follows rather than precedes the motor activity, a finding that does not permit interpretation within verbal mediation theory.

One possible answer is that verbal activity facilitates remembering of the anticipated goals of motor actions, so that the outcomes of motor actions can be evaluated relative to the anticipated goals and compensatory or corrective actions can be engaged in if needed. Thus verbal activity plays a role in guiding motor activity, but not an initiating or directing role. The developmental antecedent to this guiding role may be the use of verbal activity in describing and communicating to the self the actual outcomes of motor activity. Some early self-regulatory function of descriptions that followed actions was suggested by Vygotsky (1934/1962), although he did not specify the mechanism by which it works. The sequence of stages outlined in this chapter is not necessarily contradictory to verbal mediation theory, but rather describes phenomena that occur earlier in development than the phenomena to which verbal mediation theory has been applied.

The investigation reported here, and particularly the finding of an association between the occurrence of verbal activity and changing from an inappropriate to a more appropriate motor activity, focuses not on discrete instances of motor activity, but rather on changes in the sequence of the child's ongoing verbal and motor activities (Atkinson and Birch, 1970). Additional investigations that consider the initiation and cessation of each activity as it occurs within the stream of the child's activities are needed. Acredolo and Wozniak (1975), McCabe (1974), Goodman (1978), and Zivin (1973) have recently emphasized sequences of motor activities. This concern with analysing temporal order is also reflected in studies reported by Meichenbaum and Goodman (Chapter 10), Roberts (Chapter 9), and Rubin (Chapter 8).

The development of the function of the semantic aspect of verbal activity, from describing the outcomes of motor actions to describing anticipated goals (which are the outcomes or products of covert activities), is consistent with dialectical interpretations of development (Meacham, 1977; Meacham and Riegel, 1978; Riegel, 1975 *a*, 1975 *b*). The child, by continuing to engage in verbal activity in order to describe the outcomes of motor activities, increases the efficiency and scope of his verbal activities so that in time they become more capable of being subordinated as operations (Meacham, 1977) for the purpose of describing anticipated outcomes. As Zaporozhets, Zinchenko, and Elkonin (1964/1971), Elkonin (1959/1969), and others have noted, this marks a qualitative change in the child's ability to guide his motor behavior. Eventually verbal activity is able to precede and presumably play an even more significant role in guiding motor activity. A further dialectical aspect is that the initial function of verbal activity as characterized in this chapter — describing and communicating outcomes to the self — is clearly developed in the course of social interactions. Thus the development of the guiding function of verbal activity within the individual reflects the cultural and historical context within which the child develops.

A unique perspective on the relationship between the development of strategies for remembering and the development of voluntary action or planned behavior is introduced in this chapter. Previously the interdependence of the development of abilities for remembering information about the past, with the development of knowledge of remembering abilities and their potential outcomes (metamemory), has been emphasized (for example, Flavell and Wellman, 1977; Meacham, 1972 *a*). In this chapter, however, the emphasis has been upon the interdependence of the remembering of goals of *future* actions with the increasingly voluntary, planned, or guided character of those actions. Research directed at understanding the development of remembering abilities in very young children has increasingly employed tasks that require remembering the goals of future actions, rather than remembering information about the past. For example, Wellman, Ritter, and Flavell (1975) asked 2- and 3-year-old children to remember for 40 sec. the location of a toy dog hidden under one of several cups. Delay period activities, such as looking at and touching the cup, were found to facilitate remembering the location of the dog.

Two comments are useful here. First, the ability required to perform this task is not identical with remembering as generally conceived, that is, as involving a claim to be able to think of, or know, something without having just learned it or without having just inferred it (Meacham, 1977; Munsat, 1966). What is required in this task and in the other investigations described is an ability to keep in mind or continue to attend to the anticipated goal of a motor action, for example, pointing to the cup that hides the dog. Second, our efforts to understand the development of remembering abilities in very young children by focusing on the remembering of information about the past may have been misdirected. The origins of early remembering abilities ought to be sought in the activities by means of which the child must remember what he plans to do (essentially the same problem has been pursued in college students by Meacham and Leiman, 1975, and Meacham and Singer, 1977). It is only later that abilities directed specifically toward the remembering of information about the past are differentiated from the preparation for future action. This developmental sequence has been captured previously by de Laguna (1937/1963):

> Memory is not originally a distinct and independent function. *It occurs first as a moment in the complete act.* The distinct living over of past experience, memory proper, becomes only gradually freed from the control of the particular act and the particular occasion, and at the same time distinguished, as the *recall* of the past from the *imagination* of the possible future. [p. 179]

References

Acredolo, C., and **Wozniak, R. H.** Developmental analysis of the verbal control of behavior in terms of activity persistence and change. [Unpublished manuscript, University of Minnesota, 1975.]

Atkinson, J. W., and **Birch, D.** *The dynamics of action.* New York: Wiley, 1970.

Birch, D. Verbal control of nonverbal behavior. *Journal of Experimental Child Psychology*, 1966, *4*, 266-275.

———. Evidence for competition and coordination between vocal and manual responses in preschool children. *Journal of Experimental Child Psychology*, 1971, *12*, 10-26.

Bronckart, J. P. The regulating role of speech: A cognitivist approach. *Human Development*, 1973, *16*, 417-439.

Conrad, R. The developmental role of vocalizing in short-term memory. *Journal of Verbal Learning and Verbal Behavior*, 1972, *11*, 521-533.

Eisner, H. C. Life-span cognitive development and the Soviet theory of self-regulation, in K. F. Riegel and J. A. Meacham, eds., *The developing individual in a changing world*, vol. I. The Hague: Mouton, 1976.

Elkonin, D. B. Some results of the study of the psychological development of preschool-age-children, in M. Cole and I. Maltzman, eds., *A handbook of contemporary Soviet psychology.* New York: Basic Books, 1969. [Originally published, 1959.]

Flavell, J. H., and **Wellman, H. M.** Metamemory, in R. V. Kail, Jr. and J. Hagen, eds., *Perspectives on the development of memory and cognition.* Hillside, N.J.: Erlbaum, 1977.

Fuson, K. C. The development of self-regulating aspects of speech: A review, in G. Zivin, ed., *The development of self-regulation through private speech.* New York: Wiley, 1979.

Gal'perin, P. Y. An experimental study in the formation of mental actions, in B. Simon, ed., *Psychology in the Soviet Union.* Stanford: Stanford University Press, 1957. [Originally published, 1953.]

______. Stages in the development of mental acts, in M. Cole and I. Maltzman, eds., *A handbook of contemporary Soviet psychology.* New York: Basic Books, 1969. [Originally published, 1959.]

Gan Kova, Z. A. The interrelation of action, image and speech in thinking of children of preschool age. *Problems of Psychology*, 1960, *1*, 26-35. [Cited by Kohlberg, L., J. Yaeger, and E. Hjertholm. Private speech: Four studies and a review of theories. *Child Development*, 1968, *39*, 691-736, p. 699.]

Goodman, S., The integration of verbal and motor behavior in preschool children. Unpublished doctoral dissertation, University of Waterloo, Ontario, 1978.

Harris, A. E. The function of speech rhythms in the regulation of non-speech activity, in K. F. Riegel and J. A. Meacham, eds., *The developing individual in a changing world*, vol. I. The Hague: Mouton, 1976.

Israel, A. C., and **O'Leary, K. D.** Developing correspondence between children's words and deeds. *Child Development*, 1973, *44*, 575-581.

Katz, M. M. The effects of aging on the verbal control of motor behavior. *International Journal of Aging and Human Development*, 1974, *5*, 141-156.

Kendler, J. S. Verbalization and optional reversal shifts among kindergarten children." *Journal of Verbal Learning and Verbal Behavior*, 1964, *3*, 428-436.

Kohlberg, L., Yaeger, J., and **Hjertholm, E.** Private speech: Four studies and a review of theories. *Child Development*, 1968, *39*, 691-736.

Laguna, G. A. de *Speech: Its function and development.* Bloomington: Indiana University Press, 1963. [Originally published, 1937.]

Leithwood, K. A., and **Fowler, W.** Complex motor learning in four-year-olds. *Child Development*, 1971, *42*, 781-792.

Leont'ev, A. N. The problem of activity in Soviet psychology. *Soviet Psychology*, 1974, *13*, 4-33. [Originally published in *Voprosy Filosofii*, 1972, *9*, 95-108.]

Lisina, M. J., and **Neverovich, Y. Z.** Development of movements and formation of motor habits, in A. V. Zaporozhets and D. B. Elkonin, eds. *The psychology of preschool children*, J. Shybut and S. Simon, trans., Cambridge, Mass: MIT Press, 1971. [Originally published, 1964.]

Luria, A. R. *The nature of human conflicts*, W. H. Gantt, ed. and trans., New York: Liveright, 1932.

______. Experimental analysis of the development of voluntary action in children, in *The central nervous system and behavior.* Bethesda: National Institutes of Health, 1960(*a*); also in M. P. David and J. C. Brengelmann, eds., *Perspectives in personality research.* New York: Springer, 1960(*a*). [Originally published, 1958.]

______. Verbal regulation of behavior, in M. A. B. Brazier, ed., *The central nervous system and behavior: Transactions of the third conference, 1960.* New York: Macy Foundation, 1960(*b*).

———. The genesis of voluntary movements, in N. O'Conner, ed., *Recent Soviet psychology,* New York: Pergamon, 1961(*a*). [Originally published in *Voprosy Psikhologii,* 1957, *3,* 3-19.]

———. *The role of speech in the regulation of normal and abnormal behavior,* J. Tizard, trans., London: Pergamon, 1961(*b*).

———. The role of speech in the formation of temporary connections and the regulation of behavior in the normal and oligophrenic child, in B. Simon and J. Simon, eds., *Educational psychology in the USSR.* Stanford: Stanford University Press, 1963. [Originally published, 1960.]

———. Speech development and the formation of mental processes, in M. Cole and I. Maltzman, eds., *A handbook of contemporary Soviet psychology.* New York: Basic Books, 1969. [Originally published, 1959.]

Luria, A. R., and **Yudovich, F. I.** *Speech and the development of mental processes in the child.* London: Staples, 1959. [Originally published, 1956.]

McCabe, A. E. Verbal-motor interaction in a thematic task. (Paper presented at the meeting of the Canadian Psychological Association, Windsor, Ontario, June 1974.)

Manuilenko, Z. M. The development of voluntary behavior in preschool age children. *Soviet Psychology,* 1975, *13,* 65-116. [Originally published in Izvestiya Akademii Pedagogicheskikh Hauk RSFSR, 1948, *14,* 89-123.]

Meacham, J. A. The development of memory abilities in the individual and society. *Human Development,* 1972(*a*), *15,* 205-228.

———. Verbal-motor interactions during sequences of motor activity. Unpublished doctoral dissertation, University of Michigan, 1972.

———. Soviet investigations of memory development, in R. V. Kail, Jr., and J. W. Hagen, eds., *Perspectives on the development of memory and cognition.* Hillsdale, N. J.: Erlbaum, 1977.

———. Verbal guidance through remembering the goals of actions. *Child Development,* 1978, *49,* 188-193.

Meacham, J. A., and **Leiman, B.** Remembering to perform future actions. (Paper presented at the meeting of the American Psychological Association, Chicago, September 1975.)

Meacham, J. A., and **Singer, J.** Incentive effects in prospective remembering. *Journal of Psychology,* 1977, *97,* 191-197.

Meacham, J. A., and **Riegel, K. F.** Dialectical perspectives on Piaget's theory, in G. Steiner, ed., *The psychology of the 20th century,* vol. 7: *Piaget's developmental and cognitive theory within an extended context.* Zurich: Kindler, 1978.

Meacham, J. A., Harris, A. E., and **Blaschko, T.** Integration of verbal and motor activities. (Paper presented at the meeting of the Society for Research in Child Development, Philadelphia, March 1973.)

Mead, G. H. *Mind, self, and society.* Chicago: University of Chicago Press, 1934.

Meichenbaum, D. Self-instructional strategy training: A cognitive prosthesis for the aged. *Human Development,* 1974, *17,* 273-280.

Meichenbaum, D., and **Cameron, R.** Training schizophrenics to talk to themselves. *Behavior Therapy*, 1973, *4*, 515-534.

Meichenbaum, D., and **Goodman, J.** Reflection-impulsivity and verbal control of motor behavior. *Child Development*, 1969, *40*, 785-797.

———. Training impulsive children to talk to themselves: A means of developing self-control. *Journal of Abnormal Psychology*, 1971, *77*, 115-126.

Meichenbaum, D., and **Goodman, S.** Clinical induction of private speech and critical questions about its study in natural settings, in G. Zivin, ed., *The development of self-regulation through private speech*. New York: Wiley, 1979.

Miller, G. A., **Galanter, E.**, and **Pribram, K. H.** *Plans and the structure of behavior*. New York: Holt, Rinehart & Winston, 1960.

Miller, S. A., **Shelton, J.**, and **Flavell, J. H.** A test of Luria's hypotheses concerning the development of verbal self-regulation. *Child Development*, 1970, *41*, 651-665.

Munsat, S. *The concept of memory*. New York: Randon House, 1966.

Riegel, K. F. Adult life crises: A dialectic interpretation of development, in N. Datan and L. H. Ginsberg, eds., *Life-span developmental psychology: Normative life crises*. New York: Academic, 1975(*a*).

———. From traits and equilibrium toward developmental dialectics, in W. J. Arnold and J. K. Cole, eds., *1974-1975 Nebraska Symposium onMotivation*. Lincoln: University of Nebraska Press, 1975(*b*).

Roberts, R. N. Private speech in academic problem-solving: A naturalistic perspective, in G. Zivin, ed, *The development of self-regulation through private speech*. New York: Wiley, 1979.

Rondal, J. A. The role of speech in the regulation of behavior. (Paper presented at the meeting of the Canadian Psychological Association, Windsor, June 1974.)

Rubin, K. H. The impact of the natural setting on private speech. in G. Zivin, ed., *The development of self-regulation through private speech*. New York: Wiley, 1979.

Strommen, E. A. Verbal self-regulation in a children's game: Impulsive errors on 'Simon Says. *Child Development*, 1973, *44*, 849-853.

Thoreson, C. E., and **Mahoney, M. J.** *Behavioral self-control*. New York: Holt, Rinehart & Winston, 1974.

Trabasso, T., and **Foellinger, D. B.** Seeing, hearing, and doing: A developmental study of memory for actions. (Paper presented at the meeting of the Society for Research in Child Development, Denver, April 1975.)

Traugott, N. N. Features of the verbal accounts given by children of preschool age in relation to newly formed motor conditioned reflexes. *Pavlov Journal of Higher Nervous Activity*, 1959, *9*, 282-289. [Cited by Kohlberg, L., J. Yaeger, and E. Hjertholm. Private speech: Four studies and a review of theories." *Child Development*, 1968, *39*, 691-736, p. 699.]

Van Duyne, H. J. Age and intelligence factors as predictors of the development of verbal control of nonverbal behavior. *Journal of Genetic Psychology*, 1974, *124*, 321-331.

Vygotsky, L. S. *Thought and language*, E. Hanfmann and G. Vakar, eds., and trans., Cambridge, Mass.: MIT Press, 1962. [Originally published, 1934.]

Wellman, H. M., Ritter, K., and **Flavell, J. H.** Deliberate memory behavior in the delayed reactions of very young children. *Developmental Psychology*, 1975, *11*, 780-787.

Wilder, L. Recent developments in Soviet research on the verbal control of voluntary motor behavior, in K. F. Riegel and J. A. Meacham, eds., *The developing individual in a changing world*, vol. 1. The Hague: Mouton, 1976.

Wohlwill, J. F. *The study of behavioral development*. New York: Academic, 1973.

Wolff, P. Autonomous systems in human behavior and development. *Human Development*, 1974, 17, 281-291.

Wozniak, R. H. Verbal regulation of motor behavior: Soviet research and non-Soviet replications. *Human Development*, 1972, *15*, 13-57.

———. Speech-for-self as a multiply reafferent human action system, in K. F. Riegel and J. A. Meacham, eds., *The developing individual in a changing world*, vol. I. The Hague: Mouton, 1976.

Zaporozhets, A. V., Zinchenko, V. P., and **Elkonin, D. B.** Development of thinking, in A. V. Zaporozhets and D. B. Elkonin, eds., *The psychology of preschool children*, J. Shybut and S. Simon, trans., Cambridge, Mass.: MIT Press, 1971. [Originally published, 1964.]

Zivin, G. Speech-for-self as a function of individual styles of central organization. (Paper presented at the Biennial Meeting of the Society for Research in Child Development, Philadelphia, March 1973.)

———. Developmental aspects of rhythm in self-regulation, in K. F. Riegel and J. A. Meacham, eds., *The developing individual in a changing world*, vol. I. The Hague: Mouton, 1976.

———. Removing common confusions about egocentric speech, private speech, and self-regulation., in G. Zivin ed., *The development of self-regulation through private speech*. New York: Wiley, 1979.

CHAPTER 8

The Impact of the Natural Setting on Private Speech

KENNETH H. RUBIN
University of Waterloo

This chapter reports two studies that seek evidence in play settings of the changes in frequency of private speech (variously called speech-for-self in current literature and originally called "egocentric speech" by Piaget, (1923/1926) that have been proposed to occur with age by the two fathers of this field of study, Piaget (1923/1926) and Vygotsky (1934/1962). Using two different age groups and two different systems for typing speech, the studies found neither the age curve of speech decline suggested by Piaget nor the one suggested by Vygotsky. However the second study did demonstrate the existence in natural settings of a nontrivial amount of self-regulating speech in preschoolers, and it highlighted the situation specificity of self-regulatory versus other private speech.[1] This latter emphasis is rare in the private speech literature.[2] Before moving through the studies to a new look at the data on speech types, it is useful to review the historical precedents for expecting speech-type distributions to vary with age (although not necessarily with action setting).

SEMINAL CONCEPTUALIZATIONS OF PRIVATE SPEECH

In his book, *The Language and Thought of the Child*, Piaget (1923/1926) described an interesting phenomenon that he labelled egocentric speech. Such speech, in contrast to social speech, was not considered to be addressed or adapted to a listener and was carried on with no apparent concern for signs of understanding by the listener. Indeed, to Piaget, no listener was necessary.

[1]This report is from a section of a larger project on role-taking and communication in children. Further description of the large-scale study may be found in Rubin, 1978.

[2]A brief review of works that do indicate the influence of setting on the presence of social versus private speech and of task type and difficulty on the appearance of types of private speech is found in Chapter 10 by Meichenbaum and Goodman. Chapter 9 examines task selection frames in a naturalistic study of private speech by Roberts.

Accordingly the young preoperational-aged child displayed nonsocial speech in potentially social situations because he/she was unable to shift perspectives (decenter) from self to other and, in addition, was unwilling to become actively involved in the communicative process. In short, to Piaget and others the concept of egocentrism served to explain empirical observations that young children have difficulty in engaging actively in cooperative, reciprocal social relationships (for example Parten, 1932). If a child is unable or unwilling to communicate effectively with his/her peers, then prosocial, cooperative, and sociodramatic behaviors should be absent from the child's behavior repertoire. Egocentric speech was thus originally thought to reflect a *social* deficit.

As readers of this volume are aware however, there is another viable position concerning the forms and functions of egocentric speech. Vygotsky (1934/1962) accepted the view that the speech of young children was replete with egocentric utterances. However he believed that over the course of development the form of egocentric speech evolved from attempts to communicate socially with others to successful attempts to regulate one's own behavior. To Vygotsky egocentric speech reflected the child's dependence on verbal stimuli to promote thinking and to mediate or regulate behavior. The following example, taken from the present author's recent research program, serves well to illustrate the self-directive function of egocentric speech — Keith, a 4-year-old boy engaged in free play with a minimally responsive adult:

> I like dose animals on dose blocks. Da numbers 'n' stuff. Le's see . . . *I should get all da number ones together* [following verbalization, puts blocks on the table]. All da wood ones are da number ones!

Not only did Vygotsky disagree with Piaget concerning the function of nonsocial speech, but he also differed concerning the ultimate fate of the phenomenon. Piaget (1923/1926) believed such speech declined with age as a consequence of social interaction. Presumably through being forced to take cognizance of the role of others, as well as through general cognitive growth, the young child's speech became less and less egocentric and subsequently more socialized. Vygotsky (1962) on the other hand proposed that egocentric speech was "a transitional stage in the evolution from spoken, self-directive speech to silent, inner speech." Thus while the older child or adult is capable of covert self-guidance, the younger child must vocalize this function.

With reference to Piaget's position that egocentric utterances represent a lack of genuine communicative intent, Vygotsky proposed that speech-for-self reflected a "parasocial" will to communicate. This notion of a parasocial communicative intent draws upon the assumption that the child, when verbalizing to himself/herself wishes to do so. However since the speech is intended for himself/herself and *not* for others (as Piaget suggested), it may be low on redundancy and may be highly abbreviated. As Luria (1969) wrote:

> Because it is 'speech for oneself,' serving above all to fix and to regulate intellectual processes, and because it has a largely predicative character, inner speech necessarily ceases to be detailed and grammatical. [p. 143.]

A nice example of such abbreviated speech may be illustrated by reading the classroom notes written by undergraduate students. These notes generally lack functors, use abbreviations, and are uninterpretable to others—unless of course those others are highly familiar with the writer's restricted language style (it should be clear that the oft-suggested recommendation, "Let's skip class and borrow Amy's notes.", should be accepted with caution unless Amy happens to be a good friend or is a copious note-taker).

Vygotsky believed that the child is able to distinguish between himself/herself as the speaker and an external listener. However the child is parasocial in that he/she does not distinguish himself/herself a *listener* and as an external listener. That is in early childhood the speaker talks to himself/herself as though he/she were talking to another. Thus early self-guiding speech is overt.

Vygotsky (1962) also suggested that speech for self followed a developmental sequence in its relationship to motor activity. At first, private speech *followed* an action and was descriptive of that action.

> For example: "Oh no, I didn't get a strike."

Later, speech-for-self occurred *simultaneously* with the action.

> For example: "I'm doin' a picture. I'm drawin' Ernie."

Finally, speech-for-self *occurred before* or at the beginning of an activity. It is this latter form of speech that has an obvious directing or planning function.

> For example: "I'm not going to play with dose things. I'm going to play with this ball."

Following Vygotsky (1934/1962) was the theory of his Russian colleague Luria (1961). Luria extended Vygotsky's original work by exploring both the incidence of the verbal regulation of behavior as well as the relationship between language ability and behavior in children. To Luria true voluntary behavior was seen as being dependent on the ability to utilize self-regulation. Such behavior had its origins in early adult-child verbal encounters. Thus initially the overt speech of others regulated the infant's or toddler's behaviors. As such the control may be conceptualized as "other-external" (Flavell, 1977), that is regulation is guided by the external verbalizations of others. During the early preschool years however the control of behaviors may be categorized as "self-external" (Flavell, 1977). Thus while regulatory speech remains overt, it is now expressed by the chld himself/herself. This second stage represents the transitional point from the external control of behaviors by others to the internal control of behaviors by the self.

Finally children of approximately 4½ years of age learn to regulate their own behavior by means of inaudible, often fragmentary speech of the nature described above. Since at this age children can differentiate themselves from others, there is no need for the speech to be overt. This form of self-regulatory speech may thus be coded "self-internal" (Flavell, 1977).

According to Luria (1961) not only does the source of behavior control change with age, but the *nature* of self-regulatory verbalizations changes as well. During the early preschool years, almost any verbalization initiates or accompanies behavior, regardless of its semantic quality. For example a child who tells himself "don't touch" when peering at his mother's crystal goblets is as likely to follow his instruction as not. Luria (1961) explained this somewhat curious behavior by noting that at 3½ to 4½ years of age the child responds to the physical rather than semantic qualities of verbal stimuli. In short only the *impulsive* aspect of the child's speech affects motor behavior. By 4½ to 5½ years of age, the child's behavior is regulated by the *semantic* nature of his verbalizations. Words have meanings which themselves are able to regulate behaviors.

At this point it should be noted that empirical findings concerning the veracity of the Vygotsky-Luria position vis-a-vis the forms and functions of speech-for-self are equivocal in nature. North American psychologists for the most part have not been able to replicate Luria's original findings (for example Miller, Shelton, and Flavell, 1970). More to the point, demonstrations of the utility of speech for self-regulatory purposes have generally been limited to laboratory settings in which children have been asked to solve puzzles or similar tasks (Deutsch and Stein, 1972; Flavell, Beach, and Chinsky, 1966; Miller et al., 1970). As both Fuson (Chapter 5) and Roberts (Chapter 9) note there appears to be a lack of naturalistic data concerning the incidence and quality of private speech forms. Thus, for one, we cannot be certain that the development of private speech forms in the natural setting resembles the Vygotskian hypothesis concerning the evolution of self-regulation from verbalizations following actions to verbalizations preceding actions. Nor can we be certain that self regulatory speech develops from "other-external" to "self-internal" (Flavell, 1977). Furthermore we know little of the validity of the Luria hypotheses concerning the evolution of self-regulatory verbalizations from impulsive to semantic control. In fact, and probably most important, unless researchers pursue the study of self-regulatory mechanisms in the natural setting, we cannot be certain whether or not speech-for-self is ever spontaneously emitted!

Let us for the moment accept the belief that self regulatory speech exists outside the confines of the laboratory setting. Given this assumption we must now ask a number of rather important questions: (1) What does egocentric and self-regulatory speech sound like when emitted in the natural setting? (2) Does the quantity and quality of egocentric and self-regulatory speech change with age? (3) Does the quantity and quality of such speech change as a function of the behavior displayed in the natural setting? Each of these questions raises further questions in turn. In an effort to respond to the questions I shall now attempt to describe a series of naturalistic studies that my colleagues and I have undertaken during the past few years at the University of Waterloo.

Seminal Predictions of Age Changes in the Appearance of Private Speech

It was Piaget's (1923/1926) belief that egocentric speech declined with age and ultimately disappeared, having evolved into social speech. Supportive empirical data concerning the fate of egocentric speech have been provided by Piaget (1923/1926) himself, as well as by a number of North American researchers during the 1930s (Adams, 1932; Fisher, 1934). More recently Glucksberg, Krauss, and Higgins (1975), in reviewing the research concerning referential communication skills (for example, Glucksberg and Krauss, 1967; Flavell, et al., 1968; Rubin, 1973), noted that children become better able to tailor and adapt verbal messages to listeners as they become older. Ostensibly this improvement in referential communicative abilities is a function of the child's growing decentration skills and of the gradual decline of egocentric thought. More recently however both Maratsos (1973) and Evans (1976) have found that when children are allowed to use gestures to supplement their verbalizations during referential communication tasks, little difference is found between the communicative skills of children ranging in age from 5-to-9 years. Similarly Shatz and Gelman (1975) have noted 4-year-olds alter their communications as a function of the age and status of their listeners. For example in the Shatz and Gelman study, speech to a 2-year-old was found to be grammatically more simplified and easier to understand than speech to either an age mate or to an adult.

What about research concerning age differences in the use of self-regulatory speech? Vygotsky believed a curvilinear relationship to exist between age and private speech concerning overt speech frequency. Thus between 2 and 4 years, the amount of private, self-guiding speech was thought to increase, thereafter gradually declining until ultimately evolving into covert, underground, inner speech. Such speech served a self-guiding rather than a social function. Supportive age-related data for the Vygotsky position comes from Flavell, Beach, and Chinsky (1966), Kohlberg, Yaeger, and Hjertholm (1968), and Rubin (1973). The latter two writers utilized a private speech coding scheme conceived of by Kohlberg, Yaeger and Hjertholm (1968). This scale will be described at length later. However at this point suffice it to say that few studies concerning the fate of self-regulatory speech have been carried out in natural settings.

One such report is that of Klein (1964) who observed 3- to 7-year-olds in pseudo-naturalistic "drawing and puzzle settings," Klein found no significant differences in the frequency of all forms of private speech with age. However with increasing age there was an increase in inaudible mutterings, and the comprehensible speech that was retained was increasingly task-relevant. In addition there appeared to be a relationship between task-relevent responses and successful puzzle completion. Taken together Klein suggested that these findings provided support for Vygotsky's hypothesis that egocentric speech has functional value for problem-solving and rather than disappearing with age, it tends to become covert (as represented by the increase of inaudible mutterings and lip movements).

The research of Kohlberg and his colleagues (1968) represents a significant departure in the private-speech literature. In their major paper the authors drew on the theories of Piaget (1923/1926), Vygotsky (1934/1962), Mead (1934), and Flavell (1966) to suggest a developmental hierarchy of private speech forms related by their self-communicative function. Kohlberg, Yaeger, and Hjertholm have suggested that the ages of children in the different levels of the hierarchy may vary, but that the order of the levels remains invariant. The developmental hierarchy suggested by Kohlberg, Yaeger, and Hjertholm (1968) and recently revised by Meichenbaum and Goodman (Chapter 10) follows below:

Level I. Presocial Self-Stimulating Language

1. *Word play and repetition.* Kohlberg and his colleague's lowest level of private speech is equivalent to Piaget's concept of echolalia. This category would include singing and humming or the repeating of words for their own sake. There is no relevance vis-a-vis self-regulation.

   For example: "Teeny tiny toe, a poonie piney poe."

Level II. Outward-Directed Private Speech

2. *Comments to absent or nonhuman others.* This Meichenbaum and Goodman (Chapter 10)of Kohlberg, Yaeger, and Hjertholm's original category of comments to nonhuman objects includes one-sided dialogues to a generalized other or to inanimate materials.

   For example: "Silly car, get back in there."

3. *Description of own activity.*[3] These comments occur *simultaneously with or following a behavior.* Moreover these comments only describe visually obvious aspects of the activity and have no obvious task-solving relevance or planning function. The category may be considered to be equivalent to Vygotsky's hypothesized first two forms of private speech described above.

   For example: "This filler truck is goin' in the gas station."

Level III. Inward-Directed or Self-Guiding Private Speech

4. *Questions asked and answered by the self.* Here the content is self-guiding. The answer may include justification for an action. Included in this category are analytic comments prefaced by "I wonder if . . ."

   For example: "What are we gonna do in here? Gonna sit at the table.

5. *Self-guiding comments.* The content of these comments is task- or goal-oriented. The speech precedes or partially precedes the action. In a sense this category sounds much like "thinking aloud."

   For example: "I'll put the dolly over there."

The following two categories were not part of the original Kohlberg, Yaeger, Hjertholm (1968) coding scheme. They were instead added for purposes of the naturalistic study described below. They may be included as part of Kohlberg, Yaeger, and Hjertholm's Level II of private speech forms.

6. *Emotional expression and tension release.*

   For example: "I did it! Yea!"; "Aw crappy!"

7. *Miscellaneous.* This category includes reading out loud to one's self; unrelated speech, and so on.

Borrowing from this extended categorization scheme, the present author recently carried out an observational study of children's self-regulatory and nonself-regulatory private speech during naturalistic, dyadic free play. The purposes of the investigation were: (1) to discover the *quantity* of private speech emitted in naturalistic settings by children ranging in age from approximately 4 to 11 years; (2) to discover whether or not the overt manifestation of private speech decreased with age as suggested by Piaget

[3]Although such description, particularly if it follows an activity, is not easily considered self-regulating through an obvious function, such as planning, Meacham (Chapter 7) argues for a type of speech of similar content that is self-regulating, but not playful. It bears similarity to Vygotsky's earliest form of self-regulating speech (description after action) whose function is explicated by Zivin (Chapter 1).

(1923/1926); (3) to discover whether or not the overt manifestation of self-regulatory speech followed a curvilinear path as suggested by Vygotsky (1934/1962); and (4) to discover whether or not the private speech of younger children is more likely than that of older children to occur simultaneously with, or follow, their playful behaviors and conversely to find out whether or not the private speech of older children is more likely than that of young children to precede playful activities.

STUDY I: SEARCH FOR PRIVATE SPEECH DECLINE, AGES 4 TO 11

Briefly, 10 dyads were formed for each of preschool, first-grade, third-grade, and fifth-grade children. All 40 dyads consisted of same-sexed, familiar classmates. The elementary school aged children were taken, two at a time, to a trailer laboratory, by a familiar adult female. They were told that they would be able to "try out" some new toys and to do "whatever you want" for about 15 minutes. The children were also informed that "some pictures will be taken while you play." The playroom, which was approximately 8 ft by 10 ft was separated from a small, video-recording room by a large one-way mirror and a paneled wall.

The preschoolers were taken to a playroom within their school building. This familiar playroom was approximately 5 ft by 7 ft in area and also had a one-way mirror through which video-taped recordings could be made. Both playrooms were equipped with a lego-set, puzzles, crayons and paper, puppets, a bowling game, and books. All equipment was geared to the ages of the dyad members.

Each dyad was video- and audio-taped for 15 minutes. Following each session the verbal and behavioral video-tape data for the first 12 minutes of the session were transcribed by the two female graduate students originally responsible for data collection. Any disagreements concerning the content of children's speech were settled through multiple reviews of the videotapes until a satisfactory agreement was reached.

Subjects

The sample included 20 children (10 males, 10 females) in each of four school grades. The mean age of the preschoolers was 53.93 months (SD = 6.21 months). The mean ages of the grade-one, -three, and -five children were 78.93 months (SD = 3.59 months), 106.64 months (SD = 5.59 months), and 129.85 months (SD = 4.15 months) respectively. All children attended schools in an urban community in southwestern Ontario.

Coding of Data

The transcribed records of each child's verbalizations were coded into utterance units. In general an utterance unit was defined according to the criteria suggested by Meichenbaum and Goodman (Chapter 10). Thus each unit was separated from the following unit by at least a one second pause, a change in topic, a logical break in speech, and/or the onset of peer speech.

From both the transcripts and the video-taped recordings, each utterance was coded as social speech, nonsocial speech, or nonscorable. Social speech utterances were units that were directed at the dyadic partner and that were characterized by some or all of the following characteristics:

1. Usually accompanied by an attention-getting device (for example use of other's name, touch other.)
2. Answer to other's command or question.
3. Comments to other during a cooperative venture or mutual engagement in an activity.
4. Part of a dialogue with other.
5. Statement of emotional release *directed at* the other.
6. Statement, command, or question followed by the expectation of a response from the other. This was indicated by a pause, establishment of eye contact, and/or repetition of the original comment in a more demanding form.

Nonsocial speech was coded as outlined above (Meichenbaum and Goodman, Chapter 10; Kohlberg, Yaeger, and Hjertholm, 1968). Nonscorable units included words or phrase fragments that defied categorization.

Results

A ratio of nonsocial speech utterance units to all utterance units was calculated for each child as follows:

$$\frac{\text{No. of nonsocial speech utterance units}}{\text{No. of nonsocial speech utterance units and social speech utterance units}}$$

The mean ratios of nonsocial speech for the preschool and grade-one, -three, and -five children were .26 (SD = .19); .19 (SD = .09); .20 (SD = .10); and .17 (SD = .14) respectively. A 4 (grade) times 2 (sex) analysis of variance (ANOVA) revealed neither significant main effects for grade nor for sex.

Each nonsocial speech unit was subsequently coded vis-a-vis the Kohlberg, Yaeger, and Hjertholm (1968) category system outlined earlier. The mean percentages of nonsocial speech units that fell into each of the seven categories are presented, by grade, in Table 1.

TABLE 1 Means and Standard Deviations for Private Speech Codes by Grade

	Grade							
	P		1		3		5	
Category	*M*	*SD*	*M*	*SD*	*M*	*SD*	*M*	*SD*
Repetition	.29	.30	.15	.15	.18	.19	.09	.14
Nonhuman or absent others	.06	.09	.08	.15	.10	.15	.05	.09
Describes activity	.25	.15	.28	.16	.23	.13	.29	.19
Questions/ answers	.06	.08	.12	.11	.08	.12	.04	.06
Self-guiding	.18	.17	.18	.14	.14	.14	.27	.22
Expletive	.15	.14	.19	.13	.24	.12	.25	.14
Miscellaneous	.01	.02	.00	.00	.03	.11	.01	.01

Note: Speech category means represent the percentage of utterance units of a particular private speech category across all private speech categories.

A series of 4 (grade) times 2 (sex) ANOVAs were calculated for each private speech category. Significant grade effects were found for:

1. Repetition: F (3, 72) = 3.38, $p < .02$.
2. Questions asked and answered by self: F (3, 72) = 3.00, $p < .04$.
3. Self-guiding comments: F (3, 72) = 2.24, $p < .09$.
4. Expletives: F (3, 72) = 3.18, $p < .03$.

Follow-up Newman-Keuls analyses (all $p < .05$) revealed preschoolers to emit a significantly greater percentage of repetitious speech-to-self than did either grade-one or grade-five children. A curvilinear pattern was evinced for the category "Questions asked and answered by the self." Thus grade-one children emitted a significantly greater percentage of this form of speechforself than did either preschool or grade-five children. Finally grade-three and grade-five children were more likely to use expletives to self than were preschool children. No other multiple comparisons proved significant.

Discussion

The results of this naturalistic, video-taped study of private speech usage in dyadic free-play settings were surprising in two major respects. First the ratios of private speech utterances to the total number of utterances did not change significantly from preschool through the fifth grade. In short Piaget's (1923/1926) contention that egocentric speech declined with age was not supported herein. These data also contradict the findings of Kohlberg, Yaeger, and Hjertholm (1968), who reported a decline of private-speech use between the ages of four and six years in naturalistic settings. However the Kohlberg, Yaeger, and Hjertholm report was flawed, in that the former authors did not observe their subjects in comparable settings. Moreover these investigators failed to control for both the familiarity of peers and the types of materials made available to the subjects.

In addition the present results are at variance with Kohlberg, Yaeger, and Hjertholm's Study II, which, in a more controlled setting, revealed a decline of egocentric speech with age, particularly between seven and ten years. The child's colleague in this second study however was an adult and the setting was of a task-oriented nature. As a result the findings cannot be compared with those presented herein. To conclude, the present data revealed that in naturalistic dyadic free-play settings, a decline in the amount of private speech was not evinced over four age groups.

Second the present data did not support Vygotsky's (1934/1962) contention that the quantity of private speech followed a curvilinear path across age groups. Significant age main effects were found only for three of the original Kohlberg, Yaeger, and Hjertholm (1968) private-speech categories, while a trend was found for a fourth category. Of those four categories reaching or approximating significance, only two could be considered self-regulatory in nature, that is (1) Questions asked and answered by the self and (2) Self-guiding comments. It is noteworthy that while the questions-answered-by-the-self category did evince a curvilinear form of development, thereby supporting Vygotsky, the number of utterances within this category was miniscule. For example in preschool only 6% of all private-speech utterances consisted of questions answered by the self. Given that this figure is but a percentage of a percentage (that is the figure represents 6% of the private-speech utterances, which themselves only represent 26% of the total number of utterances), few psychologically significant conclusions could be drawn from the data.

The only other likely effect for self-regulatory utterances in the natural dyadic play situation was the trend found for self-guiding comments. While a glance at Table 1 reveals such regulatory utterances to actually *increase* at the grade-five-level, post-hoc comparisons indicated no significant mean grade differences. This increase in overt self-regulatory comments at the age of 11 years (albeit not statistically significant) actually runs counter to the Vygotskyian claim that such speech becomes internalized at about 7 to 8 years.

Finally it should be noted that expletives constituted a rather large proportion of all private-speech utterances at each grade level. Moreover, such utterances tended to *increase* significantly with age. Since expletives were often uttered as "anxiety reducers," they may actually have served in some self-regulatory capacity. That is expletives, when uttered, may have brought the child's mental state back to a homeostatic level following an introduction to a novel and possibly anxiety-provoking situation. For the older, grade-five children, this anxiety state may have led to the regressive use of overt speech for self (as in self-guiding comments). Original theorists (for example, Vygotsky, 1934/1962; Luria, 1961) and recent researchers (for example Deutsch and Stein, 1972; Zivin, 1972) have reported an increase in overt private speech use when children experience frustrating and anxiety-oriented circumstances.

Why should the pseudo-laboratory play setting be more anxiety provoking for older rather than younger children? For the preschoolers, who differed significantly from the grade-three and grade-five children in the use of expletives, the fact that they were attending a laboratory school where they were often taken by strangers into playrooms may have served an anxiety-habituation role in the present study. Alternatively it may be that the elicitation of expletives simply increases with the development of mature verbal repertoires, and that such speech does not, in any obvious way, play a regulatory role.

All in all the data reported herein do indicate that private speech does exist in naturalistic, dyadic encounters. However it is important to note that very little of the private speech emitted took on a truly self-regulatory character. Furthermore there were few data to support the argument that the private speech of younger children was more likely to occur simultaneously with or following action and that such speech was less likely to precede their behaviors than that of older children. These data counter arguments concerning the existence and the significance of regulatory speech for self in childhood, at least in nonlaboratory, nontask-oriented situations.

Perhaps one reason for the general lack of regulatory speech eminated from the dyadic social situation utilized in this study. It may have been that the play-partners denied or inhibited the use of speech-for-self by the children in the present study. For that matter it may have been that in some cases the verbal output of the play-partners regulated the behavior of the children — a possibility that receives support from recent naturalistic studies of children's requests for action in dyadic communication (for example Garvey, 1977). Such requests are found to be highly prevalent in the conversations of preschoolers. Given that the play-partner may have somehow undermined the expression of self-regulatory statements, a second study was carried out in a free, but nonconversational play setting.

STUDY II: SETTING AND TIMING OF PRESCHOOL PRIVATE SPEECH

Study II was designed to discover the nature of private speech in a free-play setting without a play-partner. Study II was also a collaborative effort with Louisa Dyck, a graduate student in the Psychology Department at the University of Waterloo. The data reported below are taken, for the most part, from Ms. Dyck's Master's thesis.

Study II differed from Study I in a number of ways. First the children observed were all preschoolers, ranging in age from 3 to 5 years. It is within this age range that one should begin to notice the development of private speech for self-regulatory purposes.

Second the children were observed while playing in a room with a minimally responsive adult rather than in dyadic peer-play. This procedure was followed in an effort to reduce any inhibitory effects a play-partner might have had on the quantity and quality of private speech emitted by a child. While a number of writers have contended that the quality of private speech would differ in an adult-child versus a child-child setting (for example Kohlberg, Yaeger, and Kohlberg 1968), there are few data to suggest that this is in fact the case. Given the general lack of self-regulatory speech found in the dyadic free-play setting in Study I, it was thought that private speech in a nonconversational setting (with a minimally responsive adult) would provide a more plentiful data base from which one could analyze the nature of verbal self-regulation.

A third distinction between the studies was the adoption of a more exhaustive category system for analyzing private-speech output in Study II. We had hoped that through the use of a more complex category system, we could more elaborately document the forms and functions of private speech that preschoolers produced while engaging in a variety of playful exercises.

Two basic questions were asked in Study II. First does the quality of private speech change with age as predicted by Vygotsky and Luria? That is does speech to the self become more self-regulatory with increasing age? To this end three age groups of preschoolers were studied. It was expected that the private speech of the youngest preschool sample (ages 3 years, 6 months to 3 years, 11 months) would occur following playful behavior, while the speech of the oldest preschool sample (4 years, 7 months to 5 years, 3 months) would occur prior to, or simultaneously with, the behavior. For purposes of the present study speech that occurred either prior to or during a behavior was considered to be regulatory. Speech which followed a related behavior was considered to be merely descriptive.

A second question asked in Study II was whether or not the playful activity the child engaged in related to the quality of private speech emitted. We know from Study I that not all private speech produced in free-play settings is regulatory in nature. Could it be that self-regulatory speech is produced prior to or during only certain forms of play, while nonregulatory private speech occurs with other forms? For example Smilansky (1968) has noted that some preschool play takes on a distinctively functional character. The child merely exercises muscle movements, as in the repetitious pushing and pulling of playdough. Another form of preschool play is that of construction, as in building a playdough structure. According to Smilansky and others (Piaget, (1946/1962; Rubin, 1977*A*) the former play form is less mature cognitively than the latter play form. Since it is likely that children do speak to themselves during both functional and constructive activities, is it possible that the quality of private speech varies given these different activities? Is speech during functional activity more likely to take on a playful, repetitious character than speech during constructive activity? Is speech during constructive play more likely to take on a self-regulatory character?

To answer these questions concerning the nature of private speech given a particular play form, a number of play categories were chosen for study. The three major categories were taken from the work of Smilansky (1968). The categories included:

1. Functional Play: simple, repetitive muscle movements with or without objects.
2. Constructive play: manipulation of objects to construct or to create something.
3. Dramatic play: the substitution of an imaginary situation to satisfy the child's personal wishes and needs.

These three particular categories of play are thought of as developing in a relatively fixed sequence with functional play appearing first and dramatic play appearing last. Recent research has indicated that the frequency of functional play emitted by a child is negatively related to his/her performance on a battery of cognitive tests, including spatial relational and classification skills, while the frequency of dramatic play positively relates to test performance (Rubin and Maioni, 1975). Moreover the model play form displayed by preschoolers in constructive play (Rubin, 1977*a*).

The three Smilansky categories described above were supplemented by three additional codes of behavior. These supplementary categories included:

4. Functional-exploratory play: investigative, exploration of the properties of an object.
5. Onlooker and unoccupied behavior.
6. Transitional behavior: changing activities, finding a new object to play with.

The private-speech coding frame utilized in the present study stemmed from the work of Kleiman (1974). Fifteen categories of speech to the self were originally documented vis-a-vis their relationship to the playful behaviors displayed by the children. For purposes of the present report only those categories of speech that were of a self-regulatory nature or that followed a related behavior were considered separately. All other private-speech categories were collapsed into a single category. A description of the private-speech categories and the methodology employed follows below.

Subjects

The preschoolers participating in the study were assigned to one of three age groups. The youngest age group (3 to 4 years) was comprised of 3 males and 4 females (*M* = 44 months; range = 41 months to 47 months). The middle age group (4 to 4½ years) consisted of 5 males and 1 female (*M* age = 52.2 months; range = 48 months to 54 months). The eldest preschool group (4½ to 5 years) had 5 males and 2 females (*M* age = 56.7 months; range = 55 months to 63 months). The children came from predominantly middle-class, professional backgrounds where English was the primary language.

Procedure

Each child was individually taken by a female graduate student to a playroom (5 ft times 7 ft) in which there was one table and one chair. On the table was a Fisher-Price farm set, playdough, table blocks, and a box of miniature plastic cars and people. On the floor there were four Tonka metal cars and trucks, a set of puppets, and stacking cups. The experimenter told each child, "Look, there are some new toys in this room. You can play with anything you wish. I have some writing to do, so I shall sit back here [in a corner of the room] while you are playing." The experimenter remained minimally responsive throughout the session, never initiating a conversation, and only responding to child's request or queries when he/she insisted that the adult reply. The play session lasted for 10 minutes and was videotaped through a one-way mirror. A second play session in the same room with the same materials was videotaped two weeks later. Thus each child was videotaped on two separate occasions for a total of 20 minutes.

Coding of Data and Initial Results

During each play session the experimenter's work consisted of transcribing the child's utterances while he/she played. This rough transcript supplemented the final transcript eventually gleaned from the video-taped recording by clarifying the content of the children's speech when the recorded utterances appeared unclear (as in whispers or softly muttered phrases). Following each play session the experimenter transcribed the child's speech, noting not only what the subject said, but also what he/she was doing. From these records each utterance was assigned to one of the following categories:[4]

1. *Analytic statements.* The child reasons out what is required in order to carry out the playful exercise. The child analyzes the structure of a task or exercise (for example "Gonna build a tunnel so I gotta get a circle one and a bunch of square ones.") Analytic statements were coded separately as occurring either (*A*) prior to or (*B*) during the relevant activity.
2. *Comments about materials.* The child comments about the materials or play objects that he/she uses. For example he/she may label an object or describe an attribute of an object. Comments about materials were coded separately as occurring (*A*) prior to (*B*) during, or (*C*) following an activity.
3. *Comments about activity.* The child describes what he/she (*A*) will do, (*B*) is doing or (*C*) has done (for example "I'm gonna get that cow.").
4. *Directions to the self.* The child tells himself/herself what to do, (for example "Don't open that door!"). Directions to self occurred prior to and during activity.
5. *Feedback.* After an action is completed the child says or implies that it was right or wrong, good or bad, fun or not fun. This category is much like an analytic statement *following* a behavior, (for example "That's a poo-poo thing I did.").
6. *Questions and conditional statements.* The child asks himself/herself a question about some aspect of the activity or comments on the probable rightness or wrongness or an activity *prior* to the engaging in it, (for example "Where that doggy goes? Oh yea, over here."). Questions and conditional statements were coded separately as occurring (*A*) prior to, (*B*) during, or (*C*) following an activity.
7. *Other.* All remaining private speech was coded as other. This category was comprised mainly of nonregulatory utterances such as fantasy statements, sound play, feeling statements, exclamations, and mutterings and whispers.

[4]An extended discussion of her private speech categories is available in Kleiman (1974). Only her self-regulatory categories have been included here.

An initial descriptive analysis was carried out to discover the utility of the aforementioned scoring frame for the study of private speech in a free-play setting. The number of utterances falling within any particular category (for example analytic comments prior to action) was divided by the total number of private-speech utterances. Calculations were carried out separately for Sessions I and II as well as across both sessions. These data are presented in Table 2. Table 3 shows the mean percentages of private speech per category for each of the three age groups (across both sessions). Finally Table 4 reveals the percentages of the various forms of private speech utterances found to occur within each play category. The data presented in Table 4 are collapsed across sessions and age groups.

Reliability

Once the experimenter had coded the utterances, the transcripts were given to the present writer in order to assess inter-rater reliability. Two hundred utterances randomly chosen by the author were recoded. After independently reviewing the videotapes, the author noted both the speech and play categories for the chosen utterances. Three sources of reliability were of interest:

1. The degree to which the two observers agreed on the coding of speech units.
2. The degree to which the two observers agreed on the coding of the play behaviors associated with the given speech units.
3. The degree to which the observers agreed on the coding of both the play and speech units.

Thus for example if a speech unit was coded by Observer A as an *analytic statement preceding functional play* and if Observer B coded that unit of speech as an *analytic statement occurring simultaneous with functional play*, the unit would be tallied as a disagreement regarding 1., as an agreement regarding 2., and as a disagreement regarding 3. The percentages of agreement were 92% for 1., 87.5% for 2., and 85% for 3. respectively.

Results

A cursory look at Tables 2, 3, and 4 reveals a number of distinct descriptive patterns concerning the quality of private-speech forms emitted during naturalistic free play.

First the percentages for each category of regulatory speech appear to be remarkably consistent from one session to the next (Table 2).

TABLE 2. Distribution of Self-Regulatory Speech among Categories for Each Play Session

Category of Speech	Session I %	Session II %	Total %
Analytic:			
prior	.96	.60	.80
during	3.14	1.20	2.20
Material comments:			
prior	.55	.30	.40
during	19.26	14.86	17.20
following	.55	.75	.60
Activity comments:			
prior	1.10	1.20	1.10
during	14.07	11.71	12.90
following	2.32	1.65	2.00
Directions to self:			
prior	7.92	5.71	6.90
during	1.36	2.25	1.80
Feedback:			
following	.55	1.95	1.20
Questions:			
prior	1.23	.75	1.00
during	5.33	2.10	3.80
following	2.32	.60	1.50
Other:	39.34	54.35	46.50
Utterances prior to action	11.76	9.04	10.20
Utterances during action	43.16	32.12	37.90
Utterances following action	5.76	4.95	5.40
Number of utterances	732	666	1398

Note: Percentages = *n* utterances within category/total *n* utterances for the session.

Second, there appear to be few differences in the percentages for each regulatory speech category across the three age groups (Table 3). The only notable differences concerned comments about materials during play, which evinced a clear curvilinear pattern. Moreover these general descriptive data were supportive of the aforementioned Vygotsky (1934/1962) position in that the overall percentages of regulatory speech demonstated a curvilinear pattern. Thus the ratios of self-regulatory utterances (analytic, material, activity, question, and directional utterances emitted prior to and during activity) to total private speech utterances were .46, .53, and .46 for the young, middle, and older preschool age groups respectively. Further preliminary support for Vygotsky's viewpoint concerning the fate of private speech stemmed from the decline of the total number of utterances emitted to the self with increasing age (556, 437, 405 utterances for the young, middle, and old preschoolers respectively).

TABLE 3. Distribution of Self-Regulatory Speech by Preschool Age Group

Category of Speech	Young %	Middle %	Old %
Analytic:			
prior	1.26	—	.99
during	2.70	1.14	2.72
Material comments:			
prior	.54	.23	.49
during	11.87	24.71	16.30
following	—	1.60	.49
Activity comments:			
prior	1.26	.92	1.23
during	14.21	14.41	9.63
following	.72	3.67	1.98
Directions to self:			
prior	6.29	7.32	7.16
during	1.44	.92	3.21
Feedback:			
following	1.08	1.37	1.23
Questions:			
prior	1.08	1.60	.25
during	4.68	2.06	4.44
following	2.16	.23	1.98
Other:	50.71	39.82	47.90
Utterances prior to action	10.43	10.07	10.12
Utterances during action	35.40	43.24	36.30
Utterances following action	3.96	6.87	5.68
Number of Utterances	556	437	405

Note: Percentages = *n* utterances within category/total *n* utterances.

The descriptive data presented in Table 4 can be used, without looking for the possibility of the self-regulatory function, to indicate in what activities children are most likely to talk themselves. It seems that they speak to themselves concerning constructive play (43.3% of all utterances) and dramatic play (27.5% of all utterances) more than concerning any of the remaining play forms. While not presented in the tables, it is noteworthy that the percentage of speech emitted concerning dramatic play increased from

17.8% of all utterances in Session I to 38.9% of all utterances in Session II. Conversely the percentage of speech emitted concerning exploration dropped from 12.2% of all utterances in Session I to 5.3% of all utterances in Session II. These speech percentages probably mirror the amount of time the children spent in the two activities. Thus, a decline in the amount of time (and speech) engaged in while exploring the environment should be expected as the children become more familiar with the setting (Weisler and McCall, 1976). Likewise an increase in dramatic play with a concomitant increase in the familiarity of the setting and materials should be expected (Rubin, 1977*a*).

When one examines the activities that are associated with self-regulatory speech, one finds that the appearance of self-regulatory speech depends on the context. The initial descriptive analysis demonstrated that speech for self-regulatory purposes, as defined herein[5], was more likely to be related to certain forms of activity than to others. For example, speech prior to and during activity was more likely to be produced around exploration, constructive play, and transitional behaviors. Clearly one quarter of all utterances emitted for exploratory purposes were in the form of questions occurring prior to or during object manipulation (for example "What's that one do?", "How's this work?").

Concerning constructive play, over 40% of all utterances were comments about materials and activities produced during the activity. Furthermore directions to the self emitted prior to a constructive act (for example "Get the circums and rectangums!") constituted 10% of all private-speech utterances for this category of play.

As for transitional behaviors (movement from one activity or play category to the next), directions to the self produced *prior* to the act constituted 21.23% of all utterances for this category.

While self-regulatory comments were not as highly represented proportionally for the dramatic, functional, and unoccupied/onlooker categories, they were not altogether absent. Thus, 125 utterances (or 35% of all utterances) emitted regarding dramatic play were of a regulatory nature, either preceding or accompanying the act. Of these utterances, 25% were material or activity comments produced during dramatic play.

In summary, the descriptive data reported above concerned the distribution of private speech among 15 categories and across 3 age groups of preschoolers. While informative in the broad sense, the comparison of speech categories is statistically problematic because a number of categories rarely occurred (for

[5]For the remaining discussion of Study II, there is a further refinement of the definition of self-regulatory speech. It henceforth refers to only those instances of the six categories derived from Kleiman (1974) that occurred before or during an activity. Instances occurring after an activity are henceforth considered to be non-self-regulatory forms of private speech. They can be appropriately considered with the "other" private-speech category.

TABLE 4. Distribution (Percentage) of Self-Regulatory Speech within Each Play Category

Category of Speech	Play Category [a]					
	Func.	Expl.	Const.	Dram.	Trans.	Unocc./ Onlooker
	%	%	%	%	%	%[b]
Analytic:						
prior	—	.81	1.15	.52	.88	—
during	—	7.26	1.82	1.82	2.65	1.07
Material comments:						
prior	1.30	1.61	—	.26	1.78	—
during	7.80	13.71	26.40	7.79	16.81	8.63
following	—	1.61	.66	.52	.88	—
Activity comments:						
prior	—	—	1.16	1.56	1.78	1.07
during	—	5.65	15.32	17.13	12.39	1.07
following	—	13.23	3.14	.78	1.78	—
Directions to self:						
prior	—	1.61	9.41	2.86	21.23	2.15
during	1.30	4.03	2.15	.78	2.65	—
Feedback:						
following	—	1.61	1.65	.78	.85	1.07
Questions:						
prior	—	3.23	.66	.52	2.65	1.07
during	9.08	20.16	1.98	1.56	1.78	1.07
following	3.90	6.45	1.65	—	—	—
Other:	76.62	29.03	32.84	63.12	31.86	82.80
Utterances prior to action	1.30	7.26	12.39	5.72	28.32	4.29
Utterances during action	18.18	50.81	47.67	29.08	36.28	11.84
Utterances following action	3.90	12.90	7.10	2.08	3.56	1.07
Number of utterances	77	124	606	385	113	93

Notes: [a]Func. = functional; Expl. = functional-exploratory; Const. = constructive; Dram. = transitional; Unocc./Onlooker = unoccupied/onlooker.
[b] %= number of utterances within speech category/total number of utterances with relevant play category.

example analytic statements, feedback). Since some of the categories had to be combined in a meaningful fashion prior to computing any inferential statistics, it was decided to concentrate on the temporal dimension of private speech. Four categories were thus formulated:

1. All regulatory speech which preceded an action.
2. All regulatory speech which accompanied an action.
3. All private speech[6] which followed an action.
4. All remaining private speech (the "other" category in Tables 2, 3, and 4).

At this point two procedural aspects require elaboration. First any utterance that began prior to an activity, but continued during play, was coded in the "prior" category. Second all speech that began during play, but continued after a particular form of play had ended, was coded in the "during" category. The distributions of these pooled data are found at the bottoms of Tables 2, 3, and 4.

Three preliminary age (3) × session (2) ANOVAs were computed in an effort to discover whether age or session experience significantly affected the amount of production of speech of differing types. For the first ANOVA, all utterances except those coded as "other" were pooled for each subject. The resulting ANOVA revealed significant main effects for neither age nor session. That is the mean number of utterances produced (minus "other" comments) did not vary systematically between the three age groups and across the two sessions. A second age (3) × session (2) ANOVA computed for *all private speech* (prior to + during + following + "other") again revealed nonsignificant main effects. Likewise an age (3) × session (2) ANOVA calculated only for the *regulatory subset of private speech* (prior to and during) produced nonsignificant main effects.

An age (3) × speech type (4—prior to, during, following, "other") × session (2) ANOVA that was computed to discover whether the *percentages* of the four categories of speech (for example number of utterances prior to behavior/total number of utterances) were distributed differently between age groups and across sessions did show that speech was not randomly distributed in time. A significant main effect was found for the speech categories, $F(3, 51) = 39.84, p < .001$. The means relevant to this main effect are found in Column 3 (Total %) at the bottom of Table 2: "Other" ($M = 46.50\%$ of all utterances); prior to ($M = 10.20\%$ of all utterances); during ($M = 37.90\%$ of all utterances); and following ($M = 5.40\%$ of all utterances). Follow-up Newman-Keuls analyses revealed

[6]The instances in this category would have been labeled self-regulatory by their content (Kleiman, 1974). However by timing criteria they follow an act and are not therefore considered self-regulatory.

significant ($p < .05$) differences between the percentage of speech emitted during an act and those percentages of speech produced either before or after an act. In short, regardless of age, the statistical norm for the appearance of self-regulatory speech was *during* a playful act. ("Other" comments likewise exceeded comments prior to and following behavior. But this may simply reflect coding conventions, which grouped together many types of speech.)

Since age and session main effects and interactions were not found to be of significance in the above analyses, these data were pooled. A series of simple one-way ANOVAs was computed for the raw number of utterances of each speech type emitted within each individual behavioral (not speech type) category. The purpose of this series of analyses was to discover whether within a given behavioral category (for example constructive play) the number of prior to, during, following, and "other" utterances differed significantly from each other. Significant differences were found for each of the following behavioral categories: functional, $F(3, 57) = 30.42, p < .001$; functional exploratory, $F(3, 57) = 7.49, p, < .001$; constructive, $F(3, 57) = 15.65, p < .001$; dramatic, $F(3, 57) = 5.81, p < .01$; and transitional, $F(3, 57) = 3.09, p < .05$.

Newman-Keuls post-hoc comparisons were subsequently calculated for the above data. The results show nonrandom fit of behavioral context and prevalent speech timing. The findings may be summarized as follows:

1. For functional-exploratory play, utterances produced during the behavior exceeded all other categories of speech.
2. Within transitional behavior, comments made following the act occurred significantly less often than comments of the prior to, during, and "other" genres.
3. For constructive play, "other" and during comments exceeded both prior to and following utterances.
4. Less interpretable is the finding that "other" comments were emitted more frequently than the remaining three speech categories for functional and dramatic play.,
5. No other multiple comparisons were statistically significant.

Discussion

In accord with the noted lack of naturalistic descriptions (Meichenbaum and Goodman, Chapter 10, and Fuson, Chapter 5), Study II presented descriptive data that allowed observations of a fairly large number of private-speech categories (Kleiman, 1974) to be related to a variety of behavioral categories. Although the data clearly indicated that the qualities of both regulatory and nonregulatory speech did not change either across the age groups studied or across play sessions separated by at least two week's time, there did appear systematic differences in the types of speech produced in the context of particular behaviors. Contextual variation of speech type has not been studied in the private-speech literature.

Before detailing the context-relevant findings, the full set of Study II's results will be reviewed. The first finding of note was the lack of support for the suggestion (Vygotsky, 1934/1962; Piaget, 1923/1926) that the quantity of overt private speech decreases with age. Although Table 3 revealed that the average numbers of utterances across sessions were 79.43, 72.83, and 57.86, for the young, middle, and old preschoolers respectively, the differences were not statistically significant. In addition the data revealed nonstatistically significant age differences for both the quantity of regulatory and nonregulatory speech forms. Perhaps the lack of significant age differences may be attributed to the fact that the *eldest* group studied averaged only 4.7 years of age. Both the positions of Piaget (1923/1926) and Vygotsky (1934/1962) propose the decline and disappearance of overt self-utterance by 7 years of age. Recall, however, that Study I, using children as old as 11 years, also found no decline. Thus a further naturalistic study of children without play-partners should use older subjects than those of Study II.

The second major finding of Study II was the consistency with which the children deployed particular forms of speech from one session to the next. The descriptive data presented in Table 2 amply demonstrate this point. While the overall percentage of regulatory speech produced during activity decreased from 43.16% to 32.12% of all private utterances from Session I to Session II, statistical analysis indicated this difference to be nonsignificant. Thus while one might expect more self-regulation upon first entry to a novel, perhaps anxiety-provoking setting, just as earlier research had shown more private speech during anxious or frustrating moments, the present data counter this proposition.

However, using speech-type frequency as an indication of what a child may be doing, it is noteworthy that the number of private comments concerning exploration dropped systematically from Session I to Session II, while an increase in utterances to the self was evinced for dramatic play. While not representing significant differences within each play category, the data probably demonstrate that, as in earlier reports, exploration decreases and symbolic play increases as the child's familiarity with a setting grows (Weisler and McCall, 1976).

The major purpose of Study II was to investigate the variety of regulatory speech forms that may be related to particular behaviors. The descriptive data presented in Table 4 demonstrate that self-regulatory utterances (that is, analytic, material, activity, question, and directional utterances that preceded or accompanied a related behavior) were most prominent during exploratory, constructive, and transitional activities. Taken across the particular speech categories, the percentages of utterances emitted for exploratory, constructive, and transitional behaviors that occurred prior to or during the act were 58.07%, 60.06%, and 60.60% respectively. That is 58.07% of the 124 utterances produced for exploratory purposes (Table 4) were self-regulatory as defined herein. Lesser percentages of self-regulatory speech were found for the categories of functional and dramatic play and for onlooker and unoccupied behaviors.

These descriptive data are noteworthy, given that most research concerning private and/or self-regulatory speech has reported data from paradigmatic and artificial laboratory settings. Moreover much of the data supporting the very existence of self-regulatory speech stems from studies concerned with constructive play activities (for example puzzle-solving and coloring, Dickie, 1973). As in these earlier reports, speech for self-regulatory purposes was found to exist, to a large degree, *during* constructive play. Children did use speech to direct their actions and to comment about the materials and activities when forming block and playdough structures or when stacking cups.

More important perhaps, and parallel to the findings of Meacham (Chapter 7), is the finding that self-guiding speech occurred to a fairly large degree when children moved from one activity to another (for example from blocks to cars) or from one mode of play to another (for example functional to constructive play). Thus 21.23% of all transitional utterances took the form of a direction to the self preceding action (Table 4). Moreover, when first encountering an object, questions concerning the functional uses of the object (during exploration) were found to be quite frequent (20.16% of all exploratory utterances).

These observations based upon descriptive data are supported by the statistical analyses performed on the pooled speech categories. Thus utterances produced *during* functional-exploratory behavior exceeded all other forms of speech related to this behavior. If these utterances were combined to form a single category with those utterances emitted *prior to* exploration, the data would certainly reveal such content-plus-timing-defined self-regulatory utterances to predominate for exploratory activity. Similarly the ANOVA for transitional behaviors revealed that utterances produced prior to and during the act were at least as plentiful as the category of miscellaneous "other" private utterances. Combining the former two categories would most likely have revealed that self-regulatory speech was a significant force for transitional behavior.

The data gathered in Study II thus suggest the following pattern. First when children are introduced to novel materials, they will be likely to explore the objects. In so doing they may question their use and describe the properties of the objects (questions + material comments during exploration + 33.87%

of all utterances related to exploration). Examples of these forms of regulatory speech should be familiar to those who observe children at play ("Hey, what's that?. Oh look, it's wiggly." "What kinda cars here? Wow, all colors!").

Second, when children move from one activity to the next, or when they switch from one play form to another (for example from functional to constructive play), their behavior may often be somewhat controlled by transitional self-verbalizations: verbalizations that direct the children to engage in particular activities ("Go get that truck now.") and verbalizations that are transitional between constructive and dramatic play ("Putting horsie in and then be Farmer Jack."). Third, as reported earlier, self-regulatory speech appears to play a major role in constructive activity.

As for the remaining play behaviors examined in Study II, it would appear that speech forms other than those of a regulatory nature are the norm. Thus "other" forms of private speech, such as fantasy statements, sound play and repetition, exclamations and remarks about feelings predominated for functional, dramatic, and onlooker/unoccupied behaviors. This is not to say that regulatory comments were not present in these activities (for example 34.80% of all dramatic play utterances were of a regulatory character as defined herein). Such comments were just less likely to occur for these behaviors than for exploratory, constructive, and transitional actions.

The upshot of this finding is rather simple, but important for conclusions about the natural incidence of private speech types. If one is to study the incidence of self-regulatory (or for that matter, private) speech, it is likely that the form of play the experimenter "pulls for" will affect the results. Thus a room filled with puzzle-type materials will more likely lead to the conclusion that self-regulatory speech is "alive and well" than will a room filled with puppets and other materials, which will pull for dramatic play. The lesson here is that one must be concerned with the activities children are allowed to engage in when attempting to provide normative data regarding the quantity and quality of private or self-regulatory speech forms.

This latter statement leads me to share with the reader the next step to be pursued with the naturalistic data source presented above. From earlier reports (for example Parten, 1933; Rubin, 1977*b*; Shure, 1963) it has been shown that certain objects (for example crayons, puzzles) have a high probability of eliciting constructive behaviors. On the other hand other materials (for example vehicles, puppets) stand a high probability of eliciting dramatic-play forms. Given the play and speech categories described in Study II, my colleagues and I now hope to review the videotapes in an effort to discover the nature of the speech and play behavior produced when children interacted with each of the seven materials provided for them. Thus our conclusions about context specificity of (private) speech should become more precise and refined.

SUMMARY

In summary, the results of Study II, as with those of Study I, indicated a lack of significant differences with regard to the type of private speech emitted by children of different ages. The Study II data were however somewhat promising for proponents of the importance of speech for self-regulatory purposes. A fairly high proportion of remarks produced concerning exploratory, constructive, and transitional activities were categorized as being self-regulatory in nature (Kleiman, 1974).

However it should be noted that a large proportion of the private speech in all behavior categories investigated in the present study, were not of a self-regulatory nature. This raises the question of the ecological significance of the rather moderate proportion of private speech that is self-regulatory.

In explaining the large amount of non-self-regulatory speech, the work of Mead (1934) may be important to note, as Kohlberg, Yaeger, and Hjertholm (1968) suggest. According to Mead, one function of private speech in early childhood is to make young speakers aware of their own actions and of their own separate existences. Thus we see (Table 2) that 5.40% of all utterances occurred after a behavior and produced some form of feedback, description, or question concerning the behavior.

Unfortunately neither the Vygotsky-Luria nor the Mead position serves to explain the 46.50% of all utterances that were clearly not regulatory. Almost half of the private speech produced by children in this study was expressive of affective and fantasy dispositions and included exclamations, fantasy statements, sound play, and repetition. Such speech serves neither to guide one's behavior nor to make one more aware of the self. Moreover such speech does not appear to represent a failure to communicate (Piaget, 1923/1926). In fact approximately 10% of the private speech produced was quite social: during dramatic play, for example, a child would oft-times talk to a puppet, change his/her tone of voice and respond as if taking the puppet's role, and then, following the puppet's "verbalization," the child would respond in turn:

Child: "Hi, how ya doin'?"

Puppet: "Not bad. How ya doin'?"

Child: "OK, 'cept I'm stuck in this room."

This "dialogue" clearly demonstrates nonegocentric role-taking and turn-taking skills—and yet is private as defined here.

In conclusion it appears that the concept of self-regulatory speech is an ecologically valid one. Given the Kleiman (1974) categories utilized in Study II, it is safe to say that analytic, material, and activity comments, as well as self-directive and questioning utterances do occur in the natural play setting. But of course not all speech to the self is self-regulatory. Moreover the quality of speech to and for the self appears to relate to the forms of behavior with which it occurs. Given the percentages of many speech types reported in this chapter, it is obviously illogical to see as pitted against each other the positions of Piaget, Mead, and Vygotsky concerning the forms and functions of private speech. Such speech has numerous forms and numerous functions. Private speech in the natural setting can be self-directive and regulatory, it can provide practice for person-to-person communicative encounters (as in speech to inanimate objects), and it can serve to better define the self. From the present corpus of data, the reader should note that private speech does play a somewhat regulatory role in the control of behavior. One important question to answer in the future is whether or not a child who fails to use the forms of regulatory speech considered in Study II would be characterized as "out of control" or hyperkinetic in the natural setting? Since the tutorial benefits of speech for self have been amply demonstrated in the laboratory (Meichenbaum and Goodman, 1971) it may now be the time to consider such practices for behavioral control in the natural setting.

References

Deutsch, F., and **Stein, A. H.** The effects of personal responsibility and task interruption on the private speech of preschoolers. *Human Development,* 1972, *15,* 310-324.

Dickie, J. Private speech: The effect of presence of others, task, and intrapersonal variables. Unpublished doctoral dissertation, Michigan State University, 1973.

Evans, M. A. Hand gestures as a communicative mode in school-aged children. Unpublished masters thesis, University of Waterloo, 1976.

Fisher, J. L. Language patterns of preschool children. *Child Development Monographs,* 1934, *15.*

Flavell, J. H. Le Language privé. *Bulletin de Psychologie,* 1966, *19,* 698-701.

______. *Cognitive Development.* Englewood Cliffs, N.J.: Prentice-Hall, 1977.

Flavell, J. H., Beach, D. R., and **Chinsky, J. M.** Spontaneous verbal rehearsal in a memory task as a function of age. *Child Development,* 1966, *37,* 283-299.

Flavell, J. H., Botkin, P. T., Fry, C. L., Wright, J. W., and **Jarvis, P. E.** *The development of role-taking and communication skills in children.* New York: Wiley, 1968.

Fuson, K. C. The development of self-regulating aspects of speech: A review, in G. Zivin, ed., *The development of self-regulation through private speech.* New York: Wiley, 1979.

Garvey, C. *Play.* Cambridge, Mass.: Harvard University Press, 1977.

Glucksberg, S., and **Krauss, R. M.** What do people say after they have learned how to talk? Studies of the development of referential communication. *Merrill-Palmer Quarterly,* 1967, *13,* 309-316.

Glucksberg, S., Krauss, R. M., and **Higgins, E. T.** The development of communication skills in children, in F. Horowitz, ed., *Review of child development research,* vol. 4. Chicago: University of Chicago Press, 1975.

Kleiman, A. The use of private speech in young children and its relation to social speech. Unpublished doctoral dissertation, University of Chicago, 1974.

Klein, W. An investigation of the spontaneous speech of children. Unpublished doctoral dissertation, University of Rochester, 1964.

Kohlberg, L., Yaeger, J., and **Hjertholm, E.** Private speech: Four studies and a review of theories. *Child Development,* 1968, *39,* 692-736.

Luria, A. R. *The role of speech in the regulation of normal and abnormal behavior,* J. Tizard, trans. New York: Liveright, 1961.

Luria, A. R. Speech development and the formation of mental processes, in M. Cole and I. Maltzman, eds., *A handbook of contemporary Soviet psychology.* New York: Basic Books, 1969.

Maratsos, M. P. Nonegocentric communication skills in preschool children. *Child Development*, 1973, *44*, 697-700.

Meacham. J. A. The role of verbal activity in remembering the goals of actions, in G. Zivin, ed., *The development of self-regulation through private speech.* New York: Wiley, 1979.

Mead, G. H. *Mind, self, and society.* Chicago: University of Chicago Press, 1934.

Meichenbaum, D., and **Goodman, J.** Training impulsive children to talk to themselves: A means of developing self-control. *Journal of Abnormal Psychology,* 1971, *77,* 115-126.

Meichenbaum, D., and **Goodman, S.** Clinical use of private speech and critical questions about its study in natural settings, in G. Zivin, ed., *The development of self-regulation through private speech.* New York: Wiley, 1979.

Miller, S. A., Shelton, J., and **Flavell, J. H.** A test of Luria's hypotheses concerning the development of verbal self-regulation. *Child Development,* 1970, *41,* 651-665.

Parten, M. B. Social participation among preschool children. *Journal of Abnormal Psychology*, 1932, *27*, 243-269.

———. Social play among preschool children. *Journal of Abnormal and Social Psychology*, 1933, *28*, 136-147.

Piaget, J. *The language and thought of the child,* M. Gabain, trans. London: Routledge & Kegan Paul, 1926. [Also available New York: Meridian, 1955. Originally published, 1923.]

Piaget, J. *Play, dreams, and imitation in childhood.* New York: Norton, 1962. [Originally published, 1946.]

Roberts, R. N. Private speech in academic problem-solving: A naturalistic perspective, in G. Zivin, ed., *The development of self-regulation through private speech.* New York: Wiley, 1979.

Rubin, K. H. Egocentrism in childhood: A unitary construct? *Child Development,* 1973, *44*, 102-110.

———. The play behaviors of young children. *Young Children*, 1977*a*, *32*, 16-24.

______. The social and cognitive value of preschool toys and activities. *Canadian Journal of Behavioural Science*, 1977*b*, *9*, 382-385.

______. Role-taking in childhood: Some methodological considerations. *Child Development*, 1978, *49*, 482-533.

Rubin, K. H., and **Maioni, T. L.** Play preference and its relationship to egocentrism, popularity, and classification skills in preschoolers. *Merrill-Palmer Quarterly*, 1975, *21*, 171-178.

Shatz, M., and **Gelman, R.** The development of communication skills: Modifications in the speech of young children as a function of listener. *Monographs of the Society for Research in Child Development*, 1973, *38*(5), Serial No. 152.

Shure, M. B. Psychological ecology of a nursery school. *Child Development*, 1963, *34*, 979-992.

Smilansky, S. *The effects of sociodramatic play on disadvantaged children: Preschool children*. New York: Wiley, 1968.

Vygotsky, L. S. *Thought and language*. E. Hanfmann and G. Vakar, eds. and trans. Cambridge, Mass.: MIT Press, 1962. [Originally published, 1934.]

Weisler, A., and **McCall, R. B.** Exploration and play: Resume and redirection. *American Psychologist*, 1976, *31*, 492-508.

Zivin, G. Functions of private speech during problem-solving in preschoolers. Unpublished doctoral dissertation, Harvard University, 1972.

Zivin, G. Removing common confusions about egocentric speech, private speech, and self-regulation. In G. Zivin, ed., *The development of self-regulation through private speech*. New York: Wiley, 1979. [See page 13 of this volume.]

CHAPTER 9

Private Speech in Academic Problem-Solving: A Naturalistic Perspective

RICHARD N. ROBERTS
University of North Carolina

At first glance a normal first-grade classroom might appear to be filled with 25 to 30 children engaging in a wide variety of random behavior. Some sit in their seats and jabber to themselves. Others talk to their neighbors. If the classroom is one with an open structure, children may be seen wandering from one activity to another. As one scans this profusion of activity, a girl is observed sitting at a desk about to begin a reading and writing assignment. She is required to choose the correct word from a list of words on the board and write the appropriate answer in the blank provided on the paper in front of her. The following sequence of events is observed: she picks up the pencil, begins to read the instructions out loud, looks at the board, plays with her hair, looks about the room, mumbles to herself that the words are too hard, stands up, and then goes over to the art corner to play.

Contrast this with another child who looks at the board, reads the sentence from the answer sheet, looks at the board again, taps the pencil on the table, reads the list of words on the board, and then writes the appropriate word in the blank. The two sequences end in quite different results: one in which the child gives up and the other in which the child successfully completes the task.

How can we observe the children's behavior in these situations and begin to make sense of the profusion of speech and motor activity that we typically observe? Such a question implies an examination of the child's behavior from two related but distinct perspectives. One question involves the degree to which such private speech exercises functional control over ongoing motor behavior in this type of academic situation. Within this same perspective it is also important to understand the degree to which ongoing motor behavior affects private speech. The child's motor activity and overt verbalizations can be seen as two distinct streams of behavior, which continually interact and influence each other. This perspective examines how one stream exerts influence on the other. How independent do the streams appear to be?

The second perspective examines the degree to which private speech serves a mediating function for the child in reaching a solution to the academic problem. In the two sequences described above the desired outcome involves a motor act of writing a correct word in the appropriate blank on the answer sheet. The occurrence of this appropriate response in the second sequence and an alternate response in the first sequence are both embedded in rich, but different, interactions of motor and verbal behavior. Any analysis should examine how these verbal and motor streams of behavior are related to each other as well as how their interaction relates to the differential outcomes.

The focus of this chapter is to demonstrate a methodology that allows such questions to be asked. Models of overt sequential processes involved in the solution of such a complex academic problem can be developed from an understanding of these relationships.

TASK SELECTION — WHY READING?

Certainly a wide range of relevant task variables affect both the outcome and the differential incidence of motor activity and private speech: type of task, task difficulty, social characteristics of the setting, and the age of the child are highly relevant to the present discussion. No attempt will be made here to discuss exhaustively all of these. Others in this book (see Meichenbaum and Goodman, Chapter 10) address these issues more completely. For the purposes of this chapter these variables will be discussed within the framework of an academic task designed for first grade children. Once the methodology has been presented, speculations can be advanced as to the various functions private speech and motor activity may serve.

Sensorimotor versus Problem-Solving Tasks

The diversity of tasks represented in the literature on private speech partly reflects its richness, but is a function of some of its confusion as well. A major distinction is between most experimental tasks that involve sensorimotor skills and naturalistic studies, which involve sequential tasks with varying degrees of problem-solving components. In the experimental line, investigations of developmental processes have used variations on the same basic laboratory method. Within a laboratory context Luria (1959) originally investigated the use of differential self-instructions and observed their effect on motoric responses, such as the rate of bulb-pressing. The bulb-pressing task has also been employed by a number of subsequent investigators (for example Jarvis, 1968; Miller, Shelton, and Flavell, 1970). Using the same experimental paradigm, Meichenbaum and Goodman (1969*a*) have used finger tapping with a telegraph key to investigate the use of covert and overt self-instructions. Wozniak's (1973) review of this self-instructional literature indicated that Meichenbaum and Goodman's (1969*a*) work represented the first clear Western replication of the Vygotsky-Luria position of a developmental theory of verbal control.

The equivocal nature of these studies has not diminished interest in the topic. Much of the persuasive evidence in Luria's own reports comes from more intense, quasi-clinical investigations, and it is possible that the laboratory methodology is inadequate for thorough exploration of verbal-motor behavior relationships (see Wozniak, 1973, for a discussion of these issues).

The second line of research employs a naturalistic approach and follows in the tradition of Piaget (1923/1955) and Vygotsky (1934/1962) who examined preschoolers' private speech as it occurs in free-play activities. These naturalistic studies frequently employ sequential age groups in order to address questions regarding differential functions of private speech. Piaget's concept of egocentric speech becoming social speech and Vygotsky's concept of private speech becoming covert internalized speech are examples of such developmental models. More recent works by Klein (1964) and Kohlberg, Yaeger, and Hjertholm (1968) continue the naturalistic and developmental traditions seeking to integrate the conflicting assumptions of Piaget and Vygotsky.

Age of the Child

Few investigators have approached the problem through an observation of performance on an academic task. In part this is a function of the age of the child who is typically studied. A major portion of the work on private speech has addressed its function for a preschool population. Puzzle-solving, a frequently used task in naturalistic work, is the equivalent of an academic task for a preschooler. The difference however involves the degree to which some form of higher cerebration is assumed to govern the end product. Older children are capable of integrating material involving longer and more complex sequences that do not have a specific concrete referent. It may be argued that the younger child requires more overt cues to perform longer sequences by virtue of having fewer exposures to this type of situation. Gal'perin's developmental model of the stages in the evolution of a mental act (Gal'perin, 1969) suggests that it is only in the higher stages that mental activity occurs in the absence of specific concrete referents. Mastery of an activity is not simply a function of remembering it but "independently repeating it with new material and obtaining a new product from this material" (p. 250). In Gal'perin's analysis there must be some reference point in any new material to link it with that previously mastered. It would make sense that these cues (referents) may be self-produced as with private speech or they may be embedded in the situation or stimulus materials. Thus one variable in task selection must be the age of the child.

A question beyond that however is whether different tasks will elicit different speech (cues) by their nature. Would private speech emitted in an academic task, such as reading, serve the same function as that emitted during other school-related activities? At present few data exist to answer such questions. Asking questions such as these implies an approach that emphasizes the contribution of the task, as well as the developmental level of the child, to the outcome. The study reported in this chapter looks at first-grade children and analyzes speech type by task difficulty and outcome.

Steps in Task Completion

With these factors in mind a reading assignment involving sentence completion is the task of study in our laboratory because it is based on behaviors regularly required of students in a classroom. The children are required to select the appropriate word to complete a sentence from a pair of words written on the board in front of them, and then to write the answer in the appropriate blank on the answer sheet. The sentences logically tell a story. In this activity there are specific elements embedded in the task that act as cues for correct responding. Performance in such a task requires a series of cognitive steps, including word recognition, breaking unfamiliar words into phonetic segments, integrating those segments into complete words, and contextual analysis of the word in the sentence. In addition few cues are provided by the task or setting for the style in which the task is to be addressed. The children perform the task as they would in a classroom, individually and with few constraints on their motor activity, verbal behavior, or the time required to complete the task. All of these variables must certainly affect the content and function of private speech.

Task Difficulty

Other investigators (for example Vygotsky, (1934/1962; Kohlberg, Yaeger and Hjertholm, 1968; Meichenbaum, 1973) have discussed the degree to which task difficulty affects the incidence of private speech in young children. These investigators have addressed the issue using a sensorimotor task. Vygotsky, for example, increased the difficulty of a normal activity, such as drawing, by placing obstructions in the child's way. No paper would be present, for instance. "By obstructing his free activity, we made him face problems" (Vygotsky, 1962, p.16). In addition to frustrating the child, these obstacles disrupted the smooth sequence of events. Vygotsky found a higher rate of speech-for-self when the child was frustrated in this manner.

As suggested by others (for example Meichenbaum, 1973) this increase is most likely to be related to the child's proficiency or competence in the task. With reference to the previous discussion of Gal'perin's view of the steps involved in mastery of a mental act, the higher incidence of private speech in harder tasks supports a view that private speech may serve in part as a self-produced cue or reference point. This reference point links skills learned in similar, easier situations with the present, more difficult one. It is most likely then in tasks involving sensorimotor skills that changes in the incidence of speech-for-self are in part a function of an interaction of *familiarity* with the skills involved in the tasks and *prior success* in similar tasks involving the same skills. More difficult or frustrating elements serve to disrupt an ongoing behavior stream.

This line of reasoning leads to an hypothesis that the higher incidence of private speech in such situations may serve as a cue to resume previous ongoing behavior. It is from this perspective that the methodology to be discussed has been developed. This variable may be even more crucial when tasks involving cognitive problem-solving are studied. For this reason I specifically developed two versions of the reading task for this work. Each consists of 12 sentences (2 practice and 10 fill-in-the-blank test sentences). The two versions differ only in the difficulty of the choice words. The children have been previously exposed to the choice words on the easier assignment through their regular reading curriculum, but not to the words on the harder version. Generally the children are equally familiar with the other words in the sentences.

Lab or Natural Setting: A Compromise

The degree to which the setting approximates the regular classroom is also a major variable. In my past work children have been videotaped individually while performing the tasks in a small room off the regular classrooms. They wear a cordless microphone and are videotaped through a one-way mirror as they complete the task. On the side of the mirror is a list of words containing the choice words, which are printed in large script. After being fitted with the wireless microphone, all children are given identical instructions that specify only the end product of writing the word in the blank and do not indicate a desired method of completion. The children are helped in the first two sample sentences by a teacher, who then leaves the room saying that she will return in 10 minutes. The children's response style, which includes verbal and motor behavior, is a function of the interaction of: task variables, individual developmental level, and past classroom experience.

Because the laboratory is an integral part of the fully operating elementary school, the children are used to individual testing situations and to wearing the wireless microphone. Nevertheless the individual nature of this setting is different from the social environment of a classroom. This difference may have both theoretical and practical implications for the findings from my past work. For example, following Piaget's model of cognitive development, egocentric speech (Piaget's term for private speech) may occur only *in social settings* after a certain developmental stage. Our children, who are first-graders, may have just passed that point. Following Piaget's logic the speech emitted individually would then be qualitatively different from that emitted in a social setting. Nevertheless the methodology as it is presented is sufficiently robust so that the translation to analysis of behavior in an ongoing classroom is possible and is, indeed, the next logical step in this ongoing research.

Though this methodology is no doubt reactive, it is virtually impossible to do naturalistic research into private speech without the use of a wireless microphone and videotape. I am essentially in agreement with the procedures for data collection discussed by Meichenbaum and Goodman in Chapter 10. I have added several technical innovations to the data collection process in order to more fully develop a complete typography of the verbal and motor streams of behavior. I use a system that generates a permanent time record on the videotape itself. The videotape is permanently altered to include a reading from a digital clock, which is superimposed on the tape. Thus when the videotape is viewed, one sees a continuous reading of the clock on the screen (Roberts, 1977). I have found this procedure to be the only method for obtaining sufficiently high interrater reliability to proceed with subsequent analyses.

PROBLEMS IN DATA COLLECTION

From Videotape to Research Protocols: Private Speech

One may well ask, "Why another coding system?" Several are presented in this book—Meichenbaum and Goodman (Chapter 10), Rubin (Chapter 8), and Fuson (Chapter 5)—in addition to those developed by previous researchers, such as Piaget (1923/1955), Kohlberg, Yaeger and Hjertholm (1968), and Klein (1963). My coding systems for speech and motor activity were developed naturalistically. That is, I looked at speech as it was emitted in the classroom, while the children were engaged in tasks similar to the one I was eventually to choose to study in more detail. In this sense my coding system examines the ecological validity of the functional and theoretical models of private speech as it relates to this type of task for this age group by examining its occurrence in the natural environment. More importantly this coding system is designed to generate data that examine the sequential and temporal relationship of private speech to ongoing motoric behavior.

The selection of a cognitive task with a specific motor component (for example writing the word in the blank) also allows an examination of the temporal relationships of speech-for-self to the motor act. In order for the emitted speech to have entered into the problem-solving process, it would seem necessary that the speech occur prior to the performance of the motor response reportedly governed by it. Prior researchers do not typically report such time-coded data, and indeed their coding systems and tasks do not tend to allow for these data to be collected.[1] The system reported here directly addresses the issue of the temporal relation of utterance and act.

Coding Speech

Relationship to Task • In categorizing children's speech, the first major distinction is between speech that is task-relevant and that should facilitate performance and task-irrelevant speech that does not seem to bear on the task and may indeed be incompatible with performance.

Task-Irrelevant Speech is best understood as either nonwords, which may or may not be compatible with task completion (a child may be humming a song, while writing the correct response) or verbalizing words, which are applicable to the task and/or may be indicative of off-task behavior. Thus the present coding system divides task-irrelevant speech into two subcategories: (1) *NonWords* and (2) *Not Applicable.*

Inevitably some of the sounds made by the children are inaudible because they are mumbled much too low to be understood. By employing videotape and wireless microphones, the incidence of such incomprehensibles is quite minimal. They are not coded in relation to relevance.

The other major coding category is *Task-Relevant Speech.* In order to gain a clearer understanding of how this speech may enter into the problem-solving process, it is further divided into four subcategories. *Evaluative Statements* indicate the children's perceptions of their performance as well as how they view the task itself ("I'm doing good." or "This is hard."). This category further indicates the natural occurrence of self-reinforcing or self-punishing statements and is of interest in relation to the child's actual performance.

In addition to the child's ongoing evaluations, another element of the overt speech may indicate the style the child develops and uses to address the academic problem. *Strategy Statements* are coded when the child is stating overtly what to do and how to do it. ("I have to do this." "Write this down.")

Much of the work on training impulsive children to mediate their behavior verbally involves teaching them to generate questions about both the task and their performance: a category of *Questions* is included to identify the frequency of the natural occurrence of this strategy.

Because the task is a reading assignment, there is a high probability that the child will read some words or parts of words aloud; thus a category for

[1]Recent and important exceptions are Goodman (1977, 1978) and Rubin (Chapter 8).

Phonemes is included. This category codes speech that is a verbal transcription of the academic task and the heading can be changed to meet the requirements of the task. (For instance if the task is composed of arithmetic problems, this category can become *Numbers*.)

Speech Reference • All task-relevant categories can be further coded according to whether the speech refers to the self, to someone else, or not to a person at all. Evaluations may be made of the self, of a friend, or of some physical object; questions may also be variously addressed; strategies may be stated for self-guidance, or they may be directed toward others in the form of instructions. Though the present task is performed individually, the task and coding system can be used for comparisons in settings involving a number of children. Therefore all speech in the task-relevant categories are recorded as statements about *Self, Other*, or *No One*.

Even when the child is alone, one may find incidents of speech that sound as though they are directed to others. This type of speech has been viewed by Piaget as a step beyond egocentric speech, and its occurrence has specific theoretical implications for his theory of cognitive development. It is indicative of the beginning of social awareness. It acknowledges and differentiates one's viewpoint from others. In a sense then Piaget views speech-for-self as developing into private speech. This is the same speech that Kohlberg, Yaeger, and Hjertholm (1968) see as necessary for developing the self through Mead's internalization of the generalized other.

Temporal Sequencing • In order to begin to understand the contribution of task-relevant speech to the problem-solving process, it is necessary to examine the temporal relationship of the speech to the motor elements of the task itself, which is defined in the current study as the physical act of writing the word in the blank on the page. If a child has begun to read "Question 1," all speech prior to writing the word physically in the blank is coded as *"Before."* All speech emitted while the child is physically writing is coded as *"During."* Any speech after the child has stopped writing, but prior to making any sound connected with the next task, "Question 2," is coded as *"After."*

Data Reduction

The data derived from this form of analysis provide information for one of the two perspectives with which this chapter was introduced. This examination of the sequencing organized around the motor act addresses the issue of the mediating function of private speech.

The hierarchical nature of this speech-coding system provides broad categories for a macroanalysis (Incomprehensible, Task-Irrelevant, Task-Related, Reading Aloud) as well as finer distinctions within each category for a microanalysis. Roberts and Tharp (1977) provided an example of its use with finer distinctions than Roberts' (1977) study, which employed only the broader categories.

The data reduction process first requires that the speech be transcribed onto speech protocols, noting both the content and time for each speech segment. Two observers working independently are required. The protocols are compared, and questions of reliability are resolved. Though this procedure is time-consuming and laborious, it appears to be the only workable solution to achieve sufficiently high reliability. The speech is then coded from reconciled protocols.

From Videotape to Research Protocols: Motor Behavior

The next stage in the process is the quantification and data reduction of the child's ongoing motor behavior. Just as the protocols are developed for the analysis of speech, a similar system is used to reduce the motor behavior on videotapes to a form permitting analysis. The ongoing motor behavior is coded from the videotapes using the coding systems developed by Roberts (1977).

Coding Motor Activity

Data are collected from several dimensions. Just as the child's speech is coded with respect to its relationship to the task, motor behavior is coded in a similar fashion. The first category is *On-Task*. In order for the child to be coded as *On-Task*, she/he must be in sufficient proximity to the desk that she/he is physically capable of writing on the paper. The child must be either looking at the board or looking at the answer sheet. *Off-Task* is a category which is mutually exclusive of *On-Task*. It is coded when the child is looking away from the board or the answer sheet and/or standing or sitting away from the desk such as that she/he would not be able to reach the paper.

The second set of mutually exclusive behaviors includes *Task-Irrelevant* and *No-Task-Irrelevant* behavior. These behaviors are of importance because they may serve to interrupt a smooth sequence and lead to off-task behavior or speech. They may also be indicative of anxiety or increased task difficulty. The category has been labelled *Task-Irrelevant* because the presence or absence of these behaviors is not a necessary condition for completion of the act of writing the response. Behaviors included in the *Task-Irrelevant* category are: touching microphone, pencil tapping, writing on paper in space other than blank, scratching oneself, standing near desk, playing with hair. The cessation of all the above behaviors is coded as *No-Task-Irrelevant*.

Other motor behaviors included a category for *Looking at Board/Choice List*. If the child glances at the stimulus materials, this category was coded.

Coding Task Outcome

Finally the outcome response itself is coded. There are four possible outcomes. These include:

1. *Task Complete—correct:* The correct response was written in the appropriate blank on the answer sheet.
2. *Task Complete—incorrect (list):* An incorrect response was written from the list of choice words.
3. *Task Complete—incorrect (made up):* An incorrect response was written that did not appear on the list of choice words.
4. *Incomplete Response:* A trial was begun, but no response was made.

The theoretical issues involved in an analysis of the various responses cannot be completely discussed here. However the relative frequency of each type of error has important implications for different theories of cognitive development. For example a child who completes a sentence with a word not from the choice list, but which makes sense in the context of the sentence, understands the material better than the child who answers incorrectly from the choice list. Gal'perin for instance would place these two children on different levels of cognitive development.

Data Reduction

The same procedures discussed for development and resolution of speech protocols are used with the development of the protocols for ongoing motor activity. Again, without the continuous timing device and videotapes, accuracy in this procedure is not possible. Some authors have suggested a modification of the reliability criterion to plus or minus five seconds (Bakeman, 1976). For our purposes this error tolerance is too large to parcel out the temporal patterns. The timing device allows for plus or minus one second resolution.

Duration versus Frequency

Ongoing motor behavior can be viewed from two perspectives as it interacts with the verbal stream. One alternative is to examine the *duration* of each coded motor act in the chain of events. Motor behavior coded in this manner can be related to the co-occurrence of verbal responses. For example one can ask, "Given the occurrence of a task-related statement, what is the probability the student is also engaging in on-task motor behavior?"

The other possibility provides different information and treats the onset of each coded motor element as a discrete event. This form of coding in which *frequency* is the major variable provides data for a sequential analysis of the interaction of the two streams of behavior (verbal and motor). From this type of analysis, hypotheses can be developed as to the degree to which behavior in one stream either cues behavior within the same stream or acts as a cue across streams. Though this type of analysis has been employed in the study of interpersonal behavior (for example, Patterson, 1964; Bakeman, 1976), it has been infrequently applied to the analysis of intrapersonal behavior (see Roberts, 1977; Goodman, 1977, 1978). It allows one to ask questions such as, "Given the occurrence of behavior *x*, what is the probability that it will be followed by behavior *y*?" If the coding system is designed with mutually exclusive and exhaustive categories for each stream, Markov chains may be the end product of the analysis (Hays, 1973; see Bakeman, 1976, for a more complete discussion of this issue.) This is not the case in the present coding system.

When these coding systems are applied to the questions addressed at the beginning of this chapter, the resulting data provide a complete typography of the verbal and motor streams of behavior. What follows is a brief presentation of some of the findings to illustrate the method and to provide an empirical basis to discuss the questions that have been raised.

PRIVATE SPEECH: A MEDIATING INFLUENCE?

Temporal Order with Respect to Task Outcome

A major theoretical question addressed by this methodology concerns the degree to which private speech governs a specific motor act. The motor behavior in this analysis consists of writing a word in a blank on an answer sheet. It is the discrete end product of a cognitive task. Prior to the execution of that act, the majority of cognitive steps have occurred. One exception is a step in which the child checks the work for accuracy. In our laboratory the children are typically given 10 minutes in a free-field setting to complete 10 sentences. In one example the speech that occurred was broken down as follows: The total number of private-speech units emitted by the 25 children was 2,271 with a mean number of verbalizations per child of 42.6 units on the easy task and 48.17 units on the hard version. Less than 5% of the total speech is categorized as *Incomprehensible* (4.5%). *Task-Irrelevant* accounts for only 10.9%, relatively evenly divided between the *Non-Words* and *Not Applicable* categories. The remaining 84% of the speech was relevant to the task. The largest subcategory was *Phonemes*, comprised of words and phrases directly from the assignment (77%). *Evaluation Statements* accounted for 4.2% of the speech. *Questions* were infrequently used. Even less frequent were *Strategy Statements*.

Speech Referent

Because the *Phoneme* category was so predominant, most speech did not refer to the behavior of self or someone else; 93% was coded as not referring to a person at all. Statements concerning the child's own behavior accounted for 6% of the speech and the remaining 1% referred to someone other than the speaker.

Temporal Sequencing

With reference to temporal order, most speech occurred "*Before*" the motor response (70.70%). The subcategory "*During*" accounted for 17.4%, and 11.9% occurred "*After*" the motor response was completed.

Comparisons were made between the frequency of responses made by boys and girls for each category. Only in the category of *Incomprehensibles* on the easy task was there a statistically significant sex difference ($t = 3.84$, $p < .001$), with girls producing more incomprehensible speech than boys (Roberts and Tharp, 1977).

Relationship to Task Difficulty

Though these percentages provide a very rough idea of the relative frequency of private speech, a much finer analysis is required to identify the relationships between its employment and outcome on the task.

Earlier a question was raised concerning the degree to which task difficulty alone may contribute to differential incidence of private speech. In this instance the children verbalize more on the hard task than on the easy task. However this increase is only with respect to the speech that is reading aloud; this is *Phonemes.* Children tend to read aloud more frequently on the hard task. Task-irrelevant speech and task-related speech (minus reading aloud) do not differ across tasks. Even without taking into account outcome, the higher incidence of this type of speech indicates that the children experience more difficulty as the task becomes harder. This lends support to the position that more difficult tasks elicit more private speech. Why then is there no increase across tasks for the task-irrelevant and / or task-relevant (minus reading aloud) speech? It is only through an analysis of the relative frequency, content, and temporal sequencing of speech with respect to outcome that one can begin to speculate on this question.

Task-Irrelevant Speech and Self-Interference in Less Competent Children

Differences begin to emerge when a comparison is made of children who make more correct responses with those who make more errors or who do not complete the trial. Children who are less competent engage in much more task-irrelevant speech than their more competent counterparts *regardless* of task difficulty. The content of this speech does not appear to be qualitatively different. Both groups engage in fantasy talk. They will tell themselves a story or construct a game with an imagined playmate (cops and robbers, monsters). The less competent child tends to tell longer stories and to become more involved in the story than the child who is answering correctly.

In addition there is a marked difference in spacing of the task-irrelevant speech. Less competent children tend to intersperse task-irrelevant speech throughout this task, but more competent children engage in this form of speech after task completion. It is not clear at this point if task-irrelevant speech serves as an interference factor or as an indicator that the child is experiencing frustration. It may well be both. The finding that task-irrelevant speech does not increase with task difficulty for less competent children argues against a frustration explanation. These children should be the most frustrated as task difficulty increases. Though the data are correlational, the interference function seems to provide a better fit. Even when the other factors such as IQ are held constant, children who respond correctly do not tend to use this form of speech.

Non-Specific Task-Relevant Speech in Less Competent Children

This same type of analysis (frequency, content, and temporal order) leads to a number of speculations as to the function of *task-related* speech. As before task difficulty does not alter the frequency of this form of speech. This is a surprising finding, given the emphasis on this type of speech in the literature. One might well expect a higher incidence of private speech in the form of strategies, evaluations, and questions as the task becomes more difficult. This is not the case for this first-grade age group and reading task.

What does occur is that the children who do poorly on the task engage in significantly more task-relevant speech than children who do well. Again at least two possible explanations exist. From a developmental perspective one might assert that children who do poorly in this problem-solving task are at an earlier developmental stage than children who do well. If this were the case, the higher incidence of task-relevant private speech would reflect that developmental difference. This reasoning assumes that this form of speech does in fact serve some mediating function in this type of task. Children who have mastered the required skills are able to shortcut the problem-solving process to eliminate the overt verbal prompts, just as Gal'perin suggests.

Evidence of advanced development (or higher competence) showing abbreviated speech would come from an analysis of the content of shortened speech and its temporal sequence with respect to task outcome: if that interpretation were supported, the content should remain the same at a higher developmental stage, but there would just be less speech or it should appear in an abbreviated form. This is not the case. Instead the content of the speech is different for children with different outcomes, which reflect different competence levels. There is little incidence of abbreviated forms.

However speech of the same type that is used by both competence levels appears to serve the same function. An example illustrates the point. Statements coded as *Evaluations* are infrequent in the speech of both competent and less competent children. These statements tend to be veridical evaluations of the child's performance. Thus a poor problem-solver is more likely to state, "I can't do this.", "This is too hard.", or "I don't know that word." A successful problem-solver is more likely to evaluate the work by stating, "All right!", "I got it.", or "There, finished."

With respect to temporal sequencing, one finds the more competent problem-solver evaluates after the task is completed, whereas the less competent child evaluates prior to task completion. This is due in part to the fact that the latter group does not finish as many of the trials that they begin. Occasionally, even in those instances when they complete the task and they know it is incorrect, they may evaluate their work veridically to themselves ("That's wrong."), but may not alter their response.

Strategy statements are made most frequently by those students who perform poorly, and they occur prior to the task completion. Again one may argue for a developmental interpretation of the use of this type of speech. However, if that were the case, and it served some facilitative function, one would also expect that its occurrence would boost performance for this less developed group. Apparently this does not happen. One explanation for this result is that the types of speech coded as *Task-Relevant* may be too diffuse for this type of task to be facilitative or to mediate the motor outcome. From the perspective discussed earlier, which viewed private speech as serving a cueing function, this type of speech may not provide sufficiently specific cues to aid in the problem-solving process.

Reading Aloud as Task-Specific Cueing in Competent Children

If the above is true, one may well look for a type of speech more specific to the task at hand. In this situation it is *Reading Aloud*. An analysis of this category reveals important differences in its differential employment. Though there is considerable individual variation in the frequency of reading aloud during the easier tasks, the variation is not specifically related to task outcome. This is not the case on the harder tasks. Even though the frequency of this type of speech increases across all subjects as task difficulty increases, the increase is larger for children who complete more correct responses. A temporal analysis indicates that this increase occurs partially prior to the act and partially after it is completed.

This would indicate that children who are more effective in the problem-solving process use this specific cue (reading aloud) differently as the task difficulty increases. Not only do they "sound out" the words more frequently but they check their responses more completely. "Sounding out" the word indicates that the word is being broken down into smaller segments. The checking response indicates that the child is making sure that the answer makes sense in the context of the sentence. Both are facilitory strategies.

ONGOING MOTOR BEHAVIOR: AN ANALYSIS BY TASK

Though data such as these are important beginning steps in providing some structure for viewing private speech, significant relationships are lost when speech is organized around only one discrete event. Private speech is but one stream of ongoing behavior that the child emits. A different topography emerges when the analysis is extended to include other streams of behavior as well. In the present case it is the verbal and motor streams that are the subject of study, and a conditional probability analysis provides the model for understanding their interaction. Though other forms of analysis have been proposed, a conditional probability model is used in the present example because it provides information with respect to the sequencing of events as well as their co-occurrence. It does not require statistical assumptions which may be difficult to meet in naturalistic work. For example a path analysis assumes that causal order is known and that relationships between variables are causally closed (Wright, 1960). These assumptions could not be met in the present example.

The conditional probability analysis may be used to examine group means as in the present case, or individual trials could be analyzed for a single-subject case study. A danger of this type of analysis is that it generates a considerable amount of data. The coding system must be compact in order for the data to be meaningfully analyzed. For the purposes of illustrating the technique, a more condensed coding system is presented to minimize the number of categories.

In the verbal stream, three categories are of interest: *Task-Irrelevant* speech, *Task-Relevant*[2] speech, and *Phoneme* or *Reading Aloud*. The motor stream includes:

1. a. On-Task
   b. Off-Task
2. a. Task-Irrelevant
   b. No-Task-Irrelevant
3. a. Looking at Board

The first two sets of motor categories are mutually exclusive.

[2] *Task-Relevant* speech here includes the three subcategories of *Evaluative Statements, Strategy Statements,* and *Questions*. It excludes the subcategory *Phonemes,* which is analyzed separately.

Motor Behavior

Raw Occurrence Task

Prior to a discussion of the interaction of the two behavior streams, it is useful to have some basic understanding of the raw occurrence of behavior in these categories. Table 1 presents such data. From this purely descriptive perspective, several points are important. Though the children attempt more trials on the easy task, they do not differ in the total amount of time they spend on the two tasks. Thus the children spend more time per trial on each hard trial than on each easy one, indicating that the hard task is indeed more difficult. One clear finding is the high percentage of time spent on-task which remains constant in both easy and hard tasks. Given the unstructured nature of the setting, it is somewhat surprising that 80% of the children's time is spent on-task. This may reflect one difference between our laboratory classroom and a regular classroom. Here the child performs the task alone. There are no other children present to offer tempting distractions.

TABLE 1. Descriptive Means for Motor Behavior on Two Task Levels

Variables	Easy Task	Hard Task
Total time per trial	383.12	431.16
Time on-task	311.56	348.08
Time off-task	72.16	83.40
Time task-irrelevant	84.84	98.04
Look-at-board	25.88	31.36
Total verbalizations		
Task-irrelevant verbalizations	5.08	4.64
Task-directed verbalizations	2.2	2.24
Reading aloud	32.52	34.96

In addition to remaining on-task for a good portion of the testing, there is also relatively little time spent in behavior which is irrelevant to task completion.

The frequency with which the children glance at the word list does not differ across tasks when analyzed by group, but does differ by individual trials. There are more glances per trial during the hard task. Other measures of gross motor behavior, such as time spent on-task and time spent in task-irrelevant behavior, remain constant across both tasks regardless of the unit of comparison.

The motor behavior of the average child can be summarized as spending the vast majority of the time working on the task, looking at the board frequently, and not engaging in much behavior that has the potential to draw him/her off task.

Differences Due to Task Difficulty

Again one may question the relative contribution of task difficulty to apparent differences in motor behavior. The difference appears to be quantitative and not qualitative. Though there is more motor behavior on the harder task, the precentages in each category remain constant over the two tasks. The harder task just takes longer and produces more behavior.

Summarizing the speech patterns, reading aloud is the primary form of speech, followed by task-irrelevant speech and task-relevant private speech. These last two categories occur very infrequently. An analysis by trial indicates that the hard task elicits more reading aloud than the easy version.

PRIVATE SPEECH AND ONGOING MOTOR BEHAVIOR: AN INTERACTIONAL APPROACH

Having described the verbal and motor streams as they exist, how does a description of the interaction of the two streams of behavior change one's perception of them?

Conditional Probability Analysis: Temporal Co-Occurrence of Behavior

Table 2 presents a summary of the simultaneous analysis of motor and speech behavior (Roberts, 1977). The conditional probabilities in this table are averages of those computed for individual subjects by trial prior to any additional data manipulation. Behaviors catalogued in the left-hand column of this table should be read as, "$P(x/y)$". For example the first behavior in that column should be read as, "The probability of on-task behavior, given the co-occurrence of task-irrelevant behavior, was equal to .17." Similarly, the next behavior should be read as, "The probability of on-task behavior, given the co-occurrence of no-task-irrelevant behavior, was equal to .83." Because the codes of *Task-Irrelevant* and *No-Task-Irrelevant* behavior form a mutually exclusive and exhaustive set, the sum of the probabilities of those two behaviors, given a target behavior X, is always equal to 1.00. The same is true for the other mutually exclusive and exhaustive set, *On-Task* and *Off-Task* behavior.

The conditional probabilities combined for hard and easy trials are presented in column 1, followed by conditional probabilities for the easy and the hard tasks computed separately in columns 2 and 3, respectively.

TABLE 2. Conditional Probability Matrix: Co-Occurrence of Behavior

Behavior	Probabilities		
	Overall	Easy Task	Hard Task
On-task			
Task-irrelevant	.17	.16	.18
No-task-irrelevant	.83	.84	.82
Off-task			
Task-irrelevant	.35	.37	.34
No-task-irrelevant	.65	.63	.66
Task-irrelevant			
On-task	.74	.75	.72
Off-task	.26	.25	.28
No-task-irrelevant			
On-task	.87	.89	.85
Off-task	.13	.11	.15
Look-at-board			
Task-irrelevant	.14	.13	.15
No-task-irrelevant	.86	.87	.85
Task-relevant speech			
On-task	.56	.59	.53
Off-task	.44	.41	.47
Task-irrelevant	.34	.28	.40
No-task-irrelevant	.66	.72	.60
Task-relevant speech [a]			
On-task	.63	.58	.69
Off-task	.37	.42	.31
Task-irrelevant	.23	.14	.33
No-task-irrelevant	.77	.86	.67
Reading aloud			
On-task	.98	.99	.98
Off-task	.02	.01	.02
Task-irrelevant	.16	.17	.16
No-task-irrelevant	.84	.82	.84

a Task-relevant speech excludes phonemes (reading aloud), which is analyzed separately.

The conditional probabilities for the criterion behaviors listed in Table 2 generally did not vary across the hard and easy tasks. The *Task-Relevant* verbalization categories are the only exceptions to this statement and will be discussed below.

Co-Occurrence of Two Motor Behaviors

The preponderance of both on-task behavior and off-task behavior occurs in the absence of task-irrelevant behavior. When task-irrelevant motor behavior does occur, it is distributed between on-task and off-task behavior in rough proportion to the occurrence of these two categories alone. This indicates that task-irrelevant behavior occurs with the same frequency whether the child is on-task or off-task.

Because looking-at-board is an on-task behavior by definition, the probability of its occurrence is not computed for on-task or off-task but only for the sets of task-irrelevant and no-task-irrelevant behaviors. Looking-at-board is most likely to co-occur when the child is not engaged in task-irrelevant behavior.

Co-Occurrence of Motor and Verbal Behavior

Task-irrelevant speech is emitted more frequently when the child is on-task and not engaged in task-irrelevant behavior than if neither of these behaviors occurs. During the hard task the probability that task-irrelevant speech will co-occur with task-irrelevant behavior increases when compared to the easy task.

If task-irrelevant speech is basically a random event, the conditional probability of its co-occurrence with on-task motor behavior should parallel the percentages of these behaviors as they occur in the task. This is not the case. It occurs more frequently during off-task behavior and less frequently during on-task behavior than expected by chance. As the task becomes more difficult, this disparity increases. This indicates a relationship between the two behaviors (task-irrelevant speech and off-task motor behavior). It also indicates that the relationships between the two streams of behavior are not always clear. A child may be on-task motorically but engaged in task-irrelevant speech.

Are any of these combinations counterproductive? One way to investigate such a question is to examine the impact of each combination on the outcome of the task. The picture becomes clearer when the conditional probability for task-irrelevant speech, given on-task or off-task behaviors, is correlated with task outcome for the two tasks. One finds differences on the easier task, but not on the harder. Increased co-occurrence of task-irrelevant speech and on-task motor behavior is correlated with success on the easy task. On the same task an increased co-occurrence of task-irrelevant speech and off-task motor behavior is correlated with failure. These patterns are not significant on the more difficult task.

As stated earlier the content and frequency of task-irrelevant speech do not appear to differ as the task becomes more difficult. Rather it is the differential employment of such speech that is significant. As long as the child remains on-task, the co-occurrence of task-irrelevant speech does not inhibit success on the easier tasks. It is the combination of off-task behavior and task-irrelevant speech that is an indication the child is only working in short spurts and does not experience success. As the task becomes more difficult, these patterns do not continue. Because the higher incidence of task-irrelevant speech is correlated with failure regardless of task difficulty, it is the task-irrelevant speech itself rather than its co-occurrence with on-task/off-task motor behavior that affects performance on the more difficult tasks.

Task-relevant private speech also occurs most frequently when the children are on-task and not engaged in task-irrelevant behavior. These relationships are stronger as the task becomes more difficult. There is a concomitant decrease in the probability of task-relevant private speech while the children are engaged in task-irrelevant or off-task behavior.

The questions raised concerning task-relevant private speech can be addressed in the same manner as the earlier discussion of task-irrelevant speech. First the probability of on-task behavior is .84 for the easy task. If task-relevant private speech is a random event, the conditional probability of its occurrence should parallel the probability of the criterion behavior. In this case that would mean the probability of task-relevant private speech, given on-task behavior, should equal .84, and the probability of task-relevant private speech, given off-task behavior, should equal .16. However this is not the case. The actual conditional probabilities are .58 for task-relevant speech, given on-task behavior, and .42 for task-relevant speech given off-task behavior. The differences between the observed and expected probabilities is greater than chance. Thus on the easy task, task-relevant private speech occurs more frequently than chance during off-task behavior and less frequently than chance during on-task behavior. As reported by Roberts and Tharp (1977), the content of task-relevant categories for the less competent children tends to be negative. They perform poorly on the task and veridically evaluate their work with such statements as, "I can't do this.", "I don't know that word.", or "This is hard." It would make sense then that these types of statements would be made when the child is off-task.

These additional clues provide an opportunity to speculate on how the co-occurrence of speech and motor behavior may affect outcome. Children who perform poorly on the task do not continue to problem-solve after they veridically evaluate their work as incorrect or difficult. The comments are more likely to be made after the child is *already* off-task. The less competent child has already been distracted or pulled off the task by something else. The verbal statement appears more to be a comment on the non-task motor behavior or a rationale for its continuation than a causal agent. For those children who do poorly on the task, these evaluations account for the higher incidence of task-related private speech during nontask motor behavior.

Children read aloud most frequently when they are on-task and not engaged in task-irrelevant behavior. The co-occurrence of reading aloud and on-task motor behavior approaches unity because it is easiest to repeat the words out loud when looking at them. Though at first glance this may seem to be so apparent as to hardly warrant discussion, it may have important implications in putting together a picture of the cognitive processes that are assumed to occur covertly. If reading aloud did not serve as a necessary link in the problem-solving process, one might find a higher incidence of word play involving the sentences and the choice words. This would most likely occur when the child is off-task motorically. However the prevalent pattern involves the child's remaining on-task motorically and continuously sounding out the words throughout the problem-solving process. Children who are more successful on harder tasks employ this strategy more often as task difficulty increases. Thus reading aloud while doing the task serves as an important cognitive strategy in reaching a solution to this academic problem. It serves to link the child's present problem-solving behavior to previously learned responses. As can be seen from this discussion, a conditional probability analysis serves to qualify and more carefully define hypotheses concerning the functional significance of the various categories of private speech.

Sequential Analysis of Behavior: Motor and Verbal Interactions

The conditional probability statements just discussed were developed by asking the question, "Given the occurrence of y, what is the probability of its co-occurrence with x?" This next analysis approaches the temporal relationship of the target and criterion behavior from a different perspective. It asks, "Given the occurrence of x, what is the probability of it being *followed* by y?" Put differently, we want to know if we can predict better than chance what behavior will immediately follow the occurrence of x.

For example, a sequence for a particular child may be:

Time	*Code*
08	On-Task onset
11	Task-Irrelevant onset
14	Look-at-Board
16	Read Aloud
18	No-Task-Irrelevant onset
20	Off-Task onset

The above chain of behavior would be analyzed as follows: On-Task, Task-Irrelevant, Look-at-Board, Real Aloud, No-Task-Irrelevant, Off-Task. The conditional probability for each behavior pair is computed by individual trial and averaged within and across subjects[3].

Does Motor Behavior Cue Motor Behavior?

Each "target" behavior can be followed by a number of other behaviors. Do any pairs occur more or less frequently than chance alone would suggest? In most instances they do not. However in those remaining cases where they do form sequential pairs, valuable information is provided in understanding the verbal-motor interaction.

On-task behavior for example is followed about a third of the time by the cessation of task-irrelevant motor behavior (four times more than chance would suggest). This chain occurs regardless of task difficulty, but is highly predictive of success on the more difficult tasks. Both behaviors are indicative of "getting down to business" and as the task becomes more difficult, the chain facilitates the problem-solving process by focusing the child's attention solely on the salient material.

[3]The major question addressed in this analysis is whether the probability of behavior y following behavior x is any different from the probability of the given behavior occurring anywhere in the behavioral chain. This addresses the question of the independence of the behaviors in the chain. Translated into a statistical question is it a test of the difference between the observed and predicted values p_{xy}, the predicted value of $p_{xy} = \frac{f_x}{f_a^+ \ldots f_n}$, and the predicted value of $f_{xy} = f_x p_{xy}$? So the difference between the predicted and observed occurrence for xy can be assessed with a binomial test where:

$$z = (x - NP/ \quad NPQ)$$

$$z = (f_{xy}(\text{observed}) - f_x p_{xy} 1/ \quad f_x p_{xy}(1 - p_{xy})$$

This z score, computed for each probability for each child on the hard and easy tasks separately, is the statistic used to correlate the probability statements with the outcome measures of number correct per task. The use of z scores allows for a stronger, more powerful analysis than the probability statements themselves. It can be used here because the sequencing of the behaviors can be assumed to be independent and the z scores are normalized, whereas in the analysis with duration as the measure, these assumptions could not be made.

Does Motor Behavior Cue Verbal Behavior?

This occurs only in one case. Approximately half the time that the children look at the board, the next response is to read aloud. This pattern makes sense. The children present a stimulus to themselves and follow it with a specific, overt verbal response. Though the frequency of reading aloud as an isolated event predicts task success and increases with task difficulty, this sequence, in which the children look at the board and then read aloud, is not a function of either of these two variables. The probability of reading aloud following a glance at the board remains constant.

Looking at the board is a motor behavior that does not cue at all nonreading task-related speech. Considering looking at the board alone, it is a motor behavior that is highly predictive of task success. In this analysis it only cues a highly specific task-related type of speech (reading aloud). With this exception motor behavior per se does not appear to cue any specific verbal behavior to form a sequential pattern for this type of task and age group. Rather it appears that if the child is already engaged in certain motor activities, there is a greater likelihood that certain types of private speech will occur (for example if on-task, then reading aloud; if off-task, then task-irrelevant or task-relevant speech).

Does Verbal Behavior Cue Motor Behavior?

Does the opposite effect occur? Does a specific verbal behavior cue any specific motor behavior? Task-irrelevant and task-relevant private speech do not serve as cues in this fashion. The motor behaviors that follow them do not suggest patterns any greater than chance. The remaining verbal category, *Reading Aloud*, does suggest a significant pattern. Approximately half the time, reading aloud is followed by looking at the board. The probability that reading aloud would be followed by looking at the board is not dependent on task difficulty or a correct response. Again both behaviors are highly specific to the task and logically follow from one another. One can begin to see a pattern emerging in which a child is *on-task*, looking at the board, reading aloud, looking at the board. . . . Both elements in this interplay are independently predictive of success. Their interchange leads to the motor activity of completing the trial.

Does Success Lead to Success?

It is not only that these two highly task-specific behaviors (reading aloud and looking at the board) lead to completion of the act; they are also the behaviors that most frequently follow a correct response. Both behaviors serve to check the response. One consists of overt speech (reading aloud) and follows a correct response 40% of the time. The other response is a silent motor activity (looking at the board). Recalling the previous discussion, it is highly probable that this motor act will be followed by the overt verbal response of reading aloud. Even if there is not overt verbalization, looking at the board indicates some overt process, which operationally serves the same function—placing the word in the context of the sentence and checking to see that the response makes sense.

WHAT MEDIATES SUCCESS? THEORETICAL CONCERNS

Specific patterns in the verbal and motor streams that relate to successful completion or to failure in academic work provide the observational base to validate a variety of theoretical assumptions regarding mediational and facilitory processes in academic problem solving.

Necessary or Sufficient Conditions for Mediation

In order to serve in any obvious mediational role, speech must precede the motor act that completes the problem solving task.[4] Certainly a major portion of the speech examined in this example does occur prior to a task's sentence completion. Though this meets one of the necessary conditions for a mediational hypothesis, is it also a sufficient condition? This does not appear to be the case. Rather some forms of speech appear to mediate the process, while other forms do not. Certainly a highly task-specific form, such as reading aloud, mediates problem-solving because its presence correlates well with success. Other forms are labeled *Task-Relevant* because their content would suggest that they serve in some mediational capacity. A closer examination and a functional analysis of speech and motor behavior question this assumption. Task-relevant speech, such as strategies, evaluations, and questions are associated with off-task motor behavior and poor performance on the task. It is difficult to support a view that this type of speech mediates a cognitive function that leads to correct responses. The speech labeled, *TaskRelevant*, does not facilitate improved performance.

Self-Regulatory Processes

These findings not only question a mediational role for this type of speech, but also raise additional questions regarding its self-regulatory function. Generally private speech in these task-relevant categories is too diffuse and nonspecific to regulate motor behavior. Asking, "What do I have to do?" does not insure the appropriate answer is within the verbal or motor repertoire. Saying, "I have to do this!" does not insure that the child can label or perform

[4]Rubin (Chapter 8) makes a similar assumption, but considers simultaneous speech as potentially mediating. Contrastingly Meacham (Chapter 7) argues for a conception of verbal selfguidance that is not planning and which resembles Vygotsky's earliest form of self-regulation (description after action), whose function is explicated by Zivin (Chapter 1).

the steps required to complete the task. Staats (1975) provides an analysis of this problem and indicates that the motor behaviors to be elicited by the task-related statements must have been previously learned by the individual and then paired with the verbal cues. In the present case task-relevant speech does not cue specific motor responses nor does it cue verbal responses that have been demonstrated to mediate task performance. For this age group, in this type of task, it is not clear what function it may serve.

One possibility is suggested by Klein (1963) and Flavell (1966) who characterize two functions for private speech: (1) cognitive self-guidance (in this case reading aloud) and (2) affective expression (in this case task-irrelevant and task relevant speech). The distinct distributions in the natural occurrence of these categories lends support to such a functional division. Evaluations, strategies, and questions express feelings and veridically evaluate performance, but do not guide the problem-solving process. Reading aloud is the only verbal element that is indicative of such a function.

Motor Behavior as Mediator

Verbal behavior is not the only stream that may serve a mediational role. In this case looking at the board is a motor behavior that is also actively involved and it is an element in a facilitory sequence. Though looking at the board is a motor behavior, it is also an overt indicator of an assumed covert process of reading silently. The act of looking at the board is an important element because it provides a necessary condition for the occurrence of a covert process—reading the choice words silently. Certainly the child may be engaged as well in other covert verbal behavior while looking at the board, but it is most likely that the looking culminates the act of reading silently.

Gal'perin's Developmental Approach

One behavior is overt, the other is indicative of a covert process. Are they developmentally linked? Gal'perin's model of the development of mental acts (Gal'perin, 1969) suggests that they may be seen as two stages in a developmental process that involves the eventual automaticity of mental activity. First comes familiarization with the task. This is followed by performance based on material objects or accompanied by material representations or signs. The third stage is one in which the act is based on audible speech, but without direct external physical support as in the preceding stage. This is followed by performance involving external speech to oneself. In the last stage the act is completed using internal speech alone. The children who are successful in the present example appear to complete the task with speech and motor patterns similar to the later stages in Gal'perin's model, when external speech is becoming internal speech. They have passed earlier stages in which the written words require some material manifestation of the concept they represent in order to be grasped. In reading the concepts have been paired with the word as the words enter the spoken vocabulary at a much earlier age. This is in contrast with other academic tasks in which the operations are new to the student. Arithmetic is such an example. When addition is first introduced, it is usually explained through apples and oranges rather than the numerical concept alone.

In support of this stage progression model, there are few instances in which the children are successful without any overt speech. In these few instances looking at the board is sufficient to complete the task. In most cases the speech has not become fully covert. In other words the act has not become completely automatic, but requires some highly task-specific external cue. Earlier, reading aloud as private speech was introduced as a cue, which aided in the problem-solving process. As the task becomes more difficult this cue acts as a reference point linking the present, more difficult material with previously mastered skills. Thus children who are more successful on the more difficult task read aloud more frequently.

Gal'perin not only addresses the developmental level of the mental act, but also the quality of its performance. One element in this assessment is the degree of its mastery. As discussed earlier, mastery involves the independent repetition of the act with new material that results in obtaining a new product. For this to occur some reference point must link old and new performances. It is more likely for a child to utilize this link if he/she has analyzed the task and understands the requisite skills that have been useful in the past. The skills and link in this example are reading aloud.

Vygotsky's Views

Vygotsky (1962) would interpret the higher incidence of reading aloud in the more difficult tasks as an indicator of a disruption of a smooth chain of cognitive activity. Harder material inhibits automatic operation, makes the individual more aware of the process, and elicits more overt speech. This is not incompatible with this present analysis. In both cases the automaticity of the over-learned process has been disrupted by the harder material and overt private speech is elicited. Overt private speech is a more primitive process in a developmental sequence and emerges as the task gets harder. The problem for Vygotsky is in explaining why the less competent child does not read aloud more, since all tasks are harder for him/her. The difference lies in the process in which the more competent child analyzes the task requirements and employs appropriate strategies that have been successful in the past.

Private speech serves a cognitive self-guidance function for Vygotsky. This function must refer to overt statements of the steps in the act itself. Reading aloud as a mediational, facilitory form of speech does not serve this function. One reason for this discrepancy might be the age difference between the first-grade children discussed here and those children discussed by Vygotsky. In large measure private speech has gone underground by first grade for

Vygotsky. It makes sense that only very task-specific speech might remain frequently overt. Speech that would serve more general cognitive self-guidance functions in this highly familiar task would no longer be overt.

This study, in applying a fine-grained temporal analysis of the two streams of behavior (motor and verbal) in natural academic problem-solving among first-grade children, has provided a critique of Vygotsky's position on self-regulatory speech. Although the very task-specific speech of reading aloud does increase with task difficulty and correlate with task success, more general and traditionally considered candidates for self-regulatory speech (evaluation, strategy statements, and questions) do not. This need not suggest that at younger ages or on nonacademic tasks, not on less familiar tasks, other children might not use these more general self-regulatory statements to mediate behavior. The analysis in this chapter however does point out the necessity of considering *task-specificity of task-related speech*, as well as task type and task familiarity as variables that, besides developmental level, may modify the applicability of Vygotsky's general developmental hypothesis of the function of self-regulatory speech.

References

Bakeman, R. Data analyzing procedures. Infancy Laboratory Technical Report no. 2, January 1975. Atlanta: Georgia State University.

Bakeman, R. Untangling streams of behavior: Sequential analysis of observational data. (Paper presented at Conference on Application of Observational-Ethological Methods to the Study of Mental Retardation, Lake Wilderness, Washington, 1976.)

Flavell, J. H. Le langage privé. *Bulletin de Psychologie*, 1966, *19*, 698-701.

Fuson, K. C. The development of self-regulating aspects of speech: A review, in G. Zivin, ed., *The development of self-regulation through private speech.* New York: Wiley-Interscience, 1979.

Gal'perin, P. Y. Stages in the development of mental acts, in M. Cole and I. Maltzman, eds., *A handbook of contemporary Soviet psychology*. New York: Basic Books, 1969.

Goodman, S. A sequential functional analysis of preschool children's private speech. (Paper presented at The Biennial Meeting of the Society for Research in Child Development, New Orleans, March, 1977.)

———. The integration of verbal and motor behavior in preschool children (Ph. D. diss., University of Waterloo, Ontario, 1978).

Hays, W. L. *Statistics for the social sciences*. New York: Holt, Rinehart & Winston, 1973.

Jarvis, P. E. Verbal control of sensory-motor performance: A test of Luria's hypothesis. *Human Development*, 1968, *11*, 172-183.

Klein, W. L. An investigation of the spontaneous speech of children during problem solving (Ph. D. diss., University of Rochester, 1963).

Kohlberg, L., Yaeger, J., and **Hjertholm, E.** Private speech: Four studies and a review of theories. *Child Development,* 1968, *39,* 691-736.

Luria, A. The directive function of speech in development. *Word,* 1959, *18,* 341-352.

______. Speech and formation of mental processes, in M. Cole and I. Maltzman, eds., *A handbook of contemporary Soviet psychology.* New York: Basic Books, 1969.

Meacham, J. A. The role of verbal activity in remembering the goals of actions, in G. Zivin, ed., *The development of self-regulation through private speech.* New York: Wiley-Interscience, 1979.

Meichenbaum, D. Theoretical and treatment implications of developmental research on verbal control of behavior. (Paper presented at the meeting of the Society for Research in Child Development, Philadelphia, April 1973.)

Meichenbaum, D., and **Goodman, J.** The developmental control of operant motor responding by verbal operants. *Journal of Experimental Child Psychology,* 1969*a, 7,* 553-565.

______. Reflection-impulsivity and verbal control of motor behavior. *Child Development*, 1969*b*, *40*, 785-797.

Meichenbaum, D., and **Goodman, S.** Clinical use of private speech and critical questions about its study in natural settings, in G. Zivin, ed., *The development of self-regulation through private speech.* New York: Wiley-Interscience, 1979.

Miller, J., Shelton, J., and **Flavell, J.** A test of Luria's hypothesis concerning the development of verbal self-regulation. *Child Development,* 1970, *41,* 651-665.

Patterson, G. R. A basis for identifying stimuli which control behaviors in natural settings. *Child Development*, 1974, *45*, 900-911.

Piaget, J. *The language and thought of the child,* M. Gabain, trans. New York: American Library, 1955. [Originally published, 1923.]

Reese, H. Verbal mediation as a function of age level. *Psychological Bulletin,* 1962, *59*, 502-509.

Roberts, R. N. The competent academic problem solver: Toward an integrated model (Ph. D. diss., University of Hawaii, 1977).

Roberts, R. N. and **Tharp, R. G.** A naturalistic study of school children's private speech in an academic problem-solving task. (Paper presented at the Annual Convention of the Association for Advancement of Behavior Therapy, Atlanta, 1977).

Rubin, K. H. The impact of the natural setting on private speech, in G. Zivin, ed., *The development of self-regulation through private speech.* New York: Wiley-Interscience, 1979.

Staats, A. W. *Social Behaviorism.* Homewood, Ill.: Dorsey, 1975.

Vygotsky, I. *Thought and language,* E. Hanfmann and G. Vakar, eds. and trans. Cambridge, Mass.: MIT Press, 1962. [Originally published, 1934.]

Wozniak, R. Verbal regulation of motor behavior: Soviet research and non-Soviet replications. *Human Development*, 1973, *15*, 13-57.

Wright, S. Path coefficients and path regressions: Alternative or complementary concepts? *Biometrics*, 16, 189-202, 1960.

Zivin, G. Removing common confusions about egocentric speech, private speech, and self-regulation, in G. Zivin, ed., *The development of self-regulation through private speech.* New York: Wiley-Interscience, 1979.

CHAPTER 10

Clinical Use of Private Speech and Critical Questions about Its Study in Natural Settings[1]

DONALD MEICHENBAUM and SHERRYL GOODMAN

University of Waterloo
Emory University

While playing alone with a doll house a 3½-year-old girl was observed to emit the following verbalizations:

> Go upstairs. Don't cry. Get off there finger. Look at this stairs. You get that going out. Alright, okay. Climb up stairs. Look what I did. Where does this go? This goes here. No. Maybe I can put them here. We have to do it again. This is a triangle, this one right here, and this one goes right here. Remember that. (Singing.)

While doing a puzzle a 4-year-old boy who performed on a trial-and-error basis, placing pieces in a haphazard fashion, made the following utterances:

> I want to take this. Oh, that's water. I'll take this man out. Oh! One leg out, two legs out. There Where does that go? Hm. Huh. That go there? Nope. That go there? Oh, oh. I don't know where this goes. There. Oh. One. Go where? Yup. It did. That? Uh, oh. Yup. Water. No. Hm. Go there? All finished.

Another 4-year-old boy who did the same puzzle, but in a planful, organized manner, said:

> I'm gonna take this out. Oh, this is Jack and Jill. This is Jack and Jill. That's the head. There. Didya put? Didya put it on? Finished?

One can often observe young children (and not infrequently one's colleagues) talking aloud to themselves, that is emitting verbalizations that

[1]The research reported in this paper was supported by grants from Canada Council, Numbers S72-2314 and S73-0034.

are unintended for a listener other than themselves. The concern of the present chapter is what shall we make of such mumblings? What is the structure and function of private speech? Do such self-verbalizations represent an inconsequential byproduct of cognitive development, an "epiphenomenon", or *do* they represent an important process in the child's cognitive development? In order to answer such theoretical questions we shall first have to address a number of methodological questions. We shall illustrate some of the problems we have encountered and the tentative solutions we have come to adopt during three years of investigating the private speech of preschoolers. The present chapter is a progress report of the private speech of two investigators who study private speech. Hopefully you will not perceive the chapter as egocentric.

METHODOLOGICAL PROBLEMS IN STUDYING PRIVATE SPEECH RESEARCH PARADIGMS

In what situations and under what circumstances should one study the child in order to unravel the interaction between his two streams of verbal and nonverbal behavior? The answer to this question is influenced by an investigator's research strategy.

Three general research approaches have been used to assess the influence of self-verbalizations on behavior. The first strategy is merely to observe the child perform a task, either in a free situation or in a laboratory, and record the naturally occurring instances of verbalizations and the ongoing behavior. The protocols reported at the beginning of this chapter illustrate this naturalistic observation. Indeed such an approach has an old tradition (McCarthy, 1930; Vygotsky, 1934/1962), but has been infrequently used in recent years.[2] Usually after noting the incidence of naturally occurring private speech the experimenter manipulates some enivironmental variable, such persons present (adults versus children) or task difficulty, and records changes in private speech. The setting may be familiar versus novel to the child, such as his preschool versus a laboratory setting.

Closely related to the naturalistic approach is an experimental paradigm derived mainly from mediation theory. The child's performance on a task is employed to infer the presence or absence of intellectual processes mediated by internal speech. For example the child may be presented with such tasks as reversal-nonreversal learning, transposition, or discrimination. The experimenter then infers the presence or absence of inner speech mechanisms

[2]See Chapter 5 by Fuson for details of specific private-speech topics on which naturalistic studies are most needed, as well as Chapter 9 by Roberts and Chapter 8 by Rubin for studies that do attempt naturalistic observation of private speech in relatively natural settings.

from the quality of performance (Kendler, Kendler, and Carrick, 1966; Reese, 1962). At times the mediational processes manifest themselves in the form of overt private speech (Flavell, Beach, and Chinsky, 1966).

A third research strategy that has been employed involves direct manipulation of the child's verbalizations with attention to resultant changes in behavior. The child's verbalizations have been manipulated by giving the child general instructions or a set, and by manipulating the content of the child's instructions to himself. In the latter case the experimenter provides the child with particular verbalizations and notes the impact on ongoing behavior. Illustrative of this approach is the work of Bem (1967), Lovaas (1964), Luria (1961), Luria and Yudovich (1959), and Meichenbaum and Goodman (1969a, 1969b). In this paradigm the child is usually required to produce a simple, repetitive, and rapid-motor response; variations in the motoric behavior are noted as a function of the accompanying verbalizations.

Since the usefulness of the latter two research paradigms have been considered elsewhere (Reese, 1962; Wozniak, 1972), the primary focus of the present chapter is on the first research strategy, studying the spontaneous verbalizations that children emit while performing some ongoing task. As noted by Fuson in Chapter 5, very little work has been done on spontaneous speech and spontaneous motor segmentation. Our discussion of methodological problems will draw predominantly on early work in our laboratory, which was preparatory to studying spontaneous motor and speech segmentation.

Recording Private Speech

In our university nursery school we have experimented with several ways of recording children's private speech in a free-play setting. For example we have placed observers in the nursery-school setting and had them transcribe all verbalizations of a particular child. We have removed the observers from the nursery-school setting and have instead used boom microphones, which hang from the ceiling to record verbalizations. We have had most success with a small lavaliere microphone that a particular child wears on his lapel. The children are told how and why they are being recorded, and they readily become accustomed to the microphone. In addition to recording the child's verbalizations it is necessary to record the child's continuous activity on videotape in order to permit delineation of the relationships, particularly temporal ones, between speech and ongoing behavior. The videotape can be engineered so it picks up the child's verbalizations as well as his motoric activity. Whenver the child's speech is recorded by means of audiotape or, preferably, videotape, we have found it necessary for the experimenter immediately to transcribe the verbalizations. This substantially reduces the frequency of such categories as inaudible mutterings or unscorables.

Recently we have begun to study the private speech of two- and three-year-olds in a situation that markedly improves comprehensible speech records. Working in the children's homes, both the experimenter and parent are present. The parent, who is more proficient than the experimenter in recognizing the referents of the child's speech, records the child's verbalizations simultaneously with the experimenter. The experimenter can then compare the two records of the child's verbalizations.

Although the free-play, situation is useful in obtaining a general description of private speech. we believe that the controls of a laboratory setting are required to discern more finely its functional aspects.

What Tasks?

What shall we ask the child to do in the laboratory in order to discern the regulative role of speech? At this time any answer at best represents a hunch. Observing children in a natural free-play situation may suggest particular characteristics of tasks that are to be brought into the laboratory. At present the characteristics of the task that we believe to be most crucial include:

1. The task should obviously be of interest to the child.
2. It should require sequential steps leading to completion—an adult analogue would be learning to drive a car or learning to ski.
3. It should be an activity to which the child can develop proficiency over trials, so that one can discern changes in the content and function of private speech with the development of skill.
4. It should be a task that can be manipulated in terms of difficulty, and presence or absence of distractors and/or supports.
5. Perhaps most importantly, it should lend itself to scoring in terms of "process' as well as "products": one must be able to unitize performance on the task in terms of degree of proficiency. Each discrete unit of performance should be able to be categorized by its efficiency, planfulness, intentionality, or some such criteria. In short the task should permit a description of the child's moment-by-moment task approach—a flow chart of the process of performance. One can then juxtapose the ongoing stream of performance in order to determine the regulative role of speech.

We have chosen the task of solving jigsaw puzzles, which meets these criteria. A number of other tasks employed by other researchers were: pegboard pounding (Wozniak, 1975), bead work (Kohlberg, Yaeger, and Hjertholm, 1968), classification tasks (Beaudichon, 1973), besides variations on puzzle-solving (Deutsch and Stein, 1972; Klein, 1964; Kohlberg, Yeager, and Hjertholm, 1968; Martin, 1975; and Zivin, 1972). Our criteria were best met with puzzles.

The point to be highlighted is that an approach that merely correlates the presence or absence of private speech with errors in overall performance is too insensitive to discern the regulative role of speech. Perhaps a bit far-fetched is our association to an observation by Claude Bernard (1957):

> If we collect a man's urine during twenty-four hours and mix all this urine to analyze the average, we get an analysis of a urine which simply does not exist; for urine, when fasting, is different from urine during digestion. A startling instance of this kind was invented by a psysiologist who took urine from a railroad station urinal where people of all nations passed, and who believed he could thus present an analysis of average European urine! [pp. 134-135]

Units of Private Speech

Now that we have examined the options concerning how and where to record private speech, the next important concern is how to unitize or score the stream of verbalizations. Although the identification of a "unit" of a given behavior has received much attention (for example Wright, 1967), our review of the literature indicates a marked oversight by investigators in failing to describe the criteria employed in the "unitizing" process. Reports generally fail to specify what constitutes a unit of private speech and the degree of reliability with which judges are able to agree on the number of units in a sample. Given that any scoring system is somewhat arbitrary, hopefully the arbitrariness is based on a logical and structural analysis of the content.

The guidelines that were employed in our laboratory to unitize the verbalizations included:

1. A speech unit generally defined by natural phrasing and sentence-structure. Any phrase or sentence comprises one unit, subject to the second criterion, below. Nonsentences and nonphrases are also unitized by the second guideline.

2. An analysis of the pauses indicated that a two-second criterion could be employed to further unitize verbalizations. If a two-second or longer pause occurred between verbalizations then they were designated as separate units, irrespective of sentence structure.

Perhaps we can illustrate the proposed guidelines for such unitization from our own data on the private speech emitted by children while doing puzzles. The two protocols offered at the beginning of the chapter of the children's verbalizations doing puzzles were unitized as follows (slashes separate units):

Protocol 1

> I want to take this./ Oh, that's water./ I'll take this man out./ Oh!/ One leg out, two legs out./ There./ Where does that go?/ Hm./ Huh./ That go there?/ Nope./ That go there?/ Oh, oh./ I don't know where this goes./ There./ Oh./ One./ Go there?. Yup./ It did./ That?/ Uh, oh./ Yup./ Water./ No./ Hm./ Go there?/ All finished./

Protocol 2

I'm gonna take this out./ Oh, this is Jack and Jill./ This is Jack and Jill./ That's the head./ There./ Didya put?/ Didya put it on?/ Finished?/

In such unitizing of children's spontaneous speech, Goodman (1975) found that judges could agree at a level of 97% using videotaped protocols. Interestingly a similar scoring format was independently developed, with slightly different emphases, by Martin and Murray (1975). They specify that a unit of private speech is discriminable by any one or combination of the following:

1. Changes in content.
2. Usual grammatical punctuation.
3. Pauses.
4. Paralinguistic cues.

For example if a child were to privately say "1,2...3.4...5,6" that would constitute one unit. But if the verbalization were, "1,2,3...1,2,3,4,5,6," it would constitute two units according to Martin and Murray, since it includes a pause and a change of content. Other examples they offer include: "A butterfly...a banana."—2 units, since it involves a change in content; "A butterfly...where does it fit?"—2 units, since it includes a change in syntactic structure; "Where does the butterfly go?"—1 unit with no change in content and no pause. Martin and Murray indicate that the rater will often rely on paralinguistic cues to discriminate units, such as pauses, shifts in rate, tone, inflection, and volume of speech. Martin and Murray report that a high degree of reliability was obtained using this scoring system.

Perhaps other guidelines could be developed for purposes of unitizing private speech, but whatever the rules, there is a need to make them explicit. The need to compare different scoring systems is apparent. One research approach being pursued in our laboratory is to ask large numbers of raters to unitize children's private speech in order to discern the naturally occurring rules guiding such unitization. While listening to an audiotape or watching a videotape of a child's private speech, raters are presented with written transcripts that lack punctuation and capitalization. By analyzing where the raters separate units, we can determine the degree of agreement in establishing units and examine the role of contextual and paralinguistic cues.

Units of Motor Behavior

In addition to unitizing verbalizations, there is also a need to develop a system for unitizing the ongoing nonverbal behavior. As mentioned above, if one wishes to examine the functional interrelationship between two different systems of behavior, then it is necessary to be able to unitize both streams of behvaior and examine the parallel events. In our work on children's puzzle-solving we were able to unitize motor behavior by defining a unit of movement as behavior occurring between the picking up of a puzzle piece and the placing it in the puzzle or returning it to the table. One could then categorize these units into various classes of proficiency, ranging from a trial and error movement to a planned movement. The interesting question then becomes, do certain categories of private speech precede, accompany, and follow certain categories of puzzle-solving?

The point to be emphasized is that in order to study the development of verbal regulation there is a need to develop both a scoring system for the child's verbalizations and a second scoring system for whatever other behavioral system one is interested in, whether motoric, perceptual, or interpersonal. One can then attempt to describe the lawful relationships between the two behavioral streams. As we shall see in the discussion of the statistical analysis of such data, new approaches may have to be considered.

Categories of Private Speech

Once one has unitized the child's verbalizations it is necessary to esstablish descriptive and functional categories. An examination of the literature inidcates that the child's private speech includes a multitude of forms with no clear common functional meaning and that there seems to be no unitary characterization of the content of such speech. A brief review of the work of Piaget and the Soviet psychologists Vygotsky and Luria will further sensitize us to the complexity of children's private speech.

Although Piaget did not study self-regulating speech, the historical confusion of his egocentric speech with Vygotsky's self-regulating egocentric speech (see Chapter 1 by Zivin), makes consideration of Piaget's categories relevant here. Piaget (1923/1955) set the precedent for theorizing about categories of private speech when he distinguished the monologue, the collective monologue, and mere repetition. Piaget defined the monologue as thinking aloud (over some activity), not speaking to anyone, and caring little if anyone is listening or hears. The child "believes that someone is listening to him; that is all he wants" (Piaget, 1923/1955, p. 31). The collective monologue is similar to the monologue, but "with the added pleasure of feeling himself an object of interest to other people" (Piaget, 1923/1955, p. 31). The presence of others serves only as a stimulus, but the others are not expected to attend, nor understand. These definitions are consistent with Piaget's notion that such instances of private speech are manifestations of the young child's failure to differentiate his own viewpoint from that of others, that is the egocentric quality of the young child's verbalizations. Perhaps some specific samples taken from

Piaget (1923/1955) will further elucidate the distinctions.

Examples of Monologue

The child simply accompanies his action with sentences spoken aloud:

> Lev sits down at a table alone and is observed saying: "I want to do that drawing, there. I want to draw something. I do. I shall need a big piece of paper to do that."
>
> Lev knocks over a game: "There. Everything's fallen down."
>
> Lev continues to work alone while thinking aloud, announcing what he is going to do, with no audience present other than himself. [p. 37]

Examples of Collective Monologue

> Lev sits at a table where a group of children are at work. Lev says, "I say, I've got a gun to kill him with. I say I am the captain on horseback. I say I've got a horse and gun as well."
>
> Lev, while working, says, "I've already done moon so I'll have to change it." [p. 41]

Piaget sees the "I say" opener as significant in that everyone is supposed to be listening. This is what distinguishes this type of remark from pure monologue. But with regard to content it is the exact equivalent of the monologue: the child is simply thinking out his actions aloud, with no desire to give anyone any information about it. (Piaget, 1923/1955, p. 41).

Thus we see in Piaget's system that private speech is a reflection of a developmental deficit resulting from egocentrism.

Piaget (1923/1955) strongly emphasizes the notion of egocentric speech representing the child's failure to differentiate between the self and others and a failure to take into account the viewpoint of the listener in formulating communication. At the same time Piaget indicates that the private speech serves a number of positive functions. These include acting as a self-command or a stimulus to excite or accelerate an action[3] as a reinforcer[4] for an action or

[3]These and the following quotations from *Language and Thought of the Child* (1923/1955) illustrate the positive functions Piaget ascribed to egocentric speech. Piaget's rather implicit attribution to speech of positive function is rarely emphasized. Intimations of planning and self-command come from Pie's "announcing his plans to himself" (p. 40) and the reference that "speech in this case functions only as a stimulus...although in some cases it accelerates action" (p. 38).

[4]"...that speech, before it can be used to socialize thought, serves to accompany and reinforce individual activity" (p. 59).

an accompanying task, or simply as an aid in marking the rhythm of an action.[5] Similarly for language in general, Piaget emphasizes the predominance of thought over language, but still ascribes positive, yet clearly secondary, functions to language. For Piaget language's symbolic nature functions to transform thought, increasing the child's ability to abstract from thought and facilitate the coordination of mental transformations. In this sense the symbolic condensation of language contributes to the interiorization of action into thought and aids the child's ability to recapitulate actions from the past and anticipate actions in the future.

It is the self-guiding role of private speech and the interiorization process that received greatest consideration from Vygotsky (1934/1962) and Luria (1961). Vygotsky's concern arose from the role language plays in the socialization of the child as reflected by the manner in which the adult's speech is repeated by the child, initially being overt private speech and then "going underground" (to use Vygotsky's term) in the form of inner speech. Accordingly private speech "serves mental orientation, conscious understanding; it helps in overcoming difficulties; it is speech for oneself intimately and usefully connected with the child's thinking" (Vygotsky, 1962, p. 113). For Vygotsky a young child's thoughts achieve reality and form through speech. Vygotsky offers as support for this notion the evidence that private speech reappears or increases when a child suddenly confronts a difficulty in a task that requires conscious reflection, an observation that has been confirmed by Kohlberg, Yaeger, and Hjertholm (1968). Vygotsky suggests that the child's private speech represents reality and serves as cognitive self-guidance in planning and executing actions. With the development of both proficiency and age the child's private speech gradually "becomes more abrupt, incomplete, and whispered speech which then completely vanishes."

Luria (1961) proposed a developmental sequence by which such an interiorization process occurs. According to Luria, the child under two years of age is not able to use speech to direct his own behavior. However the speech of others can initiate, direct, and control the child's behavior, but cannot inhibit or stop an ongoing behavior. During a second stage the child can to some extent use his own speech to control his behavior. Luria suggests that the child's speech has an impulsive component that, at this second stage, helps initiate motor behavior, but will not inhibit it, regardless of the semantic content of the speech. It is only in the third stage that the *content* of the child's speech-for-self becomes dominant, directive, and internalized. On the basis of Luria's proposal we should expect to observe changes in the content and function of private speech with age.

The brief foray into the views of Piaget, Vygotsky, and Luria further highlights the complexity and sensitivity required of any category system. How

[5]"...the child will often talk with the sole aim of marking the rhythm of his action"

shall one categorize the host of different verbalizations that include singing, chanting, the emission of real and nonsense words, verbalized fantasies, and the expression of a variety of motivational and affective states? Flavell's (1964) attempt to bring order to this task resulted in his suggestion that private speech has at least two functions: (1) a cognitive-perceptual function, which includes instances of verbal mediation and regulation and (2) an expressive function, which includes motivational and affective verbalizations.

A more comprehensive and differentiating category system was offered by Kohlberg, Yaeger, and Hjertholm (1968), who suggested that a developmental category scheme based on Mead's (1934) theory might functionally unify the diverse speech forms. They offered four major categories to classify children's private speech and suggested that these should be considered as a developmental hierarchy. The Kohlberg, Yaeger, and Hjertholm scheme includes the following categories:

> *Level I.* Presocial self-stimulatory language, including word play, repetition, animal noises, and singing.
>
> *Level II.* Outward-directed private speech, including remarks addressed to nonhuman objects and descriptions of the child's own activity, similar to Piaget's category of collective monologue.
>
> *Level III.* Inward-directed private speech, including questions answered by self and self-guiding comments.
>
> *Level IV.* External manifestations of inner speech, including inaudible mutterings. This is consistent with Vygotsky's conceptualization of the interiorization process.

Although Kohlberg, Yaeger, and Hjerthom provided some evidence to support the developmental nature of the classes of private speech, several investigators, including Kohlberg and his associates, have had difficulty in using the category scheme. Self-answered questions, commanding objects, and self-stimulation were infrequently exhibited by Kohlberg, Yaeger, and Hjertholm's subjects, resulting in insufficient verbalizations to allow their complete analysis. Kohlberg and his coworkers reported that the separate categories of describing own activity and self-guiding comments were found to be difficult to distinguish reliably. Rubin, Hultsch, and Peters (1971) studied the Kohlberg, Yaeger, and Hjertholm system and found significant interrater reliabilities only on four categories: word play, remarks addressed to nonhuman objects, questions answered by self, and inaudible mutterings. They found however, that only the self-stimulatory category had a significant test-retest reliability coefficient. One can also question whether all inaudible mutterings should be treated as belonging in the most developmentally mature category, as Kohlberg does.

Benefitting from the schemes already developed and the criticisms offered (Dickie, 1973; Klein, 1964), we have tried to develop a comprehensive category system that builds upon the work of Kohlberg, Yaeger, and Hjertholm.[6] The experimental situation used to develop the scheme was the one involving a preschooler performing a puzzle in a laboratory room with the experimenter sitting in one corner of the room, occupying herself with some work. The category system used to classify the child's verbalizations consisted of:

(A) *Social Speech.* Utterances addressed to the experimenter. Two clusters of social speech appeared to be present. Many of the verbalizations were comments or questions to the examiner, referring to the puzzle task or pertinent to the content or activity of solving the puzzle, that is *social speech: task-relevant.*

However a second group of verbalizations were offered that seemed irrelevant to the ongoing task and appeared to approximate the generalized social speech of a preschool child conversing with an adult, such as "We're going to Niagara Falls next week.", "This is my new dress." A number of these *task-irrelevant* verbalizations were in the form of free associations elicited by pictures on the puzzle, such as "We have birdies at home." or "Is it snack time?" Thus the category of experimenter-directed speech was broken down into: (1) social speech: relevant and (2) social speech: irrelevant. (The reason the experimenter was kept in the testing room with the child was because the experiment required multiple trials using several puzzles; moreover, the experimenter was present to deal with the exigencies of working with preschoolers.)

Note that the presence of the experimenter in the room results in the necessity of distinguishing social speech from private speech. However, such a distinction can be readily and reliably made by the criteria noted below. In two studies Goodman (1975, 1977) reported interjudge reliability coefficients ranging from .79 to 1.00 on differentiating social from private speech. The problem in differentiating these two classes of speech is reduced by having the experimenter sit out of the direct gaze of the child and being occupied with taking notes.

The criteria used to describe a unit of speech as social speech included: (1) the child's looking at the experimenter and/or making eye contact; (2) a verbalization by the child that made reference to the experimenter in the context of the statement; (3) a repetition of the statement when no response was offered by the examiner. Once the verbalization was categorized as social speech it was further subcategorized as task-relevant or task-irrelevant.

(B) *Private Speech.* Those verbalizations not considered to be social speech

[6]Compare with Study I in Rubin's chapter (p. 265). He used this modification of the Kohlberg, Yaeger and Hjertholm (1968) categories.

were classified as private speech. Within this range of verbalizations, six clusters emerged, all fairly consistent with the Kohlberg, Yaeger, and Hjertholm (1968) categories:

Word play

Description of activity or labeling

Comments to absent or nonhuman others

Questions and answers to self

Verbalizations of ongoing cognitive activity

Expletives

Unscorable

Two notable divergences from the Kohlberg scheme are the addition of expletives and the deletion of inaudible mutterings. Some of the category names were changed to reflect more directly the phenomena rather than the underlying theoretical assumptions. The importance of emotional expressions or expletives was suggested by Flavell (1964) and Klein (1964) and by our repeated observation of verbalizations such as, "I did it.", "I sure can.", "Hurrah!".

The category of inaudible mutterings was not needed in the laboratory study. With the aid of the transcribed audio record, the problem of undecipherable whispered comments was eliminated, and this task did not create inarticulateness in the children's productions. The use of preschool children may have also contributed to the absence of inaudible mutterings. This possibility is highlighted by the fact that Murray (1975) reported that when school-age children were observed doing a formboard puzzle task, 45% of their private speech fell into a class of inaudible mutterings. It is not clear whether this high incidence of mutterings was a function of the laboratory recording conditions or the children's age.

Finally there are some verbalizations (less than 3%) that could not be categorized as either experimenter-directed or private speech. These comments were often incomplete phrases or sentence beginnings, the meaning of which was not clear. In addition a few comments were spoiled by mechanical failures, such as noise on the tape or in the background.

Following are the definitions and examples of the respective categories:

(A) *Word play.* Includes singing or humming and the repetition of words or phrases for their own sake. Examples are:

Jack and Jill went up the hill.

Shoes, shoes, shoes.

A doggie, doggie, doggie.

(B) *Description of activity*: This is applied to two types of units—*labeling* and *describing* ongoing and/or immediately past activity. In *labeling*,[7] the child emits a verbalization that describes visually obvious aspects of his activity and does not have an apparent planning function. The child may label or describe the whole puzzle, or any piece, or describe the content. Examples are:

They've got no clothes on.

That's a little doggie.

Ah, the bus puzzle.

Here is the boy.

The description of activity must always accompany the action, be simultaneous, or follow it—but not precede the action. The timing of the verbalization in relation to the action is critical in using this category. Thus if one is to discriminate the category of "description" from other categories it is necessary to score it from the videotape. Scoring only from a written transcript will lead to misclassification. Examples of such ongoing descriptions include:

There, I got it.

The head goes like that.

(C) *Comments addressed to absent or nonhuman others*: These remarks are spoken as if to another person or object, as indicated by the content of the verbalization. The child's verbalizations sound like a one-sided dialogue addressed to a generalized other or to the puzzle. Many of these comments would be categorized as social speech if eye contact and an apparent desire or demand for a response were present. In Goodman's (1975) study these comments usually invloved the child's talking to the puzzle, but sometimes they occurred when the child seemingly addressed an absent other. Examples are:

Lookit, here's a doggie.

Hey, I got it in.

Consistent with Piaget's category of collective monologue, the words "look" and "hey" imply an audience.

(D) *Questions asked and answered by self*: These remarks are addressed to self and the content conveys self-guiding or planning and often implies a justification for action. Often the verbalization may not be phrased as a question, for example "I wonder if...". Examples are:

[7]Note that Meacham (Chapter 7) gives a specific self-guiding, but nonplanful function for this type of content. It is similar in conception to Vygotsky's earliest form of self-regulating speech (description after action) whose regulating function is explicated by Zivin (Chapter 1).

Where does this one go?

Here.

Do you know why we wanted to do that?

Because I need it to go a different way.

How does this go?

Maybe it goes that way.

Oh, yeah, it does.

(E) *Verbalization of ongoing cognitive activity*: The content of these verbalizations is task- or goal-related. The speech precedes the activity and the content sounds like "thinking aloud" such that it: (1) conveys an abstract cognitive analysis of the situation, for example "I don't know where this goes.", "I got to be fast.", "I need to start all over again."; (2) gives the reasons for action or inaction, for example "Maybe it goes here.", "I think this is upside down.", "I'm having a hard time here."; (3) reflects planning, for example "Try another one.", "I'll put this piece in here first.", or (4) involves self-guiding comments (description of activity preceding the action) or feedback to self, for example "This goes here.", "I'm getting the piece in."

(F) *Expletive*: This category involves the expression of feeling about the task, success, failure or frustration, and/or reflects a positive or negative evaluation and/or statements expressing satisfaction or dissatisfaction with performance. The verbalization is accompanied by cues of increased affect and usually consists of one-, two-, or three-word units. Examples are:

Ta da.

There.

I did it.

I can't. [whiny complaint]

This describes one system of scoring private speech. See Appendix to this chapter for examples of how the scoring system has been applied to the protocols that were offered at the outset of the chapter.

One other categorical system of private speech bears mention before we shift to other methodological concerns. Martin and Murray (1975), whose unitizing procedures were discussed earlier, adapted Beaudichon's (1973) system to include the following four categories:

> *Task-relevant*: (1) description of material details, (2) searching for solutions, (3) anticipating actions, (4) references to completed actions, (5) references to concurrent actions, (6) statement of consequences of behavior or contingency relationships.

Task-irrelevant: (1) incidental verbal activity, (2) description of irrelevant stimuli, (3) comments directed toward nonpresent experimenter.

Affective: (1) positive and negative evaluations of overall performance and (2) comments about the difficulty of the task.

Mutterings: any utterance not loud or clear enough to be ascribed a specific semantic content.

At present it is not clear whether the four-category system of Martin and Murray is sufficient, collapsing as it does the different types of task-relevant speech into one category, or whether one should keep separate the respective components of task-relevant and task-irrelevant private speech. What constitutes useful categories or response classes has yet to be established. One factor in answering this question will be the relative reliabilities for the respective categories, a topic to which we now turn our attention.

Reliability of Scoring Private Speech

One would expect that the literature would be replete with information concerning such questions as the reliability of unitizing and categorizing private speech. Well it is not. In part the problem derives from how reliabilities are reported. Hall and van de Castle (1966) indicate that such statistics as correlation coefficients of the judges' scores can mask the more subtle areas of disagreement. For example Kohlberg, Yaeger, and Hjertholm (1968) reported a correlation of .85 between two sets of scores using only the original Piagetian categories of repetition, monologue, and collective monologue. However when using the whole hierarchy of forms, Kohlberg, Yaeger, and Hjertholm report that "agreement on subcategories was not systematically calculated" (p. 727). Rubin, Hultsch, and Peters (1971), in calculating the reliability of the individual subcategories, were unable to obtain significant reliability for the categories: description of activity; self-guiding comments; and questions-to-self, which was used infrequently. Thus one overall correlation coefficient of rater agreement, summarizing all categories, may be misleading. For example Dickie (1973) reports a reliability coefficient between raters of .92. What we fail to learn from such a statistic is whether the two judges are placing the exact unit of speech in the same category. Thus two judges might have scored 25 units of speech in the comments to others category, but there is no guarantee that the sum 25 represents the same cluster for each judge. Goodman (1975) reported a percent agreement between judges using the category system described earlier. Observation of children performing the puzzle task yielded 532 units of private speech. Two independent judges were able to agree in the placement of 518 units and disagreed only on 14 units.

One could also specify those particular classes of verbalizations that contribute most to the unreliability. (In Goodman's case they included questions to self and self-guiding comments.) If coding continues over more than one week, it is also necessary to have repeated reliabilities reported. In summary we require a much more detailed description of the procedures used in determining the rater reliability.

Analyzing Private Speech

How shall we summarize or characterize the speech samples we have collected? Piaget (1923/1955) suggested that we compute a "coefficient of egocentrism" to reflect the amount of the child's private speech. His "coefficient of egocentrism" is simply the percentage of comments classified as egocentric (or as private speech) out of the total number of comments made in a situation. This procedure, in contrast to a simple frequency measure, purpotedly controls for the general factor of individual differences in talkativeness. Potential problems associated with the use of the coefficient were illustrated by Kohlberg, Yaeger, and Hjertholm (1968). In their study many subjects were eliminated from further data analysis when they made fewer than six comments and thus attained egocentrism coefficients of zero.

Caution in the use of this measure was also suggested by Schachter, et al., (1974). These authors point out that "while raw frequency scores distort in the direction of giving excess weight to the scores of the talkative child, percent conversion distorts in the direction of giving excess weight to the scores of the quiet child" (p. 11). Schachter, et al., suggest as an alternative the use of an "interval score," which is the total number of observation intervals in which private speech occurs out of the total number of observation intervals per child. It is apparent then that even the choice of a quantitative measure for private speech may influence the research findings.

The research task becomes even more complicated when one keeps in mind that the purpose in developing scoring procedures for the child's verbalizations is to demonstrate their functional interdependence on another ongoing stream of behavior. If we are interested in speech regulation, our task is to first develop a sensitive and reliable scoring system for speech and a similarly sensitive system for the other stream of behavior. Now we can begin to ask the interesting question, how these two streams interact? What is interesting about this question is the relation between two or more concurrent behavioral systems within the same individual in order to note the rules of regulation. At present we feel that a first step in treating the child's verbalizations is not to use such summary statistics as the coefficient of egocentrism. What is required is a descriptive analysis of which categories of private speech occur when, in terms of the ongoing behavior. Going back to our puzzle-solving task, do certain categories such as questions to self and self-guiding speech precede, accompany, or follow a trial-and-error movement on the puzzle? Do such instances of private speech change or drop out as the child develops proficiency on the puzzle?

Only when we have developed sensitive scoring systems for different behavioral systems over time will we be able to answer the critical questions of speech regulation. Hopefully this chapter will encourage such research. For now let us examine the nature of the research to date on the determinants and correlates of private speech.

DETERMINANTS AND CORRELATES OF PRIVATE SPEECH

Age

The variable that has received most attention has been chronological age. In part the interest in this variable derives from the different predictions offered by Piaget and Vygotsky concerning the developmental patternings of private speech. As first explicated by Kohlberg, Yaeger, and Hjertholm (1968), Piaget and Vygotsky predict differently shaped age curves. Piaget (1923/1955) argued that private speech would show a monotonically decreasing incidence with age, that it would peak in the 6- to 7-year-old child and then gradually disappear. In support of this view Piaget reported that preschool egocentric speech comprises a significant part of all expressions of children, reaching as high as 56% in the third year and dropping to 27% toward the seventh year. From Piaget's viewpoint egocentric speech plays a dominant role during the earlier years and is gradually replaced by socialized forms of speech. This replacement occurs because of the child's adjustment to the socialized thinking of adults.

Vygotsky (1934/1962) hypothesized a curvilinear relationship between the incidence of private speech and age. He suggested a rise in the percentage of private speech in the 2- to 4-year-old period, followed by a gradual decline as private speech develops into covert (inaudible) self-guiding thought.

The evidence to support the respective positions is equivocal. For example, Kohlberg, Yaeger, and Hjertholm (1968) present data in support of Piaget's notion of a monotonically decreasing function whereas Vygotsky's theorized curvilinear relationship was supported by Flavell, Beach, and Chinsky (1966) and Gratch (1966). Perhaps part of the reason for the discrepancies may result from the use of one overall index of private speech, the coefficient of egocentrism, rather than looking at the developmental trends of each category of private speech. Another likely reason is the nonidenticality of the two sets of speech referred to by Piaget and by Vygotsky (see Zivin, Chapter 1).

Flavell (1964) argued that neither Piaget's nor Vygotsky's theory accounts for all the forms, functions, and developmental trends of private speech. Consistent with this suggestion, Dickie (1973) demonstrated that different categories of private speech have different developmental trends. She differentiated two categories: (1) a lower level of private speech that included self-stimulation, remarks to nonhuman objects, and describing activity and (2) a higher level that included questions answered by self, self-guiding comments, and inaudible mutterings. Each of these classes of private speech differed functionally, the lower levels being consistent with Piaget's conceptualization, while the higher levels were more consistent with Vygotsky's conceptualization of private speech. Although these important findings require replication, they underscore the observation that private speech is not a unitary phenomenon. This variation is further highlighted when we consider such variables as mental age, situational factors, and cognitive style.

Intellectual and Cognitive Maturity

Some researchers have tried to account for the reported age-related decline in private speech as a result of the child's increasing level of cognitive maturity. Other explanations consider the role of other forms of age-related learning or maturation. Kohlberg, Yaeger, and Hjertholm (1968) reported mental age data in support of Vygotsky's hypothesis of a curvilinear development of private speech for children rated as average on IQ and Piagetian tasks, whereas it declined monotonically in bright verbal children. These authors suggested, on the basis of their data, that the age development of private speech was primarily a function of cognitive level, as reflected in mental age, rather than of other physical or environmental correlates of IQ and it was not merely a reflection of chronological age. The developmental trends of private speech were more clearly paralleled by mental rather than chronological age.

Dickie (1973) found the relationship between cognitive development (as measured by the Peabody Picture Vocabulary Test) and private speech to be dependent on the form of private speech. Increasing cognitive development was associated with a decrease in outward-directed private speech, but there was no association between cognitive development and inner-directed speech. Goodman (1975) found no relationship between IQ and mental age scores on the Peabody test and any private speech measure. Indeed, one might again suggest that, whereas cognitive level seems to tap the private-speech phenomenon better than chronological age, some variable other than these individual difference variables might exist which would more adequately account for the observed relationships.

The Setting

Instead of focusing on the individual per se (that is person variables) to explain the developmental changes in private speech, perhaps we should turn our attention to situational factors in the form of the setting. The situationality of private speech had been highlighted in Vygotsky's early work where he noted changes in the incidence of egocentric speech as a result of situational manipulations. Zaporozhets and Elkonin (1964/1971) described a series of experiments by Vygotsky that was designed to assess the impact of the social context or milieu on private speech. After having determined the incidence of private speech, children were either placed into a group of children who were totally noncommunicative (deaf and dumb), or who spoke a different language, or were unfamiliar, or they were isolated from other children, or put in a situation where they worked alone. In each one of these cases the incidence of private speech dropped substantially, in a ratio of 6 to 1. Even though the different methods for the exclusion of any type of interpersonal interaction varied—or as Zaporozhets and Elkonin say, the "illusion of understanding" was manipulated—there was a consistent tendency for the incidence of private speech to decrease whenever the possibilities for social interaction are reduced:

> These facts led Vygotsky to the well-founded assertion that egocentric speech is social by its nature and stems from the womb of social speech, being isolated but not yet completely separated from social speech in its own distinct form. [Zaporozhets and Elkonin, 1964, p. 123-124]

Other investigators have also observed that preschool and kindergarten children engage in substantial amounts of egocentric or private speech in social settings, though this amount varies widely from one situation to another. For example Kohlberg, Yaeger, and Hjertholm (1968) found in a task situation with a minimally responsive adult, preschoolers emitted 18% egocentric speech, whereas in a free-play situation with peers they emitted 32%. In contrast McCarthy (1930) and Davis (1937) report only an incidence of 2 to 3% of egocentric speech in a structured situation with a responsive adult. The differences between the Kohlberg and McCarthy findings on incidence (18 versus 2%) may be the manner with which the adult interacted with the children, engaging in parallel play in the Kohlberg study. Another variable that influences the incidence of egocentric speech is the task the child is performing.

The Task

The importance of the task variable is indicated in a study by Soviet investigator Syrinka. Syrinka (1934) analyzed children's private speech while doing such tasks as drawing and problem-solving in the presence of adults. It was found that the most typical function of private speech during drawing is a statement (naming of objects or narration accompanying the course of drawing) and that the speech has a number of connected sentences and relatively few fragmentary words. In contrast during the problem-solving activity the child's private speech was characterized by an emphasis on plans and analyses (planning of anticipated activity and analysis of failure) associated with the difficulties of task and conveying a tendency to seek the help of those present. During the problem-solving the dominant form of speech was exclamations followed by fragmentary words. Thus during the task the child seems to use his private speech to secure help from the adults when confronting difficulties.

The relationship between task difficulty and the nature of the utterances has been examined by a number of investigators. Vygotsky's suggestion that the incidence of private speech would increase when the child confronts a difficult task has been generally supported. Kohlberg, Yaeger, and Hjertholm (1968) presented data that showed that the general incidence of private speech increased with task demands for cognitive activity and, in particular, speech judged to be self-guiding in nature also increased with task difficulty. Thus puzzle-solving elicited significantly more self-guiding speech than two sensorimotor tasks (bead stringing and block building). Dickie (1973) also reported a higher incidence of private speech during puzzle and coloring tasks than in a period of free-play with toys. The more cognitively demanding the tasks the higher the evidence of private speech, especially self-guiding speech. This pattern becomes even more obvious as the child becomes older. For example Klein (1963) observed the spontaneous incidence of private speech of 3- to 7-year-old children while doing a puzzle task. He found an increase in task-relevant private speech with age and this was positively associated with success in completing the puzzle. Beaudichon (1973) observed that school-age children who performed on Piaget seriation and classification tasks produced a high proportion of regulatory utterances and that this incidence was higher for older than younger children. Zivin (1972) however, while finding an increase in utterance frequency with task difficulty on finger mazes by 4-year-olds, interpreted them as emotional reactions to failure and frustration.

The clearest demonstration of the role of difficulty and failure in affecting the incidence and content of private speech comes from Deutsch and Stein (1972). They manipulated the task difficulty by arranging conditions for personal failure (due to faulty performance), task interruption (due to faulty materials), and success (completion of the task). The personal failure condition resulted in greater amounts of private speech than the other two conditions. Deutsch and Stein interpreted the greater incidence of private speech in the personal-responsibility-for-failure-condition as reflecting an aroused achievement motivation, which was expressed in the form of private speech.

Goodman (1975) repeated the Deutsch and Stein personal failure condition and also found the amount of private speech to increase following failure. Of most interest was the differential effect of failure on the content of speech. The categories of social speech that were task-relevant, description-of-activity, and unscorables each increased significantly following failure and decreased with task success.

As suggested previously, if one wishes to note the functional role of private speech, it is necessary to look at exactly when during the task private speech occurs. Zivin (1972) recorded preschool children's private speech while performing on finger mazes. She reported that private speech tended to occur least often when the child had a more adequate problem-solving approach and most often occurred when the child manifested confusion at the task. The majority of utterances appeared immediately after errors. Lyublinskaya (1948, as cited by Zaporozhets and Elkonin, 1964/1971) also showed that private speech functions to formulate the problems during periods of difficulty and more generally facilitates planning. Her preschool children showed speech increasingly concentrated in the beginning of an activity and also at points of failure, rather than throughout. These results suggest that private speech functions to formulate the problem during a period of difficulty and to plan a course of action.

Yet the function of private speech should change as the child develops proficiency at a task. Some suggestions for this were offered by Goodman (1975). She was able to differentiate preschool children on their ability to do jigsaw puzzles. The children differed in whether they performed the task in a trial-and-error fashion or in a planful, mediated fashion in which they would look at each puzzle piece, search the puzzle, and intentionally replace the pieces. Children who performed in a mediated, competent fashion emitted few, if any, instances of private speech. In contrast children designated as performing in a trial-and-error fashion, emitted significantly more instances of private speech, and in particular, their speech fell into the categories of social speech that were task-relevant, description of activity, questions to self, and self-guiding private speech.

Although the Goodman results are interesting, the design of the study is inadequate to describe fully the developmental changes as the child develops proficiency. Research is now under way to observe children performing a task, such as jigsaw puzzles, over trials, noting when the child talks to himself and which categories of private speech change with the development of proficiency at the task. The experimental paradigm requires the child to be presented with a task that he has to work at to achieve competence, and once proficient, he is confronted with a more difficult task.

Cognitive Style

The final correlate of private speech to be reviewed is that of cognitive style. Luria (1961) and Homskaja (1956) have suggested from their experiments on verbal control, that hyperactive, impulsive children manifest less verbal control of their behavior. This relationship between impulsivity and inability to control behavior verbally was also found by Meichenbaum and Goodman (1969*a*). They assessed impulsivity by means of Kagan's (1966) Matching Familiar Figures (MFF) test, which requires the child to select one figure (such as a cowboy) that matches a standard figure from an array of six figures. The cognitively impulsive child tends to make many errors and respond quickly, whereas cognitively reflective children tend to make few errors and respond slowly.

Meichenbaum (1971) observed preschool children who had been identified as either impulsive or reflective on the MFF test. The children were matched for IQ and socioeconomic status. Their private speech was recorded in a freeplay situation. The impulsive children had twice as much private speech as did the reflective children, although both emitted equal amounts of communicative (social) speech. However when the private speech was analyzed it became apparent that the impulsive children used more self-stimulating private speech, whereas the reflective children used more self-guiding private speech. Similarly Zivin (1972) found styles of maze-solving in preschoolers that resembled impuslive versus reflective processing styles and interpreted the more frequent private speech of reflectives as potentially self-distracting. This relationship between impulsivity and private speech was partially supported by Dickie (1973), who used two different measures of impulsivity, a picture absurdities test and a game requiring the child to follow directions to drive a truck slowly and carefully along a track (similar to Maccoby, et al., 1965). Dickie found that the impulsive children used more self-stimulating and outer-directed private speech, but there was no difference between impulsive and nonimpulsive children in the amount of inner-directed speech. Kleiman (1974) also found a positive relationship between preschoolers' matching accuracy and the rate of self-directed speech emitted while working on puzzles.

Goodman (1977) assessed preschoolers' cognitive style by means of the Kansas Reflection-Impulsivity Scale for Preschoolers (Wright, 1972) and related performance on this measure to incidence of private speech while doing puzzles. Although she found no general association between these two indices when including the total population of preschoolers, an examination of the five most impulsive and five reflective preschoolers (matched on age, IQ, and sex) did reveal significant differences. The cognitively impulsive preschoolers emitted a higher percentage of private speech, especially in categories of description of activity, questions to self, and self-guiding. Once again the child's proficiency at the task seemed to influence the style and incidence of private speech.

The relationship between impulsivity and private speech has been recently examined by Camp (1975). She identified groups of aggressive and nonaggressive first- and second-grade boys and recorded instances of private speech during a variety of nonverbal performance tasks as well as the MFF. The aggressive-impulsive boys emitted significantly more task-irrelevant, immature instances of private speech and they were less able to regulate their behavior through covert (whispered) private speech.

Perhaps one variable that influences the functional value of private speech is the child's ability to listen. Berner (1971) used a delayed auditory feedback technique to measure the child's awareness of his verbal behavior, as indicated by the amount of disruption in the child's speech when the feedback from his own voice was delayed for a fraction of a second. Berner found that good listeners, those who made many errors during the disruption from the feedback, used more private speech on a jigsaw puzzle task than nonlisteners, and the private speech was more often of the self-guiding form.

At this point one is reminded of Jensen's (1966) definition of verbal mediation as:

> consisting of talking to oneself in relevant ways when confronted with something to be learned, a problem to be solved, or a concept to be attained. In adults the process generally becomes quite automatic and implicit; only when a problem is quite difficult do we begin 'thinking out loud'. Most mediational processes take place subvocally below our level of awareness. [p. 101]

Meichenbaum (1975*a*) has suggested that impulsive children do not characteristically analyze their experiences in mediational (that is verbal or imaginal) terms. Then perhaps a training program that is designed to teach such mediational skills will enhance performance and foster self-control. We now turn our attention to that possibility.

USING PRIVATE SPEECH TO CHANGE BEHAVIOR AND THINKING STYLES

Thus far our concern has been how naturally occurring instances of private speech relate to nonverbal behavior and the thinking process. Perhaps one further example in the form of a personal anecdote will underscore this developmental relationship and also suggest how the modification of private speech can be used for therapeutic and educational purposes. The anecdote comes from observations of the senior author's two-year-old son, David.

David has a yen for apples, which my wife and I readily supply. The only problem is that he dislikes the apple skin and he is disposed to spitting the skin on the floor. In fact when I come home from the office I feel like the woodsman in Hansel and Gretel following the path of—apple skins.

"See David, apple skin, dirty. I throw the skin into the garbage can and not on the floor." At this point David usually applauds my performance.

Our solution to this problem seemed quite straightforward: (1) give him apples without skin, (2) teach him to swallow the skins, or (3) set up some management program for discarding the skins involving modeling and reinforcement.

However an interesting event occurred one day when my wife went to the beauty parlor and took David with her. In order to keep David occupied she had brought an apple for him. He began to spit the skins on the floor at which point my wife said "David, no, dirty, see the skins go in the ashtray." (my wife is more influenced by my cognitive modeling than is my son). The ashtray was constructed so that you had to press a button to open the top and it would quickly reclose making a clapping sound (a highly reinforcing event for David). What happened next is the reason we offer this anecdote.

David then spontaneously performed two acts simultaneously. He spit the apple skin on the floor, looked at it, and then while picking it up and depositing it in the ashtray said to himself "Bappy . . . door . . . all done." This sequence was repeated except now the phrase "Bappy . . . door" was verbalized while he was merely looking at the apple skin on the floor and "all done" followed the behavioral act. Over several trials the verbalizations dropped out of the repertoire and the appropriate behavior was maintained and even generalized to other settings and other foods.

You should know that "Bappy" is David's word for garbage and he uses "door" as equivalent to the concept, "open," such as opening doors, bottles, envelopes, pockets, and so on. I'm even thinking of using it in the process of toilet training.

This anecdote helps to focus our attention on the complex developmental relationship between language, thought, and behavior. David's behavior also nicely illustrates the developmental progression which Vygotsky (1934/1962) and Luria (1961) have offered to explain the socialization of children. As indicated, Luria (1961) had proposed three stages by which the initiation and inhibition of voluntary motor behaviors come under verbal control. During the first stage the speech of others, usually adults, controls and directs a child's behavior. The second stage is characterized by the child's own overt speech becoming an effective regulator of his behavior. Finally the child's covert or inner speech comes to assume a self-governing role.

In other words, early in the mastery of a voluntary act, speech serves a useful supportive guiding function. With practice these verbalizations disappear. Besides the authors of Soviet-inspired studies reviewed in this volume, a number of other theorists with widely different orientations have implicated a similar progression in the development of skills. For example Kimble and Perlmutter (1970) speak of the sequence of the "automatization of voluntary acts," while Tompkins (1968) describes the "miniaturization" process that accompanies the acquisition of a skill, and Lashley implies the logical necessity of the process in his famous Hixon Symposium paper (1951). However the Soviet neuropsychologist Gal'perin (1969) most adequately describes this sequence. In his description of the stages in the development of mental acts he highlights the "abbreviation" process by which:

> the first form of a mental act is clearly developed as external speech to oneself . . . as soon as external speech to oneself is sufficiently mastered . . . speech to oneself quickly passes to its highest form, that of internal speech. [p. 263]

Gal' perin hypothesizes that speech fragments, which may appear strange to an observer, are nothing more than "particles" of external speech to oneself in the process of becoming internal speech:

> These fragments characteristically appear when it is necessarv to arrest the automatic flow of thought and once again to discern some part of the objective content of the action in order to adapt it to the individual condition or the task. [p. 264]

Gal'perin's description of contextual effect can be applied to many common examples. As an instance, you are more prone to talk to yourself (either aloud or covertly) when driving when you see a police car or an accident, indicating that some environmental stimulus may be the occasion for you to engage in inner speech. Think of such automated acts as shaving—and you cut yourself! Or in the case of the senior author, recently learning to ski: "What am I doing on this hill? Now slowly, line the skis up, good. Bend, lean back." "With proficiency (and this took some time) these verbalizations dropped out of the repertoire.

Indeed he was actually learning cross-country skiing and the hill was the top of a mound overlooking a sand trap on a golf course, but after a short while talking aloud, "left arm, right foot," and so on, interfered with his performance. Once the verbalization goes "underground," it is better to leave it there. To illustrate this point developmentally Meichenbaum and Goodman (1969) demonstrated that if you force older children (first-graders) to talk aloud to themselves while doing a motor task, it interferes with their performance, whereas younger children (kindergarteners) benefit from the opportunity to talk aloud to themselves while doing the same task.

Perhaps the sequence by which cognition becomes automatic, abbreviated, and rapid, without requiring extensive or explicit self-instructions at each stage, is best illustrated by an 11-year-boy who answered Mischel (1975):

> If I had to teach a plan to someone who grew up in the jungle—like a plan to work on a project at 10 A.M. tomorrow—I'd tell him what to say to himself to make it easier at the start for him. Like if I do this plan (emphasized word) on time I'll get a reward and the teacher will like me and I'll be proud. But for myself, I know all that already so I don't have to say it to myself—besides it would take too long to say and my mind doesn't have the time for all that—so I just remember that stuff about

> why I should do it real quick without saying it—it's like a method I know already in math; once you have the method you don't have to say every little step. [p. 40]

"Once you have the method you don't have to say every little step." But can't we teach talking to ourselves over and above its natural amount, content, and timing initially to guide and later to train behavior that causes us (or a client) problems? Indeed in our laboratory over the last 10 years we have sought to use language in the form of self-instructional training to modify the behavior of a host of different clinical populations including hyperactive children, adult schizophrenics, and neurotics. (See Meichenbaum and Cameron, 1974, for a description of this research.)

In order to have children develop self-instructional control of their behavior, a training regimen was established which included:

1. An adult model performing a task while talking aloud to himself (cognitive modeling).
2. The child performing the task under the directions of the model's instructions (overt guidance).
3. The child whispering the instructions to himself as he went through the task (faded self-guidance).
4. The child performing the task while guiding his performance by way of private speech (covert self-instruction).

Over a number of training sessions the package of self-statements modeled by the trainer and rehearsed by the child (initially aloud and then covertly) was enlarged by means of response chaining and successive approximation procedures. For example in a task that required the copying of line patterns, the examiner performed the task while cognitively modeling as follows:

> Okay, what is it I have to do? You want me to copy the picture with the different lines. I have to go slowly and carefully. Okay, draw the line down, down, good; then to the right, that's it; now down some more and to the left. Good, I'm doing fine so far. Remember, go slowly. Now back up again. No, I was supposed to go down. That's okay. Just erase the line carefully. . . . Good. Even if I make an error I can go on slowly and carefully. I have to go down now. Finished. I did it!

In the thinking-out-loud phase the model displays several performance relevant skills:

1. Problem definition—"What is it I have to do?"
2. Focusing attention plus response guidance—"Be careful . . . draw the line down."

3. Self-reinforcement—"Good, I'm doing fine."
4. Self-evaluating coping skills plus error-correcting options—"That's okay . . . even if I make an error I can go slowly."

Such training, provided over a number of different tasks, was successful in causing hyperactive children to employ mediational processes and to develop verbal control of behavior (Meichenbaum and Goodman, 1971). In short the goal was to teach the hyperactive child to think before acting and not be given over to the first impressions of the task. This viewpoint maintains that target behaviors that are habitual in nature (that is not premeditated) should first be returned to a deautomatized condition, in which the habitual maladaptive behaviors and inadequate performances come to be preceded by cognitive activity occurring within the child's awareness.

Such forced meditation increases the separation between stimuli or task presentation and responses (that is performance) and thereby provides an additional opportunity for interrupting the behavioral sequence. In this way one can impose an interruption of the response chain at an earlier stage and foster production of task-relevant thoughts, images, and behaviors. Meichenbaum (1977) has further described how this treatment can be implemented.

Other investigators have also successfully trained children to bring their behavior under self-instructional and imagery control (Bem, 1967; Camp, et al. 1977; Douglas, et al., 1976; Palkes, Stewart and Kahana, 1968; Bornstein and Quevillon, 1977; Ridberg, Parke and Hetherington, 1971; Monahan and O'Leary, 1971; Palkes, Stewart and Freedman, 1972; Denney, 1972; Finch, et al., 1975; Hartig and Kanfer, 1973; Freyberg, 1973; Goodman, 1973; Mischel, 1974; Saltz and Johnson, 1974; Schneider, 1977; Spivack and Shure, 1974). In each of the studies self-control was enhanced by making involuntary acts voluntary. This was accomplished by bringing the child's behavior under his own cognitive control through the emission of deliberate self-statements and images.

In short, by teaching children how to talk to themselves, by altering the content of their private speech in terms of both the self-statements and images, we can influence the child's behavior and thinking style. A number of behaviors have been modified by such self-instructional training, including:

1. Self-control behaviors (Meichenbaum and Goodman, 1971).
2. The distribution of attention deployment or how the child uses his eyes on a search task (Goodman, 1973).
3. Improving reading comprehension (Bommarito and Meichenbaum, 1977; Wozniak, 1973).
4. Increasing creative problem-solving (Meichenbaum, 1975*c*).

At the same time that language can be used successfully to alter some behaviors it is important to appreciate what language training cannot do. One is reminded of the experiments by Sinclair-de-Zwart (1969) who tried to train the operation of conservation via language, and failed, suggesting that learning the appropriate language terms is insufficient for learning the cognitive operation. Although language alone cannot result in the development of a new cognitive structure, Sinclair-de-Zwart did indicate that language can direct the child's attention or control perceptual activities relevant to the task:

> Language can direct attention to pertinent factors of a problem, just as it can control perceptual activities, as Luria and his collaborators have shown. In this way, language can prepare an operation but is neither sufficient nor necessary to the formation of concrete operations. [Sinclair-de-Zwart, 1967, p. 62]

Instructions and Self-Instructions

In order to appreciate the functional value of overt self-verbalizations or self-instructions, Meichenbaum (1976) has suggested that we consider research from a variety of areas, including interpersonal instructions, problem-solving, appraisal of stress, and cognitive factors in autonomic conditioning. For example several investigators (Gagne, 1964; Marlatt, 1972; Simkins, 1963; Sutcliffe, 1972) have speculated about the role of interpersonal instructions in controlling behavior. They emphasized both the instigational and directive functions of such instructions in controlling behavior; instructions both initiate or facilitate performance in a general sense, and direct attention to stimulus coinditions and to specified performance requirements in a task. Moreover instructions control extraneous behaviors by directing subjects not to engage in certain responses. So far the role of others' verbalizations has been seen only as a developmental starting point for the (transferred) effectiveness of the child's own verbalizations, particularly in Soviet-inspired research.

Gagne (1964), working within a problem-solving framework, has viewed instructions as serving the following functions:

1. Motivating the subject by eliciting an achievement set.
2. Helping the subject identify the criterion performance and the salient parts of the stimulus situation.
3. Aiding recall of relevant subordinate performance capabilities necessary to the task.
4. Channeling thinking in terms of task-relevant hypotheses and controlling extraneous thoughts and behaviors. In this way instructions provide the subject with a rule or principle by which he can mediate his behavior.

In describing the role of overt, self-verbalizations, or self-instructions, in a problem-solving task, McKinney (1973) offered the following list of functions —the overt self-instructions:

1. Increase distinctiveness of the stimulus attributes.
2. Direct subject's attention to the relevant dimensions.
3. Assist the subject in forumlating a series of hypotheses.
4. Maintain information in short-term memory.

The similarity between the Gagne and McKinney lists of psychological functions for inter- and intra-personal instructions is noteworthy. This leads to the roundabout support from other theories of the Soviet view of the external origin of self-guidance: that self-instructions operate in a similar fashion to interpersonal instructions. As noted earlier Vygotsky (1934/1962) and Luria (1961) have theorized that developmentally, the child comes to exercise verbal control of his behavior by incorporating adults' instructions. But the incorporation of adult instructions does *not* mean that the process of internalization and abbreviation should be viewed merely as a process of faded speech. Instead the transformation from interpersonal speech to thought represents qualitative diffferences in structure. How instructions modeled by a therapist or parent change into the child's own private speech and thought is a primary theoretical and practical question. The answer to this question will have major implications for the potential of self-instructional training with children. It is suggested that researchers should examine the power of interpersonal instruction as a source of continuously relevant hypotheses about the specific function of self-instructions.

Finally let us conclude with a caveat. In discussing the use of private speech to modify behavior and thinking styles it is important to make a distinction between the proposed sequence by which verbal control naturally develops and the manner in which such a sequence can be deliberately employed for the modification of behavior. Just because we can use the child's private speech to alter behavior, we cannot conclude that private speech plays a similar role developmentally. The answer to the question as to whether private speech does play a role in development must be examined through, among other paradigms, naturalistic studies—such as that by Roberts (Chapter 9) and that by Rubin (Chapter 8)—which find that self-guiding private speech actually occurs with sufficient frequency to be taken seriously.

APPENDIX

In order to illustrate the scoring procedures described in this chapter the three protocols that were offered at the beginning of the chapter are scored.

The slashes represent the different units of speech and following each passage the units are categorized. The unitizing is in part influenced by the paralinguistic properties, such as extended pauses. The assignment of a particular unit to a given category is in part influenced by its relationship to the ongoing behavior, namely, whether it precedes, accompanies, or follows the behavioral act. The following is offered as an example of the scoring guidelines described in this chapter.

> Go upstairs. / Don't cry. / Get off there finger. / Look at this stairs. / You get that going out. / Alright, okay. / Climb up stairs. Look what I did. / Where does this go? / This goes here. / No. / Maybe I can put them here. / We have to do it again. / This is a triangle / this one right here / and this one goes right here. Remember that. / (Singing.)

Unit of Speech	*Category*
Go upstairs	Comments to (absent or nonhuman) others
Don't cry	Comments to others
Get off there finger	Comments to others
Look at this stairs	Comments to others
You get that going out	Comments to others
Alright, okay	Verbalization of ongoing cognitive activity
Climb up stairs	Comments to others
Look what I did	Comments to others
Where does this go?	Questions and answers to self
This goes here	Questions and answers to self
No	Questions and answers to self
Maybe I can put them here	Ongoing activity
We have to do it again	Ongoing activity
This is a triangle	Description of activity (or labeling)
This one right here	Description of activity
and this one goes right here	Ongoing activity
Remember that	Ongoing activity
Singing	Word play
I want to take this	Verbalization of ongoing cognitive activity
Oh, that's water	Description of activity (or labeling)
I'll take this man out	Description of activity
Oh	Expletive
One leg out, two legs out	Description of activity
There	Description of activity
Where does that go?	Questions and answers asked to self
Hm	Expletive

Unit of Speech (contd)	*Category (contd)*
Huh	Expletive
That go there?	Question and answer to self
Nope	Question and answer to self
That go there?	Question and answer to self
Uh, oh	Expletive
I don't know where this goes	Social speech relevant
There	Question and answer to self
Oh Expletive	
One	Description of activity
Go there?	Question and answer to self
Yup	Expletive
It did	Social speech relevant
Uh, oh	Expletive
Yup	Expletive
Water	Description of activity
No	Description of activity
Hm	Expletive
Go there?	Question and answer to self
All finished	Social speech relevant
I'm gonna take this out	Verbalization of ongoing cognitive activity
Oh, this is Jack and Jill	Social speech relevant
This is Jack and Jill	Social speech relevant
That's the head	Description of activity
There	Description of activity
Didya put?	Question and answer to self
Didya put it on?	Question and answer to self
Finished?	Social speech relevant

REFERENCES

Beaudichon, J. Nature and instrumental function of private speech in problem solving situations. *Merrill-Palmer Quarterly,* 1973, *19,* 117-131.

Bem, S. L. Verbal self-control: The establishment of effective self-instruction. *Journal of Experimental Psychology,* 1967, *74,* 484-491.

Bernard, C. *An introduction to the study of experimental medicine,* H. C. Green, trans. New York: Dover, 1957.

Berner, E. Private speech and role-taking abilities in preschool children. (Paper presented at the Biennial Meeting of the Society for Research in Child Development, Minneapolis, 1971.)

Bommarito, J., and **Meichenbaum, D.** Enhancing reading comprehension by means of self-instructional training. [Unpublished manuscript, University of Waterloo, 1977.]

Bornstein, P., and **Quevillon, R.** The effects of self-instructional package with overactive preschool boys. *Journal of Applied Behavior Analysis,* 1976, *9,* 176-188.

Camp, B. Verbal mediation in young aggressive boys. *Journal of Abnormal Psychology*, 1977, *86*, 145-153.

Camp, B., Blom, G., Herbert, F., and **Van Dooninck, W.** Think Aloud: A program for developing self-control in young aggressive boys. *Journal of Abnormal Child psychology,* 1977, *5,* 157-169.

Davis, E. The development of linguistic skill in twins, singletons with siblings and only children from age five to ten years. *Institute of Child Welfare Monograph,* Serial no. 14. Minneapolis: University of Minnesota Press, 1937.

Denney, D. Modelling effects upon conceptual style and cognitive tempo. *Child Development,* 1972, *43,* 105-119.

Deutsch, F., and **Stein, A.** The effects of personal responsibility and task interruption on the private speech of preschoolers. *Human Development,* 1972, *15,* 310-324.

Dickie, J. *Private speech: The effect of presence of others, task and intrapersonal variables.* Unpublished doctoral dissertation, Michigan State University, 1973.

Douglas, U., Parry, P., Marton, P., and **Garson, C.** Assessment of a cognitive training program for hyperactive children. *Journal of Abnormal Child Psychology,* 1976, *4,* 389-410.

Finch, A., Wilkinson, M., Nelson, W., and **Montgomery, L.** Modification of an impulsive cognitive tempo in emotionally disturbed boys. *Journal of Abnormal Child Psychology,* 1975, *3,* 49-53.

Flavell, J. Private speech. (Paper presented at the Annual Meeting of the American Speech and Hearing Association, San Francisco, November 1964.)

______. **D. Beach**, and **J. Chinsky**. Spontaneous verbal rehearsal in a memory task as a function of age. *Child Development,* 1966, *37,* 283-299.

Freyberg, J. Increasing the imaginative play of urban disadvantaged kindergarten children through systematic training, in J. Singer, ed., *The child's world of make believe.* New York: Academic, 1973.

Fuson, K. C. The development of self-regulating aspects of speech: A review, in G. Zivin, ed., *The development of self-regulation through private speech.* New York: Wiley, 1979.

Gagne, R. Problem solving, in A. Melton ed., *Categories of human learning.* New York: Academic, 1964.

Gal'perin, P. Stages in the development of mental acts, in M. Cole and I. Maltzman, eds., *A handbook of contemporary Soviet psychology.* New York: Basic Books, 1969.

Goodman, J. Impulsive and reflective behavior: A developmental analysis of attentional and cognitive strategies. Unpublished doctoral dissertation, University of Waterloo, Ontario, Canada, 1973.

Goodman, S. Children's private speech and their disposition to use cognitive mediational processes. Unpublished masters thesis, University of Waterloo, Ontario, 1975.

Goodman, S. A sequential functional analysis of preschool children's private speech. (Paper presented at the Biennial Meeting of The Society for Research in Child Development, New Orleans, March 1977.)

Goodman, S. The integration of verbal and motor behavior in preschool children. Unpublished doctoral dissertation, University of Waterloo, Ontario, 1978.

Gratch, G. The use of private speech by headstart and middle class preschoolers. (Paper presented at the Annual Meeting of the Southwestern Psychological Association, Arlington, Texas, April 1966.)

Hall, C., and **Van de Castle, R.** *The content analysis of dreams.* New York: Appleton-Century-Crofts, 1966.

Hartig, M., and **Kanfer, F.** The role of verbal self-instructions in children's resistance to temptation. *Journal of Personality and Social Psychology,* 1973, *25,* 250-267.

Homskaja, E. On the problem of the role of speech in the compensation of motor reactions, in A. Luria, ed., *Problems of the higher neural activity of the normal and abnormal child.* Moscow: Moscow Press, 1956.

Jensen, A. Verbal mediation and educational potential. *Psychology in the schools,* 1966, *3,* 99-109.

Kagan, J. Reflection-impulsivity: The generality and dynamics of conceptual tempo. *Journal of Abnormal Psychology,* 1966, *71,* 17-24.

Kendler, T., **Kendler, H.**, and **Carrick, M.** Verbal labels and inferential problem solution of children. *Child Development,* 1966, *37,* 740-763.

Kimble, G., and **Perlmutter, L.** The problem of volition. *Psychological Review,* 1970, *77,* 361-384.

Kleiman, A. The use of private speech in young children and its relation to social speech. Unpublished doctoral dissertation, University of Chicago, 1974.

Klein, W. An investigation of the spontaneous speech of children. Unpublished doctoral dissertation, University of Rochester, 1964.

Kohlberg, L., **Yaeger, J.**, and **Hjertholm, E.** The development of private speech: Four studies and a review of theories. *Child Development,* 1968, *39,* 691-736.

Lashley, K. S. The problem of serial order in behavior, in L. A. Jeffress, ed., *Cerebral mechanisms in behavior: The Hixon Symposium.* New York: Wiley, 1951.

Lovaas, O. Cue properties of words: The control of operant responding by rate and content of verbal operants. *Child Development,* 1964, *35,* 245-256.

Luria, A., and **Yudovich, F.** *Speech and the development of mental processes in the child.* New York: Staples, 1959.

______. *The role of speech in the regulation of normal and abnormal behavior,* J. Tizard, trans. New York: Liveright, 1961.

McCarthy, D. The language development of the preschool child. *Institute of Child Welfare Monograph,* Serial no. 4. Minneapolis: University of Minnesota, 1930.

Maccoby, E., **Dowley, E.**, **Hogan, J.**, and **Degerman, R.** Activity level and intellectual functioning in normal school children. *Child Development,* 1965, *36,* 761-770.

McKinney, J. A developmental study of the effects of hypothesis verbalizations and memory load on concept attainment. [Unpublished manuscript, University of North Carolina, Chapel Hill, 1973.]

Marlatt, C. Task structure and the experimental modification of verbal behavior. *Psychological Bulletin*, 1972, *78*, 335-350.

Martin, R. Spontaneous private speech and the mediation of behavior in a resistance-to-temptation paradigm. Unpublished doctoral dissertation, University of Rochester, 1975.

Martin, R., and **Murray, J.** Manual for scoring private speech. [Unpublished manuscript, University of Rochester, 1975.]

Meacham, J. A. The role of verbal activity in remembering the goals of actions, in G. Zivin, ed., *The development of self-regulation through private speech.* New York: Wiley, 1979.

Mead, G. *Mind, self, and society*. Chicago: University of Chicago Press, 1934.

Meichenbaum, D. The nature and modification of impulsive children. (Paper presented at the Biennial Meeting of the Society for Research in Child Development. Minneapolis, 1971.

______. Theoretical and treatment implications of developmental research on verbal control of behavior." *Canadian Psychologist*, 1975*a*, *16*, 22-27.

______. Self-instructional methods, in F. Kanfer and A. Goldstein, eds., *Helping people change*. New York: Pergamon, 1975*b*.

______. Enchancing creativity by modifying what subjects say to themselves. *American Education Research Journal*, 1975*c*, *12*, 129-145.

______. Toward a cognitive theory of self-control, in G. Schwartz and D. Shapiro, eds., *Consciousness and self-regulation: Advances in research.* New York: Plenum, 1976.

______. *Cognitive-behavior modification: An integrative approach.* New York: Plenum, 1977.

Meichenbaum, D., and **Cameron, R.** The clinical potential of modifying what clients say to themselves. *Psychotherapy: Theory, Research, and Practice,* 1974, *11,* 103-117.

Meichenbaum, D., and **Goodman, J.** Relection-impulsivity and verbal control of motor behavior. *Child Development,* 1969*a, 40,* 785-797.

______. The developmental control of operant motor responding by verbal operants. *Journal of Experimental Child Psychology,* 1969*b, 7,* 553-565.

Meichenbaum, D., and **Goodman, J.** Training impulsive children to talk to themselves: A means of developing self-control. *Journal of Abnormal Psychology, 77,* 115-126.

Mischel, W. Processes in delay of gratification, in L. Berkowitz, ed., *Advances in experimental social psychology,* vol. 7. New York: Academic, 1974.

Mischel, W. Delay of gratification in choice situations. [Unpublished manuscript, Stanford University, 1975.]

Monahan, J., and **O'Leary, D.** Effects of self-instruction on rule breaking behavior. *Psychological Reports,* 1971, *79,* 1059-1066.

Murray, J. Spontaneous private speech and the mediation of behavior in a delayed match-to-sample task. Unpublished doctoral dissertation, University of Rochester, 1974.

Palkes, H., Stewart, M., and **Freedman, J.** Improvement in maze performance on hyperactive boys as a function of verbal training procedures. *Journal of Special Education,* 1972, *5,* 337-342.

Palkes, J., Stewart, M., and **Kahana, B.** Porteus maze performance of hyperactive boys after training in self-directed verbal commands. *Child Development,* 1968, *39,* 817-826.

Piaget, J. Language and thought from the genetic point of view. *Acta Psychologica,* 1954, *10,* 88-98.

Piaget, J. *The language and thought of the child,* M. Gabain, trans. New York: Meridian, 1955. [Originally published, 1923.]

Reese, H. Verbal mediation as a function of age level. *Psychological Bulletin,* 1962, *59,* 502-509.

Ridberg, E., Parke, R., and **Hetherington, M.** Modification of impulsive and reflective cognitive styles through observation of film mediating models. *Developmental Psychology,* 1971, *5,* 369-377.

Rubin, K. H. The impact of the natural setting on private speech, in G. Zivin, ed., *The development of self-regulation through private speech.* New York: Wiley, 1979.

Rubin, K., Hultsch, D., and **Peters, D.** Non-social speech in four-year-old children as a function of birth order and interpersonal situation. *Merrill-Palmer Quarterly,* 1971, *17,* 41-50.

Saltz, E., and **J. Johnson.** Training for thematic-fantasy play in culturally disadvantaged children. *Journal of Educational Psychology,* 1974, *66,* 623-630.

Schachter, F., Kirshner, K., Klips, B., Fredericks, M., and **Sanders, K.** Everyday preschool interpersonal speech usage: Methodological developmental, and sociolinguistic studies. *Monographs of the Society for Research in Child Development,* 1974, *39,* Serial No. 156 (Whole No. 3).

Schneider, M. Turtle technique in the classroom. *Teaching Exceptional Children,* Fall, 1974, 22-24.

Simkins, L. Instructions as discriminative stimuli in verbal conditioning and awareness." *Journal of Abnormal and Social Psychology,* 1963, *66,* 213-259.

Sinclair-de-Zwart, H. *Language et opérations: Sous-systèmes linguistiques et opérations concrètes.* Paris: Dunod, 1967.

———. A possible theory of language acquisition within the general framework of Piaget's developmental theory, in D. Elkins and J. Flavell, eds., *Studies in Cognitive Development.* London: Oxford University Press, 1969.

Spivack, G., and **Schure, M.** *Social adjustment of young children: A cognitive approach to solving real-life problems.* San Francisco: Josey-Bass, 1974.

Sutcliffe, J. On the role of 'instructions to the subject' in psychological experiments. *American Psychologist,* 1972, *27,* 755-758.

Syrinka, V. *Problem of egocentric speech in the investigation of Piaget.* Moscow: 1934.

Tompkins, S. A theory of memory, in J. Antrobus, ed., *Cognition and affect.* Boston: Little, Brown, 1968.

Vygotsky, L. *Thought and language,* E. Hanfmann and G. Vakar, eds. and trans., Cambridge, Mass.: MIT Press, 1962. [Originally published, 1934]

Wozniak, R. Verbal regulation of motor behavior, Soviet research and non-Soviet replications: A review and explication. *Human Development,* 1972, *15,* 13-57.

______. Reading improvement through training in verbal self-instruction. [Unpublished manuscript, University of Minnesota, 1973.]

Wright, H. *Recording and analyzing child behavior.* New York: Harper & Row, 1967.

Wright, J. *The Kansas reflection-impulsivity scale for preschoolers: A manual for users.* St. Ann, Missouri: Cemrel, 1972.

Zaporozhets, A., and **Elkonin, D.** *The psychology of preschool children,* J. Shybut and S. Simon trans., Cambridge, Mass.: MIT Press, 1971. [Originally published, 1964.]

Zivin, G. Functions of private speech during problem-solving in pre-school children. Unpublished doctoral dissertation, Harvard University, 1972.

______. Removing common confusions about egocentric speech, private speech, and self-regulation, in G. Zivin, ed., *The development of self-regulation through private speech.* New York: Wiley, 1979.

Author Index

Subject Index